AN INQUIRY INTO
FIRST PRINCIPLES

TOWARD

CONSCIOUS PARTICIPATION

IN AN UNFOLDING REALITY

Hakim Ibn Adam

Centre for Studies in Matter, Mind, and Meaning

threerosespublishing.com

ISBN: 978-1-9990656-6-9

AUTHOR'S NOTE

This is a publication of the "Centre for Studies in Matter, Mind, and Meaning", a division of Three Roses Publishing. The Centre's mission is to produce scholarly work that integrates scientific inquiry, philosophical analysis, and spiritual reflection.

CONTENTS

DEDICATION...xxiv

A Reader's Guide to This Inquiry 1

The Purpose of This Guide..1

The Central Question and Methodological Framework 2

Structural Organization 2

Navigation Strategies for Different Readers........................3

Evaluative Criteria 4

The Triadic Method in Practice....................................4

Reading as Participatory Inquiry..................................5

Scholarly Apparatus and References................................5

Expectations and Outcomes...6

Scope and Limitations...6

Conclusion..7

PART I 9

Chapter 1: What Are First Principles? 9

1.1 The Search For Certainty 9

1.2 Defining First Principles 10

1.3 Historical Development 13

1.4 The Architecture Of Knowledge 16

1.5 Modern Applications.. 19

1.6 Why First Principles Matter 22

Chapter 2: The Problem of Foundation 25

2.1 Introduction: The Paradox Of Foundations.................... 25

2.2 The Infinite Regress Problem 27

2.3 Circular Reasoning And Self-Reference 30

2.4 The Architecture Of Assumptions 33

2.5 Domain-Specific Approaches 37

2.6 The Limits Of Certainty... 40

2.7 Living With Foundational Uncertainty................................... 43

Chapter 3: Three Paths to Truth **48**

3.1 The Triadic Structure Of Human Knowledge 48

3.2 Science: The Empirical Path.. 50

3.2.1 Foundations of Scientific Knowledge............................. 50

3.2.2 Methodological Naturalism and Its Scope 51

3.2.3 The Boundaries of Empirical Investigation.................... 52

3.3 Philosophy: The Rational Path 54

3.3.1 The Domain of Pure Reason 54

3.3.2 Transcendental Arguments and Necessary Conditions 55

3.3.3 The Interplay of Reason and Experience........................ 56

3.4 Religion: The Revelatory Path 58

3.4.1 Experiential and Revelatory Foundations 58

3.4.2 Faith as Epistemic Virtue and Rational Foundation..................... 59

3.4.3 The Scope and Limits of Religious Understanding....................... 60

3.5 historical tensions and convergent possibilities 62

3.5.1 Beyond the Warfare Metaphor 62

3.5.2 Positivist Reduction and Its Limitations......................... 63

3.5.3 Fundamentalist Responses and Interpretive Sophistication 64

3.6 Toward Epistemic Integration 65

3.6.1 Complementarity and Hierarchical Organization 65

3.6.2 Convergent Truth and Mutual Enrichment 66

3.6.3 Frameworks for Productive Integration 68

3.7 Conclusion: The Convergent Quest For Understanding................... 69

PART II 72

Chapter 4: The Laws of Physics.. 72

4.1 The Architecture Of Physical Reality 72

4.2 Conservation Principles: The Mathematical Foundation Of
Constraint.. 74

4.2.1 The Logical Structure of Conservation............................. 74

4.2.2 Noether's Theorem and the Unity of Symmetry and Conservation
.... 75

4.2.3 Discrete Symmetries and the Limits of Conservation 76

4.3 Thermodynamics: Statistical Foundations And Temporal Asymmetry
.... 77

4.3.1 The Emergence of Irreversibility 77

4.3.2 Cosmological Implications and the Past Hypothesis............ 78

4.3.3 Information Theory and Modern Thermodynamics 78

4.4 Quantum Mechanics: Probability, Measurement, And The
Foundations Of Physical Reality 79

4.4.1 The Probabilistic Revolution 79

4.4.2 Entanglement and Nonlocal Correlations 80

4.4.3 Interpretational Frameworks and Ontological Implications....... 81

4.5 Relativity: Spacetime Structure And Gravitational Geometry 82

4.5.1 Special Relativity and the Unity of Space and Time 82

4.5.2 General Relativity and Dynamic Spacetime.......................... 83

4.5.3 The Challenge of Quantum Gravity...................................... 84

4.6 The Epistemic Status Of Physical Law...84

4.6.1 Mathematical Realism and the Discovery Hypothesis 84

4.6.2 The Case for Construction and Contextuality............................85

4.6.3 Toward a Dialectical Understanding 86

4.7 Synthesis And Future Directions 87

Chapter 5: Mathematical Foundations 89

5.1 The Ontological Status Of Mathematical Truth..........................89

5.2 Set Theory And The Architecture Of Mathematical Foundations 91

5.3 Logical Pluralism And The Foundations Of Reasoning.....................93

5.4 Gödel's Incompleteness Theorems And The Limits Of Formalization
....95

5.5 The Applicability Problem And Mathematical Explanation 97

5.6 Constructive Mathematics And Computational Foundations...........99

5.7 Mathematical Practice And The Sociology Of Mathematical Knowledge 100

5.8 Implications For First Principles Methodology 102

5.9 Mathematical Foundations And The Theological Horizon 104

Chapter 6: The Origin Problem.....................................106

6.1 The Epistemological Boundaries Of Cosmological Inquiry 106

6.2 Big Bang Cosmology: Empirical Achievement And Explanatory Limits..108

6.3 The Fine-Tuning Problem: Cosmic Specialness And Its Implications
....110

6.4 Multiverse Theories: Scientific Hypothesis Or Metaphysical Speculation?...113

6.5 The Existence Question: Ultimate Boundaries Of Scientific

Explanation 115

6.6 Multiverse Cosmology And The Problem Of Cosmic Hierarchy.... 118

6.7 Scientific Naturalism And Its Explanatory Limits............................ 119

6.8 Toward Integrative Understanding... 121

PART III **123**

Chapter 7: The Certainty of Existence....................................... **123**

7.1 The Epistemological Foundation: Seeking Indubitable Knowledge 123

7.2 The Cartesian Revolution: Systematic Doubt And Existential
Certainty.. 126

7.3 Consciousness As Epistemic Foundation: The Immediacy Of
Phenomenal Experience.. 128

7.4 The External World Challenge: Bridging The Epistemic Gap 131

7.5 The Problem Of Other Minds: Solipsism And Intersubjective
Knowledge... 134

7.6 Mapping Epistemic Territory: Certainty, Probability, And Fallible
Knowledge... 136

Chapter 8: The Nature of Being... **139**

8.1 The Fundamental Ontological Enterprise 139

8.2 Aristotelian Foundations And Categorical Frameworks.................. 140

8.3 The Cartesian Legacy: Substance Dualism And Its Contemporary
Assessment 142

8.4 Materialist Metaphysics: From Identity Theory To Contemporary
Physicalism.. 144

8.5 Consciousness And The Contemporary Mind-Body Problem........ 145

8.6 Personal Identity And The Metaphysics Of Persistence.................. 147

8.7 Abstract Objects And Mathematical Ontology................................. 148

8.8 Process Metaphysics And Dynamic Ontologies.................................. 150

8.9 Metaontological Reflections: Pluralism, Deflation, And Conceptual Relativity 151

8.10 Conclusion: Ontological Commitment And Philosophical Method 152

Chapter 9: The Structure of Knowledge..154

9.1 The Foundational Challenge: Epistemology As Philosophical Prerequisite.. 154

9.2 Classical Foundations: The Empiricism-Rationalism Dialectic....... 155

9.2.1 Empiricist Foundations and Their Sophistication 155

9.2.2 Rationalist Insights and Contemporary Developments 156

9.2.3 The Kantian Revolution and Its Contemporary Legacy............. 157

9.3 The Problem Of Induction: Skeptical Challenges And Contemporary Responses... 158

9.3.1 Hume's Challenge and Its Systematic Development.................... 158

9.3.2 Bayesian and Probabilistic Responses... 159

9.3.3 Pragmatic and Naturalistic Solutions... 160

9.4 The Architecture Of Justified Belief: Contemporary Structural Approaches.. 160

9.4.1 Beyond the Classical Analysis: Gettier Problems and Their Resolution 160

9.4.2 Foundationalism and Its Contemporary Developments............ 161

9.4.3 Coherentism and Holistic Approaches.. 162

9.4.4 Externalist and Reliabilist Approaches 162

9.5 Virtue Epistemology And The Normative Dimension 163

9.5.1 Aristotelian Foundations and Contemporary Developments ... 163

9.5.2 Social Virtue Epistemology and Epistemic Injustice 164

9.5.3 Religious and Contemplative Epistemology 164

9.6 Testimony, Trust, And Social Epistemology 165

9.6.1 The Epistemology of Testimony.. 165

9.6.2 Trust, Authority, and Epistemic Dependence 166

9.6.3 Indigenous and Non-Western Epistemologies............................ 166

9.7 Cross-Cultural Epistemological Perspectives.................................... 167

9.7.1 Indian Philosophical Epistemology 167

9.7.2 Buddhist Epistemological Analysis.. 167

9.7.3 Islamic Epistemological Traditions.. 168

9.7.4 Chinese Philosophical Approaches.. 168

9.8 Skeptical Challenges And Their Epistemological Significance 169

9.8.1 Contemporary Skeptical Arguments 169

9.8.2 Epistemological Responses to Skepticism 169

9.9 Implications For First Principles: Epistemological Constraints And
Possibilities.. 170

9.9.1 Methodological Pluralism and Epistemic Humility 170

9.9.2 Social and Political Dimensions of Knowledge 171

9.9.3 Integration and Convergence Criteria.. 171

9.9.4 Dynamic and Developmental Understanding............................. 171

9.10 Conclusion: Knowledge As Foundation For Philosophical Inquiry
.... 172

Chapter 10: Logical Foundations.. 174

10.1 The Architecture Of Reason 174

10.2 The Classical Laws Of Logic 175

10.2.1 The Law of Identity 175

10.2.2 The Law of Non-Contradiction 176

10.2.3 The Law of Excluded Middle 177

10.2.4 The Foundational Role.. 178

10.3 The Nature Of Logical Laws: Descriptive Or Prescriptive? 178

10.3.1 The Descriptivist Position 178

10.3.2 The Prescriptivist Response 179

10.3.3 The Middle Path: Logical Pluralism 180

10.4 Modal Logic And The Structure Of Possibility 181

10.4.1 Necessity and Possibility... 181

10.4.2 Applications to First Principles 181

10.5 Logic And Reality: The Metaphysical Connection 182

10.5.1 Historical Perspectives 182

10.5.2 Contemporary Perspectives 183

10.6 Beyond Classical Logic: Alternative Traditions 184

10.6.1 Asian Philosophical Traditions.................................... 184

10.6.2 Dialectical and Process Logics 185

10.6.3 Contemporary Non-Classical Logics 186

10.7 Implications For First Principles... 186

10.7.1 The Bootstrapping Problem 187

10.7.2 Logical Pluralism and First Principles 187

10.7.3 The Limits of Formalization.. 188

10.7.4 Integration with Other Domains................................. 188

10.7.5 The Unity and Diversity of Reason 189

10.8 Conclusion 189

PART IV 192

Chapter 11: The Sacred and Transcendent 192

11.1 The Irreducible Sacred 192

11.2 The Phenomenology Of The Sacred.................................... 193

11.2.1 Otto's Numinous and Its Critics................................... 193

11.2.2 Sacred Space and Time 194

11.2.3 Varieties and Commonalities 194

11.3 Mystical Experience And Epistemology 195

11.3.1 The Perennialist-Constructivist Debate 195

11.3.2 Reformed Epistemology and Religious Perception 195

11.3.3 Neuroscience and Consciousness 196

11.4 The Finite-Infinite Relationship 197

11.4.1 Classical Formulations.. 197

11.4.2 Contemporary Models... 197

11.5 Religious Awareness And Epistemic Pluralism 198

11.5.1 Multiple Modes of Knowing 198

11.5.2 Contemplative Science.. 199

11.6 Implications For First Principles....................................... 199

11.6.1 Dimensional Pluralism 199

11.6.2 Relational Ontology 199

11.6.3 Unity-in-Difference 200

11.7 Conclusion 200

Chapter 12: Creation and Ultimate Ground 202

12.1 The Universal Question Of Origins.................................... 202

12.2 Creation Narratives Across Traditions 204

12.2.1 The Abrahamic Model: Creation *Ex Nihilo* 204

12.2.2 Hindu Cosmology: Emanation and Cycles 205

12.2.3 Buddhist Perspectives: Dependent Origination 207

12.2.4 Indigenous and African Traditions 208

12.3 The Concept Of Ultimate Reality 210

12.3.1 Absolute Being and the Ground of Existence 210

12.3.2 Apophatic and Cataphatic Approaches 211

12.4 Divine Attributes And Logical Necessity 212

12.4.1 Classical Theistic Attributes 212

12.4.2 Logical Arguments for Divine Attributes 212

12.5 Eastern Perspectives: Beyond Personal Deity 213

12.5.1 Brahman: Existence-Consciousness-Bliss 213

12.5.2 The Dao: The Nameless Source 213

12.6 Synthesis: Convergent Insights And Critical Challenges 213

12.7 Implications For First Principles 214

12.7.1 The Principle of Sufficient Reason 214

12.7.2 The Principle of Plenitude 214

12.7.3 The Principle of Participation 214

12.8 Conclusion 214

Chapter 13: Revelation and Authority **216**

13.1 Introduction: The Epistemological Challenge 216

13.2 The Nature Of Revelation 217

13.2.1 Defining Revelation Across Traditions 217

13.2.2 Modes of Revelatory Communication 218

13.2.3 The Problem of Recognition and Validation 219

13.3 Scripture As Revelation 220

13.3.1 The Formation of Sacred Texts 220

13.3.2 Canonization and Authority...................................... 221

13.3.3 Interpretation and Hermeneutics 221

13.4 Tradition And Transmission..................................... 222

13.4.1 Oral Tradition and Living Memory........................... 222

13.4.2 Apostolic Succession and Transmission Lines 222

13.4.3 The Role of Community... 223

13.5 Natural Theology: Reason's Reach.............................. 223

13.5.1 Classical Arguments for Divine Existence 223

13.5.2 The Limits of Natural Reason 224

13.5.3 Reformed Epistemology 224

13.6 Revealed Theology: Beyond Reason's Grasp 225

13.6.1 The Content of Revelation 225

13.6.2 The Grammar of Faith... 225

13.6.3 Miracles and Signs.. 226

13.7 The Faith-Reason Synthesis.. 226

13.7.1 Historical Approaches 226

13.7.2 Modern Challenges and Responses........................... 227

13.7.3 Contemporary Integration.. 227

13.8 Authority And Interpretation 228

13.8.1 Institutional Authority... 228

13.8.2 Charismatic Authority and Innovation...................... 228

13.8.3 Interpretive Pluralism and Authority........................ 229

13.9 Synthesis: Revelation As First Principle...................... 229

Chapter 14: Moral First Principles **231**

14.1 The Moral Dimension Of Reality: Foundational Questions 231

14.2 The Objectivity Debate: Realism And Its Critics 232

14.2.1 The Case for Moral Realism 232

14.2.2 Evolutionary and Neurobiological Challenges 233

14.2.3 Constructivist and Expressivist Alternatives 234

14.3 Sources And Methods Of Moral Knowledge 236

14.3.1 Natural Law Theory: Reason and Human Nature 236

14.3.2 Divine Command Theory: Theological Foundations 237

14.3.3 Moral Intuition and Rational Insight 238

14.4 Universal Patterns In Moral Judgment 239

14.4.1 Cross-Cultural Convergence and Moral Foundations 239

14.4.2 Evolutionary Psychology and Moral Universals 239

14.5 Moral Agency: Free Will And Responsibility 240

14.5.1 The Determinism Challenge 240

14.5.2 Compatibilist Responses 241

14.5.3 Strawsonian Responsibility and Moral Relationships 242

14.6 Neuroscience, Psychology, And Moral Judgment 243

14.6.1 Neural Substrates of Moral Cognition 243

14.6.2 Psychopathy and Moral Agency 243

14.6.3 Moral Development and Neuroplasticity 244

14.7 Synthesis: Convergence Across Traditions 244

14.7.1 Universal Moral Principles 244

14.7.2 Toward Integration 245

PART V **247**

Chapter 15: Where Science, Philosophy, and Religion Meet 247

15.1 Introduction: The Convergence Hypothesis 247

15.2 Shared Epistemological Foundations 249

15.2.1 Commitment to Truth and Reality 249

15.2.2 Critical Realism Across Domains........................... 250

15.3 The Intelligibility Of The Universe............................. 251

15.3.1 Mathematical Effectiveness and Cosmic Rationality............... 251

15.3.2 Philosophical Analysis of Intelligibility....................... 252

15.3.3 Religious Perspectives on Cosmic Rationality........................... 252

15.4 Consciousness: The Interdisciplinary Convergence Point............. 253

15.4.1 The Hard Problem and Its Implications 253

15.4.2 Philosophical Analysis of Consciousness...................... 254

15.4.3 Contemplative Traditions and First-Person Investigation 255

15.5 Fine-Tuning And The Anthropic Principle 255

15.5.1 The Fine-Tuning Evidence.............................. 255

15.5.2 Scientific Responses and Multiverse Theories..................... 256

15.5.3 Philosophical and Theological Perspectives 257

15.6 Challenges To Reductive Materialism............................. 257

15.6.1 Philosophical Problems with Physicalism..................... 257

15.6.2 Information, Meaning, and Abstract Objects........................... 258

15.6.3 Alternative Metaphysical Frameworks....................... 258

15.7 Methodological Pluralism And Integration 259

15.7.1 Complementarity Across Domains........................... 259

15.7.2 Criteria for Evaluation 259

15.7.3 Future Directions 260

15.8 Conclusion: Toward Comprehensive Understanding 260

Chapter 16: Competing Worldviews 262

16.1 Introduction: The Interpretive Framework Of Reality 262

16.2.1 The Physicalist Framework 264

16.2.2 Sophisticated Physicalist Responses... 265

16.2.3 Interpretive Implications... 266

16.3 Theistic Realism: Reality As Divine Creation................................. 267

16.3.1 Classical Theistic Arguments 267

16.3.2 Epistemological Approaches.. 268

16.3.3 Contemporary Challenges... 269

16.4 Idealistic Philosophies: Consciousness As Fundamental............... 270

16.4.1 Classical and Contemporary Idealism 270

16.4.2 Contemporary Developments.. 271

16.4.3 Explanatory Advantages and Difficulties 272

16.5 Process Philosophy And Panentheistic Worldviews 272

16.5.1 Whiteheadian Process Metaphysics.. 272

16.5.2 Process Theology and Panentheism.. 273

16.5.3 Process Interpretation of First Principles................................... 274

16.6 Eastern Non-Dualistic And Pragmatic Alternatives....................... 275

16.6.1 Buddhist Philosophy and Dependent Origination................... 275

16.6.2 Daoist and Advaitic Perspectives... 276

16.6.3 Pragmatic Approaches 277

16.7 The Hermeneutical Structure Of Worldview Interpretation 278

16.7.1 Theory-Ladenness and Interpretive Frameworks..................... 278

16.7.2 Tradition-Dependent Rationality.. 279

16.7.3 Phenomenological Variation 280

16.8 Criteria For Worldview Evaluation 280

16.8.1 Internal Consistency and Logical Coherence 280

16.8.2 Explanatory Scope and Depth 281

16.8.3 Existential and Practical Adequacy............................. 282

16.8.4 Empirical Fruitfulness and Research Productivity 282

16.9 Conclusion: The Hermeneutical Challenge Of First Principles..... 283

Chapter 17: The Unity of Truth.. 285

17.1 The Metaphysics Of Truth... 285

17.2 The Convergence Thesis And Its Critics 288

17.3 Hierarchical Integration And Emergent Properties...................... 291

17.4 Methodological Strategies For Epistemic Integration.................... 294

17.5 Addressing Persistent Challenges 297

17.6 Toward Comprehensive Understanding 299

17.7 Conclusion 301

PART VI **303**

Chapter 18: Living with First Principles 303

18.1 The Ontological Structure Of Lived Experience.......................... 303

18.2 Decision-Making Architectures And Practical Reasoning............ 305

18.3 Moral Psychology and the Foundations of Ethical Life 307

18.4 Existential Meaning and the Architecture of Significance 308

18.5 Suffering, Mortality, and the Limits of Human Existence.............. 309

18.6 Temporal Orientation and the Question of Progress.................... 310

18.7 Practical Integration and the Synthesis of Worldviews 311

18.8 Conclusion 311

Chapter 19: The Ongoing Quest..**313**

19.1 The Dialectical Structure of Knowledge Expansion 313

19.2 The Historical Contingency of Foundational Frameworks............ 316

19.3 Contemporary Frontiers and Emerging Paradigms 319

19.4 Epistemic Virtues and the Methodology of Inquiry........................ 322

19.5 The Hermeneutics of Cross-Domain Integration............................ 324

19.6 Future Trajectories and Emerging Syntheses 325

19.7 Conclusion: The Quest as Constitutive Principle 326

Chapter 20: Conclusions – The Ground of Reality...................**328**

20.1 The Architecture of Inquiry.. 328

20.2 Convergent Patterns Across Domains 331

20.3 Irreducible Tensions and Complementarity.................................... 334

20.4 Provisional Affirmations 336

20.5 The Participatory Universe 337

20.6 Toward Integral Methodology.. 339

20.7 The Recursive Nature of Inquiry.. 339

20.8 Living Ground: Process and Emergence 340

20.9 Implications for Continued Inquiry 341

20.10 Conclusion: The Continuing Quest.. 342

Glossary of Key Terms **344**

References **369**

DEDICATION

To the obstacles and failures that opened the door to this inquiry.

A READER'S GUIDE TO THIS INQUIRY

The Purpose of This Guide

This monograph undertakes an ambitious intellectual journey across disciplinary boundaries, engaging historical and contemporary problems through multiple methodological lenses. The scale and scope of the investigation—spanning physics, philosophy, theology, and the human sciences—necessitate explicit guidance regarding its architecture, argumentative strategy, and optimal navigation. This orientation serves both practical and philosophical purposes: it clarifies the work's central thesis, delineates its structural organization, identifies appropriate entry points for readers from diverse intellectual backgrounds, and articulates the participatory stance that the inquiry itself advocates.

The investigation advances a fundamental claim that challenges conventional epistemological assumptions: inquiry does not merely extract objective facts from an external world but constitutes a form of conscious participation in an unfolding reality. This thesis carries profound implications for how we conceive first principles, evaluate evidence across domains, and adjudicate between competing worldviews. This guide explicates how the argument develops across twenty chapters and enables readers to extract maximum value from the work, whether approaching it comprehensively or selectively.

The Central Question and Methodological Framework

Every intellectual discipline operates from foundational commitments that function as first principles. These range from explicit axioms in logic and conservation laws in physics to tacit assumptions about what constitutes legitimate explanation or evidence. Disagreements about specific conclusions often reflect deeper divergences regarding these starting points. This work contends that such foundational commitments can be surfaced, analyzed, and evaluated through systematic comparison without succumbing to either relativism or dogmatism.

The investigation proposes that human inquiry has historically proceeded along three primary pathways, each offering distinct but complementary access to truth. The empirical path provides disciplined attention to the world through observation, measurement, and experimental manipulation. The rational path offers conceptual analysis, logical inference, and examination of the meta-criteria governing explanation itself. The revelatory path encompasses the domains of meaning disclosed through conscience, symbol, scripture, and those experiences through which communities claim access to moral and metaphysical insight.

The central methodological wager maintains that these three approaches need not remain isolated in disciplinary silos but can be brought into principled dialogue. The work provides systematic scaffolding for such dialogue and establishes evaluative criteria: coherence, explanatory scope, depth of engagement with fundamental structures, fruitfulness in generating new insights, and existential adequacy in orienting human action and understanding.

Structural Organization

The twenty chapters are organized into six major parts, each addressing a distinct aspect of the foundational inquiry while contributing to the cumulative argument. This architecture permits both linear progression and strategic entry at points most relevant to particular disciplinary interests.

Part I (Chapters 1-3) establishes the philosophical framework by examining why first principles matter, how problems of regress and circularity challenge foundational projects, and how the triadic methodology provides a constructive response to these challenges.

Part II (Chapters 4-6) examines first principles within physics and cosmology, analyzing conservation laws, quantum mechanics, relativity, and cosmological fine-tuning. These chapters demonstrate how our most successful scientific theories simultaneously constrain and provoke metaphysical interpretation.

Part III (Chapters 7-10) develops the conceptual apparatus necessary for rigorous cross-domain comparison, examining consciousness, ontology, epistemology, and logical foundations. Here, the criteria for evaluating first principles receive their most detailed articulation.

Part IV (Chapters 11-14) engages religious and moral dimensions of foundational inquiry, analyzing sacred experience, creation narratives, revelatory authority, and moral first principles. This section demonstrates how revelatory claims can enter public discourse under shared evaluative criteria without reductionism.

Part V (Chapters 15-17) undertakes a comparative evaluation of major worldviews, testing the convergence thesis against contemporary alternatives, including naturalistic materialism, theistic realism, idealism, and process philosophy. These chapters apply the developed criteria to assess competing interpretive frameworks.

Part VI (Chapters 18-20) addresses practical implications, examining how foundational commitments shape lived experience, how disciplines might collaborate without sacrificing their distinctive contributions, and what questions remain for future inquiry.

Navigation Strategies for Different Readers

The work's interdisciplinary scope permits multiple productive paths through the material, depending on readers' backgrounds and interests.

Readers approaching from the natural sciences might begin with Part II to observe how physical theories generate foundational questions, proceed to Part III for the conceptual framework, advance to Part V for worldview comparison, and then return to Part I for meta-theoretical reflection before concluding with Part VI's practical implications.

Those grounded in philosophy should commence with Part I's articulation of the foundational problem and Part III's conceptual architecture, then examine Part II as a testing ground for philosophical commitments. Part V's comparative evaluation and Part IV's treatment of revelatory domains should follow, concluding with Part VI's synthetic proposals.

Readers from theological or religious studies backgrounds might enter through Part IV's treatment of revelation and moral foundations, then engage Part III's conceptual framework and Part II's scientific constraints. Part V's comparative evaluation provides a crucial perspective before returning to Part I's framing and Part VI's practical synthesis.

Evaluative Criteria

The investigation employs explicit criteria for assessing claims across all domains, ensuring public accountability and enabling productive disagreement:

Coherence: encompasses internal consistency, absence of vicious circularity, and clarity regarding necessary self-reference, particularly concerning logical and epistemological foundations.

Explanatory scope: evaluates how comprehensively a framework illuminates relevant phenomena without ad hoc modifications or arbitrary restrictions.

Depth: measures proximity to reality's structural features, distinguishing fundamental principles from surface regularities or contingent generalizations.

Fruitfulness: assesses a framework's capacity to generate new questions, unify previously disparate problems, and yield practical benefits for inquiry and human flourishing.

Existential adequacy: examines whether a framework can orient meaningful action, sustain moral seriousness, and address lived experience without collapsing into subjectivism.

Integrative capacity: evaluates whether a framework can engage productively with other methodological approaches without silencing or trivializing their distinctive contributions.

The Triadic Method in Practice

The three paths of inquiry function not as separate domains but as complementary disciplines of attention. The empirical path maintains contact with reality beyond human preferences, resisting speculative overreach and demanding conceptual precision when theories encounter measurement. The rational path safeguards inferential rigor, making explicit the warrants connecting data to theory, theory to explanation, and explanation to metaphysical commitment. The revelatory path preserves dimensions of meaning and value essential to human orientation, while submitting claims to criteria capable of engaging rival interpretations.

Individual chapters typically employ a triangulation strategy, examining phenomena through each register sequentially, articulating competing interpretations, and applying evaluative criteria to assess relative strengths and weaknesses. Where the three paths converge on mutually reinforcing insights, the investigation identifies genuine convergence rather than claiming narrow proof. Where divergence occurs, the analysis maps disagreements explicitly rather than obscuring them through premature synthesis.

Reading as Participatory Inquiry

The work's central thesis—that inquiry involves participatory engagement rather than detached observation—carries implications for the reading process itself. Engaging the text participatorily means attending to how one's own interpretive stance, background assumptions, and evaluative commitments shape what becomes visible in the argument. This does not entail capitulation to subjectivism but rather recognition that all observation occurs from particular vantage points within specific conceptual frameworks.

When encountering challenging concepts, readers should consider what stance or framework makes them intelligible. When claims appear self-evident, examining the background assumptions that generate this appearance often proves illuminating. When revelatory or metaphysical claims enter the discussion, allowing them to speak within their own grammar while applying shared criteria prevents both uncritical acceptance and premature dismissal.

Scholarly Apparatus and References

The extensive citation apparatus serves essential functions beyond academic convention. In-text citations locate claims within ongoing scholarly conversations, enabling readers to verify sources and pursue deeper engagement with particular debates. Cross-references between chapters reveal the argument's cumulative structure and reward following conceptual threads across sections. The bibliography maps active dialogues in multiple fields, with recurring citation clusters indicating particularly significant debates.

The comprehensive Glossary of Key Terms provides an invaluable resource for navigating the work's interdisciplinary vocabulary. Given the investigation's range across physics, philosophy, theology, and related fields, technical terms often carry distinct meanings in different disciplines. The glossary clarifies these distinctions and establishes the specific senses employed throughout the argument. Readers should consult it whenever encountering unfamiliar terminology or when familiar terms appear to function in unexpected ways. The glossary entries themselves often illuminate conceptual connections that might otherwise remain implicit.

Technical discussions, while occasionally demanding, represent crucial sites where theoretical costs and benefits become measurable. When encountering technical passages, identifying the specific question they address often clarifies their necessity and reveals how appropriate conceptual precision can simplify apparently complex debates.

Expectations and Outcomes

Readers who engage seriously with this inquiry should emerge with enhanced capacities for foundational analysis. These include the ability to articulate one's own first principles and justify their foundational status, to specify and defend criteria for theory choice and worldview evaluation, to translate productively between empirical, rational, and revelatory registers, to diagnose whether disagreements stem from empirical, conceptual, or ultimate commitments, and to identify where further inquiry promises greatest fruitfulness.

Whether readers ultimately endorse the work's convergence thesis or develop alternative positions, these analytical capabilities possess enduring value for intellectual work across disciplines. They enhance precision in laboratory research, clarity in philosophical argument, depth in theological reflection, and wisdom in practical judgment.

Scope and Limitations

This investigation does not attempt to provide final, demonstrative proof for any single worldview against all competitors. Neither does it reduce any domain to another through eliminative strategies. The work acknowledges that evaluative criteria alone cannot determine all intellectual commitments—historical, cultural, and existential factors legitimately influence judgment.

The investigation's goal is simultaneously more modest and more ambitious: to articulate explicit standards for productive comparison across worldviews, to clarify why thoughtful people reach different conclusions from shared evidence, and to enhance both the quality of disagreement and the possibility of genuine progress in foundational understanding.

Conclusion

This work invites sustained engagement rather than passive consumption. It respects the intellectual traditions that have generated our current understanding while maintaining hope that deeper integration remains possible without erasing legitimate differences. Readers who grant each methodological register a fair hearing—allowing empirical evidence to challenge metaphysical assumptions, rational analysis to test favored theories, and revelatory claims to demonstrate cognitive content under shared standards—will find their questions sharpened, their criteria clarified, and their horizons of understanding expanded.

The inquiry does not promise arrival at a predetermined destination but offers instead more precise tools for navigation, clearer recognition of where paths converge and diverge, and enhanced capacity for that patient, disciplined attention through which truth discloses itself across the multiple registers of human understanding. In this methodological contribution lies the work's most enduring value, transcending particular conclusions to enrich the practice of inquiry itself.

PART I

CHAPTER 1: WHAT ARE FIRST PRINCIPLES?

1.1 THE SEARCH FOR CERTAINTY

Throughout human history, thinkers across cultures have sought bedrock truths upon which all other knowledge could securely rest. This quest for certainty—for principles so fundamental they require no further justification—represents one of humanity's most enduring intellectual pursuits (Popkin, 2003). Whether examining the mathematical architecture of modern physics, the systematic structures of philosophy, or the foundational claims of religious traditions worldwide, we discover at their base certain irreducible commitments that serve as starting points for all subsequent reasoning (Shapiro, 2000).

The concept of first principles offers a methodological key to understanding how human knowledge is structured and validated across diverse intellectual traditions. Indigenous philosophical systems have long recognized this need for foundational understanding, with Native American traditions emphasizing the interconnectedness of all existence as a fundamental principle underlying both spiritual practice and ecological wisdom (Deloria, 1999). African philosophical traditions similarly identify ubuntu—the principle that individual identity emerges through community relationships—as foundational to understanding human nature and moral obligation (Mbiti, 1990). These non-Western approaches challenge the assumption that first principles must follow Aristotelian or Cartesian models, revealing alternative foundations for systematic knowledge (Wiredu, 1996).

Rather than accepting inherited assumptions or building upon potentially flawed foundations, first principles thinking demands that we trace our beliefs back to their most basic origins. This methodological approach has proven transformative across disciplines and cultures, from Aristotle's systematization of logic to Buddhist analysis of consciousness, from the axiomatic method in mathematics to contemporary technological innovation (Rescher, 2010). Indigenous science perspectives demonstrate how traditional ecological knowledge operates from first principles about natural relationships that Western science has only recently begun to recognize and validate (Whyte, 2017).

This chapter establishes the conceptual framework for investigating reality's foundations through a critical examination of first principles methodology. We examine what philosophers across traditions mean by "first principles," tracing the concept from ancient Greek and Asian philosophy through medieval synthesis to contemporary epistemology. We explore how different domains of inquiry—scientific, philosophical, and religious—employ first principles reasoning, each with distinct methods yet sharing fundamental commitments to truth and coherence. The analysis addresses both the power and limitations of first principles approaches, engaging with skeptical challenges while demonstrating why this ancient methodology remains vital for contemporary thought, particularly as we confront questions about consciousness, cosmology, and the ultimate nature of existence.

1.2 DEFINING FIRST PRINCIPLES

The term "first principles" derives from the Greek *archai*, meaning beginnings or origins, which Aristotle employed to denote the fundamental bases from which things are known (Shields, 2016). In the *Metaphysics*, Aristotle distinguished between knowledge that depends on prior premises and knowledge that is immediate and self-evident, arguing that "there is a principle of demonstration that is not itself subject to demonstration"

(Aristotle, 384-322 BCE/1984). A first principle, in this technical sense, constitutes a foundational truth that cannot be deduced from any prior or more fundamental truth—it represents where explanation necessarily terminates to avoid infinite regress (Barnes, 1994).

Contemporary philosophy of science has refined this classical understanding while acknowledging its complexities. Chakravartty (2017) argues that first principles in science function as "constitutive principles" that define theoretical frameworks rather than empirical claims subject to direct verification. This conception finds parallel development in consciousness studies, where philosophers have identified fundamental principles about the nature of subjective experience that resist reduction to simpler components. The "hard problem of consciousness"—explaining how and why physical processes give rise to subjective experience—points toward first principles about the mind-matter relationship that may be irreducible (Chalmers, 1995). This suggests that consciousness itself may represent a fundamental feature of reality requiring its own explanatory principles rather than emerging from purely physical processes (Nagel, 1974).

Buddhist philosophy developed sophisticated frameworks for understanding foundational truths through the distinction between *paramartha-satya* (ultimate truth) and *samvriti-satya* (conventional truth), identifying fundamental principles about reality's nature that underlie all conventional understanding (Siderits, 2007). Classical Indian epistemology, as analyzed by Matilal (1986), systematized knowledge sources (*pramanas*) that serve as first principles for valid cognition, including perception (*pratyaksa*), inference (*anumana*), and testimonial knowledge (*sabda*). The Nyaya school's analysis provides particularly sophisticated frameworks for understanding how foundational principles operate across different epistemic domains, establishing criteria for distinguishing genuine first principles from mere assumptions (Phillips, 2012).

The Daoist concept of *dao* as the ineffable source and pattern of all existence represents another approach to first principles—one that emphasizes the limits of conceptual articulation while maintaining that fundamental reality can be apprehended through direct realization (Graham, 2010). The *Daodejing* articulates this principle as simultaneously transcendent and immanent, beyond ordinary conceptualization yet accessible through contemplative practice: "The dao that can be spoken is not the eternal Dao" (Ames & Hall, 2003). This paradoxical formulation highlights how some first principles may transcend linguistic expression while still serving as foundations for systematic understanding.

Mathematical axiom systems provide the clearest illustration of explicit first principles in operation. When Euclid demonstrated properties of triangles, he relied on more basic propositions about lines and angles, which themselves depended on fundamental definitions and axioms—such as "things equal to the same thing are equal to each other"—that could not be proven without circularity (Mueller, 1981). These axioms represent first principles within Euclidean geometry: necessary starting points without which geometric reasoning cannot commence. Hilbert's (1971) subsequent formalization demonstrated how different axiom systems could generate distinct but equally valid geometric theories, revealing that first principles define conceptual frameworks rather than absolute truths about physical space.

In empirical science, researchers identify fundamental laws—conservation principles, thermodynamic laws, quantum mechanical postulates—that serve as explanatory bedrock for complex phenomena (Lange, 2017). Bell's theorem demonstrates how quantum mechanical first principles about measurement and reality lead to counterintuitive but experimentally verified conclusions about local realism, forcing revision of classical assumptions about the nature of physical reality (Bell, 1964). These principles achieve validation not through mathematical proof but through their explanatory power and empirical adequacy across diverse phenomena (van Fraassen, 2008).

The identification of genuine first principles requires careful distinction from merely familiar assumptions, a challenge that has generated extensive epistemological debate. Block's (2007) analysis of consciousness reveals how seemingly obvious distinctions between access consciousness and phenomenal consciousness reflect different foundational assumptions about mental phenomena. What appears as a first principle in one theoretical framework may be revealed as derivative when viewed from a more fundamental perspective, suggesting that the identification of first principles is itself theory-dependent (Friedman, 2013). This raises critical questions about whether first principles can be objective or whether they are inevitably relative to particular conceptual schemes—a debate that continues to divide philosophical opinion (Boghossian, 2006).

1.3 HISTORICAL DEVELOPMENT

The systematic investigation of first principles emerged independently across multiple philosophical traditions, each developing distinct methodologies while converging on similar foundational questions. In ancient Greece, pre-Socratic philosophers sought to identify the *arche*—the fundamental substance or principle underlying all reality. Thales proposed water as the universal substrate, Anaximander posited the boundless (*apeiron*), while Heraclitus emphasized perpetual flux governed by *logos* (Kirk, Raven, & Schofield, 2007). These early attempts established the intellectual pattern of seeking irreducible explanatory principles beneath phenomenal diversity, though they disagreed fundamentally about whether these principles were material or formal (Lloyd, 1970).

Parallel developments in ancient Indian philosophy produced sophisticated analyses that continue to influence contemporary thought. The Upanishads articulated Brahman as the ultimate ground of being—"that from which all beings arise, through which they live, and into which they return" (Olivelle, 1998). Early Buddhist thought developed comprehensive analyses of consciousness and causation through the principle of dependent origination (*pratītyasamutpāda*), which identifies the interconnected conditions underlying all phenomena without positing a permanent substrate (Gethin, 1998). Bhattacharyya's (1956) seminal analysis demonstrates how different Indian philosophical schools approached first principles through distinct methodologies—the Samkhya through enumeration of fundamental categories, the Vaisheshika through atomic analysis, the Vedanta through consciousness—while maintaining shared commitments to systematic inquiry and logical rigor.

Chinese philosophy developed distinctive approaches to foundational principles that emphasized practical wisdom and social harmony. Confucian concepts of *ren* (humaneness) and *yi* (righteousness) served as first principles for ethical and political philosophy, grounded in assumptions about human nature's inherent orientation toward virtue (Ivanhoe & Van Norden, 2005). The Daoist notion of *wu wei* (non-action) emerged as a fundamental principle for harmonious existence, derived from observations about natural processes rather than abstract reasoning (Slingerland, 2003). Hall and Ames (1987) demonstrate how Confucian thought operates from correlative rather than causal first principles, emphasizing patterns of relationship and resonance rather than linear chains of cause and effect—a fundamentally different approach from Greek philosophical traditions.

Plato advanced Greek philosophy through his theory of Forms, proposing that sensible reality derives from eternal, immutable principles accessible through dialectical reasoning. The Form of the Good served as the ultimate first principle—"that which makes both knowledge and truth possible" (Plato, 1997). This metaphysical approach profoundly influenced subsequent philosophy by establishing a template wherein first principles transcend empirical reality and are discovered through rational contemplation rather than sensory investigation (Fine, 2019). Critics from Aristotle onward have challenged this separation of first principles from empirical reality, generating a debate that continues to shape contemporary metaphysics (Schaffer, 2009).

Aristotle systematized the study of first principles across multiple domains with unprecedented rigor. In logic, he identified the law of non-contradiction as "the most certain principle of all," arguing that it cannot be demonstrated because any demonstration would necessarily presuppose it (Aristotle, *Metaphysics*). In natural philosophy, he proposed four causes—material, formal, efficient, and final—as fundamental explanatory categories that jointly account for change and persistence in nature (Lennox, 2017). In ethics, he grounded human flourishing (*eudaimonia*) in the actualization of distinctively human capacities, particularly rational activity in accordance with virtue (Kraut, 2018). This comprehensive approach established first principles thinking as essential to systematic philosophy while raising enduring questions about the relationship between logical, metaphysical, and ethical foundations.

Medieval scholars across religious traditions achieved remarkable syntheses of philosophical and theological approaches to first principles. Thomas Aquinas integrated Aristotelian philosophy with Christian theology, distinguishing between principles accessible through natural reason and those requiring divine revelation, arguing that "grace does not destroy nature but perfects it" (Aquinas, 1265/1981). His Five Ways demonstrate how philosophical first principles can establish God's existence while acknowledging that God's nature transcends rational comprehension (McGrath, 2011). This dual approach—affirming reason's capacity while recognizing its limits—became paradigmatic for subsequent natural theology.

Islamic philosophers developed particularly sophisticated analyses of the relationship between philosophical and religious first principles. Al-Ghazali's systematic critique in the *Tahafut al-falasifa* (The incoherence of the philosophers) challenged the sufficiency of purely rational first principles for understanding ultimate reality while maintaining rigorous standards for theological inquiry (Al-Ghazali, 1095/2000). His comprehensive approach in the *Ihya 'ulum al-din* (The revival of the religious sciences) demonstrates how spiritual first principles can ground systematic understanding across domains, including ethics, psychology, and social relations (Al-Ghazali, 1106/2014). Avicenna's metaphysical system, as analyzed by McGinnis (2010), exemplifies the sophisticated integration of Aristotelian and Islamic approaches, particularly his distinction between essence and existence that became foundational for subsequent philosophy across religious traditions.

Jewish philosophers explored how rational first principles could illuminate scriptural truth while maintaining revelation's primacy. Maimonides (1963) argued in the *Guide for the Perplexed* that apparent conflicts between philosophy and scripture arise from misunderstanding either reason or revelation, proposing hermeneutical principles for reconciling them. Novak's (1998) analysis reveals how natural law thinking in Judaism provides first principles for ethical reasoning that bridge philosophical and religious approaches without reducing one to the other. Islamic intellectual traditions developed sophisticated methodologies for evaluating religious authority and textual interpretation, establishing first principles for hadith criticism that balanced authenticity, transmission, and coherence (Brown, 2014).

The modern period witnessed revolutionary reconceptions of first principles. Descartes' (1641/1996) method of systematic doubt sought absolutely certain foundations by doubting everything possibly doubtful, leading to the *cogito ergo sum*—"I think, therefore I am"—as the indubitable first principle for reconstructing knowledge. This methodological innovation transformed philosophy by making epistemological certainty the primary criterion for first principles, though critics argued it led to problematic dualisms and solipsistic tendencies (Cottingham, 2008). The Cartesian emphasis on clear and distinct ideas as markers of truth established new standards for philosophical rigor while generating debates about the relationship between psychological certainty and logical necessity that persist in contemporary epistemology (Williams, 2014).

The empiricist tradition challenged rationalist approaches by arguing that sensory experience provides the only legitimate foundation for knowledge. Locke's (1689/1975) *tabula rasa* thesis denied innate principles, proposing that all knowledge derives from sensation and reflection. Hume's (1748/2007) radical empiricism revealed fundamental problems with empiricist first principles, demonstrating that even seemingly obvious principles like causation cannot be justified without circularity: "When we look about us towards external objects, and consider the operation of causes, we are never able, in a single instance, to discover any power or necessary connexion". This skeptical critique precipitated Kant's critical philosophy, which identified synthetic *a priori* principles—categories of understanding that make experience possible while transcending it—as necessary conditions for the possibility of knowledge (Kant, 1781/1998; Guyer, 2006).

1.4 THE ARCHITECTURE OF KNOWLEDGE

Contemporary epistemology recognizes first principles as structurally essential to knowledge systems while vigorously debating their nature, justification, and scope. Foundationalism argues that knowledge necessarily rests on basic beliefs requiring no further justification to avoid infinite regress or circular reasoning (BonJour, 2010). Strong foundationalists claim these basic beliefs must be infallible, self-evident, or incorrigible—immune from error through their immediate givenness to consciousness. Moderate foundationalists accept that basic beliefs may be defeasible yet still properly basic if they possess sufficient initial credibility without requiring inferential support (Audi, 2011). This position faces the challenge of specifying non-arbitrary criteria for basicality—explaining why certain beliefs qualify as foundational while others do not—without presupposing the very foundations being justified (Williamson, 2000).

Virtue epistemology offers innovative approaches to understanding first principles through intellectual character rather than propositional foundations. Zagzebski (1996) argues that intellectual virtues such as intellectual courage, thoroughness, and open-mindedness serve as first principles for reliable belief formation, grounding epistemology in human excellences rather than abstract logical relationships. This approach provides more naturalistic foundations for knowledge claims while addressing concerns about the cultural and psychological dimensions of epistemic practices. Sosa's (2007) performance epistemology extends this framework by analyzing knowledge as apt belief—true belief whose correctness manifests competence—thereby grounding first principles in reliable cognitive capacities rather than foundational propositions.

Social epistemology reveals how first principles operate within communities of inquiry rather than individual minds alone, challenging traditional individualistic assumptions. Goldman's (1999) veritistic social epistemology demonstrates how social processes of testimony, expertise, and collective investigation shape which principles function as foundational within particular knowledge communities. Longino's (1990) analysis of scientific objectivity shows how social criticism and methodological pluralism can improve the reliability of foundational assumptions, suggesting that first principles gain epistemic authority through communal validation rather than individual intuition. This perspective reveals irreducibly social dimensions of foundational knowledge that purely individualistic approaches cannot adequately address (Kusch, 2002).

Naturalized epistemology, as developed by Kornblith (2002), argues that understanding knowledge requires empirical investigation of actual cognitive processes rather than purely *a priori* philosophical analysis. This approach treats first principles as evolved cognitive dispositions that have proven reliable for navigating natural and social environments, providing evolutionary grounding for foundational commitments. Quine's (1969) influential argument for naturalizing epistemology challenged the traditional distinction between philosophy and empirical science, proposing that epistemology should be "contained in natural science, as a chapter of psychology". While critics argue this approach conflates descriptive and normative questions, defenders maintain it provides more realistic foundations for understanding how knowledge actually functions (Kitcher, 1992).

Coherentism offers a systematic alternative to foundationalism, arguing that beliefs achieve justification through mutual support within coherent systems rather than linear derivation from basic principles. From this perspective, "first principles" are simply beliefs most deeply embedded in our web of belief—those whose rejection would require the most extensive systematic revision (Quine & Ullian, 1978). BonJour (1985) developed sophisticated coherentist criteria including logical consistency, probabilistic consistency, explanatory power, and comprehensiveness. However, coherentism faces significant challenges, including the possibility of equally coherent but incompatible belief systems, the problem of circular justification, and difficulties explaining the special epistemic status of observational beliefs (Sosa, 2007). Recent developments in inferentialist semantics attempt to address these challenges by grounding meaning and justification in patterns of inference rather than foundational reference (Brandom, 2000).

Feminist epistemologists have mounted influential critiques of traditional approaches to first principles as reflecting masculine biases toward abstraction, universality, and detachment from social context. Standpoint theory argues that knowledge is inevitably situated and that marginalized perspectives may reveal different foundational truths than those recognized by dominant groups (Harding, 1991). This challenges the claimed universality of first principles while maintaining that some perspectives provide a more accurate understanding of social reality. Longino's (2002) contextual empiricism demonstrates how background assumptions function as *de facto* first principles in scientific research, often reflecting social values and interests rather than pure logic or observation. These critiques have prompted increased attention to the politics of knowledge and the role of power in determining which principles achieve foundational status (Fricker, 2007).

Mathematical systems provide paradigmatic examples of explicit first principles functioning as axioms, though even here, foundational questions persist. The development of non-Euclidean geometries in the nineteenth century demonstrated that different, mutually incompatible axiom systems could each be internally consistent and applicable to different domains (Torretti, 1978). Gödel's (1931) incompleteness theorems proved that any formal system complex enough to include arithmetic must be either incomplete (unable to prove all truths) or inconsistent (proving contradictions)—revealing fundamental limitations to axiomatic approaches even in mathematics (Smith, 2013). These results suggest that complete foundations for knowledge may be impossible in principle rather than merely difficult to achieve.

Category theory offers alternative foundations for mathematics that emphasize structural relationships and mappings rather than set-theoretic membership, suggesting that mathematical first principles concern patterns rather than objects (Awodey, 2010). Homotopy type theory extends this approach by integrating topological and logical structures, providing new foundations that some argue better capture mathematical practice (The Univalent Foundations Program, 2013). These developments reveal how different choices of first principles generate distinct but equally valid mathematical frameworks, highlighting conventional elements in seemingly objective foundations while raising questions about mathematical pluralism versus monism (Balaguer, 1998).

Scientific methodology employs first principles both explicitly and implicitly at multiple levels. Explicitly, sciences operate with fundamental laws, conservation principles, and symmetries that constrain theoretical development. The standard model of particle physics is built on gauge symmetry principles that determine the fundamental forces and their interactions (Weinberg, 1995). Implicitly, science assumes methodological principles including the uniformity of nature, the reliability of induction, and the independence of observer and observed. These cannot be scientifically proven without circularity yet seem necessary for empirical inquiry (Ladyman, 2002). The underdetermination of theory by evidence suggests that empirical adequacy alone cannot determine which first principles to adopt, requiring additional criteria such as simplicity, unification, and fertility (Stanford, 2017).

1.5 MODERN APPLICATIONS

Contemporary physics exemplifies sophisticated applications of first principles reasoning through symmetry principles and conservation laws that constrain possible theories. Noether's theorem establishes a profound connection between continuous symmetries and conservation laws: temporal symmetry yields energy conservation, spatial symmetry yields momentum conservation, and gauge symmetries generate charge conservation (Noether, 1971). These serve not merely as empirical generalizations but as foundational constraints that any viable physical theory must respect. Modern gauge theories extend this approach, with fundamental forces arising from requirements of local symmetry—electromagnetic force from $U(1)$ symmetry, weak force from $SU(2)$, and strong force from $SU(3)$ (Weinberg, 2015). The search for grand unified theories attempts to identify more fundamental symmetry principles from which known forces emerge as low-energy manifestations (Georgi, 1999).

General relativity illustrates how revolutionary insights emerge from reconsidering first principles previously taken as absolute. Einstein's recognition that the equivalence principle—the empirical observation that gravitational and inertial mass are equal—could serve as a foundational principle rather than a coincidence led to understanding gravity as spacetime curvature rather than a force (Carroll, 2004). This reconceptualization required abandoning the Newtonian first principle of absolute space and time, demonstrating how questioning apparently settled foundations can open entirely new theoretical territories. The ongoing search for quantum gravity theories requires reconciling the incompatible first principles of general relativity (smooth spacetime) and quantum mechanics (discrete quantum states), suggesting that even more fundamental principles may await discovery (Rovelli, 2004).

Quantum mechanics reveals particularly profound challenges to classical first principles about measurement, causality, and reality. Bell's (1964) analysis of quantum entanglement demonstrates that local realism—the conjunction of locality (no superluminal influences) and realism (properties exist independently of measurement)—must be abandoned to accommodate quantum phenomena. Experimental violations of Bell inequalities confirm that nature violates these seemingly obvious first principles (Aspect, Dalibard, & Roger, 1982). The measurement problem in quantum mechanics highlights how the transition from quantum superposition to classical definiteness challenges first principles about the nature of physical properties and the role of observation (Maudlin, 2019). Various interpretations—Copenhagen, many-worlds, de Broglie-Bohm—adopt different first principles about reality, measurement, and probability, demonstrating that empirical adequacy underdetermines foundational commitments (Wallace, 2012).

Complex systems science reveals how simple first principles can generate extraordinary complexity through iteration, interaction, and emergence. Cellular automata demonstrate how complex patterns and computational universality emerge from elementary rules applied locally (Wolfram, 2002). Holland's (1995) analysis of complex adaptive systems identifies common first principles—including adaptation, self-organization, and edge-of-chaos dynamics—operating across biological, economic, and social systems. Deacon's (2011) theory of emergent dynamics demonstrates how higher-level properties arise from but cannot be reduced to lower-level principles, suggesting hierarchical organization of first principles across different levels of description. This challenges both strong reductionism and substance dualism, pointing toward process-based first principles that emphasize relationships and transformations rather than static entities (Ellis, 2016).

In technology and engineering, first principles thinking enables breakthrough innovation by challenging inherited assumptions and reasoning from fundamental constraints. Elon Musk's approach to rocket design exemplifies this methodology: rather than accepting that rockets must be expendable, SpaceX engineers returned to physical and economic first principles to develop reusable launch vehicles (Vance, 2015). The development of lithium-ion batteries required abandoning incremental improvements to existing technologies and returning to electrochemical first principles about ion transport and energy density (Yoshino, 2012). This method—decomposing problems to constituent elements and reasoning forward from basic constraints—drives innovation across industries from biotechnology to artificial intelligence (Ries, 2011).

Business strategy increasingly employs first principles thinking to identify sustainable competitive advantages in rapidly changing markets. Rather than benchmarking competitors, strategists examine fundamental customer needs, economic principles, and technological possibilities. Porter's (1985) five forces framework identifies first principles of industry competition—buyer power, supplier power, threat of substitutes, threat of entry, and rivalry—that determine profitability regardless of specific industry details. Christensen's (2016) theory of disruptive innovation reveals how breakthrough business models emerge from reconsidering first principles about customer value rather than incremental improvement of existing solutions. Companies that focus on unchanging human needs as first principles—such as Amazon's emphasis on low prices, fast delivery, and wide selection—build strategies robust to technological change (Rossman, 2019).

Artificial intelligence research illustrates both the power and limitations of first principles approaches in understanding intelligence. Early symbolic AI attempted to encode human knowledge as explicit rules—first principles of intelligent behavior—but achieved limited success in complex, open-ended domains (Dreyfus, 1992). Contemporary machine learning systems discover patterns from data without explicit programming, yet still embody implicit first principles in their architectures, optimization objectives, and training procedures (Goodfellow, Bengio, & Courville, 2016). The tension between principled and empirical approaches reflects deeper questions about whether intelligence can be reduced to formal principles or requires irreducibly embodied and contextual understanding (Marcus & Davis, 2019). Recent advances in large language models suggest that scale and data may substitute for explicit principles in some domains, though debates continue about whether these systems truly understand or merely pattern-match (Bender & Koller, 2020).

1.6 WHY FIRST PRINCIPLES MATTER

The enduring relevance of first principles thinking stems from its capacity to cut through accumulated assumptions and reveal foundational truths beneath surface complexity. In an era characterized by information overload, exponential technological change, and cultural pluralism, the ability to distinguish fundamental principles from contingent details becomes increasingly valuable for navigation and decision-making (Floridi, 2014). First principles thinking provides cognitive tools for managing complexity by identifying essential features versus merely conventional arrangements, enabling more effective problem-solving and innovation.

Religious and spiritual traditions demonstrate how first principles about ultimate reality provide frameworks for meaning and moral guidance that transcend particular cultural contexts while addressing universal human concerns. James's (1902/2002) phenomenological analysis of religious experience reveals how mystical encounters often involve direct apprehension of fundamental principles about reality's nature and human purpose that resist propositional articulation yet transform understanding. Otto's (1958) investigation of the sacred identifies the experience of the numinous as pointing toward first principles about transcendence that appear across diverse religious traditions, suggesting universal features of human spiritual awareness. Contemporary neuroscience of religious experience provides converging evidence for common neural substrates underlying spiritual experiences across cultures, though debates continue about reductive versus non-reductive interpretations (Newberg & d'Aquili, 2001).

Tillich's (1957) method of correlation demonstrates how religious first principles about ultimate concern can ground systematic theology while remaining open to philosophical and scientific insights. His approach reveals how religious first principles need not conflict with rational inquiry but can provide existential foundations that orient comprehensive understanding. Taylor's (2007) analysis of secularity shows how even explicitly non-religious worldviews operate from implicit first principles about meaning, value, and human flourishing that function analogously to religious foundations. This suggests that the question is not whether to adopt first principles but rather which principles to embrace and how critically to examine them.

Innovation particularly benefits from first principles reasoning because breakthrough advances often require transcending established paradigms rather than optimizing within them. Kuhn's (1996) analysis of scientific revolutions demonstrates how paradigm shifts involve reconsidering fundamental assumptions rather than accumulating incremental improvements. Most progress occurs through normal science operating within established frameworks, but revolutionary advances require returning to foundational questions. This explains why outsiders sometimes revolutionize fields: unburdened by disciplinary socialization, they more readily recognize which "constraints" are merely conventions (Simonton, 2004). Historical examples from continental drift to quantum mechanics illustrate how resistance to reconsidering first principles can delay scientific progress for decades (Oreskes, 1999).

First principles serve critical functions in detecting and correcting systematic errors that accumulate when foundational assumptions go unexamined. The 2008 financial crisis partly resulted from risk models built on first principles about market efficiency and rational expectations that failed to account for systemic risks and behavioral factors (Taleb, 2007). Failures in medical research reproducibility often trace to unexamined assumptions about statistical significance and causal inference that violate first principles of scientific methodology (Ioannidis, 2005). Examining foundational assumptions can reveal such hidden vulnerabilities before they manifest as crises, though cognitive and institutional biases often resist such fundamental questioning (Kahneman, 2011).

Cross-cultural dialogue increasingly requires identifying shared first principles beneath surface disagreements about specific practices and institutions. While beliefs and customs vary dramatically across cultures, certain fundamental concerns—human dignity, social cooperation, truth-seeking, fairness—appear universal, though their specific interpretations differ (Brown, 1991). Sen's (2009) capability approach reveals how different cultural traditions can converge on shared first principles about human development and flourishing despite disagreeing about specific institutional arrangements. This suggests that productive cross-cultural engagement requires excavating implicit first principles rather than debating surface manifestations (Nussbaum, 2011).

Indigenous wisdom traditions offer particularly valuable perspectives on first principles that challenge Western assumptions while addressing contemporary crises. Kimmerer's (2013) analysis of indigenous botanical knowledge reveals first principles about reciprocal relationships between humans and nature that provide alternatives to extractive approaches to natural resources. Whyte's (2017) work on indigenous climate science demonstrates how traditional ecological knowledge operates from relational first principles that emphasize responsibilities and kinship rather than rights and resources. These alternative frameworks become increasingly relevant as humanity confronts ecological and social challenges that may require fundamental shifts in how we understand our place in natural and social systems (Berkes, 2012).

The quest for first principles ultimately reflects humanity's deep need for understanding that transcends mere description or prediction. We seek not simply to catalog phenomena but to comprehend the underlying order that makes them possible and meaningful (Rescher, 2000). Whether investigating physical laws, moral truths, or spiritual realities, identifying first principles represents an attempt to touch bedrock reality—to find, beneath the flux of experience and the diversity of perspectives, something solid upon which we can build reliable understanding. This ancient quest remains urgently relevant as we confront unprecedented challenges—from artificial intelligence to climate change, from biotechnology to social fragmentation—that require both technical innovation and wisdom grounded in the deepest truths about reality, consciousness, and human purpose. The integration of diverse approaches to first principles—scientific, philosophical, religious, and indigenous—may prove essential for developing the comprehensive understanding necessary to navigate an increasingly complex and interconnected world.

CHAPTER 2: THE PROBLEM OF FOUNDATION

2.1 INTRODUCTION: THE PARADOX OF FOUNDATIONS

Every edifice of human knowledge, from the most abstract mathematical theorem to the most concrete scientific observation, ultimately rests upon foundations that cannot themselves be proven within the system they support. This paradox—that certainty requires starting points that themselves cannot be made certain—represents one of the deepest challenges in epistemology (Moser, 1989). Like ancient cartographers who could map distant lands but never the ground on which they stood, we find ourselves unable to fully justify the very principles we use to justify everything else.

This foundational problem transcends abstract philosophical speculation and manifests as a practical challenge shaping knowledge pursuit across all domains. Williamson's (2000) analysis of knowledge and its limits reveals how even our most basic epistemic concepts resist foundational analysis, demonstrating that the concepts of knowledge, evidence, and justification form an interdependent circle resistant to reductive analysis. Scientists must assume the reliability of observation and the uniformity of nature without being able to prove these assumptions scientifically (Friedman, 2001). Mathematicians must accept axioms that cannot be proven within their systems (Shapiro, 2000). Religious believers must grapple with the circularity of using scripture to validate scripture or experience to validate

25

experience (Alston, 1991). Even our most successful theories and practices rest upon assumptions that, when examined closely, reveal themselves to be acts of intellectual faith rather than demonstrable certainties.

The foundational problem emerges with particular clarity in Stroud's (1989, 2000, 2018) analysis of how we understand human knowledge in general. Any attempt to achieve a completely general understanding of knowledge faces what Stroud calls the "problem of the external world": such understanding must itself be achieved through the very cognitive capacities whose legitimacy is in question. This creates a distinctive philosophical predicament wherein we cannot step outside our epistemic situation to validate it from a neutral standpoint, yet remaining within it seems to preclude the kind of objective assessment that philosophical understanding demands. As Stroud argues, "We can never satisfy ourselves that we know anything about the world around us" when we adopt the detached philosophical perspective.

Contemporary epistemologists have increasingly recognized that the foundational problem may not be a puzzle to be solved but rather a permanent feature of human cognition. Sosa (2009) argues that the problem reveals the inherently perspectival nature of knowledge—we can achieve reflective knowledge about our first-order knowledge, but this reflective knowledge itself requires foundations that cannot be established without circularity. This recursive structure suggests that complete epistemic self-transparency may be impossible in principle rather than merely difficult in practice.

This chapter explores the various manifestations of the foundational problem and examines how different domains of inquiry have attempted to address or circumvent it. We investigate the infinite regress that threatens any attempt at ultimate justification, the varieties of circular reasoning that emerge in foundational contexts, and the hidden assumptions that undergird even our most rigorous systems of thought. Through critical analysis of both classical and contemporary approaches, we demonstrate that understanding these challenges proves essential for approaching the quest for first principles with appropriate intellectual humility and methodological sophistication.

2.2 THE INFINITE REGRESS PROBLEM

The ancient skeptic Agrippa, as reported by Sextus Empiricus, articulated what has become known as Agrippa's trilemma or the Münchhausen trilemma—a foundational challenge that remains unresolved after two millennia (Sextus Empiricus, 2000). The trilemma states that any attempt to justify a belief leads to one of three equally problematic outcomes: infinite regress, circular reasoning, or dogmatic assertion. If we demand justification for every belief, we embark on an endless chain of justifications, each requiring further support. If we allow beliefs to justify each other reciprocally, we fall into circularity. If we simply stop at certain "foundational" beliefs, we seem to embrace arbitrary dogmatism. As Barnes (1990) demonstrates, this trilemma applies not only to empirical knowledge but also to logical and mathematical reasoning.

Aristotle's *Posterior Analytics* provides the classical foundation for understanding this problem, establishing the framework that continues to shape contemporary debates (Aristotle, 384-322 BCE/1984). Aristotle recognized that demonstration (*apodeixis*) requires prior knowledge and that an infinite regress of demonstrations is impossible for finite beings. His solution involved identifying first principles (*archai*) that are "true, primary, immediate, better known than, prior to, and causes of the conclusion" (71b20-22). These principles must be grasped through intellectual intuition (*nous*) rather than demonstration, a faculty that apprehends necessary truths directly. However, as Irwin (1988) notes, Aristotle's account faces the challenge of explaining how nous can provide certain knowledge of first principles without itself requiring justification.

The regress problem manifests concretely in scientific reasoning. Consider a scientist claiming that smoking causes cancer. When asked for justification, she cites epidemiological studies. But why trust these studies? Because they use reliable statistical methods. Why are these methods reliable? Because they have successfully identified other causal relationships. How do we know those identifications were correct? Because subsequent interventions based on them were successful. But why does practical success indicate truth? At each step, the demand for justification pushes us further back, with no obvious stopping point that does not appear arbitrary (Klein, 1999). This regress threatens to undermine even our most well-established scientific knowledge.

The Cartesian tradition attempted to solve this problem through methodological doubt, seeking indubitable foundations that could withstand the most rigorous skeptical challenge. Descartes' (1641/1996) systematic doubt in the *Meditations on First Philosophy* led him to the *cogito ergo sum* as an absolutely certain foundation for knowledge. Yet even this apparently certain principle has been challenged. Frankfurt (1970) argues that the cogito involves an implicit inference that requires justification, while Hintikka (1962) contends that it is performatively self-verifying rather than logically certain. The regress problem thus reasserts itself at the supposedly foundational level, suggesting that even Cartesian certainty cannot escape the trilemma.

The British empiricist tradition, while rejecting Cartesian rationalism, faced similar challenges. Berkeley's (1965) idealism attempted to ground knowledge in immediate perception, arguing that *esse est percipi*—to be is to be perceived. However, this foundation requires assumptions about the nature of perception and minds that are themselves questionable. As Pappas (2000) demonstrates, Berkeley's account of immediate perception involves theoretical commitments about the relationship between ideas and minds that cannot be established through perception alone. Hume's (1748/2007) more radical skepticism revealed that even basic empirical beliefs about causation and induction cannot be justified without circularity, leading to what he called "mitigated skepticism"—a practical acceptance of beliefs we cannot rationally justify.

Kant's (1781/1998) transcendental philosophy represented a sophisticated attempt to circumvent the regress problem by identifying conditions that make experience possible. The *Critique of Pure Reason* argues that certain synthetic *a priori* principles—such as causality and substance—are necessary conditions for coherent experience rather than empirical generalizations requiring justification. These transcendental principles escape the regress problem because they are presupposed by the very possibility of empirical knowledge. However, as Stroud (1968) argues, Kantian foundations face their own challenges: How do we establish which principles are genuinely transcendental without presupposing the very knowledge they are meant to ground? The transcendental deduction itself seems to require the kinds of justification it is meant to provide.

Different philosophical traditions have developed distinct responses to the regress problem. Indian epistemology, particularly in the Nyāya school, developed sophisticated analyses of *pramāṇa* (means of knowledge) that ground justification in reliable sources rather than infinite chains of inference (Matilal, 1986). The Nyāya system identifies four valid sources of knowledge—perception (*pratyakṣa*), inference (*anumāna*), comparison (*upamāna*), and testimony (*śabda*)—each with its own sphere of validity and criteria for reliability. As Phillips (2012) explains, this pluralistic approach avoids the regress by recognizing multiple foundational sources while maintaining rigorous standards for each, though it faces challenges in explaining how these different sources are coordinated and how conflicts between them are resolved.

Islamic philosophers explored how certain knowledge (*'ilm al-yaqīn*) might be achieved through spiritual insight when rational justification reaches its limits. Al-Ghazali's (1095/2000) analysis in *The Incoherence of the Philosophers* distinguishes between knowledge acquired through rational demonstration (*burhān*) and knowledge achieved through direct spiritual experience (*dhawq*). His comprehensive treatment in *The Revival of the Religious Sciences* argues that mystical experience can provide foundational knowledge that transcends discursive reasoning (Al-Ghazali, 1106/2014). This approach suggests that the regress problem may appear intractable only within the confines of discursive rationality, while other modes of knowing offer alternative foundations.

Contemporary epistemologists have proposed various solutions, each facing distinctive challenges. Foundationalism maintains that certain beliefs are properly basic, justified without requiring justification from other beliefs. Contemporary modest foundationalists like Audi (2011) accept that basic beliefs may be defeasible yet still foundational, grounded in experiences or rational intuitions that provide *prima facie* justification. However, experimental philosophy has revealed significant variation in intuitions across cultures, genders, and socioeconomic backgrounds, undermining their claim to universality (Weinberg, Nichols, & Stich, 2001). Machery (2017) extends this critique, arguing that the unreliability of philosophical intuitions undermines any foundationalist project that relies on them.

Coherentism rejects the foundationalist structure entirely, arguing that beliefs are justified by their mutual support within a coherent system. BonJour's (2010) coherentist theory maintains that justification emerges from systematic connections, including logical consistency, probabilistic coherence, explanatory relationships, and analogical connections. However, coherentism faces the isolation objection developed by Fumerton (1995)—how can a coherent system of beliefs connect with reality if coherence is purely internal? The plurality objection, articulated by Sosa (1991), demonstrates that multiple incompatible systems might achieve equal coherence, leaving no grounds for choosing between them.

Infinitism, defended by Klein (2014), embraces the infinite regress, arguing that justification is a potentially infinite process that provides increasing warrant without ever reaching bedrock. Klein argues that finite beings can have justified beliefs even if they cannot complete infinite chains of justification, provided they can continue the justificatory process when challenged. As Turri and Klein (2014) explain, infinitism treats justification as arising from the availability of reasons rather than their actual possession. However, Ginet (2005) objects that this solution makes justified belief psychologically impossible for creatures with finite cognitive resources and finite time.

The persistence of these debates suggests that the regress problem may reveal something fundamental about the nature and limits of human knowledge itself. Rather than a technical puzzle awaiting solution, the regress problem might reflect an inherent feature of finite rational beings attempting to achieve complete understanding of their epistemic situation. As Williams (2001) argues, the problem may arise from an impossible demand for a kind of justification that would require us to occupy a standpoint outside our own epistemic practices—a "view from nowhere" that is necessarily unavailable to situated knowers.

2.3 CIRCULAR REASONING AND SELF-REFERENCE

Not all circles are vicious. In mathematics, recursive definitions can be perfectly legitimate and productive. The natural numbers can be defined recursively: zero is a natural number, and if n is a natural number, then n+1 is a natural number. This definition is circular in that it uses the concept of natural number to define natural numbers, yet it successfully specifies a unique mathematical structure (Enderton, 2001). Similarly, hermeneutic circles in interpretation, where understanding parts requires grasping the whole while understanding the whole requires grasping the parts, can lead to deepening comprehension rather than sterile repetition (Gadamer, 2004).

The key distinction lies between virtuous circles that generate understanding and vicious circles that merely presuppose what they purport to establish.

The problem of the criterion, articulated by Chisholm (1982), illustrates how circularity emerges at the foundations of epistemology itself. To identify instances of knowledge, we seem to need criteria for what counts as knowledge. But to establish these criteria as correct, we need to know that they successfully identify genuine knowledge. As Cling (2009) demonstrates, this problem affects not only the identification of knowledge but also the justification of any epistemic principle or method. Ancient skeptics recognized this problem: we cannot determine what we know without criteria for knowledge, yet we cannot establish criteria without already knowing what counts as knowledge. This circle appears inescapable and affects every attempt to ground epistemology non-circularly.

Russell's (1912) analysis in *The Problems of Philosophy* reveals how foundational circularity infects even basic beliefs about the external world. We believe in the existence of physical objects based on sensory experience, yet we validate sensory experience by appealing to physical facts about perception and cognition. This circularity extends to memory: we trust memory to inform us about the past, including the past reliability of memory itself. Russell concluded that such circular reasoning, while logically unsatisfying, may be pragmatically unavoidable for finite beings embedded in the world they seek to understand.

Self-referential paradoxes reveal deeper foundational problems that challenge the coherence of our most basic logical and semantic concepts. Russell's paradox—concerning the set of all sets that do not contain themselves—exposed fundamental flaws in naive set theory and necessitated a complete reconceptualization of mathematical foundations (Russell, 1903). The strengthened liar paradox ("This statement is not true") resists standard solutions and has motivated various non-classical logics (Field, 2008). Tarski's (1944) work on semantic paradoxes showed that truth cannot be coherently defined within the languages to which it applies, necessitating hierarchical approaches that distinguish object language from metalanguage. These paradoxes suggest that self-reference creates insurmountable obstacles for any system that attempts complete self-description.

Priest (2006) and other dialetheists argue that such paradoxes reveal genuine contradictions in reality, challenging the law of non-contradiction itself. Priest's approach suggests that some contradictions might be true, particularly those arising from self-reference and semantic paradoxes. The logic LP (Logic of Paradox) allows for true contradictions while avoiding explosion—the principle that from a contradiction, anything follows. However, as Beall (2009) notes, this solution faces the challenge of explaining how contradictory information can be cognitively processed and how practical reasoning can proceed when contradictions are accepted. The revenge problem also arises: even paraconsistent logics generate new paradoxes when they attempt to express their own semantic concepts.

Scientific theories often exhibit subtle circularities that become visible only under philosophical scrutiny. We validate scientific methods by their success in discovering truths about nature, yet we identify these truths using the very methods we seek to validate. As Ladyman (2002) argues, this methodological circle cannot be broken without abandoning scientific inquiry altogether. The theory-ladenness of observation, emphasized by Hanson (1958) and developed by Kuhn (2012), suggests that what we observe depends partly on the theories we hold, yet these theories are supposedly justified by observations. This circularity may not be eliminable without undermining the entire scientific enterprise, suggesting that some forms of circular justification may be inevitable in empirical inquiry.

Davidson's (2001) work on radical interpretation reveals how circularity emerges in understanding meaning and belief. To interpret another person's utterances, we must make assumptions about their beliefs, but to identify their beliefs, we must understand what their utterances mean. Davidson's solution involves the principle of charity—interpreting others as largely rational and correct—but this principle itself involves circular assumptions about the nature of rationality and truth. As Lepore and Ludwig (2005) demonstrate, Davidson's approach reveals deep connections between meaning, belief, and truth that resist non-circular analysis.

Religious epistemology faces distinctive circular challenges that have generated sophisticated philosophical responses. Appeals to religious experience to validate religious beliefs assume the reliability of such experiences, while appeals to revelation presuppose the authenticity of the source. The Islamic concept of *tawātur* (multiple attestation) attempts to break this circle by grounding religious knowledge in widely attested transmission, though as Hallaq (1999) notes, this ultimately depends on assumptions about the reliability of the initial witnesses and the transmission process. Some theologians embrace a kind of virtuous circularity, arguing that faith and understanding mutually reinforce each other in a spiral of deepening comprehension (Helm, 2000).

. As Ferreira (1986) explains, Newman's account provides resources for understanding how circular patterns of justification might be acceptable in contexts where linear justification is impossible.

Hofstadter's (1979) exploration of strange loops suggests that self-reference and circularity may be inevitable features of sufficiently complex systems. Consciousness itself may represent the ultimate strange loop—the mind attempting to understand itself using itself as the instrument of understanding. As Hofstadter (2007) later developed, the emergence of self-reference in sufficiently complex formal and cognitive systems may be a fundamental characteristic rather than an unfortunate accident. This suggests that foundational circularities might not be bugs to be eliminated but features inherent in any system complex enough to model itself.

Contemporary approaches to circular justification distinguish between different types of circularity and their epistemic implications. Bergmann (2004) differentiates between malignant circularity—where the conclusion is explicitly presupposed in the premises—and benign circularity—where background assumptions necessary for any reasoning are implicitly present. Pryor (2004) argues that some forms of question-begging are dialectically inappropriate without being epistemically vicious, suggesting that circular arguments might fail as persuasion while succeeding as justification. These distinctions reveal that blanket condemnations of circular reasoning may oversimplify a complex epistemological landscape.

2.4 THE ARCHITECTURE OF ASSUMPTIONS

Every system of thought is built upon a foundation of assumptions, though these often remain invisible until challenged. Understanding the different types of foundational commitments—axioms, postulates, definitions, presuppositions, and background beliefs—is essential for evaluating any claim to knowledge or truth. As Rescher (2005) demonstrates, these distinctions matter because different types of assumptions play different roles in our cognitive architecture and may require different forms of justification or may be immune to certain types of critique.

In formal systems, axioms represent explicit foundational assumptions chosen for their usefulness rather than their self-evidence. The development of non-Euclidean geometries in the nineteenth century revealed that incompatible axiom systems could each be consistent and applicable (Torretti, 1978). Riemann's geometry, with its rejection of the parallel postulate, proved essential for Einstein's general relativity, demonstrating that axioms once thought to represent necessary truths about space were actually contingent choices suited to particular contexts. As Gray (2007) documents, this discovery transformed mathematics from a science of absolute truth to a discipline exploring the consequences of different foundational choices.

Scientific theories embed numerous assumptions, many of which are unrecognized until anomalies force their examination. Classical mechanics assumed that mass is invariant, space is Euclidean, and time is absolute—assumptions so fundamental they seemed like necessary truths rather than theoretical commitments (DiSalle, 2006). Only when confronted with electromagnetic phenomena and high-speed motion did these assumptions become visible and questionable. As Friedman (2013) argues, the history of science is partly a history of discovering and revising hidden assumptions, from the assumption of circular planetary orbits to the assumption of deterministic causation.

Duhem's (1906/1991) analysis of physical theory reveals how theoretical assumptions form interconnected networks resistant to decisive falsification. The Duhem-Quine thesis maintains that scientific theories face the tribunal of experience not individually but as corporate bodies. When predictions fail, we cannot identify which specific assumption is responsible without making additional theoretical commitments. As Ariew (2014) explains, this holism means that even apparently basic assumptions can be preserved by modifying auxiliary hypotheses, revealing the complex architecture underlying seemingly simple theoretical commitments.

Quine's (1951) critique of the analytic-synthetic distinction extended Duhem's insights to encompass all knowledge claims. According to Quine's holism, our beliefs form a web where any statement can be revised if doing so better accommodates experience. Even logical laws might be modified, as some interpretations of quantum mechanics suggest when proposing quantum logic (Putnam, 1968). This view implies that the distinction between foundational assumptions and derived beliefs is pragmatic rather than absolute. As Hylton (2007) demonstrates, Quinean holism challenges traditional epistemological categories and suggests that foundations are relative to particular conceptual schemes.

Carnap's (1950) work on linguistic frameworks reveals how metaphysical assumptions operate in formal and scientific contexts. Carnap argues that ontological questions are properly understood as questions about which linguistic framework to adopt rather than questions about mind-independent reality. The choice of framework involves pragmatic considerations about utility, simplicity, and fruitfulness rather than correspondence to metaphysical truth. As Friedman (1999) explains, this approach suggests that foundational assumptions might be better understood as tools for organizing experience rather than claims about ultimate reality.

Putnam's (1981) analysis of reason, truth, and history demonstrates how assumptions about reference and meaning shape our entire conceptual apparatus. Putnam's model-theoretic argument suggests that even our most basic logical and semantic concepts involve theoretical commitments that could, in principle, be revised. The impossibility of a "God's eye view" means that our foundational assumptions are always made from within particular historical and cultural contexts. As Ebbs (2017) argues, this internalist perspective reveals that objectivity must be understood as emerging from within our practices rather than as correspondence to practice-independent reality.

Social epistemology reveals how assumptions are shaped by communities and contexts. Longino (1990) demonstrates how background assumptions in science often reflect social values, particularly regarding gender, race, and human nature. These assumptions influence everything from problem selection to interpretation of data. Fricker's (2007) work on epistemic injustice shows how credibility judgments rest on assumptions about whose testimony counts as reliable—assumptions often shaped by prejudice and stereotypes. As Anderson (2020) argues, these social dimensions do not necessarily undermine objectivity but demand recognizing that knowledge production is always socially situated and that achieving reliability requires diverse perspectives and critical scrutiny of background assumptions.

Hacking's (1983) analysis of representing and intervening reveals how scientific assumptions operate at multiple levels—theoretical, experimental, and instrumental. Hacking distinguishes between theories about phenomena and the experimental practices used to investigate them, showing how assumptions about experimental reliability, instrument function, and laboratory procedures interact with theoretical assumptions in complex ways. The stability of scientific knowledge depends not only on theoretical coherence but also on the robustness of experimental practices and the reliability of material technologies. As Radder (2003) demonstrates, this reveals multiple layers of assumptions that must work together for scientific knowledge production.

Lakatos's (1978) methodology of scientific research programmes provides a sophisticated account of how assumption-structures evolve while maintaining continuity. Each programme contains a "hard core" of protected assumptions surrounded by a "protective belt" of auxiliary hypotheses. When anomalies arise, the protective belt is modified while the core remains intact—until the programme degenerates and is replaced. As Zahar (1973) explains, this model shows how foundational assumptions can be both stable and revisable, neither permanently fixed nor arbitrarily replaceable. The progressive or degenerative nature of a research programme depends on whether modifications to the protective belt lead to novel predictions or merely accommodate known facts.

The role of metaphysical assumptions deserves special attention. Every scientific theory presupposes certain metaphysical commitments about causation, laws of nature, properties, and objects. As Mumford (2004) demonstrates, these assumptions are not empirically testable in isolation but shape what counts as an acceptable explanation. The debate between realists and instrumentalists about scientific theories reflects different metaphysical assumptions about what science aims to achieve—truth about unobservable reality or merely empirical adequacy (van Fraassen, 2008). Chakravartty (2017) argues that such metaphysical assumptions are ineliminable from science and that recognizing their role is essential for understanding scientific practice.

Moore's (1925, 1939) defense of common sense reveals how foundational assumptions operate in ordinary contexts. Moore argues that certain beliefs—such as the existence of material objects and other minds—are more certain than any philosophical argument that might be brought against them. His "proof of an external world" by holding up his hands suggests that some assumptions are so fundamental to human thought that questioning them is pragmatically self-defeating, even if logically possible. As Baldwin (1990) explains, Moore's approach reveals tensions between philosophical skepticism and practical certainty that may be irresolvable within purely theoretical frameworks.

2.5 DOMAIN-SPECIFIC APPROACHES

Different domains of inquiry have developed distinct strategies for managing foundational problems, each reflecting the particular challenges and goals of that domain. Understanding these varied approaches illuminates both the universality of foundational issues and the plurality of possible responses. As Kitcher (2011) argues, this diversity suggests that foundational problems may require different solutions in different contexts rather than a single universal approach.

Mathematics confronted foundational problems most directly during its "foundational crisis" in the early twentieth century. The discovery of paradoxes in naive set theory prompted three major research programmes. Logicism, championed by Frege (2013) and Russell (1903), sought to reduce mathematics to logic but foundered on the need for non-logical axioms like infinity and choice. As Burgess (2005) demonstrates, the logicist programme revealed deep connections between logic and mathematics while showing that pure logic alone cannot generate mathematical content. Formalism, developed by Hilbert (1971), treated mathematics as the manipulation of meaningless symbols according to precise rules, seeking to establish consistency through finitary methods. However, Gödel's (1992) incompleteness theorems demonstrated that consistency cannot be proven within any system capable of expressing basic arithmetic, revealing fundamental limitations to the formalist programme.

Intuitionism, advocated by Brouwer (1975), grounded mathematics in mental construction and temporal processes of thought, requiring the rejection of classical principles like the law of excluded middle for infinite sets. As Dummett (1977) explains, intuitionism offers a coherent alternative to classical mathematics but at the cost of rejecting many standard mathematical results. Contemporary philosophy of mathematics has largely abandoned the search for absolute foundations, embracing pluralism and focusing on mathematical practice rather than foundational reduction (Shapiro, 2000). This pragmatic turn suggests that foundational problems, while philosophically important, need not paralyze mathematical research.

The sciences adopt a pragmatic approach, accepting methodological assumptions that have proven fruitful while remaining open to revision. Laudan's (1984) normative naturalism argues that scientific methods are justified by their track record of solving problems and generating successful predictions rather than by *a priori* philosophical foundations. This approach faces the challenge of circularity—using scientific methods to validate scientific methods—and the pessimistic meta-induction that current theories will likely be replaced just as past theories were abandoned (Stanford, 2006).

Hacking's (1983) analysis of scientific realism reveals how experimental practices provide a form of foundation distinct from theoretical justification. The ability to manipulate theoretical entities in reliable ways—using electrons to investigate other phenomena, for example—provides pragmatic grounds for belief that transcend purely theoretical considerations. As Cartwright (1983) argues, this interventionist approach suggests that foundational justification in science may come through successful practice rather than logical demonstration. The reliability of experimental techniques provides a different kind of foundation than theoretical coherence.

Contemporary scientific realism debates center on which aspects of successful theories we should consider foundational. Worrall's (1989) structural realism argues that scientific revolutions preserve mathematical structure while abandoning ontological commitments, suggesting that structural relationships provide more secure foundations than beliefs about specific entities. However, as Frigg and Votsis (2011) demonstrate, this approach faces challenges in specifying exactly what structure is preserved and why mathematical relationships should be considered more fundamental than physical entities.

Religious epistemology offers unique perspectives on foundational problems that challenge standard philosophical assumptions. Plantinga's (2000) reformed epistemology argues that belief in God can be properly basic—foundational without requiring evidence from other beliefs. The *sensus divinitatis* provides direct awareness of God analogous to perceptual awareness of physical objects. As Beilby (2005) explains, this approach has been developed into a broader religious epistemology that includes religious experience, testimony, and tradition as legitimate sources of foundational knowledge. Critics argue that this makes religious belief immune to rational critique, though defenders maintain that properly basic beliefs can still be defeated by counterevidence.

The Anselmian tradition attempts to ground religious belief in rational insight rather than empirical evidence or authority. Anselm's (2007) ontological argument seeks to establish God's existence through pure conceptual analysis, suggesting that certain truths about ultimate reality might be accessible through reason alone. As Oppy (2018) demonstrates, while the argument remains controversial, it illustrates how religious thought can engage seriously with foundational questions using philosophical methods. Contemporary modal versions of the argument, developed by Plantinga (1974), reveal sophisticated engagement with questions about necessity, possibility, and existence.

Aquinas (1947) represents a sophisticated synthesis of philosophical and religious approaches to foundations. The *Summa Theologica* distinguishes between truths accessible to natural reason (*praeambula fidei*) and those requiring divine revelation (*articuli fidei*), while maintaining that both sources of knowledge ultimately derive from God. As Kretzmann (1997) explains, this approach suggests that different domains might legitimately employ different foundational methods while participating in a unified quest for truth. The Thomistic synthesis provides resources for understanding how faith and reason might complement rather than compete.

Eastern philosophical traditions provide alternative frameworks that often reject the Western emphasis on foundations. Buddhist epistemology, particularly Madhyamaka philosophy, embraces the absence of ultimate foundations through the doctrine of emptiness (*śūnyatā*). As Siderits (2007) explains, rather than seeking secure foundations, this approach recognizes the conventional, interdependent nature of all truth claims while maintaining their pragmatic validity. The doctrine of two truths—conventional and ultimate—provides resources for navigating practical life without requiring metaphysical foundations.

The Daoist concept of *wu wei* (effortless action) suggests that some knowledge comes through non-conceptual engagement rather than foundational reasoning. The *Zhuangzi's* perspectivism recognizes the relativity of all conceptual frameworks while maintaining that skilled practitioners can navigate reality effectively without fixed foundations (Ziporyn, 2009). As Hansen (2000) demonstrates, this approach suggests that foundational problems might arise from excessive attachment to conceptual analysis rather than from fundamental features of reality.

Indian philosophy developed sophisticated analyses of knowledge sources (*pramāṇas*) that avoid reducing all knowledge to a single foundation. The Nyāya school identifies perception, inference, comparison, and testimony as valid means of knowledge, each with its own criteria and limitations (Ganeri, 2001). As Mohanty (1992) explains, this pluralistic approach maintains rigorous standards for each source while recognizing that different types of knowledge require different types of justification. The debates between different schools about the number and nature of *pramāṇas* reveal sophisticated engagement with foundational questions.

The notion of *svataḥ prāmāṇya* (intrinsic validity) in Mīmāṃsā philosophy suggests that knowledge claims are valid unless defeated—reversing the Western assumption that all beliefs require positive justification (Phillips, 2012). As Arnold (2005) demonstrates, this approach distributes epistemic burdens differently, requiring justification only when knowledge claims are challenged rather than demanding foundational support for all beliefs. This reveals alternative ways of conceptualizing the relationship between knowledge and justification.

Contemporary virtue epistemology shifts focus from properties of beliefs to properties of believers, grounding knowledge in reliable cognitive faculties rather than foundational propositions. Sosa's (2007) performance epistemology evaluates beliefs as performances that can be accurate, adept, and apt—achieving truth through competent exercise of cognitive abilities. As Greco (2010) explains, this approach offers resources for addressing foundational problems by locating justification in reliable processes rather than chains of inference, though questions about what makes faculties reliable ultimately raise their own foundational issues.

2.6 THE LIMITS OF CERTAINTY

The twentieth century witnessed profound discoveries about inherent limits to formal systems and human knowledge—discoveries that transformed our understanding of what can be known with certainty. These results do not merely identify practical limitations but reveal necessary constraints on any system of knowledge, suggesting that the quest for absolute foundations may be impossible in principle (Horsten, 2015).

Gödel's (1992) incompleteness theorems demonstrated that any consistent formal system capable of expressing basic arithmetic must be incomplete—there exist true statements that cannot be proven within the system. Moreover, no such system can prove its own consistency without falling into contradiction. As Franzén (2005) explains, these results shattered Hilbert's programme of establishing mathematics on completely secure foundations and revealed that formal systems cannot be both complete and consistent. The implications extend beyond mathematics: any system complex enough to model itself faces inherent limitations in what it can establish about itself.

The incompleteness theorems reveal deep connections between self-reference and foundational limitations. As Smullyan (1992) demonstrates, any system powerful enough to encode statements about itself will contain undecidable propositions—statements that can neither be proven nor disproven within the system. This suggests that complete self-understanding may be impossible for sufficiently complex systems, including human cognitive and cultural systems that attempt to understand themselves. Lucas (1961) controversially argued that Gödel's theorems show that human minds transcend computational systems, though this interpretation remains disputed.

Quantum mechanics introduced fundamental uncertainty into our understanding of physical reality. Heisenberg's (1983) uncertainty principle establishes limits on simultaneous knowledge of complementary properties—not merely practical limitations of measurement but fundamental features of quantum reality. As Busch, Heinonen, and Lahti (2007) demonstrate, modern formulations of uncertainty relations reveal deep connections between information, measurement, and physical reality. The measurement problem in quantum mechanics raises deeper questions about the emergence of definite outcomes from quantum superpositions. Different interpretations—Copenhagen, many-worlds, objective collapse theories—offer incompatible answers, suggesting that even our most successful physical theory lacks clear foundations (Maudlin, 2019).

Bell's (1987) analysis of quantum entanglement demonstrates that local realism cannot be maintained in the face of quantum phenomena. Bell's theorem shows that any theory reproducing quantum mechanical predictions must violate either locality or realism, challenging fundamental assumptions about the nature of physical reality. As Brunner et al. (2014) explain, experimental violations of Bell inequalities confirm that nature violates our classical intuitions about separability and independence. This uncertainty is ontological rather than merely epistemological, suggesting that reality itself may lack the kind of determinate structure that classical physics assumed.

Einstein's (2015) theories of relativity revealed that even basic concepts like simultaneity, length, and duration depend on reference frames, undermining the classical notion of absolute space and time. The general theory of relativity demonstrates that gravitational effects arise from spacetime curvature rather than forces, requiring fundamental reconceptualization of physical foundations. As Rovelli (2018) argues, these discoveries show that concepts once considered foundational—absolute space, time, and causation—are actually relative to observational contexts and may need further revision in quantum gravity theories.

Penrose's (2004) analysis suggests that understanding consciousness may require new physical principles that transcend current theory. The hard problem of consciousness—explaining how and why physical processes give rise to subjective experience—may indicate fundamental limits in materialist foundations. Penrose's orchestrated objective reduction theory proposes that consciousness involves quantum gravitational effects, suggesting that foundational physical principles may need revision to accommodate mental phenomena. While controversial, this approach highlights potential limits to purely physicalist foundations for understanding reality.

Computational limits constrain what can be known through algorithmic processes. Turing's (1936) proof that the halting problem is undecidable has implications for artificial intelligence and the computational theory of mind. As Copeland (2015) explains, these results suggest fundamental limits on what can be known through any mechanical process. The Church-Turing thesis identifies the class of effectively computable functions, while results about computational complexity reveal that many problems, while theoretically solvable, require resources that exceed physical possibilities.

Chaitin's (1987) work on algorithmic information theory reveals that most mathematical truths are random in the sense that they cannot be compressed into shorter proofs. As Calude (2002) demonstrates, the probability that a randomly chosen mathematical statement can be proven approaches zero as statement length increases. This suggests that mathematical knowledge, despite its reputation for certainty, contains irreducible elements of randomness that resist foundational systematization. Chaitin's constant Ω embodies this incompressibility in a single number whose digits cannot be computed by any algorithm.

Popper's (1963) falsificationism reconceived scientific knowledge as inherently provisional. While we can definitively falsify universal claims through counterexamples, we can never definitively verify them through any finite number of observations. This asymmetry means scientific knowledge advances through eliminating error rather than establishing truth. As Miller (1994) explains, even our best-confirmed theories remain conjectural, forever open to revision or replacement. Popper's approach dissolves the problem of induction by denying that science requires inductive justification, but at the cost of abandoning certainty even for our most successful theories.

Complexity science reveals additional limits arising from sensitive dependence and computational irreducibility. As Kellert (1993) demonstrates, chaotic systems, though deterministic, are unpredictable because arbitrarily small measurement errors grow exponentially. Wolfram (2002) identifies systems that are computationally irreducible—their future states cannot be predicted faster than simulating their entire evolution. Climate systems, ecosystems, and economies exhibit these properties, suggesting that even perfect knowledge of laws and initial conditions may be insufficient for prediction. These discoveries imply that reductionist foundations, even if achieved, might not enable understanding of complex phenomena.

Social epistemology identifies limits arising from our nature as socially embedded knowers. Goldman's (1999) work shows how knowledge depends on testimony, trust, and social institutions—dependencies that introduce new sources of uncertainty. Kitcher's (1993) analysis of the division of cognitive labor reveals how scientific knowledge emerges from communities rather than individuals, making foundations inherently social rather than purely logical or empirical. As Longino (2002) argues, these social dimensions do not necessarily undermine objectivity but complicate any attempt to ground knowledge in individual rationality alone. The social character of knowledge introduces irreducible elements of trust and dependence that cannot be eliminated through methodological reform.

2.7 LIVING WITH FOUNDATIONAL UNCERTAINTY

Given the apparent impossibility of securing absolute foundations, how should we proceed? Rather than viewing foundational problems as obstacles to overcome, we might recognize them as defining features of the human epistemic condition—constraints that shape but need not cripple our pursuit of understanding. Various philosophical traditions offer strategies for living productively with foundational uncertainty while maintaining intellectual rigor and practical effectiveness (Rescher, 2009).

Pragmatism offers one response: foundations matter less than consequences. James (1907/1975) argued that beliefs should be evaluated by their practical fruits rather than their foundational justification. The "will to believe" doctrine maintains that in forced, living, and momentous decisions, practical considerations can legitimately influence belief formation even absent sufficient evidence (James, 1896). As Putnam (2002) developed, pragmatism need not conflate truth with utility but can recognize that our conception of truth is shaped by our purposes and practices. Contemporary pragmatists like Rorty (1979) suggest abandoning the search for foundations entirely, viewing knowledge as social practice rather than a foundational structure. However, as Haack (2009) argues, pragmatism faces challenges in explaining how successful practices connect with reality and in providing resources for criticizing established but problematic beliefs.

Dewey's (1929) analysis reveals how the traditional philosophical search for eternal foundations may reflect psychological needs for security rather than genuine epistemic requirements. Dewey argues that knowledge should be understood as intelligent inquiry that reconstructs problematic situations rather than as correspondence to fixed reality. As Hickman (2007) explains, this approach treats foundational problems as artifacts of philosophical abstraction rather than genuine obstacles to effective thinking and action. The experimental method provides sufficient grounding for practical purposes without requiring metaphysical foundations.

Peirce's (1877) method for the fixation of belief provides an alternative framework emphasizing the social and temporal dimensions of inquiry. Peirce argues that genuine doubt arises from real problems rather than methodological skepticism, and that inquiry aims at establishing stable habits of action rather than passive representation. As Misak (2013) demonstrates, this approach suggests that foundational problems matter only insofar as they create genuine obstacles to effective inquiry and action. The community of inquirers, extended over time, provides the context within which beliefs are tested and refined.

Coherentism provides another framework, evaluating beliefs by their fit within comprehensive systems. Sellars's (1956) critique of the "myth of the given" challenges foundationalist assumptions by arguing that even basic perceptual beliefs involve conceptual content presupposing linguistic and social practices. As deVries (2005) explains, this insight suggests that foundational problems arise from attempting to isolate individual beliefs from the networks of practice and commitment that give them meaning. Knowledge is holistic rather than atomistic, making foundations unnecessary.

Haack's (1993) foundherentism combines insights from both foundationalist and coherentist traditions, recognizing that experiential beliefs play a special anchoring role while maintaining that justification involves both empirical grounding and systematic coherence. Like a crossword puzzle where clues and entries mutually support each other, beliefs gain justification through multiple interconnected sources. As Haack (2009) develops, this approach acknowledges the importance of empirical constraint while recognizing the inherent fallibility and interdependence of all beliefs.

McDowell's (1994) analysis offers resources for understanding how experience can provide rational constraint on belief without serving as an infallible foundation. McDowell argues that experience has conceptual content that can serve as a "tribunal" for belief revision while remaining fallible and revisable. As Thornton (2004) explains, this approach suggests that we can maintain both empirical constraint and fallibilism without falling into the oscillation between coherentism and foundationalism that plagued earlier epistemology.

Brandom's (1994) inferentialist approach treats meaning and content as emerging from social practices of giving and asking for reasons rather than from foundational representations. This approach suggests that foundational problems arise from mistaken assumptions about the priority of representation over inference. As Wanderer (2008) demonstrates, by focusing on the normative structure of reasoning practices, inferentialism promises to dissolve rather than solve traditional foundational problems. The social practices of reason-giving provide all the grounding knowledge requires.

The notion of reflective equilibrium, developed by Rawls (1971) and Goodman (1955), suggests an iterative process of mutual adjustment between particular judgments and general principles. We begin with considered judgments and provisional principles, then refine both through reciprocal modification until achieving stable equilibrium. As Daniels (2020) explains, this process never reaches bedrock but can achieve sufficient stability for practical purposes. The method has been extended beyond ethics to epistemology and philosophy of science, offering a model for foundational inquiry that is neither arbitrary nor absolute.

Bayesian epistemology offers a probabilistic framework that sidesteps some foundational problems by focusing on belief revision rather than absolute justification. By updating probability assignments based on evidence using Bayes' theorem, agents can approach truth without requiring certain foundations. As Talbott (2016) demonstrates, subjective Bayesians accept that prior probabilities may be somewhat arbitrary while maintaining that convergence occurs given sufficient evidence. Objective Bayesians seek to constrain priors through principles like maximum entropy. However, the problem of priors reveals that even probabilistic approaches cannot entirely escape foundational questions.

Critical rationalism, developed from Popper's philosophy, embraces foundational uncertainty as a spur to intellectual progress. By holding all beliefs open to criticism while acting on the best-tested theories available, we can make progress without foundations. As Miller (1994) explains, this approach requires what Bartley (1984) called "pancritical rationalism"—the willingness to subject even our commitment to criticism itself to critical scrutiny. This stance avoids both dogmatism and relativism while acknowledging the absence of ultimate foundations.

Wittgenstein's (1969) later philosophy suggests that foundational problems arise from misunderstanding the role of basic propositions in human practices. In *On Certainty*, Wittgenstein argues that certain propositions function as hinges around which inquiry turns rather than as foundations requiring justification. These hinge propositions are neither true nor false in the ordinary sense but form the inherited background against which truth and falsity become possible. As Moyal-Sharrock (2004) explains, this approach suggests that dissolving foundational problems requires understanding their origin in philosophical misunderstanding rather than solving them through theoretical construction.

Perhaps most importantly, recognizing foundational uncertainty cultivates intellectual humility—increasingly recognized as an epistemic virtue. Acknowledging that our most basic beliefs rest on uncertain foundations should make us more open to alternative perspectives, more willing to revise our views, and more tolerant of disagreement. As Roberts and Wood (2007) argue, intellectual humility does not imply relativism—some foundations are more reliable than others—but it does counsel against dogmatism. Fricker's (2007) work reveals how overconfidence in our foundational assumptions can lead to epistemic injustice, systematically discrediting the knowledge of marginalized groups.

The problem of foundations ultimately reveals something profound about human knowledge: we are beings in the middle, unable to secure absolute starting points or reach final conclusions, yet capable of building remarkably successful systems of understanding. As Rescher (2003) argues, this epistemic finitude need not lead to skepticism but can motivate a pragmatic pluralism that embraces multiple approaches to knowledge while maintaining critical standards. The next chapter examines how three great domains of human inquiry—science, philosophy, and religion—have developed distinct yet complementary paths to truth, each offering essential insights while acknowledging the foundational challenges explored here. These three paths, rather than competing for the single correct foundation, may together provide a richer, more complete approach to understanding reality than any could offer alone.

CHAPTER 3: THREE PATHS TO TRUTH

3.1 THE TRIADIC STRUCTURE OF HUMAN KNOWLEDGE

The quest for understanding reality has consistently manifested through three primary epistemological pathways: empirical science, rational philosophy, and revelatory religion. Each represents a distinct yet complementary mode of inquiry, offering unique access to different dimensions of truth while employing methodologies suited to their particular domains. While contemporary discourse often frames these approaches as competitive or mutually exclusive, careful examination reveals their fundamental interdependence and the impoverishment that results from reducing human knowledge to any single methodology (Harrison, 2015; McGrath, 2019).

The persistence of these three approaches across diverse cultures—from ancient Greek philosophy to Chinese Daoism, from Islamic science to Indigenous wisdom traditions—suggests something profound about both reality's structure and human cognition. McGrath (2019) demonstrates in his analysis of the territories of human reason that the natural sciences, philosophy, and theology each engage with reality at different explanatory levels, employing methodologies suited to their particular domains while contributing to a comprehensive understanding that transcends any single approach. This tripartite division reflects what Barbour (1997) identifies as different but complementary ways of knowing that address distinct aspects of human experience and reality.

This triadic structure reflects what Smart (1983) identifies as the multidimensional nature of human experience, encompassing empirical, rational, and experiential dimensions that require different investigative approaches. The recognition that reality itself may be sufficiently complex to require multiple modes of access represents a first principle about the nature of knowledge—an epistemological foundation that acknowledges both the unity of truth and the plurality of valid approaches to discovering it. As Polkinghorne (1998) argues, the quest for understanding requires what he terms "binocular vision," combining different perspectives to achieve depth perception about reality's nature.

Consider how each approach addresses the phenomenon of human consciousness. Neuroscience maps neural correlates and brain activity patterns, revealing the material substrates of mental phenomena through sophisticated imaging technologies and experimental protocols (Koch, 2004). Philosophy analyzes the conceptual puzzles of qualia and intentionality, examining what Chalmers (1996) identifies as the "hard problem" of consciousness—why there should be subjective experience at all given the existence of neural processes. Religious traditions explore consciousness as soul, spirit, or Buddha-nature, investigating its ultimate nature and destiny through contemplative practices refined over millennia (Wallace, 2007). None alone captures consciousness fully; together they approximate its mystery through complementary investigations illuminating different aspects of this fundamental phenomenon.

Indigenous epistemologies, as analyzed by Smith (2012) and Whyte (2017), offer additional perspectives that challenge Western disciplinary boundaries by integrating empirical observation, rational analysis, and spiritual insight within holistic frameworks recognizing the interconnectedness of all phenomena. These approaches demonstrate that the triadic structure of knowledge, while universal in its basic form, can be organized and integrated in culturally specific ways reflecting different metaphysical assumptions about reality and human understanding. As Deloria (1999) demonstrates, Indigenous knowledge systems often refuse the compartmentalization characteristic of Western approaches, instead maintaining integrated frameworks where empirical, rational, and spiritual insights inform each other continuously.

3.2 SCIENCE: THE EMPIRICAL PATH

3.2.1 Foundations of Scientific Knowledge

Science grounds itself in systematic observation and controlled experimentation, constructing theories that explain and predict phenomena through mathematical modeling and empirical testing. This methodology combines inductive reasoning from observations with deductive testing of predictions, creating what Psillos (1999) characterizes as a sophisticated epistemic practice that has proven remarkably successful in revealing regularities across scales from quantum particles to galactic clusters. The scientific method's power lies in its combination of creative hypothesis formation with rigorous empirical testing, creating what Hempel (1966) describes as the hypothetico-deductive model of scientific explanation.

The strength of scientific methodology lies in its self-correcting mechanisms and commitment to what Popper (1963) established as falsifiability—the requirement that scientific theories must be capable of being proven wrong through empirical testing. This criterion distinguishes scientific claims from metaphysical assertions while ensuring that scientific knowledge remains perpetually revisable. Far from representing a weakness, this provisional nature constitutes science's greatest epistemic virtue, enabling progressive approximation to truth through error elimination. As Lakatos (1978) demonstrates through his methodology of scientific research programmes, scientific progress occurs through competition between research programmes that make novel predictions and solve empirical problems.

However, as Hanson (1958) demonstrated through his analysis of theory-laden observation, the notion of purely objective empirical data has been thoroughly discredited. Scientific observation occurs within theoretical frameworks that shape what counts as relevant data and how phenomena are interpreted. This insight, developed further by Kuhn (1996) in his analysis of paradigm shifts, reveals that scientific practice involves irreducibly interpretive elements that cannot be eliminated through methodological reforms alone. The Duhem-Quine thesis further complicates this picture by demonstrating that theories face empirical tests as wholes rather than individually, making it impossible to identify which specific theoretical component is responsible for predictive failure (Duhem, 1906/1991; Quine, 1951).

Contemporary philosophy of science has moved beyond naive empiricism to recognize the complex relationship between theory and observation. Hacking's (1983) analysis of experimental practice demonstrates how scientific knowledge emerges through the interaction of theoretical frameworks and material interventions, with experimental techniques serving as mediators between concepts and phenomena. This approach reveals how scientific realism can be grounded in the successful manipulation of theoretical entities rather than purely theoretical considerations. As Cartwright (1983) argues, the reality of theoretical entities is best established through our ability to use them as tools to investigate other phenomena.

The mathematical structure of scientific theories raises profound questions about the relationship between formal systems and physical reality. Wigner's (1960) famous essay on the "unreasonable effectiveness of mathematics" in the natural sciences points toward deep connections between mathematical structures and physical laws that remain philosophically puzzling. This effectiveness suggests either that reality itself possesses inherent mathematical structure, as argued by Tegmark (2014), or that human cognition is somehow attuned to mathematical aspects of nature—either conclusion points toward first principles about reality and knowledge transcending purely empirical investigation.

3.2.2 Methodological Naturalism and Its Scope

Modern science operates under methodological naturalism, investigating natural causes without invoking supernatural explanations while maintaining agnosticism about ultimate metaphysical questions (Ruse, 1982). This self-imposed limitation has proven extraordinarily fruitful, enabling cumulative knowledge growth through shared standards of evidence and reasoning. However, as Numbers (2009) emphasizes in his analysis of science-religion relationships, methodological naturalism should not be confused with metaphysical naturalism—the philosophical claim that only natural entities exist.

The success of methodological naturalism depends on philosophical assumptions that cannot themselves be empirically validated. The uniformity of nature, the reliability of inductive reasoning, and the applicability of mathematics to physical reality represent foundational commitments that make scientific practice possible while remaining beyond scientific justification (Friedman, 2001). These assumptions, while reasonable and practically successful, require philosophical examination and support. As Plantinga (2011) argues, the reliability of our cognitive faculties in tracking truth represents a deep assumption that naturalistic evolution alone struggles to justify.

Van Fraassen's (2002) constructive empiricism offers a sophisticated analysis of how science can maintain empirical adequacy without requiring commitment to the truth of theoretical claims about unobservable entities. This approach suggests that scientific knowledge might be more modest in its metaphysical commitments than scientific realists typically assume, focusing on empirical adequacy rather than theoretical truth. However, this position faces challenges from Musgrave (1985) and others in explaining the predictive success of scientific theories and the apparent reality of theoretical entities that can be manipulated experimentally.

Cartwright's (1999) analysis of the "dappled world" reveals how scientific laws apply within limited domains rather than representing universal truths about nature. This perspective suggests that scientific knowledge consists of locally applicable generalizations rather than universal principles, challenging traditional assumptions about the unity of science while maintaining commitment to empirical rigor within specific domains. Dupré (1993) extends this critique through his "disorder of things," arguing that the world's complexity resists reduction to simple unified theories.

Complex systems science has revealed fundamental limitations in reductionist approaches that attempt to understand phenomena through analysis of component parts. Anderson's (1972) insight that "more is different" demonstrates how emergent properties arise at higher levels of organization that cannot be predicted from knowledge of lower-level components alone. This recognition points toward what Mitchell (2009) characterizes as the irreducible complexity of many natural and social phenomena, requiring integrative approaches that complement traditional reductionist methods.

3.2.3 The Boundaries of Empirical Investigation

Science excels at describing natural processes and identifying causal relationships within the domain of empirical phenomena, yet it encounters principled limitations when addressing questions of ultimate origin, purpose, and value. These limitations arise not from temporary gaps in scientific knowledge but from the methodological constraints that define scientific practice itself (Haught, 2006).

The scientific method cannot validate its own foundations without falling into circularity. The reliability of perception, the uniformity of nature, and the applicability of mathematical reasoning represent presuppositions that make scientific investigation possible while remaining beyond scientific demonstration. As Ladyman (2002) argues in his analysis of scientific methodology, these foundational assumptions require philosophical rather than empirical justification. This creates what Stenmark (2004) identifies as the "limits of science"—boundaries that are not merely practical but principled.

Scientific investigation faces distinctive challenges when studying singular historical events, subjective experiences, and normative questions. The origin of life, the emergence of consciousness, and the foundations of moral value involve aspects that resist experimental manipulation and controlled testing (Nagel, 2012). While science can illuminate causal mechanisms and evolutionary processes, questions about ultimate significance and meaning require different analytical approaches. As Midgley (2014) argues, the attempt to derive meaning and value from purely scientific descriptions commits what she terms the "reductive fallacy."

Wheeler's (1990) investigations into the role of information in physics suggest deep connections between physical processes and information-theoretic principles that may require a fundamental reconceptualization of scientific ontology. Similarly, Lloyd's (2006) analysis of the universe as a quantum computer reveals how information-processing perspectives might transform our understanding of physical reality. These developments suggest that the boundaries of scientific investigation may be more fluid than traditionally assumed, yet they also reveal how scientific advances often generate new philosophical questions rather than eliminating them.

The quantum measurement problem exemplifies how successful scientific theories can generate foundational puzzles requiring philosophical analysis. Despite quantum mechanics' empirical success, the relationship between quantum superposition and classical definiteness remains theoretically unresolved, with different interpretations offering incompatible accounts of fundamental reality (Albert, 1992; Maudlin, 2019). This situation illustrates how scientific progress can intensify rather than resolve foundational questions about reality's nature.

3.3 PHILOSOPHY: THE RATIONAL PATH

3.3.1 The Domain of Pure Reason

Philosophy employs systematic rational analysis to examine questions transcending empirical investigation, utilizing conceptual analysis, logical argumentation, and thought experiments to explore necessary conditions for knowledge, existence, and value. Unlike empirical sciences, philosophy provides access to *a priori* truths—knowledge independent of sensory experience yet informative about reality's structure (BonJour, 1998).

Kant's (1781/1998) critical philosophy established that synthetic *a priori* judgments combine analytic necessity with synthetic informativeness, revealing universal and necessary features of human experience. Space and time as forms of intuition, causality as a category of understanding, and the moral law as a practical postulate represent philosophical insights providing the conceptual architecture making empirical investigation intelligible. Without these foundational frameworks, neither scientific practice nor everyday experience would be coherent. As Allison (2004) demonstrates, Kant's transcendental idealism provides resources for understanding how synthetic *a priori* knowledge is possible while avoiding both dogmatic rationalism and skeptical empiricism.

Contemporary modal logic and metaphysics, as developed by Kripke (1980) and Williamson (2013), demonstrate how philosophical analysis can reveal necessary truths about identity, possibility, and reality's structure itself. The necessity of identity, the contingency of existence, and the nature of properties represent philosophical discoveries that constrain scientific theorizing while remaining independent of empirical investigation. Fine's (2005) work on modality and essence shows how philosophical analysis can reveal metaphysical structures that empirical investigation presupposes but cannot establish.

The phenomenological tradition, initiated by Husserl (1983) and developed by Merleau-Ponty (1945/2012), offers sophisticated analyses of consciousness and embodied experience, revealing structural features of human cognition. These investigations demonstrate how philosophical analysis can illuminate conditions making scientific objectivity possible while revealing dimensions of experience that scientific methodology cannot adequately capture. Zahavi's (2003) analysis of the phenomenological method shows how first-person investigation can reveal essential structures of consciousness that third-person approaches miss.

Contemporary philosophy of mind addresses fundamental questions about consciousness, intentionality, and the relationship between mental and physical phenomena with profound implications for scientific understanding. Kim's (1998, 2005) analysis of mental causation reveals deep problems in reconciling the causal efficacy of mental phenomena with physical causal closure. These investigations demonstrate how philosophical analysis can identify conceptual problems constraining scientific theorizing about mind-brain relationships. As Hasker (1999) argues, the emergence of consciousness may require recognizing genuinely novel causal powers irreducible to physical processes.

3.3.2 Transcendental Arguments and Necessary Conditions

Philosophy's distinctive contribution lies in identifying transcendental conditions—necessary presuppositions for any possible experience or knowledge. The principle of non-contradiction, the persistence of identity through time, and the reliability of causal reasoning represent insights underwriting all forms of inquiry while remaining beyond empirical justification (Stern, 2000).

Stroud's (1968) analysis of transcendental arguments reveals both their power and limitations in establishing substantive conclusions about reality. While these arguments can demonstrate what must be true if certain types of experience or knowledge are possible, they face challenges in establishing that such experience or knowledge is actually possible or necessary. This limitation suggests that transcendental arguments provide conditional rather than absolute foundations for knowledge. However, as Cassam (1987) argues, modest transcendental arguments can establish important conclusions about the necessary conditions of experience without claiming to prove the external world's existence.

Davidson's (2001) work on radical interpretation demonstrates how basic logical and semantic principles must be presupposed in any attempt to understand linguistic meaning or propositional content. The principle of charity—interpreting others as largely rational and correct—emerges as a transcendental condition for interpretation's possibility itself. This analysis reveals how fundamental logical principles are not arbitrary conventions but necessary features of any possible system of thought. Lear's (1984) complementary analysis shows how the principle of sufficient reason operates as a transcendental condition for rational inquiry itself.

Eastern philosophical traditions contribute unique perspectives on transcendental conditions, differing significantly from Western approaches. Buddhist philosophy's analysis of dependent origination (pratītyasamutpāda) offers sophisticated accounts of causation and identity, challenging Western assumptions about substance and independence (Garfield, 1995). These traditions demonstrate how transcendental analysis can proceed from different starting points while addressing universal questions about experience and knowledge's conditions. As Siderits (2003) demonstrates, Buddhist philosophers developed rigorous arguments about the conditions for knowledge that parallel yet differ from Western transcendental arguments.

The Madhyamaka tradition's analysis of emptiness (śūnyatā) reveals how all phenomena lack independent existence while maintaining conventional reality, offering a middle way between eternalism and nihilism with profound implications for understanding the relationship between ultimate and conventional truth (Siderits, 2007). This approach suggests transcendental conditions differing markedly from Western philosophical assumptions while addressing similar foundational questions. Westerhoff's (2009) analysis shows how Nāgārjuna's arguments function as a form of transcendental analysis, revealing the conditions for conceptual thought itself.

Indian philosophical traditions developed sophisticated epistemological frameworks identifying multiple sources of valid knowledge (pramāṇas) while analyzing their scope and limitations. Ganeri's (2001) comprehensive analysis demonstrates how classical Indian philosophy developed rigorous methods for identifying necessary conditions for knowledge while maintaining pluralistic approaches, recognizing different types of epistemic access to reality. Matilal's (1986) work reveals how Indian philosophers anticipated many contemporary epistemological debates while developing distinctive solutions.

3.3.3 The Interplay of Reason and Experience

Philosophy cannot operate in isolation from empirical considerations, as Quine's (1951) critique of the analytic-synthetic distinction demonstrates. Even apparently *a priori* truths prove revisable in light of empirical discoveries, as the development of non-Euclidean geometry and its application in relativity theory illustrates. This suggests that the distinction between rational and empirical knowledge is pragmatic rather than absolute. Maddy's (2007) "second philosophy" extends this naturalistic approach while maintaining philosophy's distinctive contribution to understanding.

Putnam's (1981) analysis of reason, truth, and history reveals how assumptions about reference and meaning shape our entire conceptual apparatus in ways with empirical implications. The impossibility of achieving a "God's eye view" means that rational analysis always occurs within historically and culturally situated contexts influencing both the questions asked and answers considered plausible. This recognition leads to what Putnam (2002) calls "pragmatic realism"—acknowledging both objectivity and the perspectival nature of knowledge.

Contemporary philosophy of language has revealed deep connections between semantic theories and empirical assumptions about human psychology and social interaction. Grice's (1989) analysis of conversational implicature and Searle's (1995) work on speech acts demonstrate how understanding linguistic meaning requires both logical analysis and empirical investigation of human communicative practices. These investigations show that philosophical and empirical methods must work together to understand language and meaning.

The relationship between philosophical and empirical investigation becomes particularly complex in areas such as personal identity, free will, and moral responsibility. Parfit's (1984) thought experiments about personal identity reveal conceptual puzzles that cannot be resolved through empirical investigation alone, yet their solutions have implications for understanding psychological continuity and moral responsibility. This suggests that philosophical and empirical approaches must collaborate to address fundamental questions about human nature. As Schechtman (1996) argues, resolving questions about personal identity requires integrating metaphysical analysis with psychological and ethical considerations.

Brandom's (1994) inferentialist approach to meaning demonstrates how semantic content emerges from social practices of giving and asking for reasons rather than purely formal logical relationships. This analysis suggests that understanding the relationship between reason and experience requires attention to the social and historical contexts in which rational practices develop and function. McDowell's (1994) complementary analysis shows how experience can provide rational constraint on belief without falling into the "Myth of the Given."

3.4 RELIGION: THE REVELATORY PATH

3.4.1 Experiential and Revelatory Foundations

Religious epistemology encompasses both individual spiritual experience and communal traditions of revelation, claiming to provide access to ultimate reality through non-inferential awareness and divine disclosure. James's (1902/2002) comprehensive analysis of religious experience documents remarkable cross-cultural patterns—unity experiences, encounters with the sacred, moral transformation—suggesting objective spiritual dimensions accessible through contemplative practice. These experiences, while interpreted through particular cultural and religious frameworks, display sufficient commonality to suggest they may provide genuine epistemic access to transcendent reality.

Religious knowledge claims rest fundamentally on revelatory disclosure—ultimate reality's self-communication to human consciousness through various modalities, including scriptural traditions, prophetic testimony, contemplative insights, and ritual encounters. As Alston (1991) argues, mystical perception may constitute a genuine epistemic practice parallel to sense perception, with sophisticated criteria for assessment developed and refined over millennia of spiritual practice. This "doxastic practice" approach suggests that religious experience can provide *prima facie* justification for belief when embedded within established traditions of spiritual formation and discernment.

Stace's (1960) comparative analysis of mystical experience reveals consistent phenomenological structures across diverse religious traditions, including claims to immediate awareness of ultimate reality transcending ordinary subject-object distinctions. However, Katz's (1978) contextualist critique demonstrates how these experiences are shaped by prior conceptual frameworks and cultural expectations, suggesting that pure unmediated experience may be impossible. Forman's (1990) response argues for the possibility of "pure consciousness events" resisting cultural conditioning, indicating ongoing scholarly debate about mystical experience's epistemological status. As Pike (1992) argues, this debate reveals fundamental questions about the relationship between experience and interpretation in religious epistemology.

Contemporary neuroscientific investigation of contemplative practices has begun to validate aspects of traditional phenomenological descriptions while raising new questions about the relationship between neurological processes and spiritual experience. Studies of long-term meditators demonstrate measurable changes in brain structure and function correlating with reported experiential changes (Lutz et al., 2004; Davidson & Lutz, 2008). However, these findings raise complex questions about the relationship between neurological correlates and spiritual content, requiring both scientific and philosophical analysis. As Newberg and d'Aquili (2001) argue, neuroscientific findings neither validate nor invalidate religious truth claims but reveal the biological substrates of spiritual experience.

The Islamic tradition's analysis of knowledge by presence ('ilm ḥuḍūrī) as distinguished from knowledge by correspondence ('ilm ḥuṣūlī) offers sophisticated epistemological frameworks for understanding direct spiritual awareness (Yazdi, 1992). This distinction suggests that immediate knowledge through spiritual experience operates according to different epistemic principles than mediated knowledge through concepts and reasoning, yet both contribute to comprehensive understanding of reality. As Nasr (1989) demonstrates, Islamic philosophy developed rigorous methods for evaluating spiritual knowledge while maintaining its distinctive character.

3.4.2 Faith as Epistemic Virtue and Rational Foundation

Plantinga's (2000) reformed epistemology challenges evidentialist assumptions by arguing that belief in God can be properly basic—rationally acceptable without requiring support from independent evidence, analogous to other foundational beliefs such as belief in other minds or the external world. This approach suggests that religious beliefs may be grounded in immediate experience of divine reality rather than inferential arguments, though such experience must satisfy appropriate conditions for reliability. The sensus divinitatis functions as a cognitive faculty producing warranted religious beliefs when functioning properly in appropriate environments.

Swinburne's (2004) systematic analysis demonstrates how religious beliefs can be supported through cumulative arguments combining empirical evidence, philosophical reasoning, and experiential testimony. The teleological argument from fine-tuning, the argument from religious experience, and the argument from miracles each contribute probabilistic support that, when combined, may provide adequate rational justification for theistic belief. This Bayesian approach shows how religious belief can be rationally supported even if no single argument provides conclusive proof.

Hick's (1989) analysis of religious epistemology argues that religious experience should be accepted as veridical unless there are sufficient grounds for doubt, following the principle of credulity governing ordinary perceptual experience. This approach treats religious experience as innocent until proven guilty rather than requiring positive justification for acceptance, though it must still satisfy criteria for distinguishing authentic from inauthentic spiritual experience. As Davis (1989) argues, this principle must be balanced with critical evaluation to avoid credulity.

Gellman's (1997) investigation of religious experience and rational belief demonstrates how experiential evidence can provide sufficient grounds for religious conviction while remaining open to critical evaluation and potential revision. This approach maintains both the cognitive content of religious claims and their revisability in light of further evidence and argument. Howard-Snyder's (2013) analysis of faith shows how it can function as a virtue enabling rational commitment in conditions of evidential ambiguity.

Medieval Islamic, Jewish, and Christian traditions developed sophisticated methodologies for integrating rational argument with revealed authority. Maimonides' (1963) analysis in *The Guide of the Perplexed* demonstrates how philosophical reasoning can illuminate scriptural meaning while maintaining revealed truth's primacy. Aquinas's (1265/1981) synthesis of Aristotelian philosophy with Christian theology shows how natural reason and revealed truth can be understood as complementary rather than competitive sources of knowledge. As McGrath (2001) argues, these medieval syntheses provide resources for contemporary integration of faith and reason.

3.4.3 The Scope and Limits of Religious Understanding

Religious traditions address existential dimensions that scientific and philosophical approaches handle only obliquely: the meaning of suffering, hope beyond death, ultimate purpose, and the ground of moral obligation (Cottingham, 2005). Religious frameworks provide comprehensive narratives integrating cosmological, anthropological, ethical, and eschatological insights into coherent worldviews shaping lived experience while offering resources for confronting finitude and mortality.

Religious truth encompasses what Lonergan (1957) characterizes as participatory knowing—transformation through relationship with ultimate reality rather than detached theoretical understanding. This performative dimension means religious truth cannot be grasped through analytical investigation alone but requires personal engagement and existential commitment. The truth of compassion, for instance, is known fully only through compassionate action and relationship. As Moser (2008) argues, this participatory dimension explains why purely theoretical approaches to religious questions often miss their essential character.

Liberation theology's emphasis on praxis demonstrates how religious understanding emerges through engaged action for justice rather than purely theoretical reflection. Gutiérrez's (1988) analysis reveals how theological reflection must emerge from concrete experience of oppression and liberation rather than abstract speculation. This approach suggests that religious truth has irreducibly practical dimensions requiring social and political engagement for adequate comprehension. As Sobrino (1988) demonstrates, the "epistemological privilege of the poor" reveals dimensions of religious truth invisible from positions of privilege.

Indigenous religious traditions offer alternative frameworks challenging Western distinctions between natural and supernatural, individual and communal, secular and sacred. Deloria's (1999) analysis of Native American spirituality demonstrates how Indigenous approaches integrate empirical observation, rational reflection, and spiritual insight within relational ontologies emphasizing interconnection rather than substance. These perspectives suggest that religious understanding may require a fundamental reconceptualization of Western epistemological categories. As Tinker (2004) argues, Indigenous spiritualities provide essential resources for ecological and social healing.

Contemporary interfaith dialogue has revealed both commonalities and irreducible differences among religious traditions, resisting simple synthesis yet enabling mutual understanding. Burrell's (2004) analysis of interfaith perspectives demonstrates how different traditions can engage productively while maintaining their distinctive insights and practices. This suggests that religious pluralism may be epistemologically necessary rather than merely politically expedient. As Heim (1995) argues, different religious traditions may provide access to different dimensions of ultimate reality.

The relationship between religious understanding and scientific knowledge remains complex and contested. While some religious claims conflict with established scientific findings, many religious insights about human nature, meaning, and moral obligation complement rather than contradict scientific understanding. Peacocke's (2004) analysis demonstrates how evolutionary biology can be understood as revealing divine creative activity rather than eliminating divine causation. As Polkinghorne and Beale (2009) argue, science and religion address different but complementary questions about reality.

3.5 HISTORICAL TENSIONS AND CONVERGENT POSSIBILITIES

3.5.1 Beyond the Warfare Metaphor

Popular discourse perpetuates warfare metaphors between science and religion based on historical misunderstandings, obscuring more complex relationships. Harrison's (2015) comprehensive analysis reveals that the concepts of "science" and "religion" as distinct domains emerged only in the modern period, making anachronistic any claims about inherent historical conflict. Many scientific pioneers—Kepler, Newton, Faraday, Mendel—were devoutly religious individuals viewing their investigations as exploring divine creation rather than opposing religious belief.

Brooke's (1991) detailed historical analysis demonstrates that science-religion relationships display remarkable complexity and contextual variation rather than consistent antagonism. The Galileo controversy involved political, personal, and hermeneutical factors beyond simple science-religion conflict, with legitimate scientific objections to heliocentrism (stellar parallax was not observed until 1838) combined with complex institutional and interpretive issues. As Finocchiaro (1989) documents, the controversy concerned biblical interpretation and ecclesiastical authority as much as astronomical theory.

The reception of Darwin's evolutionary theory illustrates the diversity of religious responses rather than uniform opposition. While some religious authorities rejected evolution, others, such as Asa Gray, saw natural selection as God's method of creation. The perceived conflict often reflected broader social anxieties about human dignity and moral authority rather than necessary theological objections to evolutionary mechanisms. As Bowler

(2001) demonstrates, many religious thinkers embraced evolution while rejecting purely materialistic interpretations.

Numbers' (2006) analysis of creationism reveals how opposition to evolution emerged primarily in twentieth-century American fundamentalism rather than representing traditional religious responses to scientific theories. This perspective suggests that apparent science-religion conflicts often reflect specific cultural and political contexts rather than inherent epistemological incompatibilities. The "creation science" movement represents a modern phenomenon rather than a continuation of historical religious approaches to nature.

Recent historical scholarship has revealed how theological commitments often motivated and shaped scientific investigation. Harrison's (2007) analysis shows how Protestant emphasis on literal biblical interpretation paradoxically encouraged empirical investigation of nature, while Catholic sacramental theology supported symbolic interpretations accommodating scientific discoveries. These findings challenge simplistic narratives of inevitable conflict between scientific and religious worldviews.

3.5.2 Positivist Reduction and Its Limitations

Logical positivism attempted to reduce legitimate knowledge to empirical science and analytical tautologies, dismissing religious and metaphysical claims as cognitively meaningless. The verification principle—statements are meaningful only if empirically verifiable or analytically true—would eliminate ethics, aesthetics, and religion as mere expressions of attitude rather than genuine knowledge claims (Ayer, 1936).

However, positivism collapsed under self-referential problems and internal contradictions. The verification principle itself could neither be verified empirically nor established analytically, revealing the self-defeating character of strict empiricist epistemology. Quine's (1951) "Two Dogmas of Empiricism" demonstrated that the analytic-synthetic distinction central to positivist philosophy cannot be maintained, while Kuhn's (1996) analysis of scientific revolutions revealed how scientific theories involve irreducibly metaphysical commitments.

Post-positivist philosophy of science recognizes that scientific theories necessarily involve metaphysical assumptions, value judgments, and aesthetic criteria that cannot be reduced to purely empirical content. Putnam's (2002) analysis of the fact-value distinction demonstrates how evaluative considerations enter scientific theorizing at fundamental levels, making impossible any sharp separation between descriptive and normative elements. As Longino (1990) argues, values shape scientific practice from problem selection through interpretation of results.

Contemporary philosophy of science acknowledges science's dependence on philosophical frameworks providing conceptual foundations for empirical investigation. The uniformity of nature, the reality of causation, and the preference for simple explanations represent philosophical commitments making scientific practice possible while requiring justification beyond purely scientific methods. As Laudan (1977) demonstrates, scientific rationality itself depends on epistemic values that cannot be scientifically validated.

Haack's (2003) analysis of scientism reveals how excessive claims for scientific authority represent epistemic imperialism, misunderstanding both science's legitimate scope and necessary limitations. This perspective suggests that defending science's integrity requires recognizing rather than denying its philosophical presuppositions and methodological boundaries. Stenmark's (2001) taxonomy of scientism shows how different forms of scientific expansionism fail to respect legitimate domains of non-scientific inquiry.

3.5.3 Fundamentalist Responses and Interpretive Sophistication

Religious fundamentalism often mirrors scientific materialism's reductionism by treating ancient texts as scientific documents, creating category mistakes, impoverishing religious understanding, and generating unnecessary conflicts. Biblical literalism represents a modern phenomenon differing markedly from traditional hermeneutical approaches recognizing multiple levels of meaning in sacred texts (Barr, 1977).

Augustine's warnings against rigid biblical interpretation contradicting demonstrated natural knowledge illustrate sophisticated traditional approaches to scriptural hermeneutics. Medieval Jewish and Islamic scholars developed elaborate interpretive methodologies, distinguishing literal, allegorical, moral, and mystical meanings, enabling integration of scriptural authority with rational investigation (de Lubac, 1998). As Grant (2004) demonstrates, medieval scholars routinely accommodated new philosophical and scientific insights through sophisticated interpretive strategies.

Contemporary biblical scholarship demonstrates how historical-critical methods can illuminate scriptural meaning while respecting religious authority. Kugel's (2007) analysis reveals how ancient interpretive traditions already recognized the complex relationship between historical and theological truth in scriptural texts. This suggests that apparent conflicts between scientific and religious approaches often result from impoverished hermeneutical methods rather than inherent incompatibilities. As Levenson (1993) argues, modern biblical scholarship can enrich rather than undermine religious understanding.

The emergence of multiple interpretive strategies within religious traditions demonstrates internal resources for engaging scientific discoveries without abandoning religious commitments. Process theology, liberation theology, and contemplative traditions offer alternative frameworks for understanding divine action, complementing rather than competing with scientific explanations. As Barbour (1997) demonstrates, sophisticated theological frameworks can incorporate scientific insights while maintaining distinctive religious perspectives.

Polkinghorne's (1998) analysis reveals how science and theology can maintain integrity while engaging in productive dialogue about shared concerns. This approach avoids both reductionist materialism and biblical literalism by recognizing the legitimate autonomy of different domains of inquiry while maintaining their ultimate unity in truth. As McGrath (2004) argues, proper understanding requires respecting both scientific and theological methods while seeking integration where appropriate.

3.6 TOWARD EPISTEMIC INTEGRATION

3.6.1 Complementarity and Hierarchical Organization

The principle of complementarity, developed initially in quantum physics to understand wave-particle duality, offers a framework for integrating scientific, philosophical, and religious perspectives without reducing them to a single approach. Bohr's (1958) recognition that complete understanding sometimes requires mutually exclusive yet jointly necessary descriptions suggests that reality itself may be sufficiently complex to require multiple analytical frameworks. As Kaiser (1992) demonstrates, complementarity provides a model for understanding how different approaches can be simultaneously necessary while appearing contradictory.

Murphy's (1990) analysis of hierarchical levels of explanation from physics through biology to psychology and theology demonstrates how each level exhibits emergent properties requiring distinctive methodologies while remaining connected to other levels through bottom-up and top-down causal relationships. This approach enables a comprehensive understanding without competitive reduction of higher-level phenomena to lower-level mechanisms. As Ellis (2016) argues, genuine top-down causation operates in complex systems, making reductionism inadequate for complete understanding.

Clayton's (2004) analysis of emergence reveals how consciousness, purpose, and values represent genuine features of reality emerging from but not reducible to physical processes. This perspective suggests that mental and spiritual phenomena require their own analytical approaches while remaining naturalistic in general orientation toward scientific understanding. Strong emergence, as Clayton and Davies (2006) argue, provides resources for understanding how genuinely novel properties can arise in complex systems.

Deacon's (2011) analysis of emergent causation demonstrates how higher-level constraints can influence lower-level processes through what he characterizes as "constitutive absence"—the causal efficacy of what is not present. This analysis provides naturalistic resources for understanding how mental and spiritual phenomena can be genuinely causal without violating physical laws. The concept of "downward" causation offers frameworks for understanding how consciousness and purpose can influence physical processes.

The recognition of hierarchical organization enables what Morin (2008) characterizes as "complex thinking" embracing both unity and multiplicity without falling into either reductionist monism or incoherent pluralism. This approach suggests frameworks for integration respecting the integrity of different levels while maintaining systematic connections among them. As Mitchell (2009) demonstrates, complex systems require multiple complementary approaches for adequate understanding.

3.6.2 Convergent Truth and Mutual Enrichment

If reality possesses fundamental unity, different approaches to truth should exhibit convergence when properly pursued, with apparent conflicts often revealing category mistakes or incomplete understanding rather than genuine contradictions. The recognition of fine-tuning in cosmological constants has prompted theological reflection on creation and anthropic principles while remaining compatible with scientific investigation of physical mechanisms (Collins, 2009; Barnes, 2012). This convergence suggests that scientific and religious perspectives can illuminate complementary aspects of cosmic reality.

Quantum mechanics' challenge to classical assumptions about determinism and locality has generated philosophical reflection on causation, consciousness, and physical reality's nature complementing rather than contradicting scientific investigation. The measurement problem requires both empirical investigation and philosophical analysis for adequate understanding (Albert, 1992; Maudlin, 2019). As Shimony (1993) argues, quantum mechanics raises philosophical questions that purely scientific approaches cannot resolve.

Contemplative traditions' sophisticated analyses of consciousness and attention now inform neuroscientific research on meditation and mental training, demonstrating how ancient wisdom can contribute to contemporary scientific understanding. Wallace's (2007) concept of "contemplative science" illustrates how first-person investigative methods can complement third-person scientific approaches in studying consciousness. As Varela, Thompson, and Rosch (1991) demonstrate, contemplative traditions provide phenomenological data essential for understanding consciousness.

Environmental challenges require integration of scientific ecology, philosophical ethics, and religious wisdom about human-nature relationships. Climate change, biodiversity loss, and ecological degradation cannot be adequately addressed through purely technical approaches but require the transformation of values and practices drawing on multiple wisdom traditions (Gottlieb, 2006). As Tucker and Grim (2014) argue, world religions provide essential resources for developing ecological consciousness and sustainable practices.

The dialogue between evolutionary biology and religious traditions has generated sophisticated theological reflection on divine action, human nature, and creation's meaning, enriching both scientific and religious understanding. Rather than eliminating religious insight, evolutionary theory has prompted deeper reflection on how divine creativity might operate through natural processes (Peacocke, 2004; McGrath, 2004). As

Haught (2000) demonstrates, evolutionary theology can deepen rather than diminish religious understanding.

Contemporary discussions of consciousness, artificial intelligence, and human enhancement require integration of scientific, philosophical, and religious perspectives on human nature and technological development. These challenges cannot be adequately addressed from any single perspective but require comprehensive approaches drawing on multiple wisdom traditions (Peters, Russell, & Welker, 2002). As Herzfeld (2002) argues, theological anthropology provides essential resources for understanding human uniqueness in an age of artificial intelligence.

3.6.3 Frameworks for Productive Integration

An adequate integration framework must respect methodological integrity while enabling productive interaction across different domains of inquiry. Different questions require different approaches—empirical methods for investigating natural phenomena, rational analysis for examining necessary truths, and contemplative practices for exploring consciousness and meaning. Rather than hierarchical subordination or compartmentalized isolation, these approaches can engage in critical dialogue, enriching understanding while maintaining disciplinary rigor (McGrath, 2019).

Habermas's (2008) analysis of post-secular philosophy suggests how religious and secular reasoning can translate insights into publicly accessible language, contributing to democratic discourse. Religious wisdom about human dignity, social justice, and moral motivation can inform public policy when articulated through rational argument and empirical evidence. Conversely, scientific and philosophical insights can purify religious understanding of superstition and ideological distortion. This model of "translation" enables mutual enrichment while respecting disciplinary boundaries.

Barbour's (1997) analysis identifies four primary models of science-religion relationships: conflict, independence, dialogue, and integration. While conflict and independence models dominate popular discourse, dialogue and integration approaches offer more sophisticated frameworks for productive engagement. Dialogue involves mutual respect and exchange of insights, while integration seeks systematic synthesis through comprehensive worldviews. As Stenmark (2004) demonstrates, these models can operate simultaneously at different levels of analysis.

The multidimensional model developed by Stenmark (2004) demonstrates how science and religion can relate through different combinations of epistemic, practical, and theoretical dimensions. This analysis reveals how apparent conflicts at one level may coexist with convergence at other levels, suggesting nuanced approaches to integration, avoiding both uncritical synthesis and unnecessary opposition. Different aspects of science and religion may relate differently, requiring sophisticated rather than monolithic approaches.

The recognition that the pursuit of first principles demands integration of multiple epistemological approaches represents a foundational insight about knowledge and reality's nature. Science reveals empirical regularities and causal mechanisms, philosophy uncovers necessary conditions and conceptual relationships, and religion explores ultimate meaning and transformative practice. Their convergence points toward a unified understanding transcending methodological boundaries while respecting legitimate disciplinary autonomy (Clayton & Simpson, 2006).

Process philosophy, as developed by Whitehead (1978) and contemporary scholars, offers metaphysical frameworks integrating scientific, philosophical, and religious insights through comprehensive visions of reality as fundamentally relational and experiential. These approaches suggest how systematic integration might proceed without eliminating distinctive contributions of different investigative traditions. As Griffin (2000) demonstrates, process thought provides resources for understanding how science and religion can be reconciled within comprehensive metaphysical frameworks.

3.7 CONCLUSION: THE CONVERGENT QUEST FOR UNDERSTANDING

The recognition that human knowledge emerges through multiple complementary pathways itself represents a fundamental epistemological principle—a first principle about understanding's nature acknowledging both truth's unity and the plurality of legitimate approaches to discovering it. By embracing methodological pluralism while maintaining critical rigor, we position ourselves to discover foundational truths underlying existence through comprehensive investigation rather than premature reduction (McGrath, 2019).

Each pathway contributes indispensable insights that cannot be adequately replaced by alternatives. Science provides empirical grounding through systematic observation and mathematical modeling, revealing patterns and mechanisms across unprecedented scales. Philosophy offers conceptual clarity through rational analysis, uncovering necessary conditions and logical relationships structuring all possible experience. Religion opens experiential depths through contemplative practice and revealed wisdom, exploring ultimate questions of meaning, purpose, and transformation, transcending purely theoretical understanding.

Taylor's (2007) analysis of the "secular age" demonstrates how purely secular approaches to human meaning and moral sources face internal tensions pointing beyond naturalistic frameworks. The human search for significance, sources of moral motivation, and responses to suffering suggests experiential depths that scientific and philosophical approaches alone cannot adequately address. This recognition does not invalidate secular inquiry but suggests its necessary supplementation through religious and spiritual investigation.

Wilson's (1998) concept of "consilience" envisions eventual unification of knowledge across different domains through systematic connection of empirical sciences with humanities and human concerns. While Wilson's approach tends toward reductionist naturalism, the underlying insight about knowledge integration remains valuable when extended to include religious and contemplative traditions alongside scientific and philosophical investigation. As Ruse (2010) argues, genuine consilience requires respecting the integrity of different knowledge domains.

Contemporary challenges, including consciousness studies, environmental crisis, technological development, and global ethics, require comprehensive approaches drawing on multiple wisdom traditions. Climate change cannot be adequately addressed through purely technical solutions but requires the transformation of values and practices engaging scientific understanding, philosophical reflection, and religious wisdom about human responsibility and natural relationships (Northcott, 2007).

As we examine specific first principles in subsequent chapters, we will repeatedly discover that a comprehensive understanding requires integration of all three epistemological approaches. Physical constants require scientific measurement but raise philosophical questions about necessity and religious questions about cosmic purpose. Logical principles require philosophical analysis but operate within scientific reasoning and religious reflection. Moral principles engage philosophical argument, psychological research, and religious wisdom about human transformation and ultimate meaning.

The three paths to truth, pursued with intellectual courage and epistemic humility, converge toward an understanding that transcends methodological boundaries while respecting disciplinary integrity. This convergence does not eliminate distinctive contributions but creates productive dialogue where empirical observation, rational analysis, and contemplative experience mutually inform and correct each other. In this integrative dialogue, we approach what Polanyi (1958) characterizes as "personal knowledge," engaging the whole person in committed yet critical inquiry.

The quest for first principles thus becomes not competition among incompatible methodologies but collaborative exploration drawing on humanity's full epistemic resources. This collaborative approach represents a fundamental insight about truth and knowledge's nature—that reality is sufficiently rich and human understanding sufficiently limited that multiple approaches are not merely helpful but necessary for adequate comprehension. The convergent quest for understanding through science, philosophy, and religion offers our best hope for discovering foundational principles underlying all existence while remaining appropriately humble about the provisional character of human knowledge and reality's inexhaustible mystery.

PART II

CHAPTER 4: THE LAWS OF PHYSICS

4.1 THE ARCHITECTURE OF PHYSICAL REALITY

The identification of fundamental physical laws represents humanity's most systematic endeavor to discern first principles governing material reality. These mathematical relationships, which describe the behavior of matter, energy, space, and time across scales from quantum to cosmic, constitute what Weinberg (1992) characterized as explanatory principles of maximal depth rather than mere empirical generalizations. The distinction proves crucial: whereas contingent facts describe particular systems under specific conditions, physical laws express invariant patterns that appear to hold without exception throughout the observable universe (Carroll, 2016; Ellis, 2007).

The conceptual architecture underlying physical law raises foundational questions about the nature of scientific explanation itself. As Butterfield and Earman (2007) demonstrate through detailed analysis of classical and quantum frameworks, physical laws serve multiple epistemic functions simultaneously: they describe observable regularities, enable predictive inference, constrain the space of dynamically possible phenomena, and provide explanatory unification across disparate domains. The remarkable economy of fundamental principles—a relatively small set of mathematical relationships accounting for nature's vast phenomenological complexity—suggests what Wilczek (2015) describes as profound underlying unity beneath surface diversity.

This apparent universality presents a central puzzle for first principles analysis. Consider gravitational interaction: the same inverse-square relationship governs terrestrial mechanics, planetary dynamics, stellar evolution, galactic structure, and cosmological expansion (Hartle, 2003). This scale-invariant universality, with laws operating identically across spatial distances spanning forty orders of magnitude and temporal intervals from microseconds to billions of years, suggests that physical principles reflect genuine structural features of reality rather than artifacts of human conceptual schemes (Ladyman & Ross, 2007). Yet this inference requires careful philosophical scrutiny.

Contemporary philosophy of physics challenges naive realist interpretations through a detailed examination of scientific practice. Cartwright (1999) argues persuasively that fundamental laws function as abstract principles requiring extensive supplementation through auxiliary hypotheses, boundary conditions, and approximation schemes before generating empirical predictions. Similarly, Morrison (2000) demonstrates that even paradigmatically successful theories like quantum electrodynamics involve complex relationships between fundamental equations and phenomenological models. This gap between abstract law and concrete application suggests that physical principles may possess a more nuanced ontological status than simple realism implies.

The debate extends to the relationship between fundamental and emergent laws. Anderson (1972) articulated the influential "More Is Different" thesis, arguing that each level of complexity involves qualitatively new principles irreducible to lower-level laws. Laughlin and Pines (2000) extend this argument through their concept of "protectorates"—higher-level organizing principles that remain robust despite microscopic variations. These perspectives challenge the assumption that fundamental physics provides uniquely privileged first principles, suggesting instead a hierarchical structure of equally valid organizational principles operating at different scales (Batterman, 2002).

4.2 CONSERVATION PRINCIPLES: THE MATHEMATICAL FOUNDATION OF CONSTRAINT

4.2.1 The Logical Structure of Conservation

Conservation laws assert the invariance of specific quantities under designated transformations, thereby establishing absolute constraints that no physical process can violate (Brading & Castellani, 2003). These principles exhibit remarkable theoretical stability, persisting through revolutionary conceptual changes—energy conservation holds equally in Newtonian mechanics, Maxwellian electromagnetism, Einstein's relativity, and quantum field theory—suggesting that conservation principles reflect deeper structural features than particular dynamical frameworks (Gross, 1996).

The epistemic priority of conservation principles over force laws requires careful analysis. As Lange (2007) argues through detailed case studies, conservation laws possess a modal strength exceeding ordinary physical laws: they specify not merely what happens but what cannot happen under any circumstances. Energy conservation categorically prohibits perpetual motion machines regardless of their mechanical details; momentum conservation constrains collision outcomes independent of interaction mechanisms; charge conservation forbids spontaneous creation or annihilation of net charge irrespective of particle physics details (Kosmann-Schwarzbach, 2011).

Modern physics recognizes a hierarchy of conservation principles operating at distinct descriptive levels. Classical conservation laws—energy, momentum, angular momentum—emerge from continuous spacetime symmetries. Discrete conservation laws—baryon number, lepton number, strangeness—govern particle physics interactions. Topological conservation laws—magnetic flux quantization, winding number conservation—constrain condensed matter phenomena (Zee, 2016). Each category provides independent constraints, collectively defining the mathematical scaffolding within which all physical processes must operate.

The relationship between exact and approximate conservation deserves emphasis. While energy and momentum conservation appear absolute, other quantities exhibit only approximate conservation. Parity conservation holds in strong and electromagnetic interactions but fails maximally in weak

74

processes (Franklin, 1986). Isospin conservation characterizes strong interactions but breaks in electromagnetic processes. Strangeness conservation governs strong and electromagnetic interactions but violates in weak decays (Griffiths, 2008). This hierarchy of conservation principles, from absolute to approximate to violated, reveals the subtle structure of physical law.

4.2.2 Noether's Theorem and the Unity of Symmetry and Conservation

Emmy Noether's 1918 theorem, which Einstein praised as the most profound mathematical result guiding physics development, establishes a precise correspondence between continuous symmetries and conserved quantities (Noether, 1971). This result transforms conservation from empirical generalization to mathematical necessity: given specific symmetry assumptions, corresponding conservation laws follow deductively (Brading & Brown, 2003).

The theorem's implications extend throughout theoretical physics. In classical mechanics, temporal translation invariance necessitates energy conservation; spatial translation invariance requires momentum conservation; rotational invariance demands angular momentum conservation (Goldstein, Poole, & Safko, 2002). In field theory, local gauge invariance generates conserved currents: $U(1)$ symmetry yields electric charge conservation; $SU(2) \times U(1)$ symmetry produces weak hypercharge conservation; $SU(3)$ symmetry ensures color charge conservation (Peskin & Schroeder, 1995).

However, Noether's framework also reveals the contingent aspects of conservation principles. As Earman (2003) emphasizes, the specific conservation laws realized in nature depend upon which symmetries characterize physical law—alternative spacetime structures or different gauge groups would yield distinct conservation principles. General relativity illustrates this contingency: energy conservation holds locally but fails globally in expanding spacetime, where temporal translation symmetry breaks (Wald, 1984). This symmetry-breaking explains cosmological phenomena like redshift while demonstrating that even fundamental conservation principles possess limited domains of validity.

The relationship between global and local symmetries proves particularly significant. Global symmetries generate conservation laws through

Noether's first theorem, while local gauge symmetries yield conserved currents via Noether's second theorem (Karatas & Kowalski, 1990). The gauge principle—requiring theories to exhibit local symmetry—has proven extraordinarily fruitful, generating the Standard Model's structure and predicting new particles subsequently confirmed experimentally (Quigg, 2013). Yet this success raises philosophical questions about whether symmetry principles are fundamental or merely effective organizing principles for phenomenological regularities.

4.2.3 Discrete Symmetries and the Limits of Conservation

Discrete symmetries—charge conjugation (C), parity transformation (P), and time reversal (T)—provide additional constraints on physical processes while revealing conservation law limitations (Sozzi, 2008). The discovery of parity violation in weak interactions (Wu et al., 1957) shattered assumptions about nature's mirror symmetry, demonstrating that conservation principles previously considered sacrosanct could fail in specific domains.

The CPT theorem, independently proven by Lüders (1954) and Pauli (1955), establishes that any local, Lorentz-invariant quantum field theory must respect combined CPT symmetry. Weinberg (1995) emphasizes this result's generality: CPT conservation follows from minimal assumptions about spacetime structure and quantum mechanics, making it more fundamental than individual symmetry principles. Experimental tests confirm CPT conservation to extraordinary precision, with antiproton-proton mass differences constrained below one part in 10^9 (Gabrielse et al., 1999).

CP violation, discovered in neutral kaon systems (Christenson et al., 1964) and subsequently observed in B mesons (Aubert et al., 2001), demonstrates that even combined discrete symmetries can fail while preserving CPT invariance. This violation provides essential ingredients for cosmological baryogenesis, as Sakharov (1967) demonstrated, linking microscopic symmetry breaking to the universe's matter-antimatter asymmetry. The pattern of discrete symmetry violations—maximal P violation, small CP violation, exact CPT conservation—suggests deep principles constraining possible theories (Pich, 2017).

4.3 THERMODYNAMICS: STATISTICAL FOUNDATIONS AND TEMPORAL ASYMMETRY

4.3.1 The Emergence of Irreversibility

Thermodynamics introduces qualitatively distinct physics through the second law's assertion that entropy never decreases in isolated systems (Callen, 1985). Unlike mechanical laws describing individual particle trajectories, thermodynamic principles emerge from statistical mechanics applied to macroscopic aggregates, exhibiting what Atkins (2010) characterizes as irreversible behavior arising from reversible microscopic dynamics.

The statistical interpretation pioneered by Boltzmann (1896) reveals entropy as a measure of microscopic disorder, quantified through the formula $S = k \ln W$ relating macroscopic entropy to microscopic multiplicity. This framework explains entropy increase through phase space arguments: vastly more microscopic configurations correspond to macroscopic disorder than order, making entropy growth overwhelmingly probable for systems with Avogadro's number of particles (Lebowitz, 1993).

Yet this statistical foundation generates conceptual puzzles. Loschmidt's reversibility paradox asks how irreversible macroscopic behavior emerges from time-reversible microscopic laws (Uffink, 2001). Poincaré's recurrence theorem proves that isolated systems must return arbitrarily close to initial conditions, seemingly contradicting perpetual entropy increase (Barreira, 2006). These paradoxes highlight the subtle relationship between microscopic dynamics and macroscopic thermodynamics.

Resolution requires distinguishing between different temporal scales and probability measures. As Jaynes (1965) demonstrated through maximum entropy methods, thermodynamic behavior represents the most probable macroscopic evolution consistent with constraints, not an absolute prohibition on entropy decrease. For macroscopic systems, fluctuations violating the second law become exponentially suppressed, with waiting times exceeding the universe's age by many orders of magnitude (Penrose, 2004). The second law thus expresses statistical tendency rather than fundamental impossibility.

4.3.2 Cosmological Implications and the Past Hypothesis

The second law's cosmological applications reveal profound puzzles about temporal asymmetry and boundary conditions. If entropy inexorably increases, the universe's initial state must have possessed extraordinarily low entropy—Penrose (2004) estimates the probability at one part in $10^{10^{123}}$, suggesting either remarkable fine-tuning or deeper explanatory principles.

Carroll (2010) argues that temporal asymmetry emerges from cosmological boundary conditions rather than fundamental dynamical laws. The "Past Hypothesis"—that the early universe possessed anomalously low entropy—combined with statistical mechanics, generates all observed temporal asymmetries: thermodynamic irreversibility, electromagnetic radiation, quantum measurement, biological aging, and psychological time perception. This view makes the arrow of time a cosmological rather than fundamental physical phenomenon.

Alternative approaches seek intrinsic sources of temporal asymmetry. Price (1996) examines whether quantum measurement or gravitational collapse might provide fundamental time direction. Schulman (1997) explores two-time boundary conditions with both low-entropy initial and final states. Zeh (2007) proposes that temporal asymmetry originates in quantum decoherence processes. However, Wallace (2010) argues convincingly that these proposals either implicitly assume special boundary conditions or fail to explain observed correlations between different temporal arrows.

The relationship between thermodynamics and cosmology remains contentious. While inflation theory potentially explains low initial entropy through exponential expansion (Guth, 1997), critics like Penrose (2010) argue that inflation merely displaces the fine-tuning problem. The multiverse hypothesis suggests our low-entropy initial conditions result from anthropic selection (Susskind, 2005), but this explanation remains controversial and potentially untestable (Ellis & Silk, 2014).

4.3.3 Information Theory and Modern Thermodynamics

Recent developments forge deep connections between thermodynamics and information theory, suggesting unified foundations for physical and computational processes. Bennett's (1982) analysis of Maxwell's demon demonstrates that information erasure necessarily generates entropy, establishing fundamental thermodynamic costs for computation. Landauer's principle quantifies this cost: erasing one bit of information requires minimum energy dissipation kT ln 2, confirmed experimentally by Bérut et al. (2012).

Black hole thermodynamics exemplifies these connections. Bekenstein (1973) and Hawking (1975) discovered that black holes possess entropy proportional to surface area rather than volume, suggesting information storage limits in gravitational systems. The holographic principle, proposed by 't Hooft (1993) and refined by Susskind (1995), extends this insight: the maximum information content of any region equals its boundary area in Planck units. This principle, if correct, would establish information-theoretic constraints as fundamental physical laws.

Quantum information theory reveals additional thermodynamic constraints. The no-cloning theorem prohibits perfect copying of unknown quantum states (Wootters & Zurek, 1982). The no-deleting theorem prevents complete erasure of quantum information (Pati & Braunstein, 2000). These results suggest that quantum mechanics imposes fundamental limitations on information processing beyond classical thermodynamic constraints (Nielsen & Chuang, 2010).

4.4 QUANTUM MECHANICS: PROBABILITY, MEASUREMENT, AND THE FOUNDATIONS OF PHYSICAL REALITY

4.4.1 The Probabilistic Revolution

Quantum mechanics fundamentally transformed physics by replacing classical determinism with irreducible probability and uncertainty (Heisenberg, 1927). The theory's core principles—superposition, complementarity, entanglement, measurement-induced collapse—violate classical intuitions while achieving unprecedented predictive accuracy, with theoretical calculations matching experiments to twelve significant figures in quantum electrodynamics (Gabrielse et al., 2006).

The mathematical formalism centers on the wave function Ψ, which encodes complete quantum state information according to the orthodox interpretation (von Neumann, 1932). The Schrödinger equation governs deterministic wave function evolution between measurements, while the Born rule relates wave function amplitudes to measurement probabilities

(Born, 1926). This dual dynamics—unitary evolution punctuated by stochastic collapse—generates the measurement problem: explaining how, when, and why definite outcomes emerge from superposed states (Schlosshauer, 2007).

Heisenberg's uncertainty principle $\Delta x \Delta p \geq \hbar/2$ establishes fundamental limits on simultaneous knowledge of conjugate observables (Heisenberg, 1927). Crucially, this uncertainty reflects ontological indeterminacy rather than epistemic limitation—Bell's theorem proves no hidden variable theory can reproduce quantum predictions while maintaining locality (Bell, 1964). Experimental violations of Bell inequalities, confirmed with increasing sophistication from Aspect et al. (1982) through loophole-free tests (Hensen et al., 2015), demonstrate that nature exhibits genuine indeterminacy rather than hidden determinism.

The probabilistic character of quantum mechanics raises profound questions about physical law. If fundamental physics is irreducibly stochastic, determinism cannot serve as a first principle. Yet quantum probabilities differ qualitatively from classical probabilities: interference phenomena reveal probability amplitudes that can cancel despite positive individual probabilities (Feynman, 1985). This suggests that quantum theory describes a novel form of physical reality rather than classical uncertainty about determinate states.

4.4.2 Entanglement and Nonlocal Correlations

Quantum entanglement generates correlations unexplainable through classical mechanisms. When particles become entangled, measurements on one instantaneously affect probability distributions for the other, regardless of spatial separation—what Einstein et al. (1935) dismissed as "spooky action at a distance" but experiments conclusively confirm (Aspect, Clauser, & Zeilinger, 2022).

Bell's theorem demonstrates that quantum correlations violate local realism: either locality or realism must be abandoned (Bell, 1964). Most physicists sacrifice realism, accepting that properties lack determinate values before measurement (Mermin, 1985). This represents a radical first principles revision: rather than definite states evolving through local interactions, quantum theory describes probability amplitudes undergoing nonlocal evolution until measurement actualizes specific outcomes.

Quantum information theory reveals entanglement as a physical resource enabling novel computational and communicational capabilities (Nielsen & Chuang, 2010). Shor's algorithm factors large integers exponentially faster than known classical methods (Shor, 1997). Quantum key distribution provides unconditionally secure communication based on fundamental quantum principles (Gisin et al., 2002). Quantum teleportation transfers quantum states using entanglement and classical communication (Bennett et al., 1993). These applications demonstrate that nonlocal correlations represent genuine physical phenomena rather than mathematical artifacts.

The implications for locality as a first principle prove particularly significant. While quantum mechanics preserves signal locality—no information transmission faster than light—it exhibits kinematic nonlocality through instantaneous correlation updates (Maudlin, 2011). This tension between dynamic locality and kinematic nonlocality suggests that traditional concepts of causal influence require fundamental revision in quantum contexts (Healey, 2017).

4.4.3 Interpretational Frameworks and Ontological Implications

Despite quantum mechanics' empirical success, its interpretation remains deeply contentious (Schlosshauer et al., 2013). The Copenhagen interpretation accepts wave function collapse without explaining its mechanism (Bohr, 1935). Many-worlds interpretation maintains unitary evolution by postulating reality branching (Everett, 1957; Wallace, 2012). Spontaneous collapse theories modify Schrödinger's equation to explain measurement (Ghirardi, Rimini, & Weber, 1986). QBism treats quantum states as subjective beliefs rather than objective features (Fuchs, Mermin, & Schack, 2014).

Each interpretation implies distinct ontological commitments. Many-worlds suggests deterministic evolution in exponentially proliferating parallel realities, potentially solving the measurement problem at severe ontological cost (Vaidman, 2018). GRW-type theories add stochastic collapse to fundamental physics, explaining definite outcomes while raising questions about energy conservation and relativistic extension (Bassi et al., 2013). QBism denies objective quantum states entirely, treating the formalism as a user's manual for rational agents rather than reality description (Fuchs & Schack, 2013).

These interpretational differences profoundly affect first principles conclusions. If many-worlds holds, apparent randomness emerges from subjective uncertainty about which branch we inhabit within deterministic reality (Saunders et al., 2010). If spontaneous collapse occurs, nature includes genuinely stochastic processes at the fundamental level (Pearle, 2015). If QBism is correct, quantum mechanics describes agent experience rather than mind-independent reality (Pienaar, 2020).

4.5 RELATIVITY: SPACETIME STRUCTURE AND GRAVITATIONAL GEOMETRY

4.5.1 Special Relativity and the Unity of Space and Time

Einstein's special relativity rests on two postulates: the principle of relativity (physical laws are identical in all inertial frames) and light-speed invariance (electromagnetic wave velocity is frame-independent) (Einstein, 1905). These seemingly modest principles yield revolutionary consequences—unified spacetime, relative simultaneity, time dilation, length contraction, mass-energy equivalence—overthrowing the absolute space and time that had anchored physics since Newton (Minkowski, 1908).

Light-speed invariance reflects spacetime structure rather than electromagnetic peculiarity. The Lorentz transformations relating inertial frames reveal space and time as projections of four-dimensional spacetime with metric signature $(+,-,-,-)$ or $(-,+,+,+)$ depending on convention (Taylor & Wheeler, 1992). The invariant spacetime interval $\Delta s^2 = c^2 \Delta t^2 - \Delta x^2 - \Delta y^2 - \Delta z^2$ replaces separate spatial and temporal distances, establishing spacetime geometry as the fundamental arena for physical processes (Rindler, 2006).

The energy-momentum relation $E^2 = (pc)^2 + (mc^2)^2$ constrains all particles, revealing rest mass as irreducible energy content. Einstein's famous $E = mc^2$ demonstrates complete matter-energy equivalence, confirmed through nuclear processes with extraordinary precision—mass-energy conversion in nuclear reactions agrees with theoretical predictions to parts per million (Rainville et al., 2005). These relations represent absolute constraints that any deeper theory must respect, suggesting intimate connections between spacetime structure and conservation principles.

Special relativity thus reveals apparently independent concepts—space, time, matter, energy—as aspects of unified structures. This conceptual unification suggests that first principles analysis must examine structural relationships rather than treating physical categories as autonomous. The geometric approach's success indicates that mathematical structure may be more fundamental than material substance, a theme developed further in general relativity (Friedman, 1983).

4.5.2 General Relativity and Dynamic Spacetime

General relativity extends the relativity principle to accelerated motion through the equivalence principle: gravitational and inertial effects are locally indistinguishable (Einstein, 1916). This insight reconceives gravity as spacetime curvature rather than force, with matter-energy determining geometry through Einstein's field equations while objects follow geodesics through curved spacetime (Misner, Thorne, & Wheeler, 1973).

Einstein's field equations $R\mu\nu - \frac{1}{2}g\mu\nu R + \Lambda g\mu\nu = 8\pi GT\mu\nu/c^4$ relate spacetime geometry (left side) to energy-momentum content (right side), making spacetime itself dynamical rather than fixed background (Wald, 1984). This represents a profound conceptual shift: the arena for physical processes becomes subject to physical law, participating in rather than merely hosting dynamics.

Experimental confirmations span from millimeter-scale laboratory tests to cosmological observations. Gravitational time dilation, measured to 10^{-18} precision using optical clocks (Bothwell et al., 2022), confirms spacetime curvature near Earth. LIGO's detection of gravitational waves from merging black holes spectacularly validated dynamic spacetime, with waveforms matching numerical relativity predictions (Abbott et al., 2016). General relativity successfully describes phenomena from GPS corrections to cosmological expansion, validating Einstein's geometric vision across forty orders of magnitude in scale (Will, 2014).

The geometric perspective suggests profound first principles implications. If spacetime is dynamical rather than fixed, the traditional distinction between container and content dissolves—geometry and matter become co-determining aspects of unified reality (Rovelli, 2004). This challenges substantivalist interpretations of spacetime while supporting structural realist approaches that emphasize relational rather than absolute properties (Ladyman, 2018).

4.5.3 The Challenge of Quantum Gravity

Despite individual successes, general relativity and quantum mechanics resist unification. At the Planck scale (10^{-35} meters), quantum fluctuations should disrupt smooth spacetime, yet no consistent quantum gravity theory exists (Kiefer, 2007). Leading approaches—string theory, loop quantum gravity, asymptotic safety, causal sets—propose radically different solutions with distinct first principles implications.

String theory replaces point particles with extended objects vibrating in higher dimensions, potentially unifying all forces and matter (Green, Schwarz, & Witten, 2012). This approach requires supersymmetry and extra spatial dimensions, suggesting our four-dimensional spacetime emerges from a more fundamental higher-dimensional structure. Critics argue that string theory's landscape of 10^{500} possible vacua undermines predictive power and potentially falsifiability (Woit, 2006; Smolin, 2006).

Loop quantum gravity quantizes spacetime geometry directly, making space discrete at the Planck scale while preserving general relativity's background independence (Rovelli & Vidotto, 2014). This approach predicts specific quantum geometry effects potentially observable in cosmology and black hole physics. However, recovering smooth spacetime and matter dynamics from discrete quantum geometry remains challenging (Thiemann, 2007).

Emergent gravity scenarios derive spacetime from more fundamental structures—quantum entanglement in AdS/CFT correspondence (Maldacena, 1999), thermodynamic entropy in entropic gravity (Verlinde, 2011), or causal networks in causal set theory (Sorkin, 2003). These approaches suggest spacetime might not be fundamental but rather emergent from deeper information-theoretic or quantum principles (Cao, Carroll, & Michalakis, 2017).

4.6 THE EPISTEMIC STATUS OF PHYSICAL LAW

4.6.1 Mathematical Realism and the Discovery Hypothesis

Mathematics's "unreasonable effectiveness" in physics, highlighted by Wigner (1960) and analyzed extensively by Steiner (1998), suggests physical laws are discovered rather than invented. Mathematical structures developed for purely abstract purposes repeatedly prove essential for physical description: complex numbers enable quantum mechanics, Riemannian geometry describes curved spacetime, and group theory classifies elementary particles (Penrose, 2004).

These convergences suggest mathematical structures exist independently, awaiting discovery through physical investigation. Tegmark's (2014) Mathematical Universe Hypothesis pushes this Platonist view to its limit: physical reality is mathematical structure, making physics literally mathematics discovery. This would explain mathematics' effectiveness by identifying physical and mathematical existence.

Predictive success strengthens the discovery hypothesis. Dirac's equation predicted antimatter before experimental confirmation (Dirac, 1928); Maxwell's equations predicted electromagnetic waves before Hertz's detection (Maxwell, 1865); Einstein's equations predicted gravitational waves a century before LIGO (Einstein, 1916). Such predictions suggest that mathematical formalism captures objective features rather than imposing human constructs (Colyvan, 2001).

However, the discovery hypothesis faces substantial challenges. Mathematical structures underdetermine physical application—the same formalism describes multiple phenomena (Pincock, 2012). Theoretical choice involves pragmatic considerations beyond empirical adequacy (van Fraassen, 2008). Physical laws require extensive interpretation connecting formalism to phenomena, suggesting human contribution beyond pure discovery (Bueno & French, 2018).

4.6.2 The Case for Construction and Contextuality

Historical analysis reveals systematic revision challenging simple discovery narratives. Newtonian absolute space yielded to Einsteinian spacetime; deterministic mechanics gave way to quantum probability; laws once considered fundamental proved approximate or domain-limited (Kuhn, 1962; Laudan, 1981). This pattern suggests laws represent evolving human constructs rather than eternal truths.

Ellis (2005) argues that laws function as effective models within specific domains rather than universal descriptions. Laboratory practice involves complex negotiations between theory, instrument, and phenomenon—we never observe laws directly, only interpreted measurements (Hacking, 1983). Multiple equivalent formulations—Newtonian, Lagrangian, Hamiltonian mechanics—suggest representational plurality rather than unique truth (North, 2009).

Emergence challenges fundamental law coherence. As Anderson (1972) argued and subsequent research confirms, higher-level regularities arise from collective behavior without direct reduction to microscopic equations. Hydrodynamics, thermodynamics, and condensed matter physics involve autonomous principles that function perfectly despite lacking fundamental status (Batterman, 2002). This suggests lawlike behavior emerges at multiple organizational levels rather than flowing from unique foundations.

Social and technological dimensions further support constructivism. Theoretical development involves choosing representations, making approximations, and establishing interpretive frameworks—inherently human activities (Galison, 1987). Experimental practice requires decisions about relevance, precision, and error that shape empirical content (Franklin, 1986). These elements suggest laws emerge from negotiation between natural constraint and human decision rather than pure discovery.

4.6.3 Toward a Dialectical Understanding

Perhaps physical laws neither exist independently nor are purely constructed but emerge dialectically from mind-nature interaction. Physical investigation encounters genuine constraints—phenomena resist arbitrary theoretical imposition—while mathematical formulation involves creative representation choices (Giere, 2006).

This dialectical view explains both objectivity and revisability. Laws exhibit objectivity through empirical constraint and mathematical consistency requirements that transcend individual preference (Chakravartty, 2017). They remain revisable because alternative formulations, expanded domains, and conceptual innovations reveal current limitations (Chang, 2012). Physical law thus represents creative engagement with natural patterns rather than pure discovery or invention.

Contemporary physics exemplifies this dialectical character. Effective field theories explicitly acknowledge scale-dependence and limited validity while successfully describing phenomena within specified domains (Hartmann, 2001). The renormalization group reveals how physical descriptions change with observation scale, suggesting laws are neither fundamental nor arbitrary but emerge from scale-relative perspectives (Butterfield & Bouatta, 2014).

4.7 SYNTHESIS AND FUTURE DIRECTIONS

Physical laws provide the most empirically successful framework for understanding material reality, with conservation principles, thermodynamics, quantum mechanics, and relativity forming an interlocking theoretical structure of extraordinary explanatory power and predictive accuracy. These frameworks establish essential constraints that any first principles account must acknowledge.

Yet profound incompleteness remains. Quantum gravity's absence leaves physics fundamentally fractured at the Planck scale. Dark matter and dark energy, comprising 95% of cosmic content, lack theoretical understanding (Bertone & Hooper, 2018). The measurement problem in quantum mechanics remains unresolved after a century of debate (Leifer, 2014). These lacunae suggest current laws represent effective principles rather than ultimate foundations.

Contemporary physics pursues unification through multiple research programs with divergent first principles implications. String theory seeks geometric unification in higher dimensions; loop quantum gravity quantizes spacetime itself; emergent approaches derive spacetime from quantum entanglement; information-theoretic frameworks ground physics in computational principles (Rickles, 2016). This theoretical plurality suggests continued foundational ferment rather than convergence toward final theory.

The implications extend beyond physics to epistemology and metaphysics. If our most successful theories remain partial and revisable, all first principles claims require epistemic humility. The ongoing search for deeper foundations reveals human knowledge as an asymptotic approach rather than achieved certainty. Physical laws thus exemplify both the power and limitations of rational inquiry into nature's fundamental structure.

The search for first principles in physics ultimately reveals a dynamic, open-ended enterprise rather than a completed achievement. Each theoretical advance resolves previous puzzles while exposing deeper questions, suggesting that foundational inquiry represents perpetual dialogue between human understanding and natural complexity rather than convergence toward final truth. As subsequent chapters examine mathematical foundations and cosmological origins, the lessons from physical law—the interplay of constraint and creativity, unity and plurality, discovery and construction—provide essential guidance for navigating the broader philosophical terrain of first principles.

CHAPTER 5: MATHEMATICAL FOUNDATIONS

5.1 THE ONTOLOGICAL STATUS OF MATHEMATICAL TRUTH

Mathematics presents a foundational challenge to any systematic account of first principles through its distinctive combination of universality, necessity, and applicability. Unlike empirical observations constrained by spatiotemporal location or cultural insights shaped by historical context, mathematical propositions exhibit invariance across all possible contexts of inquiry (Shapiro, 1997). The infinitude of prime numbers, demonstrated through Euclid's elegant proof, requires no experimental verification, admits no cultural variation, and transcends contingent features of human psychology or neurobiology (Hardy, 1940). This characteristic universality has led philosophers from Plato through contemporary mathematical realists to regard mathematics as revealing structural features inherent in reality itself rather than artifacts of human conceptual schemes (Linnebo, 2017).

Wigner's (1960) analysis of the "unreasonable effectiveness of mathematics" in physics articulates a profound epistemological puzzle that remains central to contemporary philosophy of mathematics. Mathematical structures developed through pure theoretical investigation, without consideration of empirical application, repeatedly prove indispensable for describing physical phenomena with extraordinary precision (Steiner, 1998). Complex numbers, initially introduced by Cardano (1545) to solve cubic equations and dismissed as "sophistic" by contemporaries, became essential for quantum mechanics four centuries later (Penrose, 2004). Riemannian geometry, developed through purely mathematical investigations into curved spaces, provided the precise framework Einstein required for general relativity fifty years after its creation (Torretti, 1978). Group theory, pursued initially for its intrinsic mathematical interest by Galois and Abel, now underlies the Standard Model's classification of elementary particles and fundamental symmetries (Zee, 2016).

This predictive success extends beyond mere applicability to generate novel empirical discoveries. Dirac's equation predicted antimatter through mathematical consistency requirements before any empirical evidence existed (Dirac, 1928). Yang-Mills gauge theories anticipated the mathematical structure of electroweak unification decades before experimental confirmation (Yang & Mills, 1954). String theory suggests eleven-dimensional spacetime and supersymmetric partners through mathematical requirements rather than empirical motivation (Green, Schwarz, & Witten, 2012). These convergences between mathematical structure and physical reality demand philosophical explanation beyond pragmatic utility.

Yet Benacerraf's (1973) dilemma poses a fundamental challenge to mathematical realism. If mathematical objects exist abstractly, lacking spatiotemporal location and causal powers, how can causally embedded human minds acquire knowledge about them? The standard causal theory of knowledge requires appropriate causal connections between known objects and knowing subjects, connections that abstract mathematical objects cannot provide (Field, 1989). This epistemological challenge becomes acute when considering that mathematical knowledge appears both more certain than empirical knowledge and more substantive than purely logical truth (Maddy, 1990).

Contemporary philosophy of mathematics has developed increasingly sophisticated responses to these foundational challenges. Mathematical structuralism, defended by Shapiro (1997) and Resnik (1997), maintains that mathematics describes abstract structures rather than specific objects, potentially avoiding some epistemological difficulties while preserving objectivity. Ante rem structuralism posits structures existing independently of instantiation, while in re structuralism grounds structures in their concrete realizations (Parsons, 2008). Modal structuralism, developed by Hellman (1989), interprets mathematical claims as assertions about possible structures rather than actual abstract entities.

Nominalist programs attempt to eliminate abstract mathematical objects from fundamental ontology while preserving mathematical applicability. Field's (1980, 2016) science without numbers program demonstrates that Newtonian gravitational theory can be reformulated without quantification over mathematical objects, though at considerable cost in complexity and expressiveness. Azzouni's (2004) deflationary nominalism accepts mathematical discourse at face value while denying ontological commitment to mathematical objects. Yablo's (2010) figuralist approach treats mathematical language as a kind of metaphorical discourse that conveys content without literal truth.

Naturalistic approaches ground mathematical methodology in evolved cognitive capacities while maintaining varying degrees of realism. Maddy's (1997, 2007) naturalized Platonism accepts mathematical objects based on their indispensability to mathematics itself rather than philosophical arguments. Kitcher's (1984) evolutionary account traces mathematical knowledge to idealized operations on physical objects. Dehaene's (1997) cognitive neuroscience research reveals specific neural substrates for mathematical cognition, suggesting biological foundations for mathematical intuition.

5.2 SET THEORY AND THE ARCHITECTURE OF MATHEMATICAL FOUNDATIONS

Modern mathematics achieves systematic unity through set-theoretic foundations that provide a common language and conceptual framework for all mathematical disciplines (Ferreirós, 2007). Cantor's revolutionary development of transfinite set theory revealed that infinity exhibits hierarchical structure—demonstrating through diagonal arguments that the real numbers form a larger infinity than the natural numbers—fundamentally transforming mathematical ontology (Cantor, 1874, 1891). This discovery established that mathematical investigation could uncover genuinely novel conceptual possibilities transcending pre-theoretical intuition (Dauben, 1979).

The early development of set theory generated paradoxes threatening mathematical coherence. Russell's (1903) paradox concerning the set of all sets not containing themselves revealed that unrestricted comprehension principles lead to contradiction. Burali-Forti's paradox about the set of all ordinals and Cantor's paradox about the set of all sets demonstrated that naive set formation principles generate inconsistency (Hallett, 1984). These antinomies indicated that mathematical foundations required more careful analysis than the informal reasoning that had previously sufficed.

The development of axiomatic set theory through Zermelo (1908) and Fraenkel (1922) provided a systematic resolution by specifying precise formation principles for legitimate sets. The resulting Zermelo-Fraenkel system with Choice (ZFC) has proven remarkably robust, supporting virtually all contemporary mathematics while avoiding known paradoxes (Jech, 2003). The axiom of extensionality ensures sets are determined by their members; the axiom of regularity prevents circular membership chains; the axiom of separation restricts set formation to definable subsets of existing sets; the axiom of pairing, union, and power set provide construction principles; the axiom of infinity guarantees infinite sets; the axiom of replacement enables transfinite recursion (Kunen, 2011).

The axiom of choice (AC) exemplifies philosophical complexity in foundational principles. AC asserts that for any collection of non-empty sets, there exists a function selecting one element from each set—intuitive for finite collections but generating counterintuitive consequences for infinite sets (Moore, 1982). The Banach-Tarski paradox demonstrates that accepting AC allows decomposing a sphere into finitely many pieces that can be reassembled into two spheres of identical size (Wagon, 1985). The well-ordering theorem, equivalent to AC, implies every set can be well-ordered, including the real numbers, despite no constructive well-ordering being known (Rubin & Rubin, 1985).

Cohen's (1963, 1966) forcing technique proved that AC and the continuum hypothesis (CH) are independent of ZFC's remaining axioms, revealing that fundamental mathematical questions may lack determinate answers within standard foundations. Different but equally consistent mathematical universes result from accepting or rejecting these principles. Gödel (1940) had earlier shown AC and CH consistent with ZFC through the constructible universe L, while Cohen demonstrated their negations are also consistent. This independence phenomenon suggests that mathematical truth exhibits a modal structure where foundational choices determine different domains of mathematical possibility (Hamkins, 2012).

Large cardinal axioms extend ZFC by postulating infinities so vast their consistency cannot be proven within ZFC itself (Kanamori, 2003). Inaccessible cardinals cannot be reached through standard set operations; measurable cardinals admit non-trivial measures; supercompact cardinals exhibit strong reflection properties; Woodin cardinals connect to determinacy principles (Koellner, 2010). These axioms form a hierarchy of consistency strength, with stronger axioms proving the consistency of weaker ones, suggesting a natural ordering among possible extensions of standard foundations (Steel, 2014).

Alternative foundational approaches challenge set-theoretic hegemony. Category theory, systematized by Mac Lane (1998) and developed by Lawvere and Rosebrugh (2003), emphasizes morphisms between objects rather than membership relations, aligning more naturally with mathematical practice in algebra, topology, and geometry. Topos theory provides categorical foundations incorporating logical and geometric insights (Goldblatt, 2014). Univalent foundations and homotopy type theory synthesize logical, computational, and topological perspectives, potentially revolutionizing mathematical foundations (Homotopy Type Theory, 2013).

5.3 LOGICAL PLURALISM AND THE FOUNDATIONS OF REASONING

The logical principles underlying mathematical reasoning—identity, non-contradiction, excluded middle—appear so fundamental that questioning them seems to undermine rationality itself. Yet the development of alternative logical systems reveals that even basic reasoning principles admit systematic variation while maintaining coherence (Beall & Restall, 2006). This logical pluralism demonstrates that logical necessity exhibits greater complexity and context-dependence than traditional monist approaches acknowledge (Shapiro, 2014).

Classical logic, formalized through Frege's (1879) Begriffsschrift and refined in Whitehead and Russell's (1910-1913) Principia Mathematica, provides the foundation for standard mathematical reasoning. The principle of bivalence assigns every proposition exactly one truth value; excluded middle asserts every proposition or its negation holds; non-contradiction prohibits simultaneous truth and falsehood; identity ensures self-identity of all objects (Burgess, 2009). These principles capture pre-theoretical intuitions about valid reasoning while enabling rigorous mathematical development.

Intuitionist logic, developed by Brouwer (1907) and formalized by Heyting (1956), rejects excluded middle for statements about infinite domains, requiring constructive proof for existence claims. The Brouwer-Heyting-Kolmogorov interpretation specifies that proving a disjunction requires proving one disjunct, proving an existential requires constructing a witness, and proving an implication requires transforming proofs of antecedent into proofs of consequent (Troelstra & van Dalen, 1988). This restriction preserves mathematical content while eliminating non-constructive reasoning, as Dummett's (1977, 1991) philosophical analysis demonstrates.

Contemporary proof assistants implementing constructive type theories—Coq, Agda, Lean—demonstrate that substantial mathematics develops within intuitionist constraints (Avigad & Harrison, 2014). The Curry-Howard correspondence reveals deep connections between constructive proofs and computer programs, suggesting computational interpretation of mathematical reasoning (Sørensen & Urzyczyn, 2006). Constructive analysis, developed by Bishop (1967) and Bridges & Richman (1987), recovers classical results through constructive methods, challenging claims that the excluded middle is essential for mathematics.

Relevance logic, systematized by Anderson and Belnap (1975) and refined by Dunn and Restall (2002), requires a genuine connection between premises and conclusions, avoiding paradoxes of material implication that plague classical logic. The principle of relevant implication demands that the antecedent be actually used in deriving the consequent, formalizing intuitions about a valid argument (Mares, 2004). Linear logic, introduced by Girard (1987), treats logical resources as consumable, providing foundations for resource-sensitive computation and quantum information theory (Abramsky & Coecke, 2004).

Paraconsistent logics, developed by da Costa (1974) and Priest (2006), tolerate true contradictions without explosive consequences that trivialize the system. Dialetheism, defended by Priest (2006) and Beall (2009), maintains that some contradictions are true, particularly those involving semantic paradoxes and vague predicates. These approaches enable reasoning about inconsistent information—common in science, law, and everyday reasoning—without logical collapse (Priest, Graham, & Tanaka, 2013).

Non-classical logics find application across mathematics and science.

Quantum logic, introduced by Birkhoff and von Neumann (1936), models quantum mechanical propositions through non-distributive lattices. Fuzzy logic handles vague predicates through continuous truth values (Zadeh, 1965). Modal logics formalize necessity and possibility, essential for philosophical analysis and computer science verification (Blackburn, de Rijke, & Venema, 2001).

The proliferation of logical systems raises fundamental questions about logical consequence and valid reasoning. Logical monism maintains that one correct logic governs all reasoning (Williamson, 2013). Logical pluralism accepts multiple legitimate logics for different domains (Beall & Restall, 2006). Logical nihilism, defended by Russell (2018), denies that any logical truths are universally valid. The choice between positions affects fundamental issues about rationality, truth, and the relationship between logic and reality (Hjortland, 2017).

5.4 GÖDEL'S INCOMPLETENESS THEOREMS AND THE LIMITS OF FORMALIZATION

Gödel's (1931) incompleteness theorems fundamentally transformed the understanding of formal systems and mathematical truth by demonstrating inherent limitations in axiomatizing arithmetic. These results revealed that mathematical truth necessarily transcends formal provability, with profound implications extending across philosophy, computer science, and cognitive science (Franzén, 2005; Smith, 2013).

The first incompleteness theorem establishes that any consistent formal system containing Robinson arithmetic includes true sentences unprovable within the system. Gödel's proof constructs a sentence asserting its own unprovability through arithmetization of syntax—encoding formal expressions as numbers—and diagonal lemma techniques (Boolos, Burgess, & Jeffrey, 2007). If the Gödel sentence were provable, the system would prove a falsehood; if disprovable, the system would disprove a truth. Therefore, in consistent systems, the Gödel sentence is true but unprovable, demonstrating that truth exceeds provability (Raatikainen, 2015).

The second incompleteness theorem proves that no consistent formal system containing Robinson arithmetic can establish its own consistency. This demolished Hilbert's program for securing mathematics through finitary consistency proofs (Sieg, 2013). Any consistency proof must use reasoning principles at least as strong as those being justified, generating either circularity or infinite regress (Detlefsen, 1986). The theorem suggests that mathematical certainty cannot be achieved through formal methods alone but requires irreducibly semantic or intuitive elements (Feferman, 1998).

Subsequent developments strengthened and extended incompleteness results. Rosser (1936) eliminated the assumption of ω-consistency through a more complex self-referential construction. Turing (1936) connected incompleteness to computability through the halting problem's undecidability. Chaitin (1987) demonstrated incompleteness through algorithmic information theory, showing that mathematical truth contains irreducible randomness where some facts have no simpler explanation than stating the facts themselves.

The philosophical implications extend beyond technical mathematics. Lucas (1961) and Penrose (1989, 1994) argued that incompleteness demonstrates human mathematical insight transcends mechanical computation, though these arguments face substantial criticism (Putnam, 1960; Shapiro, 2003). Hofstadter (1979, 2007) explored connections between self-reference, consciousness, and incompleteness, suggesting that sufficient complexity necessarily generates undecidability. However, careful analysis reveals that broader philosophical conclusions require additional premises beyond the mathematical results (Lindström, 2001; Franzén, 2005).

The incompleteness theorems constrain but do not eliminate foundational programs. Proof theory, developed by Gentzen (1936) and extended by Takeuti (1987), analyzes consistency through transfinite induction up to ordinals beyond the system being studied. Reverse mathematics, systematized by Simpson (2009), determines the minimal axioms required for mathematical theorems, revealing that most ordinary mathematics requires only weak subsystems of second-order arithmetic. These programs demonstrate that incompleteness is compatible with substantial foundational insight (Feferman, 2000).

Contemporary research explores incompleteness across mathematical domains. Paris and Harrington (1977) found natural combinatorial statements independent of Peano arithmetic. Harvey Friedman's Boolean relation theory generates concrete finite statements whose truth requires large cardinal axioms (Friedman, 1998). The continuum hypothesis and Whitehead problem exemplify independence in set theory and algebra, respectively (Shelah, 1974). These results suggest that incompleteness pervades mathematics rather than being confined to artificial self-referential constructions (Stillwell, 2010).

5.5 THE APPLICABILITY PROBLEM AND MATHEMATICAL EXPLANATION

Mathematics' extraordinary success in describing, predicting, and explaining physical phenomena constitutes what Steiner (1998) calls the "applicability problem"—a challenge that resists resolution through purely pragmatic considerations and demands systematic philosophical analysis. The problem encompasses both the descriptive success of mathematical physics and the discovery of novel phenomena through mathematical reasoning (Bangu, 2012).

Historical analysis reveals remarkable convergences between pure mathematics and empirical discovery that transcend mere coincidence. Maxwell's electromagnetic theory emerged from mathematical analysis of Faraday's experimental results, with Maxwell's equations predicting electromagnetic waves before Hertz's detection (Buchwald, 1985). Einstein's general relativity required Riemannian geometry, developed fifty years earlier without physical motivation (Norton, 1985). Quantum mechanics depends essentially on Hilbert spaces, spectral theory, and group representations developed within pure mathematics (von Neumann, 1932).

Mathematical prediction of novel phenomena strengthens the puzzle. Dirac's relativistic wave equation predicted antimatter through mathematical consistency before experimental discovery (Pais, 1986). The Higgs mechanism emerged from gauge-theoretic requirements decades before experimental confirmation (Higgs, 1964). Black hole thermodynamics predicted Hawking radiation through mathematical analysis combining general relativity and quantum field theory (Hawking, 1975). These successes suggest that mathematical reasoning reveals physical possibilities invisible to purely empirical investigation (Morrison, 2000).

Tegmark's (2008, 2014) Mathematical Universe Hypothesis provides a radical resolution by identifying physical reality with mathematical structure entirely. Under MUH, the universe is not described by mathematics, but literally is mathematics—physical existence equals mathematical existence. This eliminates the applicability problem by denying any distinction between mathematical and physical reality. However, MUH faces significant challenges: consciousness resists mathematical reduction; the hypothesis appears empirically untestable; the relationship between mathematical and physical existence remains obscure (Hut, Alford, & Tegmark, 2006).

Structural realism offers a more moderate approach. Worrall (1989) introduced structural realism to preserve predictive success while accommodating theoretical change. French and Ladyman (2003) developed ontic structural realism, maintaining that structure exhausts physical reality. According to OSR, mathematics succeeds because physical reality consists of mathematical structures instantiated in spacetime. This preserves mathematical applicability while avoiding commitment to mathematical Platonism (Ladyman & Ross, 2007).

Alternative approaches emphasize the role of idealization and abstraction. Batterman (2002, 2010) argues that mathematical effectiveness stems from asymptotic reasoning and dimensional analysis rather than direct correspondence. Pincock (2012) analyzes mathematical representation through mapping accounts, showing how mathematics captures relevant features while ignoring irrelevant complexity. Morrison (2015) emphasizes the role of mathematical unification in scientific explanation beyond mere description.

The indispensability argument, refined by Colyvan (2001) and Baker (2005), provides a naturalistic approach to mathematical ontology. If mathematical entities are indispensable to our best scientific theories, and we should believe our best scientific theories, then we should believe in mathematical entities. This approach grounds mathematical existence in scientific practice rather than *a priori* philosophical argument. Critics like Melia (2000) and Leng (2010) argue that mathematics functions as useful fiction without ontological commitment.

Recent work explores enhanced indispensability arguments appealing to mathematical explanation in science. The hexagonal structure of honeycomb, the prime-numbered life cycles of cicadas, and the FitzHugh-Nagumo model of neural activity appear to involve essentially mathematical explanations (Baker, 2009; Lyon & Colyvan, 2008). These cases suggest that mathematics contributes to scientific understanding beyond mere description or prediction (Lange, 2013).

5.6 CONSTRUCTIVE MATHEMATICS AND COMPUTATIONAL FOUNDATIONS

Constructive mathematics prioritizes explicit construction and computational content over abstract existence, providing alternative foundations that illuminate relationships between mathematical truth, effective procedure, and physical reality (Bridges & Richman, 1987). This tradition, extending from Brouwer's intuitionism through contemporary type theory, challenges classical mathematics' reliance on non-constructive reasoning while maintaining mathematical rigor (Troelstra & van Dalen, 1988).

Brouwer's (1907, 1912) intuitionist program rejected excluded middle for infinite domains, requiring constructive proof for all existence claims. Mathematical objects exist only through mental construction; propositions are true only with explicit proof construction; choice sequences and spreads replace classical continuum concepts (van Atten, 2018). Brouwer's philosophy grounds mathematics in temporal intuition and mental construction rather than timeless abstract truth, fundamentally reconceiving mathematical ontology and epistemology (Posy, 2020).

Contemporary constructive analysis, initiated by Bishop (1967) and developed by Bishop and Bridges (1985), demonstrates that substantial mathematics develops within constructive constraints. Constructive measure theory, functional analysis, and algebra recover classical results through constructive methods, challenging claims that non-constructive reasoning is essential (Bridges & Vîță, 2006). The constructive approach often yields additional computational information invisible in classical treatments, suggesting that constructivity enhances rather than restricts mathematical content (Richman, 1990).

Martin-Löf type theory provides foundations where propositions-as-types correspondence identifies mathematical propositions with data types and proofs with programs (Martin-Löf, 1984). This approach unifies logic, mathematics, and computation within a single framework, enabling machine-verified proof while maintaining philosophical coherence (Nordström, Petersson, & Smith, 1990). Homotopy type theory extends MLTT by incorporating topological and higher-categorical insights, potentially revolutionizing mathematical foundations (Univalent Foundations Program, 2013).

Proof assistants implementing constructive type theories demonstrate the practical viability of constructive foundations. Coq, based on the calculus of inductive constructions, has verified the four-color theorem and odd-order theorem (Gonthier, 2008; Gonthier et al., 2013). Agda implements dependent type theory for programming and verification (Norell, 2007). Lean combines classical and constructive reasoning for mathematical formalization (de Moura et al., 2015). These systems show that constructive mathematics supports both theoretical development and practical application (Avigad & Harrison, 2014).

Realizability theory, developed by Kleene (1945) and extended by contemporary researchers, provides semantic foundations for constructive mathematics through computational interpretation (van Oosten, 2008). Recursive realizability interprets mathematical statements through recursive functions; modified realizability handles higher-order constructions; categorical realizability provides topos-theoretic models (Longley & Normann, 2015). These interpretations demonstrate that constructive mathematics admits rigorous model-theoretic treatment while maintaining computational significance.

The relationship between constructive and classical mathematics exhibits surprising subtlety. The double-negation translation shows that classical theorems translate to constructive theorems about double-negated statements (Gödel, 1933). Many classical theorems have constructive versions with identical statements but different proofs. Some classical principles, like the intermediate value theorem, have multiple constructive versions with different computational content (Bridges, 1999). This suggests that constructive and classical mathematics explore different aspects of mathematical reality rather than contradicting each other (Rathjen, 2005).

5.7 MATHEMATICAL PRACTICE AND THE SOCIOLOGY OF MATHEMATICAL KNOWLEDGE

Mathematical development exhibits patterns of discovery, justification, and conceptual change that illuminate general features of rational inquiry while challenging purely formal accounts of mathematical knowledge (Kitcher, 1984). Contemporary studies of mathematical practice reveal social, historical, and cognitive dimensions that complement logical analysis, suggesting that mathematical knowledge emerges through complex interactions between formal reasoning and human practices (Mancosu, 2008).

Lakatos's (1976) methodology of mathematical research programs demonstrated through historical case studies that mathematical development involves conjecture, refutation, and concept refinement rather than monotonic accumulation of proven theorems. The evolution of Euler's polyhedron formula through counterexamples and proof modifications reveals that mathematical concepts undergo substantial revision in response to mathematical discovery. This quasi-empirical view challenges both formalist and Platonist accounts by showing that mathematical knowledge exhibits fallibility and historical development (Corfield, 2003).

Contemporary sociology of mathematics examines how mathematical communities establish standards of rigor, evaluate proofs, and determine research directions. The acceptance of computer-assisted proofs like the four-color theorem required renegotiating standards of mathematical evidence (MacKenzie, 2001). The classification of finite simple groups, spanning thousands of pages across hundreds of papers, challenges traditional notions of surveyable proof (Gorenstein, Lyons, & Solomon, 1994). These developments show that mathematical knowledge depends on community judgment and social processes beyond individual rationality (Heintz, 2000).

Cognitive science research reveals psychological and neurological foundations of mathematical reasoning that constrain and enable mathematical practice. Dehaene's (1997) studies identify specific neural circuits for numerical cognition, suggesting biological bases for mathematical intuition. Lakoff and Núñez (2000) argue that mathematical concepts arise through conceptual metaphor and embodied cognition rather than direct apprehension of abstract truth. These findings challenge Platonist epistemology while explaining both universality and variation in mathematical thinking (Carey, 2009).

The role of visualization, intuition, and informal reasoning in mathematical discovery resists complete formalization. Thurston's (1994) geometrization program relied heavily on geometric intuition, later formalized by Perelman. Grothendieck's revolutionary contributions to algebraic geometry emerged from reconceptualizing basic notions rather than proving difficult theorems (McLarty, 2007). These examples demonstrate that mathematical creativity involves cognitive processes beyond formal derivation (Giaquinto, 2007).

Cross-cultural studies of mathematical development reveal both universal patterns and cultural variation. All cultures develop counting systems and basic arithmetic, suggesting universal cognitive foundations (Butterworth, 1999). However, different cultures emphasize different mathematical concepts and methods—the Chinese remainder theorem, Indian contributions to trigonometry, and Islamic developments in algebra (Joseph, 2011). This pattern suggests that mathematical knowledge combines universal structural constraints with culturally specific developments (Ascher, 1991).

The increasing role of computation in mathematical research challenges traditional epistemology. Computer algebra systems enable calculations beyond human capability; automated theorem provers discover new results; experimental mathematics uses computation to generate conjectures (Borwein & Bailey, 2004). These developments raise questions about mathematical understanding versus mere calculation and the role of human intuition in computer-mediated mathematics (Avigad, 2008).

5.8 IMPLICATIONS FOR FIRST PRINCIPLES METHODOLOGY

Mathematical foundations provide crucial insights for understanding the nature and limits of systematic inquiry into first principles across all domains. The complex relationships between formal rigor and substantial truth, systematic theory and inherent limitations, universal validity and contextual application revealed through mathematical investigation illuminate general features of foundational inquiry (Shapiro, 2000).

Gödel's incompleteness theorems demonstrate that formal systems necessarily encounter fundamental limitations that cannot be overcome through increased rigor or expanded axiomatization. Truth transcends provability in any consistent formal system capable of expressing arithmetic, suggesting that systematic approaches to first principles must acknowledge irreducible incompleteness (Raatikainen, 2015). This result extends beyond mathematics: if our most rigorous formal domain exhibits essential incompleteness, we should expect analogous limitations in theological systems, philosophical frameworks, and scientific theories attempting comprehensive explanation (Chaitin, 2005).

Independence results in set theory revealing that fundamental questions may lack determinate answers within established frameworks, not through ignorance but through underdetermination by accepted principles. The independence of the continuum hypothesis and the axiom of choice from ZFC demonstrates that basic mathematical questions require additional foundational commitments beyond logical deduction (Koellner, 2010). This suggests that first principles inquiry must acknowledge the role of foundational choice in determining what questions can be answered and what answers are possible—apparent necessity may reflect adopted axioms rather than absolute requirement (Hamkins, 2012).

The extraordinary applicability of mathematics to physical reality, combined with ongoing debates about its explanation, suggests that formal structures can exhibit predictive and explanatory power transcending their apparent domain while leaving fundamental questions unresolved. Mathematical physics' success does not definitively support either Platonist realism or nominalist reduction, indicating that effective principles may be compatible with divergent metaphysical interpretations (Leng, 2010). This implies that agreement on operational principles need not require consensus on ultimate foundations.

The development of alternative foundations—intuitionist, constructive, categorical—demonstrates that systematic rigor accommodates fundamental pluralism about basic concepts and methods. Different foundational approaches capture different aspects of mathematical reality, proving useful for different purposes without any single approach claiming exclusive validity (Bell, 2011). This suggests that first principles inquiry should remain open to multiple systematic approaches rather than seeking unique foundational truth, recognizing that different frameworks may illuminate complementary aspects of reality (Awodey, 2010).

The social and cognitive dimensions of mathematical practice reveal that even our most rigorous knowledge involves irreducibly human elements beyond formal systematization. Mathematical proof, concept formation, and problem selection involve community judgment, historical development, and cognitive constraints that complement but cannot be reduced to logical analysis (Ferreirós, 2016). This indicates that first principles inquiry must integrate systematic analysis with informed judgment, recognizing that fundamental insights emerge through interaction between formal reasoning and human understanding rather than pure deduction (Mancosu, 2008).

The relationship between constructive and classical mathematics suggests that apparent contradictions between foundational approaches may reflect different perspectives on shared mathematical reality rather than genuine inconsistency. Classical and constructive mathematics often prove equivalent results through different methods, with constructive proofs providing additional computational information (Bridges, 1999). This complementarity model may extend to other domains where seemingly incompatible approaches—empirical and rational, scientific and religious— might capture different aspects of unified truth (Bishop & Bridges, 1985).

5.9 MATHEMATICAL FOUNDATIONS AND THE THEOLOGICAL HORIZON

The philosophical investigation of mathematical foundations points toward questions that transcend purely mathematical or philosophical analysis, suggesting connections between mathematical truth and ultimate reality that have engaged thinkers from Pythagoras through contemporary philosophy of mathematics (Heller, 2016). The apparent objectivity and universality of mathematical truth, combined with systematic limitations revealed through incompleteness and independence results, suggest a reality that both supports and transcends finite systematic inquiry (Gödel, 1995).

Mathematical Platonism's assertion that abstract mathematical objects exist independently raises profound questions about the relationship between mind and reality that parallel traditional theological concerns. If mathematical truths exist in an abstract realm accessible through rational insight, this suggests a conception of reality transcending purely physical or psychological categories (Brown, 2008). The reliability of mathematical intuition in discovering objective mathematical truth might indicate that human reason participates in a rational structure that grounds both mathematical and physical reality (Katz, 1998).

The applicability problem—mathematics' unreasonable effectiveness in describing physical reality—suggests systematic connections between rational structure and empirical phenomena that may point toward deeper unifying principles. The capacity of abstract mathematical reasoning to predict novel empirical phenomena implies that reality exhibits rational structure accessible to finite minds through mathematical investigation (Tegmark, 2014). This rational transparency of nature to mathematical description has historically motivated theological interpretations of mathematics as divine language or thought (Davies, 1992).

Yet incompleteness and independence results reveal that no finite systematic approach can exhaust mathematical truth, suggesting that mathematical reality transcends complete human comprehension. The existence of unprovable truths, undecidable questions, and dependence on unprovable axioms might reflect the relationship between finite and infinite rather than mere technical limitations (Myhill, 1952). This systematic incompleteness parallels theological traditions emphasizing divine transcendence and the limits of rational theology (Pickover, 2009).

CHAPTER 6: THE ORIGIN PROBLEM

6.1 THE EPISTEMOLOGICAL BOUNDARIES OF COSMOLOGICAL INQUIRY

Contemporary cosmology represents humanity's most ambitious intellectual achievement in understanding cosmic structure and evolution, successfully mapping the universe across 13.8 billion years with extraordinary precision (Planck Collaboration, 2020). The Lambda-CDM model integrates diverse observational phenomena—from cosmic microwave background anisotropies to large-scale structure formation—within a mathematically rigorous framework that has withstood decades of empirical testing (Weinberg, 2008). Yet this remarkable empirical success encounters fundamental epistemological boundaries when addressing ultimate origins, boundaries that reflect not temporary technological limitations but principled impossibilities inherent in scientific methodology itself.

The observable universe presents cosmology with multiple horizons that fundamentally constrain empirical access to primordial conditions. The cosmic microwave background radiation, emitted approximately 380,000 years after the initial singularity when the universe first became transparent to electromagnetic radiation, creates an opaque barrier that no conceivable observational technology can penetrate (Dodelson, 2003). This surface of last scattering represents an absolute observational limit for electromagnetic astronomy. While gravitational wave astronomy and neutrino detection offer alternative observational windows, they too face fundamental limitations in accessing the universe's earliest epochs (Abbott et al., 2016).

The Planck era—encompassing the first 10^{-43} seconds after the putative initial singularity—represents a temporal regime where quantum gravitational effects dominate and known physics breaks down catastrophically (Rovelli, 2004). At the Planck scale, where quantum mechanical uncertainty meets gravitational collapse, spacetime itself may exhibit a discrete or foam-like structure that defies classical geometric description (Wheeler & Ford, 1998). Current physical theories, when extrapolated backward, predict their own invalidity at precisely the epoch most crucial for understanding cosmic origins, creating what Butterfield and Isham (2001) term the "problem of quantum gravity."

Ellis's comprehensive methodological analysis emphasizes these unique epistemic challenges facing cosmological inquiry. The discipline confronts what he terms "the uniqueness problem"—cosmology studies exactly one universe, cannot manipulate initial conditions experimentally, and cannot access spacetime regions beyond the particle horizon (Ellis, 2007). Unlike particle physics, which conducts repeatable experiments under controlled conditions, or stellar astrophysics, which observes millions of stars at different evolutionary stages, cosmology investigates a unique, unrepeatable historical sequence without comparative cases or experimental controls.

This methodological distinctiveness has profound implications for cosmological epistemology. Kragh (1996) traces how cosmology's scientific status remained contested throughout much of the twentieth century, with philosophers like Popper initially questioning whether cosmology qualified as genuine science given its inability to conduct controlled experiments. While modern cosmology has established its scientific credentials through successful prediction and observation, fundamental questions about its scope and limits persist.

Van Fraassen's constructive empiricism provides crucial philosophical context for understanding these limitations. Scientific theories, he argues, aim for empirical adequacy—correctly describing observable phenomena— rather than providing literally true descriptions of unobservable reality (van Fraassen, 2002). When cosmological theories posit conditions or entities fundamentally beyond observational access, such as the multiverse or pre-Big Bang states, they may exceed the legitimate bounds of empirical science regardless of their mathematical elegance or theoretical appeal.

Cartwright's analysis of science's "dappled world" further illuminates this boundary problem. Scientific knowledge operates successfully within specific domains of applicability, but attempts to extend scientific methods beyond their natural limits may generate what she terms "imperialism of physics"—pseudo-explanations that appear scientifically grounded while actually transcending empirical constraints (Cartwright, 1999). The origin problem may represent precisely such a boundary case, where scientific methodology encounters questions that exceed its conceptual framework.

6.2 BIG BANG COSMOLOGY: EMPIRICAL ACHIEVEMENT AND EXPLANATORY LIMITS

The Big Bang model stands as modern science's most comprehensive and empirically successful cosmological theory, unifying diverse observational phenomena within a mathematically precise framework grounded in general relativity and quantum field theory (Weinberg, 2008). The model's development through iterative refinement in response to observational discoveries exemplifies mature scientific practice while simultaneously revealing fundamental explanatory limitations that may be inherent rather than temporary.

The historical trajectory from Hubble's initial observations of galactic recession to contemporary precision cosmology illustrates the productive interplay between theoretical prediction and empirical discovery. Hubble's discovery of the velocity-distance relationship, interpreted through Friedmann-Robertson-Walker solutions to Einstein's field equations, established the empirical foundation for cosmic expansion (Hubble, 1929). The subsequent prediction and discovery of cosmic microwave background radiation by Penzias and Wilson (1965) provided dramatic confirmation of hot Big Bang cosmology, while the detection of primordial light element abundances validated theoretical predictions about Big Bang nucleosynthesis (Alpher, Bethe, & Gamow, 1948).

Contemporary observations have refined these early discoveries with extraordinary precision. The Wilkinson Microwave Anisotropy Probe and Planck satellite missions have measured cosmic microwave background temperature fluctuations to parts per million, confirming theoretical predictions about primordial density perturbations while constraining cosmological parameters to percent-level accuracy (Bennett et al., 2013;

Planck Collaboration, 2020). These measurements establish the universe's age at 13.799 ± 0.021 billion years, its spatial geometry as flat to within 0.4%, and its composition as approximately 5% ordinary matter, 27% dark matter, and 68% dark energy.

Big Bang nucleosynthesis provides the model's most stringent quantitative test, successfully predicting primordial abundances of light elements based solely on nuclear physics and cosmological expansion rates. During the first three minutes of cosmic evolution, when temperatures ranged from 10^{10} to 10^9 Kelvin, nuclear reactions synthesized approximately 75% hydrogen and 25% helium-4 by mass, with trace amounts of deuterium, helium-3, and lithium-7 (Cyburt et al., 2016). These theoretical predictions match observational determinations across diverse astrophysical environments—from metal-poor stars to distant quasar absorption systems—with remarkable precision, though the "lithium problem" regarding lithium-7 abundance remains unresolved (Fields, 2011).

The discovery of cosmic acceleration through Type Ia supernovae observations revolutionized cosmological understanding while demonstrating the model's capacity for accommodation of unexpected phenomena (Riess et al., 1998; Perlmutter et al., 1999). This discovery, recognized with the 2011 Nobel Prize in Physics, necessitated introducing dark energy as the dominant component of cosmic energy density. Yet dark energy's nature remains profoundly mysterious, with its observed value differing from quantum field theory predictions by approximately 120 orders of magnitude—the worst prediction in the history of physics (Weinberg, 1989).

Despite these empirical successes, the Big Bang model encounters fundamental explanatory limitations that appear principled rather than temporary. The model describes cosmic evolution from an initial singularity but cannot explain that singularity's existence, properties, or causal origin. As Vilenkin (2006) emphasizes, the initial singularity represents a boundary to spacetime itself where known physics becomes undefined rather than merely complicated. The model requires precisely specified initial conditions—entropy, density, curvature, and field configurations—that appear as unexplained inputs rather than consequences of deeper principles.

Cosmic inflation, proposed by Guth (1981) to address the horizon, flatness, and monopole problems, successfully explains several puzzling features of Big Bang cosmology while introducing new explanatory challenges. Inflation requires a scalar field with precisely calibrated potential energy that drives exponential expansion for at least 60 e-foldings before gracefully exiting to standard Big Bang evolution (Liddle & Lyth, 2000). The mechanism triggering inflation, the field's initial conditions, and the process ensuring successful reheating remain poorly understood despite decades of theoretical development.

The Borde-Guth-Vilenkin theorem demonstrates that inflationary spacetimes cannot be past-eternal, requiring a beginning that inflation itself cannot explain (Borde, Guth, & Vilenkin, 2003). This theorem, which applies to any spacetime with average expansion rate $H > 0$, shows that extending the Big Bang model through inflationary mechanisms does not eliminate the need for initial conditions but merely pushes explanatory requirements to an earlier epoch. As Guth himself acknowledges, "inflation does not explain how the universe began, but only how it evolved after it began" (Guth, 1997).

6.3 THE FINE-TUNING PROBLEM: COSMIC SPECIALNESS AND ITS IMPLICATIONS

The apparent calibration of fundamental physical constants and initial conditions for the emergence of complexity presents contemporary physics with its most profound interpretive challenge. Multiple parameters governing physical interactions must fall within extraordinarily narrow ranges to permit atomic stability, stellar nucleosynthesis, and the chemical complexity necessary for biological evolution (Barrow & Tipler, 1986). This observed fine-tuning, while subject to ongoing debate regarding its significance and interpretation, raises fundamental questions about the nature of physical law and cosmic existence that transcend purely empirical investigation.

Carter's introduction of anthropic reasoning to cosmological discourse provided the initial conceptual framework for addressing apparent cosmic fine-tuning. His weak anthropic principle represents a logical tautology— observers necessarily find themselves in regions of spacetime compatible with their existence (Carter, 1974). The strong anthropic principle, more controversially, suggests that the universe must possess properties allowing observers to emerge at some stage in its evolution. These principles, while philosophically distinct, both highlight the non-trivial relationship between observed cosmic properties and the requirements for observation itself.

Contemporary analyses have identified numerous examples of apparent fine-tuning across different physical domains. Rees (1999) emphasizes six dimensionless numbers whose values appear calibrated for complexity: the cosmic density parameter Ω, the cosmological constant Λ, the amplitude of primordial fluctuations Q, the baryon-to-photon ratio η, the nuclear efficiency parameter ε, and the number of spatial dimensions D. Each parameter exhibits sensitive dependence on precise values, with small variations eliminating the possibility of complex structure formation.

The strong nuclear force illustrates fine-tuning's quantitative precision. If the strong force coupling constant were increased by 2%, diproton formation would proceed efficiently, eliminating free hydrogen and preventing stellar evolution as observed (MacDonald & Mullan, 2009). If decreased by 5%, deuterium would become unstable, blocking nucleosynthesis pathways beyond hydrogen. The observed value permits both hydrogen abundance for stellar fuel and helium production for stellar nucleosynthesis, falling within a narrow window compatible with cosmic chemistry.

The cosmological constant problem exemplifies fine-tuning's most extreme manifestation. Quantum field theory predicts vacuum energy density of order the Planck scale, approximately 10^{120} times larger than the observed value driving cosmic acceleration (Weinberg, 1989). This discrepancy—larger than any other in physics—suggests either fundamental theoretical misunderstanding or extraordinarily precise cancellation between independent contributions. Weinberg's anthropic bound, derived before dark energy's discovery, predicted $\Lambda < 10^{-120}$ in Planck units based solely on galaxy formation requirements, remarkably close to the subsequently observed value.

Collins (2009) provides a systematic analysis of fine-tuning across multiple parameters, demonstrating that life-permitting values typically occupy minute fractions of physically possible parameter space. The ratio of electromagnetic to gravitational force strengths, approximately 10^{36}, must fall within this range to permit both atomic stability and stellar evolution. Significantly stronger electromagnetic forces would prevent nuclear fusion in stellar cores, while weaker forces would destabilize atomic structure. The existence of stable stars requiring both nuclear fusion and radiation pressure represents a non-trivial constraint on fundamental force ratios.

Several interpretive frameworks compete for explaining apparent fine-tuning, each facing distinct challenges. The necessity hypothesis proposes that fundamental constants derive from deeper theoretical principles, eliminating free parameters through mathematical constraints. String theory initially promised such unification but instead revealed a vast landscape of approximately 10^{500} metastable vacua, each corresponding to different low-energy physics (Susskind, 2005). Rather than explaining fine-tuning through necessity, the string landscape may exacerbate the problem by demonstrating the enormous range of physically possible but life-incompatible universes.

The multiverse hypothesis attempts to dissolve fine-tuning through observer selection effects operating across unlimited cosmic diversity. If universe-generating mechanisms produce all possible parameter combinations, observers necessarily find themselves in rare life-permitting regions regardless of typical cosmic properties (Tegmark, 2014). However, this explanation faces what Barnes (2012) terms the "inverse gambler's fallacy"—observing a particular outcome provides no evidence for multiple trials unless the trials' existence is independently established.

Design arguments interpret fine-tuning as evidence for purposeful cosmic architecture, whether through traditional theistic creation or contemporary simulation hypotheses (Bostrom, 2003). These proposals avoid multiplying entities unnecessarily but require accepting intentional agents or programmers whose existence and properties themselves demand explanation. The design inference also faces challenges from evolutionary arguments suggesting that observers might adapt to various cosmic conditions rather than requiring specific parameter values.

Stenger (2011) challenges fine-tuning arguments by claiming that simultaneous variation of multiple parameters maintains life-compatibility across broader ranges than single-parameter analyses suggest. However, technical responses by Barnes (2012) and Lewis and Barnes (2016) demonstrate that multi-parameter fine-tuning may be even more restrictive than single-parameter cases, with life-permitting regions forming thin sheets or curves in multi-dimensional parameter space rather than extended volumes.

6.4 MULTIVERSE THEORIES: SCIENTIFIC HYPOTHESIS OR METAPHYSICAL SPECULATION?

Multiverse hypotheses have emerged as prominent theoretical responses to fine-tuning puzzles, quantum measurement problems, and string theory's landscape challenge, positing vast ensembles of universes exhibiting diverse physical properties (Carr, 2007). These proposals attempt to naturalize apparent cosmic specialness through observer selection effects while raising fundamental questions about scientific methodology, empirical constraint, and the boundaries between physics and metaphysics.

Contemporary physics provides multiple independent routes to multiverse conclusions, suggesting either convergent truth or shared conceptual limitations. Eternal inflation, developed by Vilenkin (1983) and Linde (1986), extends standard inflationary cosmology by proposing that inflation never completely terminates globally but continues eternally, generating infinite sequences of thermalized regions or "pocket universes." Each pocket universe, formed through localized reheating when inflation ends locally, potentially exhibits different low-energy physics determined by scalar field values during symmetry breaking.

The string theory landscape provides another pathway to multiverse structures. String theory's extra spatial dimensions must be compactified to match observed four-dimensional spacetime, with different compactification schemes yielding different effective field theories (Douglas, 2003). Flux compactifications generate approximately 10^{500} distinct metastable vacua, each corresponding to different particle physics and cosmological parameters. If cosmic dynamics explores this landscape through eternal inflation or other mechanisms, vast numbers of universes with varying properties become physically realized (Susskind, 2005).

Quantum mechanical interpretations generate additional multiverse structures. Everett's relative state formulation, commonly termed the many-worlds interpretation, proposes that quantum measurement never collapses the wave function but generates branching world-lines corresponding to all measurement outcomes (Everett, 1957). Each branch represents a complete universe with its own observers experiencing definite outcomes, while the universal wave function evolves unitarily without collapse. Contemporary advocates like Wallace (2012) argue this interpretation emerges naturally from quantum mechanics' mathematical formalism without additional postulates.

Tegmark's comprehensive classification organizes multiverse proposals into four hierarchical levels with increasing generality and decreasing empirical accessibility (Tegmark, 2003, 2014). Level I comprises regions beyond our Hubble volume within infinite space, statistically realizing all initial conditions compatible with observed physics. Level II encompasses eternal inflation's pocket universes with potentially different constants and effective laws. Level III includes quantum mechanical parallel worlds generated through measurement-like processes. Level IV posits the mathematical universe hypothesis—that all mathematically consistent structures exist physically, making mathematical existence equivalent to physical existence.

Each multiverse level faces distinct empirical and conceptual challenges. Level I multiverses remain within standard cosmology's domain and may eventually become partially observable through cosmic microwave background observations of super-horizon correlations (Kleban, 2012). Level II proposals depend on extrapolating inflation beyond empirically constrained regimes, with different inflation models generating different multiverse structures. Level III interpretations involve fundamental questions about quantum measurement, probability, and identity that resist decisive empirical resolution. Level IV hypotheses transcend empirical constraint entirely, making physical existence coextensive with mathematical consistency regardless of observational access.

The scientific status of empirically inaccessible theories has generated sustained methodological debate within physics and philosophy of science. Ellis and Silk (2014) argue that accepting theories without unique testable predictions threatens to undermine science's empirical foundations, potentially transforming physics into "ironic science" that tells stories about inaccessible domains rather than investigating observable reality. If theoretical elegance and explanatory scope suffice without empirical constraint, the demarcation between science and metaphysical speculation dissolves.

Defenders of multiverse theories propose modified criteria for scientific legitimacy when direct testing proves impossible. Dawid (2013) develops "non-empirical theory assessment" based on theoretical uniqueness, explanatory scope, and meta-inductive support from the success of similar theoretical strategies. If string theory represents the only mathematically consistent quantum theory of gravity, its landscape implications might warrant acceptance despite empirical inaccessibility. Carroll (2016) argues that multiverse theories qualify as scientific if they emerge as necessary consequences of empirically successful frameworks, analogous to accepting quarks or black hole interiors based on successful theories despite direct unobservability.

Smolin (2006) critiques multiverse theories as "theories of anything" that sacrifice predictive power for explanatory scope. In infinite multiverses containing all possibilities, any observation becomes equally probable, eliminating genuine prediction. The measure problem—defining probability distributions over infinite ensembles—remains unsolved despite decades of effort, potentially rendering multiverse theories mathematically ill-defined rather than merely empirically inaccessible (Albrecht & Sorbo, 2004).

6.5 THE EXISTENCE QUESTION: ULTIMATE BOUNDARIES OF SCIENTIFIC EXPLANATION

The fundamental question of existence—why there is something rather than nothing—represents the ultimate challenge to scientific cosmology and potentially to rational inquiry itself. While physics successfully describes cosmic evolution from specified initial conditions, explaining existence itself appears to transcend the conceptual framework within which empirical science operates (Grünbaum, 2009). Various attempts to bring existence questions within science's purview illuminate both the power and the principled limitations of physical explanation.

Contemporary physics has proposed several mechanisms by which "nothing" might naturally generate "something," attempting to naturalize existence through quantum processes. Tryon's pioneering proposal suggested the universe might represent a quantum fluctuation from vacuum, exploiting the possibility that total energy—including negative gravitational binding energy—equals zero (Tryon, 1973). This zero-energy hypothesis permits universe creation without violating conservation laws, making cosmic existence a natural quantum phenomenon rather than requiring external causation.

Vilenkin developed sophisticated quantum cosmological models where universes tunnel from zero-radius initial states through quantum mechanical processes: "The universe is created from literally nothing" (Vilenkin, 1982). These scenarios employ path integral formulations of quantum gravity to calculate transition amplitudes from non-existence to classical spacetime, providing mathematical descriptions of creation events without assuming pre-existing causal structures. The Wheeler-DeWitt equation, quantum gravity's analog of the Schrödinger equation, governs these transitions with solutions describing universe creation from quantum vacuum (DeWitt, 1967).

The Hartle-Hawking no-boundary proposal offers an alternative approach by eliminating temporal boundaries entirely rather than explaining them (Hartle & Hawking, 1983). Using Euclidean path integrals where time becomes imaginary near the origin, spacetime possesses finite extent without boundaries, analogous to Earth's surface having finite area without edges. Time emerges gradually from an initial regime of pure spatiality, avoiding singularities and the need for external creation. This proposal makes the universe self-contained, neither created nor destroyed but simply existing as a four-dimensional structure.

Krauss (2012) popularized these quantum cosmological ideas, arguing that modern physics demonstrates how universes arise naturally from quantum vacuum states through well-understood processes. Virtual particle production, vacuum energy, and quantum tunneling allegedly show that "nothing" possesses creative potential, making universe creation not merely possible but inevitable given quantum mechanics. The discovery of dark energy driving cosmic acceleration suggests that empty space contains substantial energy density, providing the resources for the universe's generation.

However, these physical approaches face fundamental philosophical objections that may be insurmountable within scientific methodology. Albert (2012) identifies a crucial conceptual confusion: quantum vacuum states are not "nothing" but particular configurations of quantum fields with definite properties, energy content, and dynamics. They exist within spacetime, obey physical laws, and exhibit complex behavior, including particle creation and annihilation. Calling quantum vacuum "nothing" represents linguistic confusion rather than a genuine explanation of existence from non-existence.

The deeper problem concerns the explanatory framework itself. Physical explanations necessarily presuppose mathematical structures, logical principles, and nomological regularities. Explaining why these frameworks exist or possess their particular characteristics would require stepping outside the framework—abandoning physical explanation entirely. As Russell (1948) noted, scientific explanation traces causal chains backward but cannot explain the chain's existence without circular reasoning or infinite regress.

Contemporary philosophers have developed sophisticated analyses of these limitations. Pruss (2006) examines the principle of sufficient reason, showing that demands for complete explanation lead either to necessary beings whose existence requires no external explanation or to brute facts that terminate explanation arbitrarily. Science, investigating contingent phenomena through contingent hypotheses, cannot reach the level of necessity that ultimate explanation appears to require. The existence question may demand metaphysical rather than physical resolution.

Some philosophers argue that the existence question itself may be meaningless or ill-formed. Grünbaum (2009) contends that "why is there something rather than nothing?" presupposes that nothingness represents the natural or expected state requiring no explanation, while existence demands justification. This assumption may be groundless—perhaps existence is natural while absolute nothingness is impossible or incoherent. The question's apparent profundity may stem from linguistic confusion rather than genuine metaphysical depth.

Information-theoretic approaches offer alternative perspectives on existence questions. Wheeler's "it from bit" hypothesis proposes that physical properties emerge from information-theoretic processes rather than material substances: "Every it—every particle, every field of force, even the spacetime continuum itself—derives its function, its meaning, its very existence entirely from binary choices, bits" (Wheeler, 1990). Lloyd (2006) develops this perspective through universe-as-quantum-computer models, where physical processes represent computational operations on quantum information.

Yet information-theoretic approaches relocate rather than resolve fundamental questions. Information requires physical instantiation, processing mechanisms, and semantic interpretation. Explaining information's existence or its particular patterns confronts the same infinite regress that plagues substance-based ontologies. The shift from material to informational foundations may illuminate physical processes without addressing ultimate existence questions.

6.6 MULTIVERSE COSMOLOGY AND THE PROBLEM OF COSMIC HIERARCHY

Multiverse theories, while offering potential solutions to fine-tuning problems, generate new conceptual challenges regarding cosmic hierarchy, probability measures, and ultimate explanation that may exceed their initial explanatory advantages (Ellis, 2011). The proliferation of universe-generating mechanisms raises questions about their own fine-tuning, potentially displacing rather than resolving fundamental problems about cosmic specialness and design.

Greene's systematic analysis reveals how different multiverse mechanisms require increasingly complex theoretical machinery while moving progressively further from empirical constraint (Greene, 2011). Quilted multiverses arising from infinite space require only spatial infinity and ergodic initial conditions. Inflationary multiverses demand specific scalar field dynamics and potential energy functions. Quantum multiverses presuppose particular interpretations of measurement and probability. String landscape multiverses require ten-dimensional spacetime, supersymmetry, and flux compactifications. Each level increases theoretical complexity while decreasing empirical accessibility.

The problem of cosmic hierarchy appears particularly acute for multiverse explanations of fine-tuning. If universe-generating mechanisms produce vast ensembles with varying properties, these mechanisms themselves require precise calibration to generate any life-permitting universes. Eternal inflation requires scalar fields with specific potential shapes, initial conditions above the Planck density, and graceful exit mechanisms ensuring successful reheating (Guth, 2007). String theory's landscape requires extra dimensions, moduli stabilization, and supersymmetry breaking at appropriate scales. These requirements suggest that multiverse-generating mechanisms may themselves be fine-tuned, undermining their explanatory purpose.

Page (2008) quantifies this "meta-fine-tuning" problem, showing that universe-generating mechanisms must satisfy stringent constraints to produce even rare life-permitting universes within vast ensembles. The fraction of possible inflation models generating life-permitting universes may be smaller than the fraction of life-permitting universes among all possible initial conditions, making inflation more fine-tuned than the problem it purports to solve. Similar arguments apply to string landscape scenarios where most flux compactifications yield cosmological constants incompatible with structure formation.

The measure problem represents multiverse theories' most fundamental technical challenge. In infinite ensembles, any finite spatial region's properties occur infinitely often, making all events equally probable without well-defined probability measures (Vilenkin, 2007). Different measure proposals—proper time, scale factor cutoff, causal diamond, and stationary—yield contradictory predictions for observable quantities like cosmological parameters and vacuum decay rates. Without solving the measure problem, multiverse theories cannot generate definite predictions even in principle, potentially rendering them mathematically ill-defined rather than merely empirically untestable.

Recent developments in quantum foundations suggest alternative approaches to apparent fine-tuning without invoking multiverses. Quantum Darwinism, developed by Zurek (2009), explains classical emergence through environmental decoherence and information proliferation without requiring parallel worlds. Relational quantum mechanics, advocated by Rovelli (1996), treats measurement outcomes as relational properties without universal wave function collapse or branching. These interpretations preserve quantum mechanics' empirical content while avoiding vast multiplicities of unobservable worlds.

6.7 SCIENTIFIC NATURALISM AND ITS EXPLANATORY LIMITS

The recognition of cosmology's inherent limitations in addressing ultimate origins has prompted sophisticated forms of scientific naturalism that acknowledge empirical methodology's boundaries while maintaining commitment to natural explanation within appropriate domains (Ladyman & Ross, 2007). This position represents intellectual honesty about science's scope rather than capitulation, with important implications for understanding the relationship between empirical investigation, philosophical analysis, and theological insight.

Contemporary naturalism increasingly acknowledges what Dupré (1993) terms the "disorder of things"—the impossibility of reducing all phenomena to fundamental physics and the need for pluralistic explanatory strategies. While particle physics successfully describes elementary constituents, emergent phenomena at higher organizational levels require autonomous theoretical frameworks. Chemistry is not merely applied physics, biology is not merely applied chemistry, and psychology is not merely applied neuroscience. Each level exhibits novel properties and regularities requiring level-specific concepts and methods.

This explanatory pluralism extends to cosmology's relationship with ultimate questions. Ellis (2007) distinguishes between cosmology's legitimate scientific domain—describing cosmic evolution within spacetime—and metaphysical questions about existence, necessity, and purpose that transcend empirical methodology. Science can trace causal chains backward to extreme conditions but cannot explain causation itself. It can describe physical laws' mathematical structure, but cannot explain their existence or effectiveness. It can map cosmic evolution, but cannot address cosmic purpose or meaning.

Alternative cosmological proposals attempting to avoid initial singularities illustrate the persistence of ultimate questions despite theoretical sophistication. Steinhardt and Turok's cyclic cosmology replaces the Big Bang with eternal cycles of expansion and contraction, eliminating temporal beginnings while preserving eternal cosmic evolution (Steinhardt & Turok, 2007). Penrose's conformal cyclic cosmology posits infinite sequences of cosmic aeons, each emerging from the previous cycle's conformal boundary (Penrose, 2010). Loop quantum cosmology replaces classical singularities with quantum bounces, connecting our expanding phase to a previous contracting phase (Bojowald, 2008).

Yet these alternatives, while avoiding particular singularities, still assume mathematical frameworks, physical laws, and cosmic existence itself. They relocate rather than eliminate foundational questions about why reality instantiates particular mathematical structures rather than others or nothing at all. The persistence of these questions across different cosmological scenarios suggests they reflect necessary features of physical explanation rather than contingent limitations of specific theories.

Information-theoretic approaches to fundamental physics, while offering novel perspectives, encounter similar explanatory boundaries. Digital physics proposals, from Zurek, W. H. (2009), calculating space to Wolfram's computational universe, suggest that reality consists of computational processes rather than material substances (Zuse, 1969; Wolfram, 2002). Tegmark's mathematical universe hypothesis radicalizes this approach, identifying physical existence with mathematical structure itself rather than its instantiation (Tegmark, 2014).

However, computational and mathematical approaches to fundamental reality face what Floridi (2008) terms the "problem of the primal cause"— explaining why particular computational or mathematical structures are instantiated rather than others. The selection problem for mathematical structures parallels the fine-tuning problem for physical parameters, potentially requiring anthropic selection or external specification. Information and computation presuppose frameworks for representation and processing that themselves demand explanation.

6.8 TOWARD INTEGRATIVE UNDERSTANDING

The origin problem reveals both remarkable achievements and inherent limitations of scientific cosmology in addressing ultimate questions about cosmic existence. Contemporary cosmology has successfully traced cosmic evolution across vast scales while revealing the universe's structure with extraordinary precision (Weinberg, 2008). The Lambda-CDM model's quantitative success in explaining diverse phenomena—from primordial nucleosynthesis to large-scale structure formation—represents a triumph of mathematical physics applied to the cosmos. Yet this empirical achievement encounters principled boundaries when addressing existence itself, the selection of physical laws, and the presence of apparent cosmic purpose.

These limitations reflect necessary features of empirical methodology rather than temporary theoretical inadequacies. Science investigates existing phenomena within governing frameworks through observational constraint and experimental manipulation. Questions about framework existence, selection, and purpose transcend empirical methodology while remaining central to comprehensive understanding. As Ellis (2007) emphasizes, acknowledging these boundaries represents intellectual honesty rather than failure, opening dialogue with complementary approaches to ultimate questions.

The convergence of independent theoretical frameworks on similar limitations suggests genuine boundaries rather than discipline-specific inadequacies. Quantum cosmology cannot explain wave function existence, string theory cannot derive the landscape's structure, and information-theoretic approaches cannot account for computational framework selection. Each approach successfully describes aspects of physical reality while encountering questions requiring different methodological tools.

This recognition points toward the need for genuinely integrative approaches combining empirical investigation with philosophical analysis and theological insight. Philosophy provides logical and conceptual resources for examining questions that transcend empirical constraint—analyzing modality, causation, existence, and explanation through rational reflection (Craig & Sinclair, 2009). Theology offers frameworks grounded in revelation and contemplative experience for addressing cosmic purpose, ultimate reality, and existence's meaning (Polkinghorne, 2007).

Rather than representing competing alternatives, these approaches can function as complementary perspectives on different aspects of ultimate questions exceeding any single methodology's scope. Science maps cosmic structure and dynamics while identifying questions requiring broader frameworks. Philosophy analyzes conceptual foundations and logical implications while respecting empirical discoveries. Theology addresses existential meaning and ultimate purpose while engaging scientific understanding. This methodological pluralism, advocated throughout this work, appears necessary for addressing first principles that span empirical, rational, and experiential domains.

The trajectory from cosmological investigation through philosophical reflection toward theological contemplation represents not retreat from rigorous inquiry but recognition that different questions require different approaches. Understanding cosmic origins demands integrating multiple perspectives while respecting each domain's integrity and limitations. This integration, challenging though it may be, offers the possibility of a comprehensive understanding that honors both scientific achievement and the irreducible mystery of existence itself.

PART III

CHAPTER 7: THE CERTAINTY OF EXISTENCE

7.1 THE EPISTEMOLOGICAL FOUNDATION: SEEKING INDUBITABLE KNOWLEDGE

The philosophical enterprise confronts a fundamental challenge that strikes at the heart of all knowledge claims: establishing reliable foundations in the face of persistent skeptical doubt. This quest for epistemic certainty transcends mere academic exercise, addressing whether any beliefs can serve as unshakeable first principles upon which systematic knowledge might be constructed. The stakes prove considerable for any comprehensive inquiry into first principles. As Audi (2011) demonstrates in his systematic epistemological framework, without some foundation of certainty, all knowledge claims face an intractable trilemma: infinite regress, circular justification, or arbitrary termination.

The challenge of foundational certainty emerges with particular force when examining first principles across domains. Ancient skeptical traditions developed sophisticated arguments that systematically undermined apparent sources of knowledge. The Pyrrhonian skeptic Sextus Empiricus articulated ten modes of epoché (suspension of judgment) that demonstrate how sensory evidence, expert testimony, and even logical reasoning succumb to doubt when subjected to rigorous scrutiny (Sextus Empiricus, trans. 2000). These modes—ranging from disagreement among philosophers to the relativity of perception—reveal genuine vulnerabilities in human cognitive processes that contemporary epistemology must still address.

The skeptical challenge extends beyond Western philosophy. Indian philosophical traditions developed equally sophisticated skeptical arguments that illuminate different dimensions of the certainty problem. Jayarāśi Bhaṭṭa, the seventh-century skeptic of the Cārvāka school, advanced devastating critiques of all pramāṇas (means of valid knowledge), arguing that perception, inference, testimony, and comparison each fail to provide indubitable knowledge when examined critically (Ganeri, 2001). His arguments anticipate many contemporary concerns about the theory-ladenness of observation and the problem of epistemic circularity. The Buddhist philosopher Nāgārjuna similarly employed prasaṅga (reductio ad absurdum) arguments to demonstrate the ultimate emptiness of all conceptual categories, including those used to establish certainty itself (Westerhoff, 2009).

Contemporary epistemology has developed increasingly sophisticated responses to these skeptical challenges through competing theoretical frameworks. BonJour's (1985) influential analysis reveals the structural dilemma facing any foundationalist program: genuinely self-evident basic beliefs must somehow avoid both the need for justification (which would undermine their foundational status) and arbitrariness (which would undermine their epistemic authority). His later work acknowledges this tension while defending a moderate foundationalism based on rational insight into necessary truths (BonJour, 2010). This evolution in BonJour's position reflects broader developments in contemporary epistemology toward more nuanced understandings of epistemic justification.

Klein's (1999) examination of the regress problem reveals additional complexities that traditional foundationalist strategies often overlook. His infinitist solution—accepting that justification requires an infinite chain of non-repeating reasons—challenges the assumption that epistemic regress necessarily constitutes a vicious problem. Klein argues that the availability of infinite justificatory chains, rather than their actual completion, suffices for knowledge. This position, while controversial, forces reconsideration of what epistemic foundations require. Aikin (2011) extends this analysis by distinguishing between vicious and benign forms of epistemic regress, suggesting that some circular justifications might be epistemically acceptable when they involve virtuous rather than vicious circles.

The phenomenological tradition offers a distinctive response to foundational challenges through methodological innovation rather than theoretical argumentation. Husserl's (1913/1983) phenomenological reduction (epoché) suspends the natural attitude's ontological commitments to examine consciousness as it presents itself prior to theoretical interpretation. This approach seeks apodictic evidence in the structures of intentional consciousness itself, independent of metaphysical commitments about external reality. The phenomenological method thus attempts to identify what Husserl terms "absolute givenness"—aspects of experience that present themselves with such immediacy that doubt becomes impossible. Sokolowski (2000) clarifies how this phenomenological approach differs from both Cartesian methodological doubt and ancient skepticism by focusing on essence intuition (Wesensschau) rather than existential claims.

Recent developments in epistemology have introduced additional perspectives that complicate traditional debates about certainty. Williamson's (2000) knowledge-first epistemology reverses traditional priorities by treating knowledge as primitive rather than analyzing it in terms of belief plus additional conditions. This approach suggests that the search for certain foundations may rest on confused assumptions about knowledge's structure. Similarly, virtue epistemologists like Zagzebski (1996) ground knowledge in intellectual virtues rather than foundational beliefs, offering an alternative to traditional foundationalist-coherentist debates.

The implications of these epistemological investigations extend beyond philosophy to fundamental questions about scientific methodology, ethical reasoning, and religious knowledge. If radical skepticism proves insurmountable, these enterprises lose their claim to objective validity. Alternatively, establishing even minimal certainties could provide sufficient epistemological grounding for broader knowledge construction while acknowledging the fallible character of most beliefs. The question becomes not whether we can achieve absolute certainty about all knowledge claims, but whether we can identify any propositions immune to coherent doubt that might serve as first principles for further inquiry.

7.2 THE CARTESIAN REVOLUTION: SYSTEMATIC DOUBT AND EXISTENTIAL CERTAINTY

René Descartes fundamentally transformed philosophical methodology through his development of systematic doubt as an instrument for discovering indubitable foundations. His approach, articulated most fully in the *Discourse on Method* (1637/1996) and *Meditations on First Philosophy* (1641/1996), represents a methodological rather than skeptical enterprise— doubt serves as a tool for establishing certainty rather than an end in itself. This crucial distinction differentiates Cartesian doubt from both ancient Pyrrhonian skepticism and contemporary forms of nihilistic doubt. As Wilson (1978) demonstrates in her careful analysis of Cartesian methodology, Descartes employs skeptical arguments strategically to clear away uncertain beliefs and reveal what cannot be coherently doubted.

The architecture of Cartesian doubt proceeds through carefully orchestrated levels of increasing radical scope. The initial level targets sensory experience based on familiar observations about perceptual error. The bent oar in water, the square tower appearing round from distance, the sun seeming small despite its immense size—these commonplace illusions demonstrate that sensory appearance can diverge from reality (Descartes, 1641/1996). Yet this level of doubt remains limited, as Descartes acknowledges that occasional sensory error does not entail systematic unreliability. The argument requires strengthening to achieve its methodological purpose.

The dream argument introduces a more radical skeptical possibility. Descartes observes that dream experiences can possess the full vividness and coherence of waking life while occurring, making the distinction between dreaming and waking states epistemically problematic (Descartes, 1641/1996). Contemporary neuroscience has confirmed that dream states can activate the same neural regions as waking perception, lending empirical support to Descartes' phenomenological observation (Hobson, 2009). However, Frankfurt (1970) argues that the dream argument proves less devastating than initially appears, as even dreams must draw their content from waking experience, preserving some connection to reality.

The evil demon hypothesis represents Descartes' most radical skeptical scenario, positing an omnipotent deceiver who systematically manipulates all experiences and beliefs. This hypothesis extends beyond empirical deception to encompass mathematical and logical truths, raising the possibility that even "2 + 3 = 5" might be false despite our irresistible conviction of its truth (Descartes, 1641/1996). Curley (1978) demonstrates how this scenario differs qualitatively from previous skeptical arguments by threatening the reliability of reason itself, not merely sensory experience.

Within this context of hyperbolical doubt emerges Descartes' foundational insight: the cogito ergo sum. The cogito's distinctive certainty derives from what Williams (1978) identifies as its self-verifying structure—the very act of doubting one's existence confirms that existence. This insight cannot be formulated as a standard syllogism without losing its distinctive certainty, as Hintikka (1962) demonstrates through his performative interpretation. The proposition "I exist" becomes necessarily true whenever thought or asserted by any particular thinker, not through logical deduction but through the existential act of thinking itself.

Recent scholarship has revealed additional nuances in the cogito's epistemic status. Peacocke (2012) argues that the cogito exemplifies a broader class of "cogito-like" thoughts that possess similar self-verifying properties, including "I am thinking" and "I am conscious." These thoughts share the characteristic that their truth conditions are automatically satisfied by the mental act of entertaining them. This analysis suggests that Cartesian certainty might extend beyond bare existence to encompass certain aspects of mental activity.

However, the transition from the cogito to broader claims about the self's nature involves additional premises that lack the cogito's immediate certainty. When Descartes moves from "I am thinking" to "I am a thinking thing (res cogitans)," he introduces substantial metaphysical commitments about substance and attribute that require independent justification (Cottingham, 2008). Markie (1992) demonstrates that this transition relies on a principle of substantial instantiation—that properties must inhere in substances—which itself requires defense against bundle theories and process metaphysics.

Contemporary critics have developed sophisticated challenges to the Cartesian project. Dennett (1991) argues that the cogito establishes far less than Descartes claimed, at most demonstrating that thinking is occurring without establishing a unified, persistent thinking subject. This deflationary reading challenges whether the cogito can support the broader epistemological construction Descartes attempts. Rovane (1998) extends this critique by arguing that the certainty of the cogito might be merely psychological rather than epistemic, reflecting the pragmatic impossibility of doubting one's existence rather than its logical indubitability.

Eastern philosophical traditions provide alternative perspectives on self-certainty that illuminate hidden assumptions in the Cartesian approach. The Buddhist doctrine of anatta (non-self) accepts the undeniability of present experience while denying that this establishes a permanent, substantial self (Harvey, 2013). The Yogācāra school's analysis of self-awareness (svasaṃvedana) acknowledges reflexive awareness while maintaining that this awareness is empty of inherent existence (Ganeri, 2012). These perspectives suggest that certainty about present experience need not entail certainty about a substantial experiencer.

Nevertheless, even minimalist interpretations of the cogito preserve something epistemologically significant: the self-refuting character of total skepticism about consciousness. As Burge (1996) argues, denying that one is thinking while thinking constitutes a kind of rational inconsistency distinct from standard logical contradiction. This pragmatic self-refutation provides a minimal but genuine foundation for epistemological construction, even if it cannot support Descartes' ambitious metaphysical conclusions.

7.3 Consciousness As Epistemic Foundation: The Immediacy Of Phenomenal Experience

Beyond the bare certainty of existence established by the cogito, consciousness presents additional epistemic features that resist skeptical dissolution. The qualitative, subjective character of experience—what philosophers term "phenomenal consciousness" or "qualia"—possesses a distinctive first-personal immediacy that provides another candidate for indubitable knowledge. This phenomenal dimension of consciousness offers epistemic resources distinct from both the formal certainty of the cogito and claims about external reality.

The irreducibly subjective dimension of consciousness received its most influential contemporary articulation in Nagel's (1974) analysis of "what it is like" to have experiences. Nagel's argument reveals that conscious experience involves an essentially subjective component that resists capture in objective, third-personal descriptions. This subjective character creates what Joseph Levine terms the "explanatory gap" between physical descriptions and phenomenal experience (Levine, 1983). Even complete knowledge of neural processes would not convey what it is like to experience red or taste coffee to someone who had never had these experiences.

Chalmers (1995) crystallized these insights through his distinction between the "easy problems" and the "hard problem" of consciousness. The easy problems involve explaining cognitive functions like attention, memory, integration of information, and behavioral control—challenges that admit computational or neural solutions in principle. The hard problem concerns explaining why there is "something it is like" to have experiences— why conscious states possess qualitative, subjective character rather than occurring "in the dark" without phenomenal properties. This hard problem persists because phenomenal consciousness seems to involve something beyond functional organization that nonetheless presents itself with immediate certainty to the experiencing subject.

Block's (1995) influential distinction between phenomenal consciousness (P-consciousness) and access consciousness (A-consciousness) further refines our understanding of what possesses special epistemic status. P-consciousness encompasses the qualitative, experiential properties of mental states, while A-consciousness involves information being available for use in reasoning, reporting, and behavioral control. Block argues these can dissociate, as demonstrated by phenomena like blindsight, where patients respond to visual stimuli without conscious visual experience (Weiskrantz, 1986). This dissociation suggests that epistemic certainty attaches specifically to phenomenal consciousness rather than to cognitive access or functional processing.

The epistemic privilege of phenomenal consciousness has been defended through various philosophical arguments. Kripke (1980) argues that the relationship between pain and the feeling of pain is one of identity rather than correlation—pain necessarily is the feeling of pain. This creates an asymmetry with physical-functional identifications, which seem contingent. McGinn (1989) develops a "cognitive closure" thesis suggesting that human cognitive faculties might be constitutionally incapable of understanding how phenomenal consciousness arises from physical processes, even though consciousness itself remains undeniable.

Eastern philosophical traditions have long emphasized consciousness's self-evident character through sophisticated analyses. The Advaita Vedanta tradition, particularly as developed by Śaṅkara (c. 800 CE), describes consciousness as svayamprakāśa (self-luminous)—requiring no external illumination to be known (Ram-Prasad, 2007). This tradition argues that consciousness cannot be doubted because doubt itself presupposes the consciousness that doubts. The Sāṃkhya system similarly posits consciousness (puruṣa) as self-evident and irreducible to material processes (prakṛti), providing a dualist framework that preserves consciousness's epistemic primacy (Larson & Bhattacharya, 1987).

However, empirical research in neuroscience and cognitive psychology has revealed complexities that challenge naive assumptions about consciousness's unity and transparency. Gazzaniga's (2005) split-brain studies demonstrate that consciousness can be divided, with separate streams of awareness in each hemisphere that cannot directly communicate. Patients with hemispatial neglect can be unaware of half their visual field while denying any deficit, suggesting that consciousness of absence and absence of consciousness can be conflated (Rees et al., 2002). These findings complicate claims about consciousness's epistemic transparency.

The phenomenon of change blindness, where observers fail to notice large changes in visual scenes, reveals that we can be mistaken about the richness of our conscious experience (Simons & Rensink, 2005). Schwitzgebel (2008) marshals extensive evidence that introspection is unreliable about many aspects of experience, including peripheral vision, imagery, and even emotional states. These findings suggest that while we cannot doubt that we are having some experience, we can be systematically mistaken about its nature and content.

Dennett's (1991) "multiple drafts" model presents a more radical challenge to consciousness's epistemic privilege. Dennett argues there is no single, continuous stream of consciousness but rather multiple parallel processes that create various "drafts" of experience, none of which has privileged status as "the" conscious experience. This view suggests that the apparent unity and immediacy of consciousness are cognitive illusions generated by the brain's interpretive mechanisms.

Contemporary predictive processing accounts add further complexity. Clark (2013) and Hohwy (2013) argue that conscious experience is actively constructed through predictive models that are constantly updated based on prediction error. What seems like direct awareness of the world or even our own mental states involves complex inferential processes. Seth (2021) extends this framework to argue that even the sense of being a self is a controlled hallucination generated by predictive processing.

Despite these empirical and theoretical challenges, a core of phenomenal certainty remains defensible. Even if consciousness is more complex, divided, or constructed than introspection suggests, the basic fact that there is something it is like to have experiences cannot be coherently denied by the experiencer. As Strawson (2006) forcefully argues, denying the reality of experience while experiencing constitutes a form of cognitive pathology rather than philosophical insight. This minimal phenomenal realism provides an epistemic foundation even while acknowledging the fallibility of introspection about conscious content.

7.4 THE EXTERNAL WORLD CHALLENGE: BRIDGING THE EPISTEMIC GAP

The transition from consciousness's certainty to knowledge of external reality generates one of philosophy's most persistent and profound challenges. This "problem of the external world" emerges from an apparent epistemic asymmetry: while we enjoy direct, immediate access to our conscious states, the external world seems known only through the mediation of these states, creating what appears to be an unbridgeable inferential gap. The problem's persistence across centuries of philosophical inquiry suggests it touches on fundamental features of the human epistemic condition.

The problem's contemporary formulation derives from what Putnam (1981) identifies as the "interface conception" of perception—the view that we directly access only mental representations while external objects remain beyond immediate experience. This creates what early modern philosophers termed the "veil of perception" between consciousness and the world. If our epistemic access is limited to our own mental states, how can we justify beliefs about an external reality that purportedly causes these states? The Chinese philosopher Zhuangzi captured this uncertainty through his famous butterfly dream paradox, which questions the criteria for distinguishing dream from reality when both present themselves with equal vividness to consciousness (Zhuangzi, trans. 2009).

Berkeley's (1710/1965) idealist solution eliminates the epistemic gap by denying the existence of mind-independent material substance. His principle that "to be is to be perceived" (esse est percipi) makes reality fundamentally mental, consisting of ideas in minds ultimately grounded in God's infinite perception. Foster (1985) provides a sophisticated contemporary defense of Berkeleyan idealism, arguing that it better explains the regularities of experience than materialist alternatives. However, Robinson (1994) demonstrates that Berkeley's system faces serious challenges in explaining the apparent causal powers of physical objects and the continuity of unperceived objects.

Kant's (1781/1998) transcendental idealism offered a more nuanced resolution through his distinction between phenomena (things as experienced) and noumena (things in themselves). Kant argued that space, time, and categories like causality are *a priori* forms through which the mind structures experience. We can have certain knowledge of phenomena because our cognitive faculties partially constitute them, while noumenal reality remains unknowable. Allison (2004) defends this as a "two-aspect" rather than "two-world" interpretation, where phenomena and noumena represent different ways of considering the same reality rather than distinct ontological realms.

Contemporary Kantian approaches have developed sophisticated responses to external world skepticism. Cassam (1997) argues that outer experience is a necessary condition for inner experience, reversing the traditional priority of self-knowledge. Stroud (2000) demonstrates that transcendental arguments can establish the necessity of belief in the external world for coherent experience, even if they cannot prove the external world's existence. These neo-Kantian strategies shift focus from proving the external world exists to showing that external world beliefs are epistemically mandatory.

Moore's (1939) "proof" of the external world takes a radically different approach by claiming that particular external world propositions possess greater certainty than philosophical arguments against them. When Moore holds up his hands declaring "Here is one hand... and here is another," he claims this provides more certain knowledge than any skeptical premise. Pryor (2000) develops a sophisticated defense of this "dogmatist" position, arguing that perceptual experiences provide immediate, non-inferential justification for external world beliefs. However, Wright (2004) objects that this response fails to engage with skepticism's real challenge about the warrant for our entire perceptual framework.

Putnam's (1981) semantic externalism offers a novel anti-skeptical argument. If we were brains in vats, our word "brain" would refer to whatever the computer simulates as brains, not to biological brains. Therefore, the thought "I am a brain in a vat" would be false when thought by an envatted brain. This argument suggests that radical skeptical scenarios might be self-refuting. However, DeRose (1999) argues that semantic externalism at best shows we can know we are not brains in vats without establishing positive knowledge about the external world's nature.

Phenomenological approaches challenge the presuppositions generating the external world problem. Merleau-Ponty (1945/2012) argues that consciousness is always already embodied and world-directed. The lived body is not an object in the world but our very means of having a world. This phenomenological analysis dissolves the internal/external dichotomy by showing that consciousness and world are co-constituted through embodied engagement. Dreyfus (1991) extends this analysis by demonstrating how skilled coping with the environment involves a form of knowledge that precedes and grounds explicit representation.

Disjunctivist theories of perception, developed by philosophers like McDowell (1994) and Martin (2004), reject the assumption that veridical perception and hallucination share a common epistemic factor. In genuine perception, we are directly presented with external objects, not with mental intermediaries. This approach promises to close the epistemic gap by making perception constitutively world-involving. However, critics like Burge (2005) argue that disjunctivism faces serious challenges from empirical psychology and fails to adequately explain perceptual error.

Enactivist approaches informed by cognitive science offer additional resources. Thompson (2007) argues that perception is not passive reception but active exploration through sensorimotor engagement. Noë (2004) develops an "actionist" account where perceiving is a kind of skillful bodily activity. These approaches suggest the external world problem rests on false assumptions about perception as internal representation rather than dynamic interaction.

7.5 THE PROBLEM OF OTHER MINDS: SOLIPSISM AND
INTERSUBJECTIVE KNOWLEDGE

The certainty of one's own consciousness raises particularly acute questions about knowledge of other minds. If our epistemic starting point is first-personal consciousness, how can we justify beliefs about other conscious beings? This problem of other minds represents a crucial test case for moving beyond solipsistic foundations toward genuinely intersubjective knowledge. The challenge proves especially pressing given that moral consideration, linguistic communication, and social cooperation all presuppose the existence of other-minded beings.

The traditional argument from analogy attempts to bridge the gap between self-knowledge and knowledge of others through inductive inference. The argument's structure appears straightforward: I observe that my mental states correlate with certain behaviors, I observe similar behaviors in others, therefore, others probably have similar mental states. However, Mill (1865) already recognized this argument's fundamental weakness—it attempts to generalize from a single case (one's own) to all other cases, violating basic principles of inductive inference. Hyslop (1995) demonstrates additional problems: the argument presupposes that behavioral similarity indicates mental similarity, but this assumption itself requires justification.

Wittgenstein's (1953) private language argument provides a powerful challenge to the framework generating other minds skepticism. If mental states were purely private, accessible only to their possessor, then no public language for describing mental states could develop. The fact that we successfully use mental state terminology suggests these concepts must have public criteria for application. Malcolm (1954) develops this into an argument that other minds are not inferred from behavior but are conceptually presupposed by our mental state concepts. However, Ayer (1954) objects that the private language argument at most establishes that we must act as if others have minds, not that they actually do.

Strawson's (1959) transcendental argument extends Wittgensteinian insights by arguing that self-ascription of mental states presupposes the ability to ascribe them to others. The concept of experience gains content only through contrast between one's own and others' experiences. This suggests that the conceptual framework enabling self-knowledge necessarily includes recognition of other subjects. Cassam (1997) refines this argument while acknowledging its limitations—it establishes the necessity of other-ascription for self-ascription but not necessarily the truth of other-ascriptions.

Theory theory, and simulation theory represent contemporary cognitive science approaches to understanding other minds. Theory theorists like Gopnik and Wellman (1992) argue that we understand others through an implicit theory of mind that develops through childhood. Simulation theorists like Goldman (2006) contend that we understand others by simulating their mental states in our own cognitive system. These approaches reframe the philosophical problem as an empirical question about cognitive mechanisms. However, Gallagher (2001) argues that both approaches problematically assume that other minds are hidden and must be inferred rather than directly perceived in embodied interaction.

Mirror neuron research has generated significant interest as potentially providing a neural basis for understanding other minds. Rizzolatti and Craighero (2004) demonstrate that the same neurons fire when performing an action and when observing others perform that action. Gallese (2001) argues that this "mirror matching mechanism" enables direct experiential understanding of others' actions and emotions. However, Hickok (2014) provides extensive criticism of interpretations that mirror neurons solve the problem of other minds, arguing they are neither necessary nor sufficient for action understanding.

The phenomenological tradition offers resources for reconceiving the problem of other minds. Husserl's (1913/1983) account of empathy (Einfühlung) describes how we experience others as conscious beings through a form of intentionality distinct from both perception and inference. Stein (1917/1989) developed a sophisticated analysis of empathy as a unique form of experience that presents others' mental states as real while maintaining their otherness. Zahavi (2014) argues this phenomenological approach avoids both the problematic assumption that other minds are hidden and the implausible claim that we have the same access to others' minds as our own.

Levinas (1961/1969) radically reconceives the problem by arguing that the encounter with the Other is primary and foundational for self-consciousness rather than derivative from it. The face-to-face encounter with another person presents an ethical demand that cannot be reduced to epistemological categories. This approach suggests the problem of other minds misconstrues the nature of intersubjective encounter by treating it as primarily a knowledge relation rather than an ethical one.

Buddhist philosophy provides distinctive perspectives that challenge the problem's presuppositions. The anatta (no-self) doctrine denies substantial selfhood for both self and others, dissolving the sharp self-other distinction generating the problem (Siderits, 2003). The Yogācāra school's analysis of ālaya-vijñāna (storehouse consciousness) posits a shared unconscious substrate underlying individual consciousness streams, providing a basis for intersubjective connection (Waldron, 2003). These approaches suggest that the problem of other minds may rest on false assumptions about the separateness of individual minds.

Contemporary social cognition research reveals that other minds are not simply theoretical posits but are engaged through multiple cognitive and affective systems. Direct social perception theory argues that we can directly perceive some mental states in others' expressions and behaviors without inference (Gallagher, 2008). Participatory sense-making approaches show how meaning emerges through interaction rather than being possessed by individual minds (De Jaegher & Di Paolo, 2007). These findings suggest that knowledge of other minds involves multiple, interacting cognitive processes rather than a single inferential mechanism.

7.6 MAPPING EPISTEMIC TERRITORY: CERTAINTY, PROBABILITY, AND FALLIBLE KNOWLEDGE

The examination of various certainty candidates reveals a complex epistemic landscape requiring careful cartography. Rather than finding bedrock certainty for all knowledge claims, we discover a terrain with varying degrees of epistemic security. This mapping proves crucial for determining which propositions can serve as first principles and which require more tentative treatment. The resulting picture suggests that absolute certainty is both rarer and less necessary than traditional foundationalism assumed.

The cogito and immediate phenomenal consciousness provide minimal but genuine certainties possessing distinctive logical and phenomenological features. These certainties exhibit what Shoemaker (1996) terms "immunity to error through misidentification"—when I judge that I am thinking or experiencing, I cannot be mistaken about who is thinking or experiencing, even if I can be mistaken about the nature of these states. However, these certainties remain remarkably thin, establishing neither substantial selfhood, memory's reliability, nor external reality's nature.

Wittgenstein's (1969) analysis of "hinge propositions" reveals another category of apparent certainties that function as framework conditions for inquiry rather than empirical hypotheses. Propositions like "The earth has existed for many years" or "I have never been to the moon" are not typically justified by evidence but rather constitute the inherited background enabling empirical investigation. Moyal-Sharrock (2004) argues these represent a form of "nonpropositional" certainty—ways of acting rather than beliefs requiring justification. This analysis suggests some apparent certainties reflect grammatical features of our conceptual schemes rather than substantive knowledge claims.

Contemporary epistemology has developed sophisticated frameworks for understanding knowledge without requiring certainty. Williamson's (2000) knowledge-first epistemology treats knowledge as a primitive mental state not analyzable into belief plus additional conditions. On this view, we can know many propositions without certainty, and demanding certainty creates artificial barriers to legitimate knowledge claims. This approach dissolves traditional problems about the relationship between knowledge and certainty by denying that knowledge requires certainty as a component.

Sosa's (2007) virtue epistemology provides a framework for distinguishing multiple epistemic levels. Animal knowledge involves apt belief—true belief produced by reliable cognitive abilities. Reflective knowledge adds understanding of what makes the belief apt. This bi-level epistemology explains how we can have genuine knowledge while acknowledging its fallibility. Greco (2010) extends virtue epistemology by analyzing knowledge as success from ability, integrating insights from both reliabilist and responsibilist approaches.

Probabilistic approaches offer tools for navigating uncertainty while maintaining rational belief. Bayesian epistemology provides formal frameworks for updating beliefs based on evidence, showing how rational belief revision can proceed without certainty (Talbott, 2016). Joyce (1998) demonstrates how probabilistic coherence constraints can guide belief formation even when certainty is unattainable. These formal approaches suggest that rationality involves managing uncertainty rather than eliminating it.

Eastern epistemological traditions offer additional perspectives on knowledge and certainty. The Jain doctrine of anekāntavāda (non-absolutism) holds that all knowledge claims are partial and perspectival, requiring qualification by syāt (perhaps) to acknowledge their conditional nature (Ganeri, 2001). This epistemic humility avoids both dogmatism and skepticism by recognizing truth's complexity. The Buddhist notion of conventional truth (saṃvṛti-satya) versus ultimate truth (paramārtha-satya) provides resources for maintaining practical knowledge while acknowledging its ultimate emptiness (Siderits, 2003).

Contemporary cognitive science reveals systematic limitations in human epistemic capacities that affect certainty assessments. The Dunning-Kruger effect demonstrates that subjective confidence often correlates negatively with actual competence (Kruger & Dunning, 1999). Confirmation bias leads us to seek confirming evidence while avoiding disconfirming evidence (Nickerson, 1998). These findings suggest that psychological certainty provides poor guidance for epistemic evaluation, requiring external checks on our confidence assessments.

This mapping suggests that certainty's boundaries are both narrower and less significant than traditional epistemology assumed. We possess genuine certainty about present consciousness and self-verifying thoughts. We may have practical certainty about framework propositions structuring coherent thought. However, most beliefs about external reality, other minds, past events, and theoretical entities involve irreducible uncertainty. Rather than paralyzing inquiry, this recognition can liberate it from impossible demands for absolute foundations.

The implications for first principles methodology prove significant. Rather than seeking indubitable foundations, we might adopt what Levi (1991) calls "full belief"—commitment sufficient for theoretical construction while acknowledging fallibility. This approach allows for revisable first principles that guide inquiry while remaining open to revision. The next chapter will explore how these minimal certainties about consciousness relate to broader questions about being's nature, examining what ontological conclusions can be drawn from our epistemic starting points.

CHAPTER 8: THE NATURE OF BEING

8.1 THE FUNDAMENTAL ONTOLOGICAL ENTERPRISE

The investigation of what exists constitutes philosophy's most fundamental enterprise, establishing the conceptual framework within which all other inquiries operate. While Chapter 7 established consciousness's epistemic certainty through rigorous phenomenological and epistemological analysis, the present chapter confronts the broader metaphysical terrain of reality itself. Ontology—the systematic investigation of being qua being—addresses not merely which entities populate the universe but the more fundamental question of what existence itself entails (van Inwagen, 2009). This inquiry transcends academic speculation, as our ontological commitments determine positions on artificial intelligence, moral responsibility, mathematical truth, and scientific realism.

The contemporary ontological landscape has undergone significant transformation through methodological innovations that challenge traditional substance-property frameworks. Fine's (2012) groundbreaking analysis of metaphysical grounding reveals hierarchical dependence relations where some truths obtain in virtue of others, illuminating reality's fundamental structure beyond mere existence claims. This framework demonstrates that ontological inquiry involves not simply cataloging existents but understanding the priority relations that structure reality. Schaffer's (2009) priority monism exemplifies this approach by arguing that the cosmos as an integrated whole grounds its parts rather than emerging from them—a position that inverts traditional atomistic assumptions while remaining consistent with scientific understanding.

The relationship between ontological commitment and theoretical adequacy proves particularly complex in light of Quine's (1948) influential criterion. According to Quine's approach, we bear ontological commitment to whatever entities our best theories quantify over—making ontology inseparable from epistemology and philosophy of science. However, Azzouni (2004) challenges this criterion by distinguishing between quantificational commitment in theories and genuine ontological commitment, arguing that mathematical and scientific indispensability arguments fail to establish existence claims. This debate reveals deep methodological questions about how theoretical utility relates to metaphysical truth.

Contemporary developments in metaontology have further complicated traditional approaches to existence questions. Thomasson's (2015) easy ontology argues that many ontological questions admit straightforward answers once we clarify relevant concepts and examine empirical facts, suggesting that complex metaphysical theorizing often obscures rather than illuminates. Conversely, Sider (2011) defends substantive metaphysics by arguing that reality possesses inherent structure that metaphysical inquiry aims to discover, with some concepts "carving nature at its joints" while others impose artificial divisions. These methodological debates shape how we approach specific ontological questions throughout this investigation.

The historical trajectory from ancient Greek investigations through medieval scholasticism to contemporary analytic metaphysics reveals both continuity and transformation in ontological inquiry. Aristotelian categories established foundational distinctions that persist in contemporary debate, while Cartesian dualism introduced the mind-body problem that continues challenging physicalist and dualist frameworks alike. Understanding this historical development proves essential for appreciating contemporary positions' sophistication and the persistent challenges they address.

8.2 ARISTOTELIAN FOUNDATIONS AND CATEGORICAL FRAMEWORKS

Aristotelian ontology established the systematic foundation for Western metaphysical inquiry through its comprehensive categorization of being's fundamental types. The *Metaphysics* presents substance (ousia) as the primary ontological category, with individual substances serving as fundamental existents that ground all other categories' existence (Aristotle, *Metaphysics*, 384-322 BCE/1984). This framework's sophistication emerges through what Shields (2016) identifies as the multiple criteria substances must satisfy: serving as ultimate subjects of predication, persisting through change, and existing independently of other entities.

The form-matter distinction (hylomorphism) provides Aristotle's solution to understanding how substances achieve unity despite compositional complexity. Contemporary neo-Aristotelian philosophers have developed sophisticated interpretations of this framework. Koslicki (2008) argues that hylomorphic analysis explains both natural kinds' unity and artifacts' ontological status through formal principles that organize material constituents. This approach avoids both eliminativist reduction and mysterious emergence by locating substances' unity in organizational principles rather than material aggregation. Johnston (2006) extends hylomorphic analysis to address contemporary problems about material constitution, demonstrating how Aristotelian resources resolve puzzles about coincident objects and temporal persistence.

Contemporary neo-Aristotelian approaches demonstrate the framework's continued vitality while addressing modern challenges. Lowe's (2006) four-category ontology distinguishes objects (individual substances), kinds (substantial universals), attributes (property universals), and modes (property instances) as irreducible ontological categories. This framework elegantly handles the problem of universals by distinguishing substantial kinds that objects instantiate from attributes they possess through modes. Lowe's system avoids both nominalist elimination of universals and Platonic reification by grounding universals in their instantiations while maintaining their genuine existence.

Armstrong's (1997) development of Aristotelian realism about universals provides systematic foundation for understanding natural laws and scientific generalizations. Unlike Platonic universals existing in separate realm, Armstrong's immanent universals exist only in their instantiations while remaining genuinely universal. This approach explains how distinct electrons share identical charge—they instantiate the same universal rather than merely resembling each other. Ellis's (2001) scientific essentialism extends this framework by arguing that natural kinds possess essential causal powers that ground natural laws' necessity, providing a metaphysical foundation for scientific realism.

However, quantum mechanics poses significant challenges to Aristotelian substance ontology's assumptions. French and Krause (2006) argue that quantum particles violate the principle of individuality fundamental to substance metaphysics—quantum statistics suggest that particles of the same type are not merely indistinguishable but genuinely lack individual identity. Ladyman and Ross (2007) develop ontic structural realism, arguing that structure rather than objects should be considered ontologically fundamental, with apparent objects emerging as stable patterns in structural relations. These challenges motivate reconsideration of whether substance-based frameworks can accommodate contemporary physics.

8.3 THE CARTESIAN LEGACY: SUBSTANCE DUALISM AND ITS CONTEMPORARY ASSESSMENT

Descartes' substance dualism fundamentally restructured ontological inquiry by positing two irreducibly distinct categories of finite substance: res extensa (extended physical substance) and res cogitans (thinking mental substance). This distinction generates the modern mind-body problem that continues shaping philosophy of mind despite widespread rejection of Cartesian dualism itself. Rozemond's (1998) careful historical analysis demonstrates that Descartes' arguments rely on sophisticated modal reasoning about conceivability and possibility that anticipates contemporary debates about consciousness.

The interaction problem remains dualism's most formidable challenge, as Elisabeth of Bohemia recognized in her correspondence with Descartes. Shapiro's (2007) analysis of their exchange reveals Elisabeth's philosophical sophistication in pressing how nonspatial mental substance could causally influence spatial physical substance. Contemporary physics exacerbates this challenge through conservation laws that appear to leave no room for mental causation. Kim's (2005) causal exclusion argument formalizes this problem: if every physical event has sufficient physical causes (causal closure), then mental causes become either epiphenomenal or must be identified with physical causes, eliminating genuine dualism.

Contemporary dualists have developed sophisticated responses that attempt to preserve mental causation while respecting scientific findings.

Hasker's (1999) emergent dualism proposes that consciousness emerges from complex neural organization as a distinct substance with novel causal powers. This emergence follows natural laws rather than requiring miraculous intervention, occurring when biological complexity reaches critical organizational thresholds. The emergent mind then exercises downward causation on neural processes, creating genuine two-way interaction. However, critics like Kim (2006) argue that emergence cannot generate genuine substances and that downward causation remains problematic given physical causal closure.

Zimmerman's (2010) exploration of spatial souls offers another strategy by arguing that souls might possess spatial location without spatial extension. This would allow direct causal interaction with extended matter while preserving souls' simplicity and indivisibility. Unger (2006) develops a similar approach through his theory of compound individuals that combine physical and mental aspects. These approaches attempt to preserve dualism's insights about consciousness while avoiding traditional interaction problems.

Swinburne's (2013) contemporary defense of substance dualism appeals to consciousness's unity and persistence as evidence for simple mental substances. The binding problem—how distributed neural processing generates unified conscious experience—suggests that physical processes alone cannot explain phenomenal unity. Swinburne argues that personal identity's apparent simplicity across time further supports substantial souls rather than mere psychological continuity. However, Bayne (2010) challenges unity-based arguments by developing sophisticated accounts of phenomenal unity within physicalist frameworks.

Recent neuroscientific findings create additional challenges for dualist approaches. Neuroplasticity research demonstrates intimate connections between brain structure and mental capacities, with physical changes producing predictable psychological effects (Schwartz & Begley, 2002). Split-brain studies reveal that consciousness can be divided through physical intervention, challenging assumptions about mental substances' indivisibility (Gazzaniga, 2005). While dualists can accommodate these findings through various strategies, the weight of neuroscientific evidence creates a strong presumption toward physicalist approaches.

8.4 Materialist Metaphysics: From Identity Theory To Contemporary Physicalism

Materialist ontology's evolution from crude reductionism to sophisticated physicalism reflects both empirical discoveries and conceptual refinements in understanding the relationship between mental and physical phenomena. Smart's (1959) type identity theory proposed direct identification between mental state types and brain state types, achieving ontological parsimony while preserving mental causation. However, Putnam's (1967) multiple realizability argument demonstrated that mental states can be implemented in diverse physical substrates, undermining type-identity claims while motivating functionalist alternatives.

Lewis's (1972) functionalist analysis defines mental states through causal-functional roles rather than physical constitution, accommodating multiple realizability while maintaining physicalist commitments. Mental states are whatever physical states play appropriate causal roles relating inputs, outputs, and other mental states. This approach preserves psychology's autonomy while grounding it in physical reality. However, Block's (1978) inverted spectrum and absent qualia arguments suggest that functional organization cannot capture phenomenal consciousness's qualitative character—systems might satisfy functional criteria while lacking or differing in conscious experience.

Davidson's (1970) anomalous monism offers a sophisticated reconciliation between mental causation and physical law through token identity without type reduction. Every mental event is identical to some physical event, ensuring causal efficacy, while the absence of strict psychophysical laws preserves psychology's autonomy. McLaughlin's (1985) analysis reveals how anomalous monism navigates between reductive physicalism and property dualism, though critics argue it ultimately collapses into epiphenomenalism by making mental properties causally irrelevant.

Contemporary physicalism has developed increasingly sophisticated positions that address consciousness while maintaining naturalistic commitments. Papineau's (2002) causal argument for physicalism demonstrates that conscious states must be physical states to avoid systematic causal overdetermination. Melnyk's (2003) realization physicalism allows mental properties to be realized by but not reduced to physical properties, preserving genuine mental causation through realization relations. These approaches show physicalism's theoretical flexibility in accommodating phenomenal consciousness without abandoning naturalism.

Eliminative materialism represents physicalism's most radical form, predicting that neuroscience will eliminate rather than reduce mental concepts. P. M. Churchland's (1981) systematic critique argues that folk psychology constitutes a failed theory comparable to vitalism or phlogiston theory. P. S. Churchland's (2002) neurophilosophical approach demonstrates how neuroscientific understanding might replace mentalistic explanation. However, critics like Horgan and Woodward (1985) argue that folk psychology's predictive success and indispensability for social interaction ensure its preservation regardless of neuroscientific advances.

The phenomenal concept strategy offers physicalists resources for addressing anti-physicalist intuitions without abandoning physicalism. Loar (1997) argues that phenomenal concepts involve special modes of presentation that create explanatory gaps without ontological gaps. Papineau (2007) develops this strategy through quotational concepts that use experiences themselves as concept constituents. However, Chalmers (2007) argues that phenomenal concept strategies fail to bridge the explanatory gap, as phenomenal knowledge involves more than alternative conceptualization of physical facts.

8.5 Consciousness And The Contemporary Mind-Body Problem

Contemporary philosophy of mind centers on consciousness's relationship to physical reality, particularly the "hard problem" of explaining phenomenal experience's qualitative character. Chalmers' (1995) formulation crystallized this challenge by distinguishing functional problems amenable to computational explanation from the hard problem of why there is "something it is like" to have experiences. This distinction shapes contemporary debates by clarifying what requires explanation and what theoretical resources prove adequate.

Phenomenal consciousness presents multiple challenges to physicalist reduction. McGinn's (1989) cognitive closure thesis argues that human cognitive architecture might be constitutionally incapable of understanding consciousness's emergence from physical processes. This "mysterian" position maintains naturalism while denying that we can comprehend the psychophysical connection. Levine's (2001) analysis of the explanatory gap demonstrates that even accepting physicalism leaves unexplained why particular physical states produce specific phenomenal experiences rather than others or none at all.

Integrated Information Theory (IIT) represents the most ambitious attempt to quantify consciousness scientifically. Tononi's (2008) mathematical framework proposes that integrated information (Φ) measures consciousness, with systems possessing consciousness proportional to their integration level. IIT makes precise predictions about which systems are conscious and explains various consciousness phenomena, including split-brain cases and anesthesia. However, Aaronson (2014) demonstrates that IIT implies panpsychism by attributing consciousness to simple systems with minimal integration, while Doerig et al. (2019) show that IIT makes incorrect predictions about conscious experience.

Property dualism offers sophisticated non-reductive approaches that preserve consciousness's irreducibility while avoiding substance dualism's problems. Chalmers' (2010) naturalistic dualism accepts causal closure while positing fundamental psychophysical laws connecting physical processes to phenomenal properties. These laws operate as systematically as laws relating different physical properties, making consciousness scientifically tractable while irreducible. Critics like Stoljar (2006) argue that property dualism faces similar problems to substance dualism regarding mental causation and theoretical parsimony.

Russellian monism attempts to reconcile consciousness with physicalism by reconceiving the physical itself. Strawson's (2006) real physicalism argues that consciousness reveals matter's intrinsic nature, which physics describes only structurally. This view preserves causal closure while making consciousness fundamental rather than emergent. Goff's (2017) phenomenal bonding solution addresses the combination problem by proposing special phenomenal relations that bind micro-experiences into macro-consciousness. However, Chalmers (2017) argues that Russellian monism faces its own hard problem of explaining how phenomenal properties yield physical structure.

Recent neuroscientific developments provide constraints on viable theories while revealing consciousness's complexity. Dehaene's (2014) global workspace theory identifies neural signatures of conscious access through widespread cortical integration. Koch's (2019) research program seeks neural correlates of consciousness while acknowledging that correlation does not establish reduction or emergence. These empirical investigations inform philosophical theorizing while highlighting persistent explanatory gaps between neural mechanisms and phenomenal experience.

8.6 PERSONAL IDENTITY AND THE METAPHYSICS OF PERSISTENCE

Personal identity through time raises fundamental questions about human nature, moral responsibility, and prudential concern that intersect with broader metaphysical issues about persistence, change, and temporal parts. The question of what makes a person at one time identical to a person at another time proves crucial for ethics, law, and practical reasoning while illuminating general principles about identity and persistence.

Psychological approaches ground personal identity in mental continuity, developing Locke's insight that consciousness constitutes personal identity. Parfit's (1984) revolutionary analysis argues that psychological continuity and connectedness matter for survival independently of identity. His thought experiments involving fission and gradual replacement demonstrate that what matters for survival—psychological continuity—can admit degrees and branching while identity cannot. Shoemaker's (2012) person life view extends Parfitian insights by treating persons as maximal psychological continuity aggregates while acknowledging identity's practical importance.

Biological approaches ground identity in organism continuity rather than psychological features. Olson's (1997) animalism argues that we are essentially biological organisms persisting through life continuity. This approach elegantly handles persistent vegetative states and early fetal development, where psychological approaches struggle. DeGrazia's (2005) enhancement of animalism addresses objections while maintaining biological continuity's primacy. However, McMahan's (2002) embodied mind account demonstrates that mere biological continuity cannot explain our special concern for future consciousness.

The constitutional view offers sophisticated reconciliation between psychological and biological insights. Baker's (2000) account treats persons as constituted by but not identical to human organisms, with the first-person perspective providing identity conditions. This approach explains why psychological features matter while acknowledging biological foundations. Shoemaker's (2011) analysis reveals how constitution views navigate between pure psychological and biological approaches while facing their own challenges about coincident entities.

Four-dimensionalist approaches reconceive persistence through temporal parts theory. Sider's (2001) stage theory treats persons as instantaneous stages connected by causal relations, dissolving many traditional puzzles while requiring revisionary metaphysics. Hawley's (2001) perdurantist account treats persons as spacetime worms extended through time. These approaches elegantly handle gradual change and fission cases but conflict with ordinary temporal experience and moral practice.

Practical identity theories ground personal identity in agency and self-constitution rather than metaphysical facts. Korsgaard's (2009) constitutivist approach argues that agents create identity through rational self-constitution and commitment to practical identities. Schechtman's (2014) person life view combines narrative self-constitution with biological and social dimensions. These approaches acknowledge identity's constructed dimension while preserving its normative significance for responsibility and prudential concern.

8.7 ABSTRACT OBJECTS AND MATHEMATICAL ONTOLOGY

Abstract objects' ontological status generates fundamental questions about mathematical truth, scientific realism, and the relationship between abstract and concrete reality. Mathematical entities appear indispensable for scientific description yet lack spatiotemporal location and causal powers, creating tension between their apparent necessity and problematic metaphysical status.

The Quine-Putnam indispensability argument provides the most influential case for mathematical realism. Colyvan's (2001) enhanced formulation demonstrates that mathematics proves genuinely indispensable across scientific domains—not merely convenient but required for formulating our best theories. Scientific realism about electrons commits us equally to mathematical entities quantified over in scientific theories. Baker's (2005) enhanced indispensability argument shows that mathematical entities play genuinely explanatory roles, as in biological cases where prime number cycles minimize predator overlap.

Benacerraf's (1973) epistemological challenge questions how causally inert mathematical objects could be known. Field's (2016) reformulation emphasizes that mathematical knowledge requires explaining the reliability of mathematical beliefs, which seems impossible without a causal connection. Linnebo's (2017) analysis reveals how this challenge extends beyond mathematics to all abstract objects, including properties, propositions, and types.

Contemporary nominalist strategies attempt to preserve mathematics without ontological commitment. Field's (1980) science without numbers program demonstrates that Newtonian gravitational theory can be reformulated without mathematical entities, suggesting that mathematics might be dispensable in principle despite practical indispensability. Melia's (2000) weaseling strategy argues that scientific theories' mathematical components can be interpreted as fictional aids rather than ontological commitments. However, Colyvan (2010) demonstrates that nominalization strategies face severe difficulties with quantum mechanics and other fundamental theories.

Structuralist approaches reconceive mathematical objects as positions in structures rather than independent entities. Shapiro's (1997) ante rem structuralism treats structures as abstract objects existing independently of instantiation. Hellman's (2001) modal structuralism eliminates abstract objects by translating mathematical claims into modal claims about possible structures. Resnik's (1997) structural relationism treats mathematical objects as positions in patterns while denying that they have properties independent of structural relations. These approaches address Benacerraf's identification problem while facing challenges about structure individuation.

Neo-Fregean approaches derive mathematical objects from logical abstraction principles. Wright's (1983) neo-logicism uses Hume's Principle to derive arithmetic from second-order logic plus definitions. Hale and Wright (2001) extend this program to other mathematical domains through additional abstraction principles. This approach promises to solve epistemological problems by grounding mathematical knowledge in logical knowledge. However, Field (2016) argues that abstraction principles themselves require ontological commitment to abstract objects, merely relocating rather than solving the problem.

8.8 PROCESS METAPHYSICS AND DYNAMIC ONTOLOGIES

Process philosophy challenges substance metaphysics' primacy by treating temporal becoming, change, and dynamism as reality's fundamental features. Rather than viewing change as an alteration of enduring substances, process approaches treat events, occasions, or becomings as ontologically basic, with apparent substances emerging as stable patterns in temporal flux.

Whitehead's (1978) systematic process philosophy presents reality as composed of "actual occasions of experience"—momentary becomings that achieve concrete actuality before perishing into "objective immortality" as data for subsequent occasions. Griffin's (2007) development shows how this framework elegantly resolves classical problems: Zeno's paradoxes dissolve if motion involves discrete occasions rather than continuous alteration, while the mind-body problem becomes a question of occasion types rather than substance interaction. Contemporary process thought extends Whiteheadian insights while addressing criticisms about panpsychism and causal efficacy.

Eastern philosophical traditions provide sophisticated process metaphysics through different conceptual frameworks. Siderits' (2007) analysis of Buddhist dependent origination (pratītyasamutpāda) demonstrates how phenomena lack inherent existence (svabhāva) while existing conventionally through causal interdependence. The Yogācāra school's ālaya-vijñāna (storehouse consciousness) provides a dynamic account of continuity without a permanent self. Garfield's (2015) examination of Madhyamaka philosophy reveals how ultimate reality consists of interdependent processes rather than independent substances, offering resources for contemporary philosophy of time and persistence.

Contemporary powers metaphysics bridges the substance and process approaches by treating causal powers as fundamental. Mumford and Anjum's (2011) dispositional essentialism locates natural necessity in powers' essential natures rather than external laws. Chakravartty's (2007) semirealism combines dispositionalist insights with structural realism, treating both properties and relations as fundamental. These approaches accommodate dynamism while preserving realist commitments about natural kinds and scientific explanation.

Complexity theory and emergence provide a scientific foundation for process thinking. Ellis's (2016) analysis demonstrates how complex systems exhibit emergent properties irreducible to components, with downward causation from higher organizational levels. Kauffman's (2016) investigation of biological organization reveals self-organizing processes that generate novel causal powers. These developments suggest that process metaphysics better captures nature's creative advance than static substance frameworks.

Chinese philosophy offers distinctive process perspectives through Daoist emphasis on transformation. Ames and Hall's (2003) analysis reveals how Daoist cosmology treats change as fundamental, with the Dao representing transformation's pattern rather than static being. The *Yijing*'s philosophy presents reality as continuous transformation through complementary processes (yin-yang) rather than substantial entities. These non-Western approaches provide valuable alternatives to substance-focused Western metaphysics while resonating with contemporary science.

8.9 METAONTOLOGICAL REFLECTIONS: PLURALISM, DEFLATION, AND CONCEPTUAL RELATIVITY

Metaontology examines what we accomplish when asking ontological questions and whether such questions admit determinate answers. This second-order reflection on ontological methodology has profound implications for first-order ontological claims and the broader enterprise of metaphysical inquiry.

Carnap's (1950) deflationary approach argues that ontological questions divide into internal questions within linguistic frameworks (trivially answered by framework rules) and external questions about framework choice (pragmatic rather than factual). Thomasson's (2015) easy ontology develops neo-Carnapian themes by arguing that existence questions often have obvious answers given relevant concepts and empirical facts. Price's (2009) functional pluralism extends deflationary approaches by treating different existence claims as serving different practical functions rather than describing a unified reality.

Ontological realists defend substantive metaphysics against deflationary challenges. Sider's (2011) argument for metaphysical structure contends that reality has inherent joints that privileged concepts carve, making some ontological theories objectively superior. Van Inwagen's (2009) meta-ontological realism maintains that ontological questions have determinate answers discoverable through philosophical analysis rather than linguistic legislation. Fine's (2009) defense of metaphysics argues that reality admits multiple legitimate descriptions while maintaining objectivity about fundamental structure.

Pluralist approaches navigate between deflation and realism by acknowledging multiple legitimate ontological frameworks. McDaniel's (2017) ontological pluralism argues that "existence" is analogical rather than univocal, with different domains exhibiting different existence conditions. Turner's (2010) analysis shows how ontological pluralism avoids both relativism and dogmatism while explaining persistent ontological disagreement. These approaches preserve substantive ontology while acknowledging conceptual scheme contributions.

Quantifier variance debates illuminate fundamental metaontological issues. Hirsch's (2011) quantifier variance thesis argues that apparent ontological disagreements often involve different quantifier meanings rather than factual disagreement. Eklund's (2009) maximalist response argues that there is a privileged quantifier meaning that captures reality's domain. These debates reveal deep connections between language, thought, and reality that affect all ontological theorizing.

The relationship between ontology and natural science raises additional metaontological questions. Ladyman and Ross's (2007) naturalized metaphysics argues that only scientifically informed metaphysics deserves credence, with physics determining fundamental ontology. Paul's (2012) defense of autonomous metaphysics maintains that philosophical analysis reveals modal and essential features that empirical science cannot access. These methodological debates shape how we integrate philosophical and scientific insights about reality's nature.

8.10 CONCLUSION: ONTOLOGICAL COMMITMENT AND PHILOSOPHICAL METHOD

The investigation of being's nature reveals profound interconnections between ontological commitments and broader philosophical positions across epistemology, philosophy of mind, ethics, and philosophy of science. Contemporary ontology demonstrates remarkable sophistication in addressing perennial questions while incorporating scientific developments and methodological innovations.

The persistence of fundamental disagreements—about consciousness, abstract objects, personal identity—reflects not philosophical failure but the genuine difficulty of these questions given human cognitive limitations and conceptual resources. Different ontological frameworks illuminate different aspects of reality's complexity without necessarily providing complete or final answers. Eastern philosophical traditions offer valuable alternatives to Western substance metaphysics that may better accommodate contemporary scientific understanding while preserving important insights about consciousness and value.

Methodological pluralism appears warranted given ontology's complexity and the partial success of various approaches. Substance ontology captures important features of medium-scale reality and scientific practice. Process metaphysics better accommodates change, emergence, and quantum phenomena. Structural approaches illuminate mathematical and scientific representation. Rather than seeking a single correct ontology, we might recognize that different frameworks serve different explanatory purposes while contributing to a comprehensive understanding.

The practical implications of ontological choices extend beyond academic philosophy to artificial intelligence, medical ethics, environmental policy, and legal theory. Our ontological commitments shape how we understand consciousness, personal identity, moral status, and natural kinds—with direct consequences for real-world decisions. This practical dimension makes ontological inquiry not merel52y theoretical but essential for navigating technological and ethical challenges.

The next chapter's examination of knowledge's structure will reveal how epistemological considerations both constrain and are constrained by ontological commitments. Understanding reality requires understanding how we know it, while understanding knowledge requires clarity about what we attempt to know. This reciprocal relationship between being and knowing demands an integrated analysis that respects both metaphysical and epistemological insights while acknowledging their ultimate interdependence.

CHAPTER 9: THE STRUCTURE OF KNOWLEDGE

9.1 THE FOUNDATIONAL CHALLENGE: EPISTEMOLOGY AS PHILOSOPHICAL PREREQUISITE

The investigation of first principles encounters an immediate methodological paradox: any attempt to establish foundational truths about reality necessarily employs cognitive faculties whose reliability remains undemonstrated. This recursive challenge—that we must use reason to validate reason, experience to justify experience—constitutes what Alvin Goldman characterizes as the "bootstrapping problem" endemic to epistemological inquiry (Goldman, 2008). The present chapter examines how contemporary epistemology addresses this foundational challenge while providing essential frameworks for evaluating competing claims about first principles across scientific, philosophical, and religious domains.

The significance of epistemological considerations for first principles inquiry extends beyond abstract philosophical concerns. As Paul Boghossian demonstrates in his analysis of epistemic relativism, the stakes of epistemological debates directly impact our ability to adjudicate between competing worldviews and knowledge claims (Boghossian, 2006). Without robust epistemological frameworks, the investigation of first principles devolves into either dogmatic assertion or paralyzing skepticism—neither conducive to genuine philosophical progress.

Contemporary epistemology has evolved substantially beyond traditional debates between empiricism and rationalism, developing sophisticated approaches to social knowledge, epistemic injustice, virtue epistemology, and the integration of cognitive science with philosophical analysis. These developments, as Jennifer Lackey's recent work demonstrates, reveal knowledge acquisition as simultaneously individual cognitive achievement and an irreducibly social phenomenon (Lackey, 2021). This dual character proves particularly relevant for understanding how scientific communities establish physical laws, philosophical traditions develop logical principles, and religious communities preserve revelatory insights.

The relationship between epistemology and first principles inquiry exhibits what Robert Audi terms "reciprocal dependency"—epistemological principles both guide and are informed by substantive investigations into reality's fundamental structure (Audi, 2011). This circularity need not be vicious; rather, it reflects what Catherine Elgin calls the "epistemic interdependence" characteristic of philosophical inquiry, where provisional commitments enable investigation that may ultimately revise those very commitments (Elgin, 2017).

9.2 CLASSICAL FOUNDATIONS: THE EMPIRICISM-RATIONALISM DIALECTIC

The historical confrontation between empiricist and rationalist epistemologies established enduring categories for analyzing knowledge sources, though recent scholarship reveals these traditions as exhibiting greater internal complexity and mutual influence than canonical narratives suggest.

9.2.1 Empiricist Foundations and Their Sophistication

Contemporary reexamination of classical empiricism reveals sophisticated treatments of knowledge that transcend crude sensationism. John Locke's Essay Concerning Human Understanding, far from reducing knowledge to passive sensory reception, articulates what Nicholas Jolley identifies as a "constructivist empiricism" wherein the mind actively synthesizes sensory materials through reflection and combination (Jolley, 2015). Locke's distinction between nominal and real essences anticipates contemporary debates about natural kinds while his treatment of sensitive knowledge provides a nuanced account of empirical certainty's limits (Locke,

1689/1975).

David Hume's empiricism, often mischaracterized as leading to radical skepticism, actually develops what Helen Beebee terms "sophisticated naturalism" about human cognitive capacities (Beebee, 2016). Hume's Treatise distinguishes natural from philosophical relations, providing a framework for understanding how associative mechanisms generate knowledge while acknowledging their contingent foundations (Hume, 1739/2000). His analysis of probable reasoning anticipates contemporary Bayesian approaches while his treatment of testimony prefigures social epistemology's insights about knowledge transmission (Traiger, 2010).

The British empiricist tradition culminates in John Stuart Mill's System of Logic, which develops what Geoffrey Scarre calls "scientific empiricism"— the view that even apparently necessary truths derive from highly confirmed empirical generalizations (Scarre, 2020). Mill's methods of experimental inquiry—agreement, difference, concomitant variation, and residues— provide a systematic framework for causal reasoning that influenced subsequent philosophy of science while maintaining empiricist commitments (Mill, 1843/2002).

However, empiricism faces persistent challenges that contemporary philosophers continue addressing. The problem of unobservable entities in science challenges strict empiricist constraints on knowledge. As Stathis Psillos argues, scientific realism requires accepting theoretical entities that transcend direct observational access, suggesting limitations to pure empiricism (Psillos, 2009). Additionally, Peter Carruthers' work on innate knowledge demonstrates that certain cognitive capacities appear to require non-empirical foundations, particularly in domains like mathematics and language acquisition (Carruthers, 2019).

9.2.2 Rationalist Insights and Contemporary Developments

Rationalist epistemology, rather than simply opposing empiricism, develops systematic criteria for distinguishing reliable from unreliable knowledge sources. René Descartes' Meditations on First Philosophy employs methodological doubt not as a skeptical endpoint but as what Gary Hatfield calls "epistemic therapy"—a process for identifying indubitable foundations (Hatfield, 2014). The cogito argument establishes what Descartes terms the "Archimedean point" from which to reconstruct knowledge on secure foundations (Descartes, 1641/1996).

Gottfried Wilhelm Leibniz's rationalism introduces crucial distinctions that continue to structure epistemological debate. His differentiation between truths of reason and truths of fact, analyzed comprehensively by Brandon Look, provides a framework for understanding necessary versus contingent knowledge while maintaining both types' objectivity (Look, 2021). Leibniz's principle of sufficient reason—that nothing occurs without adequate explanation—remains influential in contemporary metaphysics and philosophy of science despite ongoing debates about its scope and justification (Della Rocca, 2010).

Contemporary rationalism has developed sophisticated responses to empiricist challenges while incorporating cognitive science insights. George Bealer's theory of rational intuition argues for what he terms "modal reliabilism"—the view that intuitions about possibility and necessity provide reliable access to modal truths when properly constrained (Bealer, 2002). This approach addresses traditional concerns about intuition's fallibility while maintaining its indispensability for philosophical and mathematical knowledge.

BonJour's defense of *a priori* justification demonstrates how rationalist insights survive empiricist and naturalist critiques (BonJour, 1998). His argument that certain propositions—logical principles, simple mathematical truths, conceptual relations—can be justified through pure rational insight provides a foundation for non-empirical knowledge while acknowledging reason's limitations in other domains. However, Timothy Williamson's critique raises questions about whether allegedly a priori knowledge might derive from highly abstract empirical generalizations, challenging sharp distinctions between rational and empirical knowledge (Williamson, 2013).

9.2.3 The Kantian Revolution and Its Contemporary Legacy

Immanuel Kant's critical philosophy fundamentally reconceptualized the empiricism-rationalism debate by arguing that knowledge requires both sensory content and rational form. His distinction between phenomena and noumena, as Henry Allison's influential interpretation demonstrates, establishes epistemic constraints rather than metaphysical claims about two worlds (Allison, 2004). The categories of understanding and forms of intuition provide what Kant terms "conditions for the possibility of experience" that structure empirical knowledge without determining its specific content (Kant, 1781/1998).

Kant's notion of synthetic *a priori* judgments—propositions that extend knowledge while possessing necessity and universality—remains contentious yet influential. Mathematical propositions like "7 + 5 = 12" allegedly combine conceptual analysis with genuine cognitive advancement, though contemporary philosophers debate whether such judgments genuinely transcend analyticity (Hanna, 2018). Michael Friedman's neo-Kantian philosophy of science argues that relativized *a priori* principles function as constitutive frameworks enabling empirical inquiry without claiming absolute necessity (Friedman, 2013).

Contemporary Kantian epistemology addresses traditional criticisms while developing new applications. Hannah Ginsborg's account of primitive normativity explains how Kantian insights illuminate rule-following and concept acquisition without requiring innate categories (Ginsborg, 2015,). John McDowell's conceptualist interpretation of Kantian themes argues that experience itself possesses conceptual content, dissolving traditional problems about the relationship between thought and reality (McDowell, 1994).

9.3 THE PROBLEM OF INDUCTION: SKEPTICAL CHALLENGES AND CONTEMPORARY RESPONSES

The problem of induction, first articulated systematically by David Hume, continues to generate sophisticated philosophical responses that illuminate fundamental issues about empirical knowledge and scientific methodology.

9.3.1 Hume's Challenge and Its Systematic Development

Hume's skeptical argument targets the rational justification of inductive inference—our practice of projecting observed regularities onto unobserved cases. The argument's force derives from what Peter Millican calls its "surgical precision" in identifying the logical gap between premises about observed cases and conclusions about unobserved ones (Millican, 2017). Neither deductive reasoning nor inductive reasoning can bridge this gap without circularity, leaving induction without a rational foundation despite its practical indispensability (Hume, 1748/2007).

Nelson Goodman's "new riddle of induction" demonstrates that Hume's problem runs deeper than initially apparent. The predicate "grue"—defined as green before future time t and blue thereafter—generates projections incompatible with standard inductive practice while remaining formally equivalent in their past confirmations (Goodman, 1955). This reveals what Goodman terms the "problem of projectibility": determining which predicates support inductive projection requires prior metaphysical or linguistic commitments that themselves demand justification (Stalker, 1994).

Contemporary developments extend these challenges through consideration of curve-fitting problems and underdetermination arguments. As Helen Beebee demonstrates, any finite data set remains consistent with infinitely many incompatible hypotheses, suggesting that successful induction requires substantial background assumptions about simplicity, uniformity, and natural kinds (Beebee, 2011). Kyle Stanford's "problem of unconceived alternatives" argues that the history of science reveals a persistent failure to consider genuine theoretical possibilities, undermining confidence in current theories' inductive support (Stanford, 2006).

9.3.2 Bayesian and Probabilistic Responses

Bayesian epistemology reconceptualizes induction through probability theory, treating evidence as updating prior probabilities rather than establishing universal generalizations. Colin Howson and Peter Urbach argue that Bayes' theorem provides "logic of scientific inference" that captures actual scientific reasoning while avoiding classical induction's problems (Howson & Urbach, 2006). This approach formalizes how evidence confirms or disconfirms hypotheses without requiring certainty or universal projection.

Contemporary Bayesianism addresses traditional objections through sophisticated frameworks. Objective Bayesianism, developed by Jon Williamson, constrains prior probabilities through principles like maximum entropy, reducing subjective elements while maintaining a probabilistic framework (Williamson, 2010). James Joyce's accuracy-based approach grounds probabilistic coherence in purely epistemic considerations about truth-conduciveness rather than pragmatic or subjective factors (Joyce, 2009).

However, Bayesian approaches face what John Norton calls the "material theory of induction" challenge—the claim that successful induction depends on local, domain-specific facts rather than universal formal principles

(Norton, 2021). Additionally, the problem of logical omniscience suggests that Bayesian agents must possess infinite computational capacity, raising questions about the framework's applicability to actual human reasoning (Garber, 1983).

9.3.3 Pragmatic and Naturalistic Solutions

Pragmatist responses to induction, initiated by Charles Sanders Peirce and developed by subsequent philosophers, shift focus from justification to vindication. Hans Reichenbach's pragmatic vindication argues that inductive methods will succeed if any method can succeed, providing practical rather than theoretical justification (Reichenbach, 1938). This approach acknowledges induction's theoretical uncertainties while maintaining its methodological indispensability.

Contemporary naturalized epistemology treats induction as an empirical phenomenon requiring scientific rather than purely philosophical investigation. Ruth Millikan's teleosemantics explains inductive success through evolutionary considerations about cognitive mechanisms designed to track environmental regularities (Millikan, 2017). Peter Godfrey-Smith's environmental complexity thesis argues that inductive capacities evolved to match environmental predictability, explaining both successes and limitations (Godfrey-Smith, 2003).

However, naturalistic approaches face what James Ladyman calls the "circularity challenge"—using empirical methods to justify empirical methods appears viciously circular (Ladyman, 2018). Responses invoking reflective equilibrium or coherence remain controversial, with critics arguing they merely relocate rather than resolve justificatory challenges.

9.4 THE ARCHITECTURE OF JUSTIFIED BELIEF: CONTEMPORARY STRUCTURAL APPROACHES

Contemporary epistemology has developed sophisticated frameworks for understanding justification's structure that move beyond traditional foundationalism-coherentism debates.

9.4.1 Beyond the Classical Analysis: Gettier Problems and Their Resolution

Edmund Gettier's counterexamples to the justified true belief analysis catalyzed what Linda Zagzebski calls the "post-Gettier industry" in epistemology (Zagzebski, 2009). Gettier cases demonstrate that justified true belief can result from epistemic luck rather than genuine knowledge-generating processes (Gettier, 1963). Contemporary responses reveal deep insights about knowledge's nature and requirements.

The defeasibility approach, developed by Keith Lehrer and Thomas Paxson, requires that knowledge be undefeated by any true proposition (Lehrer & Paxson, 1969). However, Peter Klein demonstrates that determining relevant defeaters generates infinite regress, suggesting this approach merely displaces rather than solves the problem (Klein, 2008).

Modal conditions offer alternative solutions through counterfactual requirements. Ernest Sosa's safety condition requires that one could not easily have been wrong in similar circumstances (Sosa, 2007). However, Juan Comesaña identifies cases where safety appears satisfied without knowledge, suggesting additional conditions are necessary (Comesaña, 2005).

Timothy Williamson's knowledge-first epistemology revolutionizes post-Gettier epistemology by treating knowledge as a primitive mental state rather than an analyzable composite (Williamson, 2000). This approach, while controversial, elegantly dissolves Gettier problems by denying their presupposition that knowledge admits of reductive analysis. Critics like Frank Jackson argue this abandons rather than solves the analytical project, though supporters contend that the project was misguided (Jackson, 2012).

9.4.2 Foundationalism and Its Contemporary Developments

Contemporary foundationalism has evolved sophisticated responses to traditional objections while maintaining core insights about justification's structure. Richard Fumerton's acquaintance foundationalism argues that direct acquaintance with facts provides non-inferential justification for foundational beliefs (Fumerton, 2001). This approach addresses Sellarsian concerns about the given by distinguishing acquaintance from conceptual judgment while maintaining genuine foundations.

Michael Huemer's phenomenal conservatism holds that seemings—intellectual or perceptual appearances—provide defeasible justification for corresponding beliefs (Huemer, 2007). This modest foundationalism avoids classical requirements for certainty while maintaining structural asymmetry between basic and non-basic beliefs. Critics like Matthew McGrath argue that seemings cannot bear justificatory weight without prior vindication, threatening regress (McGrath, 2013).

Ali Hasan's classical foundationalism attempts to resurrect stronger foundationalist claims through careful analysis of rational insight and acquaintance (Hasan, 2013). His argument that certain beliefs about consciousness and simple necessary truths possess genuine indubitability challenges prevailing skepticism about classical foundationalist resources. However, critics question whether alleged foundations possess claimed epistemic properties or merely psychological conviction.

9.4.3 Coherentism and Holistic Approaches

Contemporary coherentism develops sophisticated accounts of how belief systems generate justification through mutual support relations. Keith Lehrer's trustworthiness coherentism emphasizes metacognitive requirements—justified belief requires not just first-order coherence but coherent beliefs about one's own trustworthiness (Lehrer, 2000). This approach addresses isolation objections by connecting coherence to truth-conduciveness through self-trust.

Erik Olsson's probabilistic coherentism formalizes coherence through probability theory, demonstrating conditions under which coherent belief sets are truth-conducive (Olsson, 2005). His impossibility results show that coherence alone cannot generate a high probability of truth, but coherence combined with individually reliable sources can amplify justification beyond individual credibilities.

Susan Haack's foundherentism integrates foundationalist and coherentist insights through her crossword puzzle analogy—beliefs receive support both from experiential "clues" and mutual "interlocking" (Haack, 2009). This approach captures intuitions about experiential constraint while acknowledging holistic dimensions of justification. Critics debate whether foundherentism genuinely transcends the foundationalism-coherentism dialectic or simply combines their features.

9.4.4 Externalist and Reliabilist Approaches

Externalist epistemologies locate justifying factors in objective features of belief-forming processes rather than subjective accessibility. Alvin Goldman's process reliabilism underwent significant refinement to address initial objections while maintaining core externalist commitments (Goldman, 2012). His two-stage theory distinguishes belief-dependent from belief-independent processes, addressing generality problems through contextual specification of process types.

Ruth Millikan's teleological reliabilism grounds justification in proper function rather than statistical reliability, connecting epistemology to philosophy of biology (Millikan, 2004). Beliefs are justified when produced by cognitive mechanisms performing their evolved or designed functions, regardless of actual reliability in non-normal conditions. This approach handles evil demon scenarios by maintaining that systematically deceived believers possess justified beliefs despite unreliability.

Sandy Goldberg's social externalism extends reliabilist insights to testimony and social knowledge, arguing that justification can depend on external social factors like testifiers' reliability (Goldberg, 2018). This approach illuminates how knowledge depends on social division of cognitive labor while raising questions about epistemic autonomy and responsibility.

9.5 VIRTUE EPISTEMOLOGY AND THE NORMATIVE DIMENSION

Virtue epistemology's emergence represents what Jason Baehr calls a "paradigm shift" in contemporary epistemology, redirecting focus from belief properties to agent excellences (Baehr, 2011).

9.5.1 Aristotelian Foundations and Contemporary Developments

Contemporary virtue epistemology draws on Aristotelian ethics while developing distinctive accounts of intellectual excellence. Linda Zagzebski's virtue responsibilism treats intellectual virtues as acquired character traits motivated by love of truth (Zagzebski, 1996). Virtues like intellectual courage, humility, and thoroughness constitute excellences of cognitive character analogous to moral virtues. This approach explains knowledge's value through the value of virtuous agency rather than purely instrumental truth-conduciveness.

John Greco's agent reliabilism combines virtue-theoretic insights with reliabilist epistemology, treating knowledge as true belief produced by intellectual virtue understood as reliable cognitive ability (Greco, 2010). This approach addresses value problems by locating knowledge's value in creditable cognitive achievement while maintaining externalist insights about reliability's importance.

Heather Battaly's pluralist virtue epistemology distinguishes responsibilist from reliabilist virtues while arguing that both contribute to epistemic excellence (Battaly, 2019). Some virtues (like perception) are faculties requiring no motivation, while others (like open-mindedness) are character traits requiring cultivation. This pluralism accommodates diverse intuitions while maintaining a unified framework.

9.5.2 Social Virtue Epistemology and Epistemic Injustice

Miranda Fricker's Epistemic Injustice initiated what Kristie Dotson calls the "epistemic injustice turn" in epistemology (Dotson, 2014). Testimonial injustice occurs when prejudice causes hearers to give deflated credibility to speakers' words; hermeneutical injustice occurs when marginalized groups lack interpretive resources for understanding their experiences (Fricker, 2007). These phenomena reveal how social power structures systematically distort knowledge practices.

José Medina's epistemology of resistance develops virtues for resisting epistemic injustice, including epistemic humility, curiosity, and openness to friction (Medina, 2013). These virtues enable privileged knowers to recognize their epistemic limitations while empowering marginalized knowers to resist dominant frameworks. The account connects individual virtue to structural reform, showing how personal and political epistemology intersect.

Gaile Pohlhaus Jr.'s analysis of willful hermeneutical ignorance reveals how dominant groups actively maintain ignorance about marginalized experiences, refusing to acquire interpretive resources that would challenge their privilege (Pohlhaus, 2012). This work demonstrates that epistemic injustice involves not just individual prejudice but systemic resistance to epistemic resources that threaten existing power structures.

9.5.3 Religious and Contemplative Epistemology

Religious epistemology examines distinctive epistemic practices and virtues within religious traditions. William Alston's doxastic practice approach argues that Christian mystical perception constitutes a socially established belief-forming practice analogous to sense perception (Alston, 1991). While lacking independent verification, such practices can be rationally engaged when they demonstrate internal consistency and practical fruits.

Alvin Plantinga's reformed epistemology, refined in his Warranted Christian Belief, argues that theistic belief can possess warrant—that property converting true belief to knowledge—through proper function of sensus divinitatis (Plantinga, 2000). This approach treats religious knowledge as a basic cognitive capacity rather than inference from evidence, challenging evidentialist assumptions about religious epistemology.

Contemporary work explores contemplative epistemology across traditions. Evan Thompson's analysis of Buddhist contemplative science argues that disciplined introspection provides systematic first-person investigation of consciousness, complementing neuroscientific third-person methods (Thompson, 2020). Michel Bitbol develops neurophenomenology, integrating contemplative practice with neuroscience, suggesting new frameworks for understanding consciousness (Bitbol, 2019).

9.6 TESTIMONY, TRUST, AND SOCIAL EPISTEMOLOGY

Recognition that most knowledge derives from testimony rather than direct experience has generated what Sanford Goldberg calls the "social turn" in epistemology (Goldberg, 2010).

9.6.1 The Epistemology of Testimony

The epistemology of testimony examines how knowledge is transmitted through communication. Jennifer Lackey's dualism distinguishes speaker testimony from hearer testimony, showing how knowledge can be generated in testimonial exchange rather than merely transmitted (Lackey, 2008). A speaker might unknowingly assert a truth that becomes knowledge for appropriately positioned hearers, challenging transmission models of testimony.

Paul Faulkner's affective trust account argues that testimonial knowledge often depends on affective trust rather than evidence about reliability (Faulkner, 2011). Such trust involves participant stance toward testifiers rather than detached assessment, explaining how testimony functions in intimate relationships where evidential assessment would be inappropriate.

The debate between reductionism and non-reductionism continues to generate insights. Elizabeth Fricker's local reductionism requires monitoring for trustworthiness indicators without demanding global reduction of testimony to other evidence types (Fricker, 2006). This position mediates between demanding excessive vigilance and accepting uncritical credulity.

9.6.2 Trust, Authority, and Epistemic Dependence

John Hardwig's analysis of epistemic dependence in science reveals how modern knowledge requires trusting expert testimony about matters beyond individual competence (Hardwig, 1991). Large-scale scientific collaborations involve trusting colleagues' contributions without the possibility of independent verification, making trust constitutive of scientific knowledge rather than an unfortunate limitation.

Linda Zagzebski's epistemic authority theory argues for rational deference to epistemic authorities based on their superior epistemic position (Zagzebski, 2012). Her preemption thesis—that authoritative testimony gives reason to believe that preempts one's own reasons—remains controversial but illuminates how expertise functions in epistemic communities.

Alvin Goldman's veritistic social epistemology evaluates social practices and institutions by their truth-conduciveness, providing a framework for assessing epistemic institutions (Goldman & Blanchard, 2018). This approach enables normative evaluation of practices like peer review, education, and media while acknowledging social knowledge's irreducibly collective dimensions.

9.6.3 Indigenous and Non-Western Epistemologies

Indigenous epistemologies offer alternative frameworks challenging Western assumptions. Kyle Whyte's indigenous climate science demonstrates how traditional ecological knowledge provides sophisticated environmental understanding, complementing Western science (Whyte, 2018). Indigenous knowledge emphasizes relationships, responsibilities, and place-based understanding, often absent from Western approaches.

Leanne Betasamosake Simpson's work on Anishinaabe epistemology reveals how indigenous knowledge systems integrate cognitive, embodied, and spiritual dimensions that Western philosophy typically separates (Simpson, 2017). These epistemologies emphasize learning through land-based practices, ceremony, and intergenerational transmission rather than abstract theorizing.

The challenge involves what Boaventura de Sousa Santos calls "epistemologies of the South"—developing frameworks that take seriously diverse knowledge traditions without imposing Western categories (Santos,

2014). This requires what he terms "ecology of knowledges," recognizing different knowledge forms' complementarity rather than hierarchy.

9.7 CROSS-CULTURAL EPISTEMOLOGICAL PERSPECTIVES

Engaging non-Western epistemological traditions reveals alternative approaches to knowledge that illuminate limitations in Western frameworks while suggesting possibilities for integration.

9.7.1 Indian Philosophical Epistemology

Classical Indian epistemology develops through pramāṇa theory—systematic analysis of knowledge sources. Jonardon Ganeri's work demonstrates how Indian philosophers developed sophisticated accounts prefiguring and sometimes surpassing contemporary Western epistemology (Ganeri, 2012). The Nyāya school's four pramāṇas—perception, inference, comparison, and testimony—provide a comprehensive framework for knowledge acquisition.

The Buddhist epistemologist Dharmakīrti developed what John Taber calls "apoha theory"—a nominalist semantics explaining how concepts apply without assuming real universals (Taber, 2018). This theory addresses problems about concept acquisition and application that continue to challenge Western philosophy while supporting Buddhist metaphysical commitments.

Contemporary developments integrate Indian and Western approaches. Anand Vaidya's work on cross-cultural epistemology demonstrates how Indian philosophy contributes to contemporary debates about intuition, testimony, and skepticism (Vaidya, 2017). These contributions suggest that philosophical progress requires genuine engagement with diverse traditions rather than mere comparison.

9.7.2 Buddhist Epistemological Analysis

Buddhist epistemology emphasizes consciousness's constructive role in knowledge. Dan Arnold's analysis of Dharmakīrti reveals sophisticated accounts of perception as non-conceptual awareness subsequently conceptualized through mental construction (Arnold, 2012). This approach anticipates contemporary cognitive science insights while supporting Buddhist claims about reality's constructed nature.

The Yogācāra school's vijñapti-mātra (consciousness-only) doctrine, as interpreted by Dan Lusthaus, provides an idealist epistemology that avoids solipsism through intersubjective karmic connections (Lusthaus, 2002). This framework addresses mind-body problems while maintaining practical engagement with conventional reality.

Contemporary Buddhist epistemology engages neuroscience and cognitive science. Evan Thompson's enactive approach draws on Buddhist philosophy to develop embodied, embedded accounts of cognition, challenging representationalist assumptions (Thompson, 2015). This work demonstrates how contemplative traditions contribute to scientific understanding rather than merely benefiting from it.

9.7.3 Islamic Epistemological Traditions

Islamic epistemology integrates revealed and rational knowledge through sophisticated frameworks. Dimitri Gutas's analysis reveals how Islamic philosophers developed what he terms "double-truth theory"—the view that philosophy and religion provide complementary rather than contradictory truths (Gutas, 2016). This approach navigates tensions between reason and revelation that continue to challenge religious epistemology.

Al-Ghazali's occasionalism, as interpreted by Frank Griffel, provides radical empiricism wherein only present experience possesses certainty while causal connections require divine sustenance (Griffel, 2009). This position anticipates Humean skepticism while maintaining a theistic framework through continuous divine action.

Contemporary Islamic epistemology engages modern challenges. Abdulkader Tayob's work on Islamic knowledge production examines how traditional epistemologies adapt to modern contexts while maintaining distinctive characteristics (Tayob, 2018). This work reveals a dynamic tradition capable of addressing contemporary challenges rather than a static historical artifact.

9.7.4 Chinese Philosophical Approaches

Chinese epistemology emphasizes practical wisdom and contextual understanding. Stephen Angle's reconstruction of Neo-Confucian epistemology reveals sophisticated accounts of moral knowledge through what Wang Yangming calls liangzhi (pure knowing)—immediate moral insight requiring cultivation rather than argument (Angle, 2018). This approach integrates cognitive and affective dimensions typically separated in Western philosophy.

Chad Hansen's interpretation of Daoist epistemology reveals a critique of conventional knowledge through what he terms "anti-language" strategy—using language to point beyond linguistic categories (Hansen, 2014). This approach challenges representationalist assumptions while suggesting alternative relationships between language, thought, and reality.

Contemporary developments explore Chinese philosophy's contributions to current debates. Karyn Lai's work on Chinese naturalism demonstrates how Chinese philosophy provides resources for understanding knowledge as embedded in natural and social contexts rather than abstract theoretical achievement (Lai, 2017).

9.8 SKEPTICAL CHALLENGES AND THEIR EPISTEMOLOGICAL SIGNIFICANCE

Contemporary skepticism continues to reveal epistemological assumptions while motivating theoretical advances.

9.8.1 Contemporary Skeptical Arguments

Contemporary skepticism develops sophisticated challenges beyond classical formulations. Barry Stroud's neo-Humean skepticism demonstrates how even modest knowledge claims presuppose substantial background assumptions vulnerable to skeptical challenge (Stroud, 2018). His work shows skepticism's persistence despite numerous attempted solutions.

The problem of criterion, revived by Michael Bergmann, reveals structural challenges to epistemological theory itself—we cannot establish criteria for knowledge without already knowing something, yet cannot know anything without criteria (Bergmann, 2015). This problem threatens epistemology's foundations rather than merely first-order knowledge claims.

Bryan Frances's disagreement skepticism argues that peer disagreement about philosophical matters undermines justification for philosophical beliefs (Frances, 2018). If equally competent philosophers disagree about epistemological principles, suspending judgment appears required, threatening epistemology itself.

9.8.2 Epistemological Responses to Skepticism

Anti-skeptical strategies continue to develop in sophistication. Duncan

Pritchard's epistemological disjunctivism argues that perceptual knowledge involves direct access to environmental facts rather than inference from experiential states (Pritchard, 2012). This approach blocks skeptical arguments by denying the assumption that good and bad cases share common epistemic factors.

Ernest Sosa's virtue perspectivism addresses skepticism through distinguishing animal from reflective knowledge (Sosa, 2017). While skeptical scenarios threaten reflective knowledge about our knowledge, they leave animal knowledge intact, preserving practical knowledge while acknowledging theoretical limitations.

Michael Williams's contextualist response argues that skeptical problems arise from the inappropriate decontextualization of knowledge claims (Williams, 2001). Knowledge attributions are inherently contextual, and skeptical contexts illegitimately abstract from conditions that make knowledge possible.

9.9 IMPLICATIONS FOR FIRST PRINCIPLES: EPISTEMOLOGICAL CONSTRAINTS AND POSSIBILITIES

The epistemological investigations surveyed provide essential guidance for approaching first principles while revealing both possibilities and limitations.

9.9.1 Methodological Pluralism and Epistemic Humility

Contemporary epistemology supports what Helen Longino calls "pluralistic empiricism"—recognition that different knowledge types require different methodological approaches (Longino, 2013). Physical principles require empirical investigation, logical principles require rational analysis, moral principles may require emotional engagement, and religious principles might require contemplative practice.

This pluralism does not entail relativism. Sandra Harding's standpoint epistemology demonstrates how different perspectives can provide objective knowledge while acknowledging their situatedness (Harding, 2015). Marginalized perspectives may reveal features of reality invisible from dominant positions, enriching rather than undermining objectivity.

9.9.2 Social and Political Dimensions of Knowledge

Charles Mills's analysis of "white ignorance" reveals how racial domination produces systematic epistemic distortions that affect even well-intentioned inquirers (Mills, 2017). Identifying first principles requires confronting how social position shapes epistemic access, particularly regarding moral and political principles.

Shannon Fyfe's work on epistemic exploitation shows how marginalized groups bear disproportionate burdens in correcting dominant groups' ignorance (Fyfe, 2023). This suggests that approaching first principles requires not just including diverse voices but restructuring epistemic labor more equitably.

9.9.3 Integration and Convergence Criteria

Nancy Cartwright's evidence pluralism demonstrates how different evidence types can support identical conclusions through independent routes (Cartwright, 2019). When empirical, rational, testimonial, and experiential evidence converge, confidence increases beyond what any single source provides.

Philip Kitcher's "modest realism" suggests that convergence across different methodologies and perspectives indicates contact with reality rather than mere agreement (Kitcher, 2012). This approach maintains commitment to truth while acknowledging fallibility and ongoing revision.

9.9.4 Dynamic and Developmental Understanding

Thomas Kuhn's developmental epistemology, refined in his later work, treats knowledge as historically evolving without abandoning objectivity (Kuhn, 2000). Scientific revolutions reveal new first principles that reconstruct previous knowledge rather than simply accumulating facts.

Hasok Chang's pragmatic realism advocates "epistemic iteration"—using current knowledge to develop better knowledge-seeking methods that reveal limitations in current knowledge (Chang, 2022). This recursive process enables progress while maintaining appropriate humility about current achievements.

9.10 Conclusion: Knowledge As Foundation For Philosophical Inquiry

This examination of knowledge's structure reveals epistemology as an indispensable foundation for investigating first principles while demonstrating the complexity and sophistication required for such investigation. Contemporary epistemology has moved far beyond simple empiricism-rationalism debates to develop nuanced frameworks addressing social knowledge, epistemic injustice, cross-cultural perspectives, and integration of diverse knowledge sources.

The epistemological landscape demonstrates that approaching first principles requires methodological pluralism rather than monistic reduction to a single epistemic approach. Different domains—physical, mathematical, moral, religious—may require different epistemic methods while remaining subject to rational evaluation and mutual constraint. This pluralism respects knowledge's diversity while maintaining commitment to truth and objectivity.

Understanding knowledge's inherently social character proves crucial for approaching first principles. Knowledge emerges through communal inquiry involving testimony, trust, and distributed cognition. Epistemic injustice reveals how social power structures systematically distort knowledge, requiring conscious effort to include marginalized perspectives and redistribute epistemic resources more equitably.

Cross-cultural epistemological engagement demonstrates that Western philosophy lacks a monopoly on epistemological insight. Indian, Buddhist, Islamic, Chinese, and Indigenous epistemologies provide sophisticated frameworks that complement and sometimes surpass Western approaches. Genuine philosophical progress requires taking these traditions seriously rather than treating them as merely historical or anthropological curiosities.

The persistence of skeptical challenges reminds us that even our most confident beliefs remain open to doubt and revision. Rather than defeating knowledge, skepticism motivates more sophisticated epistemological theories and appropriate intellectual humility. We can maintain commitment to truth while acknowledging fallibility and the ongoing need for inquiry.

As the investigation proceeds to examine specific first principles in subsequent chapters, these epistemological insights provide essential guidance. They remind us that identifying first principles requires employing our full range of cognitive capacities—empirical, rational, testimonial, experiential—while maintaining critical awareness of their limitations. The quest for first principles emerges not as a straightforward discovery of self-evident truths but as a complex, ongoing, communal enterprise requiring intellectual virtue, social awareness, and epistemic humility.

CHAPTER 10: LOGICAL FOUNDATIONS

10.1 THE ARCHITECTURE OF REASON

Logic constitutes the foundational architecture of rational inquiry, providing the structural framework within which all other first principles— whether scientific, philosophical, or religious—receive articulation, evaluation, and systematic relation. The priority of logical principles manifests in their pragmatic inescapability: any attempt to argue against logic must employ logical argumentation, creating what Putnam (1981) termed a "performative contradiction". Before asserting energy conservation, consciousness existence, or divine manifestation, we necessarily employ logical principles to structure these claims coherently and assess their internal consistency.

This foundational status generates profound philosophical questions directly impacting our investigation of first principles. The central debate concerns whether logical laws constitute discovered features of reality analogous to physical constants, or represent human constructs— conventional tools imposed to organize experience (Maddy, 2014; Sher, 2016). If logic proves contingent or culturally relative, then all principles derived through logical reasoning inherit similar contingency. Conversely, if logical principles reflect reality's necessary structure, they provide secure foundations for systematic knowledge construction across domains.

The present chapter examines logic as potentially the most fundamental first principle—the foundation upon which all other foundations necessarily rest. Through systematic analysis of classical logical laws, their metaphysical status, modal extensions, and alternative traditions, we assess whether logical principles represent bedrock features of reality or useful cognitive tools helping finite minds navigate an ultimately trans-logical cosmos. This investigation reveals unexpected complexity in logic's foundational role while confirming its indispensability for rational inquiry.

10.2 THE CLASSICAL LAWS OF LOGIC

Three principles have traditionally constituted fundamental logical laws in Western philosophy: identity, non-contradiction, and excluded middle. While Aristotle extensively discussed these principles, their explicit formulation as a foundational triumvirate emerged through centuries of philosophical development (Łukasiewicz, 1971; Smith, 2019). These laws purport to describe reality's most general structural features while establishing conditions for correct reasoning.

10.2.1 The Law of Identity

The law of identity states that everything is identical to itself: A = A. This apparently trivial principle establishes crucial logical and metaphysical foundations. For any object, concept, or proposition to remain intelligible across contexts, it must maintain self-identity. Without stable identity conditions, reference becomes impossible—we cannot meaningfully speak about entities lacking determinate self-identity (Russell, 1903; Strawson, 1959).

Leibniz (1714/1989) refined this principle through his law of the identity of indiscernibles: if two entities share all properties without exception, they are numerically identical. As he argued, "There is no such thing as two individuals indiscernible from each other". This formulation connects logical identity directly to metaphysical identity, suggesting logic describes not merely cognitive organization but reality's structure. Contemporary discussions of identity across time, personal identity, and quantum mechanical identity presuppose this basic principle while revealing its complexities (Wiggins, 2001; Sider, 2001; French & Krause, 2006).

The law enables definition, classification, and systematic knowledge construction. Scientific practice depends fundamentally on stable identities—electrons must remain electrons rather than spontaneously transforming into muons. Mathematical discourse requires that numerical entities maintain self-identity across legitimate contexts. Even religious discourse assumes divine identity, as Aquinas argued: "God is altogether immutable" (Summa Theologiae). Contemporary perfect being theology continues to develop these identity conditions (Rogers, 2000; Nagasawa, 2017).

Contemporary physics complicates simple identity assumptions. Quantum mechanical wave-particle duality challenges classical notions of self-identical objects existing independently of measurement contexts. As Albert (1992) demonstrates, "quantum mechanics describes a world in which the very idea of objective properties becomes problematic". The Ship of Theseus paradox questions identity persistence through material change. These puzzles suggest identity might be more contextually complex than classical logic assumes, though not necessarily undermining the principle's general validity (Fine, 2016; Morganti & Tahko, 2017).

10.2.2 The Law of Non-Contradiction

Aristotle characterized non-contradiction as "the most certain of all principles" (Metaphysics, 384-322 BCE/1984), stating that contradictory propositions cannot simultaneously be true in the same respect: nothing can be both A and not-A under identical conditions. A particle cannot simultaneously be an electron and not an electron; a proposition cannot be both true and false under the same interpretation.

This principle appears indispensable for meaningful discourse. If contradictions were generally permissible, any statement could be proven through the principle of explosion. Lewis and Langford (1932) demonstrated that accepting both P and not-P within classical systems allows the derivation of any arbitrary conclusion Q. Without non-contradiction constraints, rational argumentation collapses into incoherence. As Tahko (2009) argues, "the law of non-contradiction serves as a transcendental condition for the possibility of thought itself".

The principle faces apparent counterexamples requiring careful analysis. Quantum superposition suggests particles exist in contradictory states before measurement, though physicists debate whether this represents genuine contradiction or descriptive framework inadequacy (Schrödinger, 1935; Griffiths, 2002). The Copenhagen interpretation maintains that quantum states do not violate non-contradiction but rather reveal measurement's constitutive role (Bohr, 1958; Faye, 2019).

Semantic paradoxes like the liar paradox ("This statement is false") appear both true and false simultaneously. Priest (2006) argues that some contradictions (dialetheia) are genuinely true, developing paraconsistent systems containing contradictions without explosion. However, Field (2008) and Beall (2009) provide alternative resolutions preserving classical consistency through semantic ascent and truth-value gaps, respectively.

Recent work on vagueness provides additional challenges. If someone with precisely 50,000 hairs is neither clearly bald nor clearly non-bald, non-contradiction faces boundary cases where contradictory predications might both apply (Fine, 2001; Keefe & Smith, 1996). Supervaluationist approaches maintain classical logic by treating vague predicates as admitting multiple precisifications (Keefe, 2000), while degree theories abandon bivalence while preserving non-contradiction (Machina, 1976).

10.2.3 The Law of Excluded Middle

The law of excluded middle states that for any meaningful proposition P, either P or not-P must be true—tertium non datur. This principle underlies classical bivalent logic, where every well-formed statement receives exactly one truth value. Combined with non-contradiction, the excluded middle establishes logic's classical architecture.

Mathematical reasoning frequently depends on the excluded middle. Proof by contradiction assumes that if not-P leads to a contradiction, then P must be true. Many fundamental results, including Euclid's proof of infinite primes, rely on this pattern (Mueller, 1981). Yet intuitionistic mathematicians reject the excluded middle for statements concerning infinite sets. Brouwer (1975) argued that we cannot assert P or not-P without constructive methods determining which alternative holds. Heyting (1956) formalized intuitionistic logic, while Dummett (1991) developed a comprehensive anti-realist philosophy of mathematics, rejecting the excluded middle.

The principle encounters empirical challenges from vague predicates and future contingents. Vague predicates resist bivalent classification—determining whether someone with 50,000 hairs is bald admits degrees rather than sharp boundaries. Zadeh (1965) developed fuzzy logic, allowing truth degrees between 0 and 1, capturing graduated properties while preserving systematic reasoning. Williamson (1994) defends classical logic through epistemic accounts of vagueness, arguing apparent vagueness reflects ignorance rather than metaphysical indeterminacy.

Future contingents challenge excluded middle—whether "a sea battle will occur tomorrow" is currently true or false remains debatable (Aristotle, De Interpretatione, 9). MacFarlane (2003) argues for relativist semantics where future contingent truth values are assessment-sensitive, while Belnap and Green (1994) develop branching time semantics preserving modified excluded middle.

10.2.4 The Foundational Role

These three laws together constitute classical logic's foundation, enabling deductive reasoning where conclusions follow necessarily from premises. All formal systems, from pure mathematics to computer science, build upon these foundations while extending them in domain-specific directions. Even sophisticated attempts to challenge these laws must employ logical argumentation, suggesting pragmatic inescapability (Strawson, 1952; Resnik, 1996).

The relationship between logical principles and mathematical foundations proves intimate and mutually reinforcing. Mathematical logic formalizes these principles rigorously, while mathematics assumes them throughout reasoning processes. Gödel's incompleteness theorems depend on classical principles for their formulation, even while revealing formal systems' limitations (Gödel, 1931; Nagel & Newman, 2001; Smith, 2013). This reciprocal dependence suggests deep connections between logical and mathematical first principles explored in Chapter 5.

10.3 THE NATURE OF LOGICAL LAWS: DESCRIPTIVE OR PRESCRIPTIVE?

A fundamental question affects logical principles' status as first principles: do they describe reality's necessary structure (descriptive) or prescribe how rational agents ought to reason (prescriptive)? This debate profoundly impacts logic's foundational status across inquiry domains.

10.3.1 The Descriptivist Position

Logical realists maintain that logical laws describe mind-independent features of reality's structure. Frege (2013) insisted: "Being true is different from being taken to be true, whether by one or many or everybody". This position treats logical principles as discoveries rather than inventions, analogous to physical laws describing matter's behavior patterns.

Contemporary logical realists argue that logical principles represent the most general metaphysical necessities. Williamson (2013) defends this through modal metaphysics, arguing logical truths constitute the broadest class of metaphysical necessities—true in all possible worlds. As he states, "Logic is universal because it is maximally general". Penrose (1989) suggests logical truths exist in a Platonic realm accessible through rational intuition, paralleling mathematical objects.

This view gains support from logic's apparent universality and indispensability for systematic inquiry. If logical principles merely reflected contingent conventions, their cross-cultural recognition and systematic power would require explanation. Maddy (2007) argues logical principles are continuous with scientific principles—both describe objective features at different generality levels. Sher (2016) develops a foundational holism where logical principles are grounded in reality's formal-structural features.

The descriptivist position faces challenges from formal systems' diversity and the apparent cultural variations in reasoning patterns. If classical logic described reality's necessary structure, coherent alternatives would seem impossible. Yet we possess intuitionistic, paraconsistent, relevance, and linear logics, each capturing different reasoning aspects while maintaining internal coherence (Haack, 1996; Russell, 2018).

10.3.2 The Prescriptivist Response

Logical conventionalists argue that logical laws are prescriptive rules adopted for organizing thought rather than discoveries about reality's structure. Carnap (1937) maintained: "In logic, there are no morals. Everyone is at liberty to build his own logic". Logic becomes pragmatic decision-making rather than metaphysical discovery.

This view gains empirical support from viable formal systems' plurality. Haack (1996) demonstrates that alternative systems can be formally rigorous while rejecting classical principles. Each serves specific purposes and captures different reasoning aspects without claiming exclusive correctness. As she argues, "the plurality of logics shows that logic is not a body of truths about a special subject matter".

Putnam (1968) argued that empirical discoveries might force logical revision, as they forced the revision of Euclidean geometry. He suggested quantum mechanics might require quantum logic, making logical principles empirically revisable rather than *a priori* necessities. Quine (1986) similarly argued that logic sits within our belief web, subject to revision through experience rather than standing outside it.

Contemporary experimental philosophy suggests logical intuitions vary across cultures and individuals, undermining universal validity claims (Weinberg, Nichols, & Stich, 2001; Machery et al., 2017). If logical principles were objective features, such variation would be surprising. However, Dutilh Novaes (2015) argues apparent variation reflects different contexts and applications rather than fundamental logical disagreement.

10.3.3 The Middle Path: Logical Pluralism

Beall and Restall (2006) advocate logical pluralism—multiple logics can be equally correct for different purposes. Classical logic might govern mathematical reasoning, while paraconsistent logic handles paradoxes, and quantum logic describes microscopic phenomena. As they argue, "there is more than one genuine deductive consequence relation". Shapiro (2014) develops similar positions, arguing that logical consequence is relative to mathematical structures and interpretive contexts.

This position suggests logical principles involve both descriptive and prescriptive elements. They arise from interactions between mind and world, shaped by reality's structure and cognitive architecture. Different reality aspects might require different logical frameworks, just as Newtonian and relativistic physics apply at different scales without undermining each other's domain-specific validity.

Russell (2018) challenges even pluralist assumptions through logical nihilism, arguing there are no logical laws—only useful reasoning patterns without metaphysical grounding. This radical position questions logic's provision of first principles, though critics argue it remains self-undermining by employing logical argumentation to deny logic's validity (Cotnoir, 2018).

Field (2009) proposes logical pluralism without metaphysical pluralism, suggesting different logics serve different purposes while reality remains univocal. This preserves logical diversity while maintaining metaphysical unity, potentially reconciling pluralism with first principles' quest.

10.4 MODAL LOGIC AND THE STRUCTURE OF POSSIBILITY

Modal logic extends classical logic by formalizing necessity and possibility, providing sophisticated tools for understanding what must be, might be, and cannot be. This enterprise reveals deep connections between logical and metaphysical first principles, bridging logical investigations with ontological concerns.

10.4.1 Necessity and Possibility

Modal logic introduces operators for necessity ($\square$) and possibility ($\lozenge$), transforming ordinary propositions into modal statements. A proposition is necessary if it must be true, possible if it could be true, and impossible if it cannot be true. These modalities structure our understanding of first principles—we seek necessary truths rather than contingent regularities.

Kripke (1963) revolutionized modal logic through possible worlds semantics, providing rigorous mathematical foundations. Under this framework, necessary truths hold in all possible worlds, while possible truths hold in at least one. This technical apparatus clarifies modal concepts and enables precise reasoning about necessity and contingency. As Kripke (1980) later demonstrated, "metaphysical necessity is necessity in the strictest sense".

The distinction between metaphysical and epistemic necessity proves crucial for evaluating first principles. Kripke (1980) showed that some truths like "water is H_2O" are metaphysically necessary despite being discoverable only empirically. This suggests mathematical truths might be metaphysically necessary even if epistemically dependent on human cognitive capacities (Chalmers, 2002; Soames, 2003).

The metaphysics of possible worlds remains contentious, with implications for understanding first principles. Lewis (1986) defended modal realism, treating possible worlds as concrete realities. Stalnaker (2012) advocates actualism, interpreting possible worlds as abstract properties. Adams (1974) proposes theistic actualism, where possible worlds are divine thoughts. These interpretations affect how we understand proposed first principles' necessity.

10.4.2 Applications to First Principles

Modal logic helps distinguish different types of first principles. Logical principles appear metaphysically necessary—true in all possible worlds. Mathematical principles might share absolute necessity if mathematical realism proves correct. Physical laws seem nomologically necessary—required by nature's actual structure but possibly different in alternative worlds. Moral principles might be metaphysically necessary if moral realism holds, contingent if ethics proves culturally relative (Fine, 2002; Rosen, 2006).

The ontological argument employs modal logic explicitly. Plantinga (1974) argues that if God's existence is possible, it must be necessary, since a maximally great being would exist in all possible worlds. This connects modal logic directly to theological first principles. Critics like Oppy (1995) question whether possibility premises can bear such metaphysical weight without independent arguments. Pruss (2018) develops new modal ontological arguments addressing these concerns.

Modal logic illuminates consciousness, free will, and personal identity puzzles bearing on first principles. Chalmers (2006) uses two-dimensional semantics, arguing for consciousness's irreducibility to physical processes, suggesting phenomenal concepts pick out referents differently from physical concepts. These applications demonstrate modal logic's importance for evaluating proposed first principles.

Fine (1994) argues that not all necessary truths are essential—some things are necessarily true without being part of reality's essential structure. This distinction between metaphysical necessity and essential nature complicates modal approaches to first principles, suggesting we need more refined tools than simple necessity (Correia & Skiles, 2019).

10.5 LOGIC AND REALITY: THE METAPHYSICAL CONNECTION

The relationship between logic and reality constitutes philosophy's deepest questions, directly affecting logic's status as a first principle. This connection links logical foundations to ontological and epistemological issues.

10.5.1 Historical Perspectives

Aristotle integrated logic with metaphysics systematically, treating logical categories as ontological categories structuring both thought and being. The categories organize reality itself rather than merely human conceptual schemes (Categories; Metaphysics). This integration assumes logical principles reflect being's fundamental structure. As Corcoran (2009) demonstrates, "Aristotle's logic is a theory of deduction as a method of gaining knowledge".

Medieval Islamic philosophers developed sophisticated accounts of logic's relationship to reality. Al-Farabi argued that logic provides tools for distinguishing truth from falsehood across all sciences (McGinnis, 2010). Avicenna (Ibn Sīnā) maintained that logical forms reflect existence's essential structure rather than arbitrary conventions. Their work influenced both Islamic and Christian traditions, establishing logic's metaphysical significance (Street, 2004; Leaman, 2009).

Aquinas synthesized Aristotelian logic with Christian theology, holding that logical principles are grounded in divine intellect and participated in by human reason (Summa Theologiae, I-II). This theological grounding suggests logical laws reflect God's rational nature. Contemporary perfect being theology continues this approach (Rogers, 2000; Speaks, 2018).

Kant (1781/1998) revolutionized this discussion by distinguishing formal logic from transcendental logic. While we cannot determine whether noumenal reality obeys logical principles, phenomena necessarily conform to logic's requirements as conditions of possible experience. This critical turn preserves logic's necessity while limiting its metaphysical scope. As Kant argued, "general logic abstracts from all content of knowledge" (A55/B79).

10.5.2 Contemporary Perspectives

Modern physics challenges simple assumptions about the logic-reality relationship. Quantum mechanics exhibits features resisting classical logical description—superposition, entanglement, and measurement-induced collapse. Some argue for quantum logic as nature's true logic (Birkhoff & von Neumann, 1936; Putnam, 1968), while others maintain classical logic remains valid with only descriptive frameworks requiring revision (Maudlin, 2019).

The consistent histories interpretation preserves classical logic by carefully specifying contexts and avoiding incompatible descriptions (Griffiths, 2002). Many-worlds interpretations maintain classical logic by denying wave function collapse, treating apparent contradictions as reflecting incomplete descriptions (Wallace, 2012). These approaches demonstrate that the logic-quantum mechanics relationship remains theoretically unsettled.

Information-theoretic approaches suggest logic emerges from information-processing constraints rather than metaphysical necessities. Floridi (2011) treats reality as fundamentally informational, with logic describing information's organizational patterns. This connects logical principles to computational and physical constraints rather than abstract metaphysical structures. Tegmark (2014) proposes the mathematical universe hypothesis, where reality is a mathematical structure, making logic constitutive of existence.

Brandom (1994) grounds logic in social practices of giving and asking for reasons rather than mind-independent reality. Logical principles emerge from discourse community norms rather than metaphysical discoveries. This pragmatist approach treats logic as foundational for human reasoning without requiring metaphysical commitments. Peregrin (2014) develops inferentialist accounts where logic codifies material inference patterns.

Contemporary grounding theory provides new tools for understanding logic's relationship to reality. Schaffer (2009) argues that logical truths might be grounded in more fundamental metaphysical facts rather than being basic themselves. This suggests logical principles might derive from other first principles rather than being foundational. Rosen (2010) and Fine (2012) develop sophisticated grounding frameworks applicable to logical principles.

10.6 BEYOND CLASSICAL LOGIC: ALTERNATIVE TRADITIONS

While classical Western logic has dominated philosophical discourse, alternative traditions offer different perspectives on foundational principles. These alternatives challenge classical logic's universality and suggest that first principles might be more culturally and contextually diverse than traditionally assumed.

10.6.1 Asian Philosophical Traditions

Buddhist logic employs different foundational principles from classical Western approaches. The catuṣkoṭi (tetralemma) allows four positions: affirmation, denial, both, and neither. Nāgārjuna used this framework in the Mūlamadhyamakakārikā, arguing that ultimate reality transcends conceptual categories (Garfield, 1995). As Westerhoff (2009) demonstrates,

"Nāgārjuna's philosophical project aims at a therapeutic dissolution of all philosophical theories".

The Buddhist doctrine of śūnyatā challenges the law of identity by denying fixed essence (svabhāva). Everything arises through dependent origination (pratītyasamutpāda), making identity relational and processual. Siderits (2007) shows how this metaphysics requires reconceptualizing logical principles fundamentally. Priest (2018) argues that Buddhist logic anticipates paraconsistent developments.

Jaina logic introduces syādvāda (conditioned predication) and anekāntavāda (non-one-sidedness) as alternatives to classical bivalence. The seven-fold predication allows complex truth conditions. Ganeri (2001) demonstrates this logic's sophistication in handling perspective-dependence and contextual variation. As he argues, "Jaina logic is a logic of qualified assertion".

Chinese philosophical traditions emphasize correlative over analytic thinking. The yin-yang framework suggests complementary opposition rather than logical contradiction. Hansen (1992) argues that classical Chinese thought lacks a substance-property metaphysics underlying Western logic, operating with part-whole frameworks, resisting classical analysis. Graham (2010) demonstrates sophisticated logical thinking in ancient China despite different emphases.

Islamic contributions proved crucial for logical development. Al-Farabi integrated Aristotelian logic with Islamic theology while developing original insights. Avicenna anticipated modal logic developments by centuries. Ibn Rushd (Averroes) defended logic's universality against theological critics while showing reconciliation with revealed religion (Street, 2004; McGinnis & Reisman, 2007).

10.6.2 Dialectical and Process Logics

Hegelian dialectical logic replaces static contradiction with dynamic development through productive resolution. The dialectical movement from thesis through antithesis to synthesis captures development that formal logic cannot accommodate. Hegel (2010) reconceived contradiction as productive tension driving systematic development. As Redding (2007) explains, "Hegel's logic is meant to capture the necessary development of thought".

Process philosophers argue reality is fundamentally processual, requiring logics of becoming rather than being. Whitehead (1978) developed process metaphysics where actual occasions are basic. Rescher (1996) develops process semantics, formalizing change as a logical primitive. These approaches suggest that first principles might be dynamic rather than static.

Contemporary temporal logic formalizes change systematically while preserving rigor. Prior (1967) developed tense logic, while Pnueli (1977) created temporal logic for computer science. These developments show that alternative frameworks can capture reality aspects that classical logic cannot accommodate without abandoning systematic reasoning.

10.6.3 Contemporary Non-Classical Logics

Paraconsistent logics allow contradictions without explosion. Priest (2006) argues that some contradictions are genuinely true at boundaries—change moments, thought limits, self-reference. These logics find applications in artificial intelligence, legal reasoning, and database management. Da Costa (1974) developed paraconsistent set theory, while Berto and Restall (2019) surveyed philosophical implications.

Relevance logics require genuine premise-conclusion connections. Anderson and Belnap (1975) developed relevant implication, ensuring authentic connections. This captures the intuition that logical consequence requires more than truth-preservation. Mares (2020) provides comprehensive philosophical foundations for relevance logic.

Linear logic treats propositions as consumable resources, modeling computational processes more accurately than classical logic (Girard, 1987). Category theory and homotopy type theory provide new foundations suggesting alternative logical space conceptions (Awodey, 2010; Homotopy Type Theory, 2013).

Substructural logics systematically explore weakening classical principles while maintaining coherent reasoning. Restall (2000) shows how different structural rules generate different systems with varied applications. This demonstrates classical logic's contingency while preserving systematic reasoning. Paoli (2002) develops philosophical implications of substructural approaches.

10.7 IMPLICATIONS FOR FIRST PRINCIPLES

Our systematic investigation yields crucial insights for identifying first principles across scientific, philosophical, and religious domains.

10.7.1 The Bootstrapping Problem

Logic faces fundamental bootstrapping: we must employ logical reasoning to investigate logic itself. Any argument for or against logical principles utilizes logical argumentation, creating apparent circularity. This differs from empirical or mathematical foundations, which can be questioned from external perspectives.

Shapiro (2000) argues this circularity is virtuous rather than vicious—logic's self-support confirms its foundational status. Others interpret it as revealing logic's conventional nature. The bootstrapping problem suggests logical first principles might be pragmatically indispensable rather than metaphysically guaranteed. Priest (2006) argues we can coherently question logic using logic, while Woods (2019) develops transcendental arguments for logical principles.

This connects to broader justification questions. If all justification employs logical principles, then logical principles cannot receive external justification without presupposing what requires justification. This suggests either foundationalism about logic or coherentist approaches treating logical principles as self-supporting (Boghossian, 2000; Wright, 2004).

10.7.2 Logical Pluralism and First Principles

If logical pluralism proves correct, singular first principles become more complex. Different reality aspects might require different logical frameworks—quantum logic for microscopic phenomena, fuzzy logic for vague predicates, paraconsistent logic for paradoxes, classical logic for mathematics. This doesn't necessarily lead to relativism; some principles might remain more fundamental (Beall & Restall, 2006; Field, 2009).

The first principle might be minimal rationality—consistency within contexts, providing reasons, avoiding arbitrary claims—rather than specific logical systems. This thin rationality conception might underlie logical diversity while maintaining normative force (Lynch, 2009; Ferrari & Moruzzi, 2020).

Alternatively, logical pluralism might indicate different first principles types operating at different analysis levels. Classical logic might govern mathematical and scientific reasoning, while alternative logics capture other human experience aspects—aesthetic judgment, religious insight, moral reasoning (Caret, 2017).

10.7.3 The Limits of Formalization

Gödel's incompleteness theorems demonstrate that sufficiently rich formal systems cannot be both complete and consistent (Gödel, 1931; Smith, 2013). No formal system can prove its own consistency. Some mathematical truths transcend formal proof capabilities. These limitations apply equally to logical systems.

These limitations suggest that first principles might include aspects resisting logical formalization—ineffable insights, mystical experiences, aesthetic intuitions, moral convictions recognized as fundamental despite resisting formal articulation. Logic's precision might exclude reality dimensions accessible through other approaches (Hofstadter, 1979; Franks, 2009).

This connects to broader questions about formal and informal reasoning relationships. While logical systems provide powerful systematic analysis tools, they cannot capture all human reasoning aspects or reality features qualifying as first principles (Govier, 1987; Johnson, 2000).

10.7.4 Integration with Other Domains

Logic provides the framework for articulating scientific laws, philosophical principles, and theological doctrines, but cannot determine their specific content independently. Conservation laws must be logically consistent, but aren't derivable from logical principles alone. Consciousness's certainty employs logical argumentation while pointing toward realities transcending formal description.

This suggests hierarchical yet interconnected relationships among first principles. Logic enables the formulation and evaluation of domain-specific principles without reducing to them. Conversely, empirical discoveries, phenomenological insights, and religious experiences might reveal reality aspects requiring new logical frameworks (Tahko, 2015; Williamson, 2016).

The integration challenge involves understanding how logical principles relate to other domain principles without either reducing everything to logic or treating logic as merely instrumental. Different first principles types might be mutually informing rather than simply hierarchically ordered (Lowe, 2013).

10.7.5 The Unity and Diversity of Reason

Despite logical diversity across traditions and contexts, significant commonalities exist in human reasoning patterns. All cultures recognize inference forms, consistency requirements, and argumentative norms. This suggests universal rationality features, possibly grounded in evolutionary pressures, cognitive architecture, or transcendental consciousness structures (Hauser, 2006; Mikhail, 2011; Mercier & Sperber, 2017).

Yet logical systems' diversity indicates no single logic exhausts rationality's possibilities. Different cognitive tasks, cultural contexts, and reality aspects might require different logical approaches. The first principle might be rationality itself—commitment to coherent reasoning—rather than specific logical rules (Davidson, 2001; Steinberger, 2019).

This unity-diversity tension appears throughout the first principles investigation. Just as scientific laws exhibit both universal and contextual features, logical principles might display both universal rational constraints and contextual variations in specific applications (van Benthem, 2008; Dutilh Novaes, 2020).

10.8 CONCLUSION

Logic presents itself as the most fundamental first principle—the unavoidable framework within which all other principles receive articulation and assessment. The classical laws of identity, non-contradiction, and excluded middle have structured Western thought for millennia, appearing to describe not merely cognitive organization requirements but reality's intelligibility conditions.

Our systematic investigation reveals unexpected complexity in logic's foundational status. The nature of logical laws remains contested between descriptive accounts treating them as mind-independent reality features and prescriptive accounts viewing them as useful thought organization tools. The plurality of viable logical systems—Eastern and Western, formal and dialectical—challenges classical principles while maintaining rational coherence, suggesting logical first principles are more diverse yet less arbitrary than traditionally assumed.

This complexity enriches rather than diminishes logic's foundational significance. Logic emerges not as a monolithic first principle but as a family of related frameworks for structuring thought and investigating reality.

Different logical systems capture different aspects of reality, too rich for any single formal system to encompass completely. The logic-reality relationship remains philosophy's deepest question, connecting fundamental issues in metaphysics, epistemology, and philosophy of science.

For our broader quest to identify first principles, logic provides both an essential foundation and an inherent limitation. It enables rigorous formulation and evaluation while constraining what can be formally expressed. It unifies human reasoning patterns while diversifying into multiple systems adapted to different domains. It appears practically necessary while remaining ultimately mysterious in its relationship to reality's structure.

The implications extend across all first principles investigation domains. Scientific theories must maintain logical consistency, though logic alone cannot determine which theories accurately describe natural phenomena. Philosophical arguments depend on logical inference, though logic cannot settle all philosophical questions independently. Religious claims must avoid contradiction within their interpretive frameworks, though those frameworks might employ non-classical logical principles. Mathematical foundations presuppose logical principles while extending beyond them into domain-specific territories.

Perhaps the deepest insight concerns logic's self-transcendent character. Gödel's theorems reveal formal systems' inherent limitations. Alternative logical traditions suggest different rational thought structuring ways. The bootstrapping problem demonstrates logic's ultimate self-dependence. These features indicate that first principles might include both what logic can capture systematically and what necessarily escapes logical formalization.

As we examine religious first principles in subsequent chapters, logic's lessons prove crucial. Religious claims must maintain consistency within their interpretive frameworks, even when those frameworks differ from classical Western logic. The diversity of logical traditions parallels and illuminates the diversity of religious approaches to ultimate reality. Logic's inherent limitations suggest conceptual space for revelations, experiences, and insights transcending formal reasoning while not contradicting it within appropriate domains.

The quest for first principles requires logic without being exhausted by logical analysis. Logic provides essential scaffolding for constructing and evaluating foundational claims across all human inquiry domains. Yet scaffolding is not the building itself. Beyond logic's necessary framework lie the specific first principles—scientific, philosophical, and religious—that logic helps us discover, articulate, and assess but does not independently determine. In recognizing both logic's foundational role and its inherent limitations, we prepare ourselves for truly comprehensive investigation of reality's ultimate foundations across the full spectrum of human knowledge and experience.

PART IV

CHAPTER 11: THE SACRED AND TRANSCENDENT

11.1 THE IRREDUCIBLE SACRED

The persistence of religious experience across human cultures and historical epochs presents a fundamental challenge to any comprehensive account of first principles. From the earliest archaeological evidence of ritual burial practices to contemporary neuroscientific studies of contemplative states, human beings consistently report encounters with dimensions of reality that transcend ordinary empirical observation and rational analysis (Eliade, 1957/1987; Newberg & d'Aquili, 2001). This universality demands serious philosophical engagement with the possibility that religious experience provides epistemic access to foundational aspects of reality's structure.

The methodological challenge proves formidable. Religious experiences resist the controlled observation and replication that characterize scientific inquiry, while their cultural mediation complicates claims to universal validity (Katz, 1978). Nevertheless, dismissing such experiences as mere psychological projection or cultural construction may prematurely foreclose investigation into potentially fundamental dimensions of reality. As William

James (1902/2002) demonstrated through his empirical study of religious experiences, the subjective character of these phenomena does not necessarily invalidate their cognitive content, any more than the subjective character of mathematical intuition invalidates mathematical truth.

This chapter examines religious experience through three complementary lenses: phenomenological analysis of sacred encounters across traditions, epistemological evaluation of mystical knowledge claims, and philosophical investigation of the finite-infinite relationship as a potential first principle. Throughout, we maintain critical rigor while remaining methodologically open to the possibility that some truths about reality's fundamental structure might be accessible primarily through modes of awareness that transcend ordinary consciousness.

11.2 THE PHENOMENOLOGY OF THE SACRED

11.2.1 Otto's Numinous and Its Critics

Rudolf Otto's (1917/1958) identification of the numinous as an irreducible element in religious experience remains influential despite significant criticism. His analysis of the mysterium tremendum et fascinans—the overwhelming yet attractive mystery—captures phenomenological features that appear across diverse religious contexts. The tremendum aspect manifests as absolute otherness that reduces the experiencer to existential humility, while the fascinans dimension paradoxically attracts consciousness toward what exceeds its comprehension.

Contemporary cognitive science challenges Otto's claim of irreducibility. Boyer (2001) demonstrates how religious concepts arise from ordinary cognitive mechanisms, including hyperactive agency detection and intuitive psychology. Barrett (2004) provides evolutionary explanations for sensing unseen presences without requiring supernatural referents. These naturalistic accounts suggest that the numinous experience emerges from standard cognitive processes operating in unusual contexts rather than from a distinct sensus numinis.

However, the evolutionary origin of a cognitive capacity does not determine the veridicality of its outputs. Mathematical cognition similarly evolved for adaptive purposes, yet discovers objective truths about abstract relationships (Dehaene, 2011). The question remains whether evolved religious capacities sometimes accurately detect transcendent realities, even if they also generate culturally specific supernatural beliefs. Cross-cultural phenomenology reveals both universal patterns and significant variations that complicate simple reductionist explanations (Hood, Spilka, Hunsberger, & Gorsuch, 2009).

11.2.2 Sacred Space and Time

Mircea Eliade's (1957/1987) analysis of sacred space and time as qualitatively distinct from profane dimensions offers insights into how religious experience structures human consciousness. Sacred space manifests as centered and meaningful rather than homogeneous, while sacred time operates cyclically and remains recoverable through ritual participation. This structuring appears across traditions despite varying cultural expressions.

Jonathan Z. Smith (1987) critiques Eliade's essentialist approach, arguing that sacredness is constructed through human practices of differentiation rather than inherent in objects or spaces. This constructivist perspective correctly identifies the role of cultural mediation but may overcorrect by eliminating any referential content from religious experience. Contemporary phenomenology suggests a middle path: sacred experiences involve both cultural construction and potential disclosure of reality's depths (Taves, 2009).

Indigenous perspectives offer valuable correctives to Western academic categories. Deloria (1999) demonstrates how Native American traditions understand sacred geography as involving genuine spiritual-material relationships rather than mere symbolic projection. These alternative frameworks challenge assumptions underlying much Western discourse about religious experience while suggesting dimensions of reality that dominant approaches may overlook.

11.2.3 Varieties and Commonalities

William James's (1902/2002) empirical catalogue of religious experiences identified recurring features despite enormous individual and cultural variation: ineffability, noetic quality, transiency, and passivity. His pragmatic evaluation by "fruits" rather than origins remains methodologically valuable—religious experiences should be assessed by their transformative effects rather than their causal mechanisms alone.

Contemporary instruments like Hood's Mysticism Scale confirm cross-cultural commonalities while revealing significant variations (Hood et al., 2009). Neuroscientific studies demonstrate measurable brain changes associated with contemplative practices, suggesting genuine transformation rather than mere subjective belief (Davidson & Lutz, 2008; Lutz, Antoine, Greischar, & Rawlings, 2004). These findings support James's insight that religious experiences involve real psychological processes with potentially epistemic import, though questions about ontological reference remain contested.

11.3 MYSTICAL EXPERIENCE AND EPISTEMOLOGY

11.3.1 The Perennialist-Constructivist Debate

The relationship between experience and interpretation stands at the center of contemporary debates about mystical knowledge. Stace (1960) argued for a universal "common core" beneath cultural variations, distinguishing between raw experience and subsequent conceptual elaboration. This perennialist position suggests that diverse traditions access the same ultimate reality through different cultural lenses.

Katz's (1978) influential critique demonstrates the inseparability of experience and interpretation—there exists no unmediated experience prior to cultural conditioning. Buddhist śūnyatā, Christian unio mystica, and Advaitic brahman-realization represent genuinely different experiences rather than varying interpretations of identical phenomena. This constructivist approach better accounts for phenomenological diversity but potentially undermines claims to transcultural truth.

Forman (1990) proposes a nuanced position acknowledging both cultural shaping and "pure consciousness events" that transcend conceptual frameworks. This approach aligns with contemplative traditions that distinguish between constructed mental states and non-conceptual awareness (Wallace, 2007). The debate's implications for first principles prove significant: if mystical experiences are entirely constructed, they reveal human psychology rather than reality's structure; if they involve genuine transcendent encounters, cultural variations might reflect different aspects of a reality exceeding any single framework.

11.3.2 Reformed Epistemology and Religious Perception

Alvin Plantinga's (2000) reformed epistemology argues that religious beliefs can be properly basic—justified without inferential support—if formed through properly functioning cognitive faculties aimed at truth. This approach treats religious perception as epistemologically parallel to sense perception, requiring no additional justification when operating reliably.

Critics identify significant disanalogies between religious and sensory perception. Sensory experience exhibits intersubjective agreement, predictive success, and technological enhancement absent from religious experience (Gale, 1991). Religious diversity poses particular challenges: if Christians, Muslims, Hindus, and Buddhists possess functioning religious faculties, why do they reach incompatible conclusions? Plantinga's appeal to sin's noetic effects appears ad hoc to critics who find it insufficiently responsive to religious pluralism.

William Alston's (1991) doxastic practice approach offers a more nuanced treatment of religious diversity. Different traditions might constitute equally legitimate practices accessing different aspects of divine reality, analogous to how different scientific methodologies reveal complementary aspects of natural phenomena. This perspectival realism maintains ontological commitment while acknowledging epistemic limitations, though adjudication between conflicting claims remains problematic.

11.3.3 Neuroscience and Consciousness

Neuroscientific research increasingly maps brain correlates of religious experience without necessarily explaining them away. Newberg and d'Aquili's (2001) neuroimaging reveals decreased parietal lobe activity during mystical states, correlating with dissolved self-boundaries. However, correlation does not establish causation's direction—brain states might facilitate rather than produce religious experiences.

The hard problem of consciousness complicates reductionist explanations (Chalmers, 1995). If neuroscience cannot explain ordinary subjective experience's emergence from neural processes, dismissing religious experience based on brain correlates seems premature. Varela's (1996) neurophenomenology argues for integrating first-person experiential reports with third-person neuroscientific data, suggesting that religious experiences might reveal normally hidden dimensions of consciousness.

Contemporary consciousness research supports this possibility. Studies of meditation demonstrate genuine neuroplastic changes enhancing attention, emotional regulation, and self-awareness (Davidson & Lutz, 2008). Psychedelic research shows that altered states can produce lasting positive transformations (Griffiths et al., 2006). These findings suggest that religious practices access real features of consciousness, though their ontological implications remain disputed.

11.4 THE FINITE-INFINITE RELATIONSHIP

11.4.1 Classical Formulations

The relationship between finite and infinite emerges consistently across religious and philosophical traditions as a potential first principle. Aquinas's participation metaphysics remains influential: finite beings exist through participation in infinite being, having rather than being existence itself (Aquinas, Summa Theologiae). This framework preserves genuine finite reality while maintaining ontological dependence on the infinite source.

The doctrine of analogy addresses how language applies across the finite-infinite divide. Terms are neither univocal nor equivocal but analogical—similar with essential difference (Burrell, 2004). This preserves meaningful discourse about transcendent reality while respecting qualitative distinction. Islamic philosophy developed parallel approaches through Avicenna and Ibn Rushd (Averroes), exploring how finite realities emanate from infinite essence while maintaining genuine existence (McGinnis, 2010).

Contemporary challenges to classical formulations include process philosophy's critique of divine immutability and feminist theology's rejection of hierarchical ontologies. Yet the basic insight—that finite existence requires infinite ground—continues to inform philosophical theology and may represent a fundamental metaphysical principle accessible through both rational reflection and religious experience.

11.4.2 Contemporary Models

Process philosophy reconceives the finite-infinite relationship as dynamic and reciprocal. Whitehead (1929) and Hartshorne (1948) propose dipolar theism, where God includes and responds to finite experiences, making the relationship genuinely interactive. This addresses classical difficulties with divine-temporal relations while preserving transcendence through distinction between God's primordial and consequent natures.

Panentheism, developed by Clayton (2004) and Peacocke (2004), locates finite reality within infinite divine life without identification. This model employs emergence analogies to conceive divine action through top-down causation compatible with natural processes. Religious naturalists like Kauffman (2008) and Goodenough (1998) naturalize the infinite as nature's creative possibilities, though questions remain about whether this preserves genuine transcendence.

These models suggest that the finite-infinite relationship might constitute a first principle bridging religious, philosophical, and scientific approaches. Quantum entanglement reveals irreducible relationality in physics (Bell, 2004), while ecology emphasizes systemic interdependence (Wilson, 1998). Religious experience might provide experiential confirmation of relational ontology discovered through other methodologies.

11.5 RELIGIOUS AWARENESS AND EPISTEMIC PLURALISM

11.5.1 Multiple Modes of Knowing

Rather than positing a single religious faculty, epistemic pluralism recognizes multiple modes of awareness contributing to comprehensive understanding. Rational intuition, emotional perception, aesthetic appreciation, and contemplative awareness might each provide partial access to transcendent dimensions through distinctive cognitive operations.

Coakley's (2013) théologie totale integrates intellectual, contemplative, and embodied practices as mutually necessary for theological knowledge. This challenges both narrow rationalism and anti-intellectual experientialism. Comprehensive understanding requires engaged capacities that correct and complement each other, suggesting that first principles might be accessible through converging perspectives rather than single methodological approaches.

Contemporary phenomenology supports this pluralistic epistemology. Merleau-Ponty's (1945/2012) analysis of embodied perception reveals aspects of reality inaccessible to pure intellection. Heidegger's (1962) investigation of being-in-the-world demonstrates how different modes of engagement disclose different dimensions of reality. Religious awareness might represent one legitimate mode among others, contributing distinctive insights while requiring integration with other approaches.

11.5.2 Contemplative Science

Research on contemplative practices provides empirical grounding for claims about expanded awareness. Long-term meditation produces structural brain changes and enhanced cognitive capacities persisting beyond formal practice (Davidson & Lutz, 2008). These findings suggest genuine consciousness transformation rather than temporary altered states or wishful thinking.

Wallace (2007) advocates "contemplative science," taking introspective methods seriously as a means of investigating consciousness. If consciousness includes dimensions inaccessible to third-person methods, contemplative practices might reveal aspects of reality—including potential first principles—hidden from ordinary awareness. This requires rigorous methodologies for evaluating contemplative claims while remaining open to discoveries challenging materialist assumptions.

Buddhist philosophy offers sophisticated frameworks for understanding consciousness that complement contemporary research. Concepts like ālaya-vijñāna (storehouse consciousness) and tathāgatagarbha (Buddha-nature) provide resources for understanding expanded awareness (Waldron, 2003). These traditional frameworks might inform consciousness studies while benefiting from scientific methodologies, suggesting productive dialogue between contemplative and empirical approaches.

11.6 IMPLICATIONS FOR FIRST PRINCIPLES

11.6.1 Dimensional Pluralism

Religious experience suggests reality includes qualitatively distinct dimensions—physical, biological, psychological, sacred—each requiring appropriate methods of investigation. This dimensional pluralism aligns with emergence theories in complexity science while preserving space for genuinely religious insights (Anderson, 1972). The sacred might emerge from but transcend lower organizational levels, exhibiting irreducible properties accessible primarily through religious awareness.

11.6.2 Relational Ontology

Religious experience consistently emphasizes relationship as fundamental rather than derivative. This challenges both atomistic and monistic ontologies in favor of relational approaches where entities exist only within networks of relationships. Quantum entanglement, ecological interdependence, and social construction converge with religious insights about reality's fundamentally relational character (Barad, 2007).

11.6.3 Unity-in-Difference

Rather than simple unity or plurality, religious experience points toward unity-in-difference as characterizing reality's structure. The One manifests as many without losing essential unity; the many participate in One without losing distinctness. This coincidentia oppositorum appears across traditions and might reflect reality's organizational pattern rather than logical contradiction (Cusanus, 1453/1997).

11.7 CONCLUSION

Our investigation reveals that religious experience, despite significant epistemological challenges, potentially provides access to first principles complementing scientific and philosophical approaches. The phenomenology of the sacred reveals recurring patterns—transcendent presence, fundamental unity, consciousness transformation—that might indicate genuine features of reality accessed through religious awareness, though always mediated through human cognitive and cultural frameworks.

The finite-infinite relationship emerges as a particularly crucial principle bridging religious and philosophical approaches. Contemporary models— participation metaphysics, panentheism, process thought—offer ways of conceiving this relationship consonant with both religious experience and rational reflection. The convergence of insights from religious experience with developments in consciousness studies, quantum physics, and systems theory strengthens claims about religious experience's potential epistemic value.

Religious awareness appears to involve genuine human capacities for apprehending transcendent dimensions, whether understood as distinct faculties, emergent properties, or modes of consciousness. These capacities manifest differently across cultures yet point toward universal features of human consciousness connecting finite awareness to infinite depths. The first principles suggested—dimensional pluralism, relational ontology, unity-in-difference—extend rather than contradict scientific and philosophical insights, pointing toward reality's greater complexity than any single methodology can capture.

As we proceed to examine specific religious concepts of ultimate reality and creation, we carry forward these insights about the sacred as a genuine dimension of human experience and potentially of reality itself. Religious experience provides not proofs but pointers—indications of first principles inviting further investigation through all available approaches. The quest for comprehensive understanding requires integrating rather than choosing between empirical, rational, and religious methodologies.

CHAPTER 12: CREATION AND ULTIMATE GROUND

12.1 THE UNIVERSAL QUESTION OF ORIGINS

The interrogation of existence itself—why there is something rather than nothing—constitutes what Robert Nozick (1981) termed philosophy's most fundamental question, one that "subsumes all other questions". This inquiry transcends disciplinary boundaries, emerging at the intersection of metaphysics, cosmology, and theology as an irreducible feature of human consciousness confronting its own contingency. While contemporary physics has achieved remarkable success in describing cosmic evolution from Planck time (10^{-43} seconds) forward, it encounters what George Ellis (2007) identifies as an "ultimate limit" at the boundary conditions of existence itself.

The explanatory asymmetry between scientific and religious approaches to ultimate origins reflects not competitive inadequacy but complementary domains of inquiry. As Ian Barbour's (1997) critical realist framework demonstrates, science addresses questions of physical process through empirical methodology, while religion engages questions of ultimate meaning and ontological ground through integrative frameworks combining reason, experience, and revelation. This distinction, refined through centuries of philosophical analysis from Aquinas through Plantinga (2011), suggests that dismissing religious creation accounts as prescientific cosmology commits what Alfred North Whitehead (1925) called the "fallacy of misplaced concreteness"—mistaking one mode of abstraction for comprehensive reality.

Contemporary cosmological discoveries paradoxically both challenge and reinforce religious intuitions about creation. The quantum vacuum's seething virtual particles, as Lawrence Krauss (2012) provocatively argues, suggest that "nothing" in the classical philosophical sense may be physically impossible. Yet as David Albert (2012) counters in his critique of Krauss, quantum field states remain fundamentally something rather than nothing, possessing specific properties, obeying particular laws, and existing within spacetime frameworks. The persistence of this explanatory gap validates William Lane Craig's (2008) observation that "the universe's beginning cannot be scientifically explained since science presupposes the universe's existence".

Religious traditions approach this explanatory lacuna through what Paul Ricoeur (1969) termed "limit concepts"—symbolic frameworks that point beyond empirical description toward ultimate reality's ineffable ground. These creation narratives function not as proto-scientific hypotheses vulnerable to empirical falsification but as what Mircea Eliade (1957/1987) identified as "paradigmatic models" establishing cosmic order and meaning. Their truth claims operate at what Ian Ramsey (1957) called the "disclosure level"—revealing dimensions of reality inaccessible to purely empirical investigation.

The fine-tuning discoveries of contemporary cosmology have unexpectedly revitalized design arguments, though in forms more sophisticated than Paley's mechanical watchmaker. Robin Collins (2009) demonstrates that fundamental constants appear calibrated within extraordinarily narrow ranges, permitting complex chemistry and biological evolution—the cosmological constant, for instance, must be fine-tuned to one part in 10^{120}. While multiverse hypotheses offer potential naturalistic explanations, they remain, as George Ellis and Joe Silk (2014) argue, "fundamentally untestable and therefore philosophical rather than scientific". This epistemic situation suggests that ultimate explanations necessarily transcend empirical methodology, vindicating religious traditions' claims to address questions science cannot adjudicate.

12.2 CREATION NARRATIVES ACROSS TRADITIONS

12.2.1 The Abrahamic Model: Creation *Ex Nihilo*

The doctrine of *creatio ex nihilo* represents Abrahamic monotheism's distinctive contribution to metaphysical thought, establishing what Langdon Gilkey (1959) termed "the ontological foundation of biblical faith". This principle, while not explicitly articulated in Genesis's opening verses, emerged through patristic reflection as theologians like Irenaeus and Tertullian confronted Gnostic dualism's challenge (May, 1994). The doctrine's philosophical sophistication appears in its simultaneous affirmation of divine transcendence and creation's genuine reality, avoiding both emanationist pantheism's dissolution of finite existence and dualistic frameworks' limitation of divine sovereignty.

Contemporary biblical scholarship reveals Genesis 1's literary sophistication in establishing this metaphysical framework. Jon Levenson (1988) demonstrates how the text systematically subverts ancient Near Eastern chaos combat myths, presenting creation not as divine struggle against primordial forces but as sovereign speech-acts bringing ordered reality into existence. The repeated formula "And God said... and it was so" establishes what Gerhard von Rad (1972) identified as "creation through word"—a principle emphasizing both divine transcendence and creation's rational intelligibility.

Thomas Aquinas's systematic articulation of creation *ex nihilo* through the real distinction between essence and existence provides an enduring philosophical framework. In created beings, Aquinas argues, essence (what something is) remains distinct from existence (that it is), while in God alone essence and existence coincide as *ipsum esse subsistens* (subsistent being itself). This metaphysical architecture, as Etienne Gilson (1952) demonstrates, resolves the ancient problem of the one and many by establishing participation metaphysics where finite beings participate in divine being without compromising divine simplicity. Contemporary Thomists like Edward Feser (2014) argue that this framework remains philosophically superior to both process theology's limitation of divine perfection and modern naturalism's inability to explain contingent existence.

Islamic theology reinforces creation *ex nihilo* through sophisticated kalām arguments, particularly as developed by Al-Ghazali (1095/2000) and refined by contemporary philosophers like William Lane Craig (2008). The kalām cosmological argument's logical structure—everything that begins to exist has a cause; the universe began to exist; therefore, the universe has a cause—gains support from Big Bang cosmology and the Borde-Guth-Vilenkin theorem demonstrating spacetime's finitude (Borde et al., 2003). Islamic philosophers like Seyyed Hossein Nasr (2015) emphasize how the Qur'anic *kun fa-yakūn* formula establishes divine command theory's metaphysical foundation, where existence itself constitutes a divine speech-act.

Jewish philosophical tradition contributes distinctive insights through creative tension between Greek philosophical categories and biblical revelation. Maimonides's Guide of the Perplexed navigates between Aristotelian eternalism and scriptural creation by distinguishing logical from temporal priority. As Kenneth Seeskin (2005) explicates, Maimonides argues that even if the world were temporally eternal, it would remain ontologically dependent on God as a necessary being—a position anticipating contemporary discussions about whether Big Bang cosmology supports theistic arguments. The Kabbalistic tradition, particularly as developed in the Zohar and systematized by Isaac Luria, introduces tzimtzum (divine self-contraction) as explaining how infinite divine reality creates space for finite existence—a concept Paul Tillich (1957) recognized as addressing the fundamental paradox of creation.

Critics of creation *ex nihilo* raise substantial philosophical challenges requiring serious engagement. Adolf Grünbaum (1989) argues that the doctrine generates insoluble puzzles about temporal creation by an eternal being, while Quentin Smith (1988) contends that quantum cosmology eliminates the need for creative cause. J.L. Mackie (1982) presses the coherence problem: how can an immaterial being causally interact with material reality? Theistic responses, developed by philosophers like Richard Swinburne (2004) and Alexander Pruss (2006), invoke agent causation, divine conservation, and analogical predication to address these challenges, though debates remain vigorous.

12.2.2 Hindu Cosmology: Emanation and Cycles

Hindu cosmological thought presents fundamentally different first principles through emanationist and cyclical frameworks that dissolve sharp Creator-creation distinctions characterizing Abrahamic traditions. The

Vedic tradition's evolutionary sophistication appears in the Nasadiya Sukta's philosophical depth, which Max Müller (1899) praised as "the earliest philosophical composition of the Indo-European race". The hymn's progression from undifferentiated unity through desire (kāma) as creative principle to epistemic uncertainty about ultimate origins establishes what Wendy Doniger (1981) interprets as "theological humility before mystery".

The Sāṅkhya system, one of Hinduism's six orthodox philosophical schools, provides systematic metaphysics distinguishing puruṣa (consciousness) from prakṛti (primordial matter) as coeternal principles. This dualistic framework, as Gerald Larson (1979) demonstrates, offers a sophisticated analysis of consciousness-matter interaction without requiring external creator. Prakṛti's three guṇas (sattva, rajas, tamas) in dynamic equilibrium explain phenomenal diversity through their various combinations and transformations. Critics like Śaṅkara challenge Sāṅkhya's dualism as philosophically unstable, arguing that only non-dualistic monism adequately explains reality's unity (Deutsch & Dalvi, 2004).

Advaita Vedanta's non-dualism represents Hindu philosophy's most influential articulation of ultimate reality. Śaṅkara's commentary tradition establishes Brahman as saccidānanda through sophisticated epistemological arguments. The sublation (bādha) principle—where higher reality levels negate lower ones upon realization—provides a framework for understanding māyā's relationship to Brahman. As Eliot Deutsch (1969) explicates, māyā functions not as a simple illusion but as "Brahman's creative power viewed from an empirical standpoint". This preserves the phenomenal world's pragmatic reality (vyāvahārika satya) while maintaining ultimate reality's (pāramārthika satya) non-dual nature.

Contemporary neuroscience unexpectedly resonates with Advaitic insights about consciousness's fundamental nature. Giulio Tononi's Integrated Information Theory suggests consciousness as an intrinsic property of appropriately organized information (Tononi, 2008), while David Chalmers's (1995) "hard problem" demonstrates consciousness's irreducibility to physical processes. These developments lead some philosophers like Philip Goff (2019) toward cosmopsychism—the view that consciousness pervades reality—positions surprisingly consonant with Vedantic metaphysics.

Rāmānuja's Viśiṣṭādvaita (qualified non-dualism) offers an alternative framework preserving both unity and difference through body-soul analogy:

finite reality constitutes Brahman's body while remaining distinct. As John Carman (1974) demonstrates, this position maintains devotional theism's personal God while avoiding crude anthropomorphism. Sri Aurobindo's (1939/2005) integral philosophy synthesizes traditional Vedanta with evolutionary thought, proposing consciousness's evolution from matter through mind toward supramental realization—a framework engaging seriously with modern science while maintaining spiritual foundations.

12.2.3 Buddhist Perspectives: Dependent Origination

Buddhism's approach to ultimate origins radically departs from both theistic creation and emanationist frameworks through pratītyasamutpāda (dependent origination), which Richard Gombrich (2009) identifies as "the Buddha's most important philosophical contribution". This principle systematically deconstructs substantialist metaphysics by demonstrating all phenomena's radical interdependence, arising through a twelve-linked chain (dvādaśāṅga-pratītyasamutpāda) from ignorance through consciousness, name-and-form, sense contacts, feeling, craving, clinging, becoming, birth, to aging-and-death.

The Buddha's refusal to answer metaphysical questions about the cosmos's ultimate origin—the fourteen unanswerable questions (avyākata)—represents not agnosticism but what Steven Collins (1982) terms "systematic metaphysical critique". Questions about whether the universe is eternal or created, finite or infinite, are rejected as based on false presuppositions assuming substantial existence. The Majjhima Nikāya's Cūḷamāluṅkya Sutta employs the famous arrow parable: someone shot with a poisoned arrow who refuses treatment until learning the archer's caste, name, and bow type will die before obtaining answers—similarly, metaphysical speculation distracts from liberation's urgent task (Ñāṇamoli & Bodhi, 1995).

Nāgārjuna's Madhyamaka philosophy radicalizes dependent origination through śūnyatā (emptiness) doctrine, demonstrating through rigorous logical analysis that nothing possesses svabhāva (inherent existence or self-nature). The Mūlamadhyamakakārikā's tetralemma (catuṣkoṭi) systematically negates four logical possibilities: things neither exist, nor non-exist, nor both, nor neither—at least as substantive entities (Garfield, 1995). This represents not nihilism but what Mark Siderits (2007) calls "metaphysical anti-realism"—denial of ultimate facts about reality's fundamental nature.

Contemporary interpretations diverge regarding śūnyatā's implications. The Gelug tradition following Tsongkhapa maintains conventional reality's validity within the emptiness framework through Candrakīrti's conventional/ultimate truth distinction (Jinpa, 2002). Japanese Zen, particularly as articulated by Dōgen, emphasizes "mountains are mountains"—emptiness not negating phenomenal reality but revealing its nature (Kim, 2004). Western Buddhist philosophers like Jan Westerhoff (2009) argue that śūnyatā anticipates contemporary anti-foundationalist epistemology and structural realism in philosophy of science.

The Yogācāra school's consciousness-only (vijñapti-mātra) doctrine offers an alternative framework emphasizing consciousness's constitutive role without positing a permanent self. The ālaya-vijñāna (storehouse consciousness) concept explains karmic continuity and experiential coherence while maintaining the impermanence doctrine. Dan Lusthaus (2002) argues that Yogācāra represents phenomenological analysis rather than metaphysical idealism—examining how consciousness constructs experienced reality without claiming the external world's non-existence.

The tathāgatagarbha (Buddha-nature) tradition introduces quasi-substantialist elements that critics argue compromise the emptiness doctrine. Texts like the Tathāgatagarbha Sūtra and Ratnagotravibhāga describe inherent luminous awareness obscured by adventitious defilements. Contemporary scholars debate whether Buddha-nature represents expedient teaching (upāya) for those unable to accept emptiness's radical implications or genuine metaphysical doctrine about consciousness's ultimate nature (Zimmermann, 2002). The Chinese Huayan school's Indra's Net metaphor—infinite jewels each reflecting all others—provides a holographic model of reality's interpenetration that contemporary physicists like David Bohm (1980) find remarkably prescient.

12.2.4 Indigenous and African Traditions

Indigenous cosmologies worldwide contribute distinctive first principles through emergence narratives and vital force concepts deserving fuller philosophical engagement than typically accorded. These traditions, as Robin Wall Kimmerer (2013) argues, embody "indigenous ways of knowing" that complement Western scientific approaches through emphasis on relationship, reciprocity, and reverence.

Pueblo emergence accounts describe humanity's journey through multiple worlds, each representing consciousness's evolutionary stage. Alfonso Ortiz's (1969) analysis of Tewa cosmology reveals a sophisticated symbolic system where six directions (including the center) correspond to colors, seasons, and spiritual principles. The emergence through successive worlds represents not linear progress but spiral development, maintaining connection with previous stages. This multidimensional reality concept resonates unexpectedly with contemporary physics' multiple dimensions and parallel universes (Cajete, 1994).

Australian Aboriginal Dreamtime concepts present creation as an eternal present rather than a past event. As W.E.H. Stanner (1979) demonstrated, Dreamtime (Tjukurpa in Pitjantjatjara) represents "everywhen"—a temporal framework where linear time dissolves into eternal now containing past, present, and future simultaneously. This challenges Western philosophy's temporal assumptions, suggesting what Nancy Munn (1973) terms "topographic time"—where landscape features embody temporal events. Contemporary philosophers like Peter Forrest (2010) argue that Aboriginal metaphysics offers resources for understanding quantum mechanics' temporal paradoxes.

African philosophical traditions, enormously diverse across the continent, generally emphasize vital force or life energy as a fundamental principle. John Mbiti's (1990) comprehensive study identifies recurring themes: reality as fundamentally religious, pervasive spiritual forces, and emphasis on community, including ancestors. The Yoruba concept of àṣẹ— divine force flowing through all things—provides dynamic rather than substantial metaphysics. As Wande Abimbola (1976) explicates, àṣẹ represents "the absolute power that makes all things possible" without being separate from creation.

Bantu philosophy, as articulated by Placide Tempels (1959) and refined by Alexis Kagame (1976), centers on vital force (in Kinyarwanda, imana) hierarchically distributed through reality. Being means possessing force; to exist more fully means increased vital force. This dynamic ontology influences ethics, where actions either increase or diminish vital force for individuals and the community. Critics like Paulin Hountondji (1983) challenge "ethnophilosophy's" homogenizing tendencies, arguing for recognizing African philosophical diversity and critical traditions.

Contemporary African philosophers increasingly engage these

traditional concepts with global philosophical discourse. Mogobe Ramose's (2002) ubuntu philosophy—"a person is a person through other persons"—develops relational ontology, challenging Western individualism. Kwame Gyekye's (1995) moderate communitarianism synthesizes individual rights with communal values. These frameworks offer resources for addressing contemporary challenges from environmental ethics to artificial intelligence's social implications.

Native American traditions contribute process metaphysics, emphasizing relationships over substances. Vine Deloria Jr. (1973) contrasts Western metaphysics' spatial orientation with indigenous traditions' temporal focus: "American Indians hold their lands—places—as having the highest possible meaning, and all their statements are made with this reference point in mind". This place-based philosophy grounds ethics in reciprocal relationships with land and non-human beings, offering alternatives to anthropocentric environmental philosophy.

12.3 THE CONCEPT OF ULTIMATE REALITY

12.3.1 Absolute Being and the Ground of Existence

The philosophical investigation of ultimate reality—that which exists necessarily and grounds all contingent existence—represents metaphysics' central concern across cultures. Contemporary analytic philosophy's renewed interest in metaphysical questions, following decades of linguistic philosophy's dominance, returns to classical questions about being qua being that Aristotle initiated in his Metaphysics. The modal distinction between necessary and contingent existence, formalized through possible worlds semantics by Saul Kripke (1980) and David Lewis (1986), provides a rigorous framework for analyzing ultimate reality concepts.

The principle of sufficient reason (PSR), articulated by Leibniz (1714/1989) as "nothing happens without a reason why it should be so rather than otherwise", drives arguments toward the ultimate ground. Alexander Pruss (2006) defends PSR against Humean skepticism through careful modal analysis, arguing that PSR denial leads to radical skepticism about causation and inductive reasoning. The PSR generates what Robert Koons (1997) terms "cosmological argument from contingency"—the existence of any contingent being requires a necessary being as ultimate explanatory ground.

Contemporary debates about grounding and fundamentality provide new resources for understanding ultimate reality. Jonathan Schaffer's (2009) priority monism argues reality has a hierarchical structure with one fundamental entity grounding all else—a position remarkably consonant with classical theism and Advaitic monism. Kit Fine's (2001) work on ontological dependence distinguishes various dependence relations— existential, essential, and explanatory—clarifying how derivative entities relate to fundamental reality. These developments suggest convergence between analytic metaphysics and perennial philosophy's insights about reality's hierarchical structure.

12.3.2 Apophatic and Cataphatic Approaches

The epistemological challenge of conceptualizing ultimate reality generates two complementary theological methods. Apophatic (negative) theology, developed by Pseudo-Dionysius and Maximus the Confessor, approaches God through systematic negation of finite categories. Vladimir Lossky (1957) argues apophasis represents not agnosticism but recognition that ultimate reality transcends conceptual categories: "God is not essence, nor person, nor will... He is more than all that". This via negativa parallels Nāgārjuna's systematic negations and Śaṅkara's neti neti (not this, not that) method.

Cataphatic (positive) theology makes affirmative statements about ultimate reality through analogical predication. Aquinas's doctrine of analogy navigates between univocal predication (using terms identically for God and creatures) and equivocal predication (using terms completely differently). When saying "God is good," the term "good" applies neither identically to divine and human goodness nor completely differently, but analogically—similar while infinitely exceeding creaturely goodness (Rocca, 2004). This preserves meaningful theological discourse while respecting divine transcendence.

Contemporary philosophers like Denys Turner (2004) argue that authentic theology requires a dialectical relationship between cataphatic and apophatic approaches—affirmation requiring negation's corrective, negation presupposing affirmation's content. This dialectic appears across traditions: the Bhagavad Gītā describes Brahman as "neither being nor non-being" yet also as saccidānanda; the Dao De Jing opens with "The Dao that can be spoken is not the eternal Dao" while offering positive characterizations of the Dao's operations.

12.4 Divine Attributes And Logical Necessity

12.4.1 Classical Theistic Attributes

Perfect being theology, initiated by Anselm of Canterbury and systematized by subsequent philosophers, derives divine attributes from the concept of maximal greatness. Richard Swinburne (2016) provides a rigorous analysis of core attributes: omnipotence (maximal power), omniscience (maximal knowledge), perfect goodness (maximal moral perfection), eternality (existence at all times or timelessly), necessity (existence in all possible worlds), and simplicity (lacking parts or composition). These attributes generate philosophical puzzles requiring sophisticated analysis.

The omnipotence paradox—can God create a stone too heavy for God to lift?—receives various solutions. Thomas Flint and Alfred Freddoso (1983) argue that omnipotence means the ability to actualize any logically possible state of affairs consistent with God's nature. George Mavrodes (1963) demonstrates that the paradox involves pseudo-task like creating square circles. Contemporary discussions focus on whether omnipotence includes power over the past, the ability to sin, or the capacity for self-limitation.

12.4.2 Logical Arguments for Divine Attributes

Modal logic provides powerful tools for analyzing divine attributes' logical relationships. Alvin Plantinga's (1974) modal ontological argument demonstrates that if maximal greatness (including necessary existence) is possible, then it is actual—since a maximally great being must exist in all possible worlds, including the actual world. While the argument's soundness depends on maximal greatness's possibility, which critics contest, it clarifies conceptual connections between divine attributes.

Robert Adams (1987) argues that divine commands constitute moral obligations' foundation, grounding objective morality in God's necessarily good nature. This divine command theory avoids the Euthyphro dilemma by locating goodness in God's essential nature rather than arbitrary commands. Critics like Erik Wielenberg (2005) propose non-theistic moral realism, while theistic philosophers respond that moral properties' normative force requires personal ground.

12.5 EASTERN PERSPECTIVES: BEYOND PERSONAL DEITY

12.5.1 Brahman: Existence-Consciousness-Bliss

The Upanishadic characterization of Brahman as saccidānanda provides a sophisticated metaphysical framework transcending personality-impersonality dichotomies. Sat (existence/being) designates Brahman as reality's ground; cit (consciousness/awareness) identifies Brahman with consciousness itself rather than unconscious substance; ānanda (bliss/fullness) indicates Brahman's self-sufficient completeness requiring nothing external. This triadic characterization, as Anantanand Rambachan (2006) demonstrates, emerges through philosophical analysis rather than mystical speculation, representing reasoned conclusions about ultimate reality's necessary features.

12.5.2 The Dao: The Nameless Source

Daoist philosophy contributes distinctive insights through the Dao concept—simultaneously source, pattern, and process of reality. The Dao De Jing's opening lines establish the Dao's ineffability while providing substantive characterizations: empty yet inexhaustible, still yet ever-moving, preceding heaven and earth yet not transcendent in the Western theistic sense. Contemporary scholars like Roger Ames and David Hall (2003) interpret the Dao through process philosophy, emphasizing creative transformation over static being. This resonates with Whitehead's process metaphysics and offers resources for dialogue between Eastern and Western philosophy.

12.6 SYNTHESIS: CONVERGENT INSIGHTS AND CRITICAL CHALLENGES

The comparative analysis reveals remarkable convergences alongside irreducible differences. Most traditions recognize: (1) contingent reality's dependence on necessary ground; (2) ultimate reality's transcendence of ordinary conceptual categories; (3) consciousness or awareness as fundamental rather than emergent; (4) value or purpose as intrinsic to reality rather than projected; (5) the inadequacy of purely material explanations for existence itself.

These convergences suggest what John Hick (1989) terms "the Real"— ultimate reality diversely experienced through different cultural-religious lenses. Critics like Gavin D'Costa (1990) argue that this pluralistic hypothesis undermines traditions' truth claims, reducing them to cultural constructs. The challenge involves maintaining both traditions' distinctive insights and recognizing convergent patterns pointing toward shared truth.

12.7 IMPLICATIONS FOR FIRST PRINCIPLES

12.7.1 The Principle of Sufficient Reason

Creation accounts across traditions implicitly affirm that contingent existence requires explanation, whether through divine creation, emanation, or dependent origination. This suggests the PSR's universality as a rational principle, though its application differs across frameworks.

12.7.2 The Principle of Plenitude

Many traditions suggest reality manifests maximal diversity within unity— creation expressing divine creativity's fullness, Brahman's līlā (divine play) generating phenomenal multiplicity, the Dao's productions being inexhaustible. This plenitude principle appears in contemporary discussions about modal realism and multiverse theories.

12.7.3 The Principle of Participation

The relationship between ultimate ground and contingent reality frequently involves participation metaphysics—creatures participating in divine being, phenomena manifesting Brahman, particular dao embodying universal Dao. This participation framework offers alternatives to both reductive materialism and substance dualism.

12.8 CONCLUSION

Investigation of creation narratives and ultimate ground concepts reveals not primitive cosmologies superseded by scientific advance but sophisticated metaphysical frameworks addressing questions beyond empirical methodology's scope. The convergences identified—recognition of contingency, affirmation of consciousness's fundamentality, commitment to reality's intelligibility and value-ladenness—suggest a possible synthetic framework honoring both scientific discoveries and religious insights.

The persistence of ultimate "why" questions despite scientific progress validates religious traditions' continued relevance for comprehensive understanding. As cosmologist Paul Davies (2006) acknowledges, "Science can explain how the universe evolved from the first fraction of a second, but it cannot explain why there is a universe at all". This explanatory gap points toward mystery at reality's heart—a mystery that religious traditions engage through symbol, ritual, and contemplative practice alongside philosophical reflection.

The dialogue between scientific cosmology and religious creation accounts need not involve conflict but can generate mutual enrichment. Science provides an increasingly detailed understanding of cosmic evolution's mechanisms; religion offers frameworks for understanding existence's meaning and purpose. Together they contribute to humanity's ongoing quest to comprehend our place in the cosmos—a quest that itself may constitute participation in the creative process underlying all reality.

CHAPTER 13: REVELATION AND AUTHORITY

13.1 INTRODUCTION: THE EPISTEMOLOGICAL CHALLENGE

The epistemological architecture of religious knowledge confronts a fundamental paradox that defines the boundaries of human cognition. If ultimate reality transcends empirical observation and rational demonstration—as religious traditions consistently maintain—then the question of epistemic access becomes paramount. This challenge extends beyond methodological curiosity to address whether transcendent dimensions of reality remain cognitively accessible through any legitimate means (Alston, 1991; Plantinga, 2000).

The concept of revelation proposes a distinctive epistemic pathway that claims to bridge the ontological gap between finite consciousness and infinite reality. As Swinburne (2007) articulates, revelation constitutes "a communication from God which tells us things of deep importance for our salvation which we could not discover for ourselves". While this definition reflects specifically theistic assumptions, it captures the universal religious claim that certain fundamental truths about reality's ultimate structure require disclosure from transcendent sources rather than human discovery through empirical or rational investigation.

Contemporary epistemology of revelation faces unprecedented challenges from multiple directions. Scientific naturalism questions the coherence of supernatural causation within a causally closed physical universe (Kim, 2005). Religious pluralism problematizes exclusive revelatory claims when multiple traditions assert contradictory truths with equal conviction (Hick, 1989). Critical hermeneutics demonstrates interpretation's cultural conditioning, challenging assumptions about objective textual meaning (Gadamer, 2004). Cognitive science offers naturalistic explanations for religious experience previously attributed to divine causation (Boyer, 2001).

These challenges demand systematic philosophical analysis that neither dismisses revelation through reductive naturalism nor accepts it through uncritical fideism. The investigation must examine revelation's phenomenological structure, epistemological status, hermeneutical complexity, and practical implications while maintaining methodological rigor appropriate to the subject matter's distinctive characteristics.

13.2 THE NATURE OF REVELATION

13.2.1 Defining Revelation Across Traditions

Revelation's conceptual architecture varies significantly across religious traditions, reflecting diverse metaphysical frameworks and anthropological assumptions about human cognitive capacities and divine-human interaction. These variations require careful phenomenological analysis to identify both convergent patterns and irreducible differences.

Within Abrahamic traditions, revelation typically involves propositional content communicated through prophetic mediation and preserved in authoritative texts. Islamic theology develops sophisticated taxonomies distinguishing *wahy* (direct prophetic inspiration), *tanzil* (descent of revelation from the divine realm), and *ilham* (general spiritual guidance) (Rahman, 1979). The Qur'anic concept of revelation emphasizes both divine transcendence and linguistic accommodation, as Rahman (1979) notes: "The Qur'an is entirely the Word of God and, in an ordinary sense, also entirely the word of Muhammad".

Christian theological reflection articulates multiple modalities of divine self-disclosure. Barth's (2004) neo-orthodox framework distinguishes three forms: Jesus Christ as revealed Word (das offenbarte Wort Gottes), scripture as written Word (das geschriebene Wort Gottes), and proclamation as declared Word (das gepredigte Wort Gottes). This triadic structure emphasizes revelation's event-character rather than static propositional content, addressing concerns about textual fundamentalism while maintaining divine sovereignty.

Eastern religious epistemologies often emphasize non-propositional disclosure through contemplative realization. Hindu distinction between śruti (heard revelation) and smṛti (remembered tradition) establishes hierarchical authority structures, with Vedic texts possessing apauruṣeya status—existing without human authorship (Flood, 1996). As Flood (1996) clarifies, "Śruti is revelation, not in the sense of a truth or proposition revealed, but in the sense of an audition of the eternal sound".

Buddhist epistemology frames revelation as discovery rather than reception, with the Buddha's enlightenment uncovering universal principles (dharma) accessible through proper methodology. This framework shifts emphasis from external divine communication to internal realization, though maintaining careful lineage transmission (paramparā) to ensure interpretive authenticity (Harvey, 2013).

Contemporary comparative analysis increasingly recognizes functional similarities beneath surface variations. Smith's (1993) influential study demonstrates that "scripture" constitutes a relational category defined through communal use rather than intrinsic textual properties, suggesting that revelation involves complex socio-cognitive processes transcending simple communication models.

13.2.2 Modes of Revelatory Communication

Religious phenomenology identifies multiple channels through which revelatory disclosure occurs, each presenting distinctive epistemological challenges requiring systematic analysis.

Direct theophany represents immediate divine manifestation, overwhelming normal consciousness. Biblical accounts—Moses at Sinai (Exodus 3), Isaiah's temple vision (Isaiah 6), Ezekiel's merkabah (Ezekiel 1)—parallel Hindu descriptions of Krishna's cosmic form (viśvarūpa) in the Bhagavad Gītā (11.5-55). Otto's (1958) phenomenological analysis identifies the *mysterium tremendum et fascinans* as characteristic of authentic numinous encounter, combining overwhelming power with irresistible attraction.

Contemporary neuroscientific research provides naturalistic correlates without necessarily eliminating transcendent causation. Newberg and d'Aquili (2001) document specific neural patterns during mystical states, while Hood, Hill, and Spilka (2009) confirm cross-cultural phenomenological commonalities through empirical measurement. These findings raise complex questions about the relationship between neurological processes and potential transcendent realities.

Prophetic inspiration involves divine communication through specially chosen individuals who receive and transmit messages for communal benefit. The Hebrew dabar Yahweh (word of the Lord) and Islamic *wahy* through angelic mediation represent paradigmatic cases. Contemporary analysis must address Hume's (1748/2007) evidential challenges while considering Swinburne's (2004) Bayesian reformulation that incorporates background beliefs about divine existence and purposes.

Dreams and visions constitute altered-state revelations appearing consistently across traditions. Bulkeley's (2008) cross-cultural research documents structural similarities in visionary dreams while acknowledging distinctive cultural elaborations. Contemporary sleep research and neuroimaging provide an increasingly sophisticated understanding of dream phenomenology without resolving ontological questions about potential transcendent content.

Inner illumination claims direct spiritual insight without sensory mediation. Christian mystical tradition describes infused contemplation, Sufi *kashf* (unveiling), and Zen satori as immediate awareness of ultimate reality. Wallace's (2007) contemplative science methodology attempts rigorous investigation of such claims through trained introspection and intersubjective validation.

Natural revelation proposes divine disclosure through creation itself. The contemporary fine-tuning argument, articulated by Collins (2009) through Bayesian analysis, suggests that physical constants' precise values indicate design rather than chance. However, multiverse hypotheses and observer selection effects provide alternative explanations requiring careful philosophical evaluation (Lewis & Barnes, 2016).

13.2.3 The Problem of Recognition and Validation

Establishing criteria for distinguishing genuine revelation from psychological projection, cultural construction, or deliberate deception presents formidable epistemological challenges that have generated diverse philosophical responses.

James's (1902/2002) empirical approach identifies four phenomenological markers: ineffability, noetic quality, transiency, and passivity. While providing useful descriptive categories, these characteristics appear in various altered states, making divine attribution problematic. Katz's (1978) constructivist critique argues that all religious experience is culturally mediated, challenging claims to uninterpreted divine encounter.

The pragmatic criterion examines revelation's moral and spiritual fruits rather than origins. This approach, traceable to Matthew 7:16, avoids some epistemological difficulties while raising questions about circular reasoning and the relationship between utility and truth (Alston, 1991).

Contemporary virtue epistemology offers promising frameworks through emphasis on intellectual virtues, enabling an appropriate response to transcendent reality. Zagzebski's (2012) analysis treats faith as exercising epistemic virtues, including intellectual courage, humility, and trust that enable knowledge acquisition in conditions of uncertainty.

13.3 SCRIPTURE AS REVELATION

13.3.1 The Formation of Sacred Texts

The transformation of oral revelation into written scripture involves complex historical processes illuminating the relationship between divine inspiration and human mediation. Contemporary biblical scholarship demonstrates textual formation's complexity while raising questions about authority and interpretation.

The Documentary Hypothesis, despite ongoing refinements, reveals the Hebrew Bible's compositional complexity through the identification of multiple sources and redactional layers (Baden, 2012). Kugel's (2007) analysis emphasizes interpretive implications: "The Bible is a fundamentally cryptic document" requiring sophisticated hermeneutical engagement.

New Testament formation involved preserving Jesus' traditions, collecting apostolic correspondence, and establishing canonical boundaries through complex ecclesiastical processes. Metzger's (1987) comprehensive analysis documents criteria including apostolic authorization, orthodox content, liturgical use, and ecclesiastical reception.

The Qur'an's distinctive claim to direct divine speech raises different questions about textual formation and preservation. Neuwirth's (2010) analysis emphasizes understanding the Qur'an as liturgical performance emerging through dialogue with its original audience, while the science of qira'āt preserves controlled textual variation within established parameters.

13.3.2 Canonization and Authority

Canonical formation reveals complex interactions between divine inspiration and human recognition, challenging simplistic models of scriptural authority.

Jewish canonization occurred gradually through communal use and rabbinic deliberation, with the tripartite structure (Torah, Nevi'im, Ketuvim) reflecting decreasing authority levels. Halbertal's (1997) analysis demonstrates how communities balance innovation and conservation through sophisticated hermeneutical strategies.

Christian canonical diversity—with Catholic, Orthodox, and Protestant variations—suggests that canonical boundaries involve theological judgment rather than self-evident divine demarcation. Wright's (2005) dynamic model treats scripture as a living voice requiring ongoing interpretive engagement rather than a static propositional repository.

Protestant *sola scriptura* faces challenges from historical consciousness and hermeneutical theory. Gregory's (2012) historical analysis argues that the Reformation's unintended consequence was interpretive fragmentation, undermining the scriptural authority it sought to preserve.

13.3.3 Interpretation and Hermeneutics

Even divinely inspired texts require human interpretation, introducing epistemological complexity that has generated sophisticated hermeneutical theories across traditions.

Jewish PaRDeS methodology acknowledges multiple semantic levels operating simultaneously, while Christian development from patristic allegory through medieval fourfold sense to modern historical-critical methods reveals evolving interpretive sophistication (de Lubac, 1998).

Islamic distinction between *tafsir* (traditional exegesis) and *ta'wil* (rational interpretation) parallels tensions in other traditions between authority and innovation. Contemporary Quranic hermeneutics engages modern linguistics and literary theory while maintaining traditional frameworks (Esack, 2005).

Gadamer's (2004) philosophical hermeneutics describes meaning emerging through "fusion of horizons" between text and interpreter, challenging objectivist assumptions while avoiding complete relativism. Ricoeur's (1976) dialectical approach balances critical suspicion with constructive retrieval.

Feminist hermeneutics reveals patriarchal assumptions shaping traditional interpretation. Schüssler Fiorenza's (1983) methodology combines suspicion toward androcentric bias with creative reconstruction of suppressed voices. Postcolonial criticism demonstrates interpretation's political dimensions through analysis of missionary hermeneutics and indigenous resistance (Sugirtharajah, 2001).

13.4 TRADITION AND TRANSMISSION

13.4.1 Oral Tradition and Living Memory

Oral preservation involves sophisticated processes, maintaining continuity while enabling adaptation. Vedic tradition's elaborate mnemonic techniques achieved remarkable accuracy across millennia, challenging assumptions about literacy's superiority (Scharfe, 2002).

Vansina's (1985) pioneering research demonstrates oral tradition's reliability and distinctive characteristics, preserving essential content while allowing formal variation. Jewish distinction between Written and Oral Torah establishes complementary rather than competing authorities, with the Mishnaic chain (shalshelet ha-qabbalah) legitimizing rabbinic interpretation through apostolic succession.

Islamic hadith criticism developed rigorous methodologies for evaluating transmission chains (*isnad*) that rival contemporary historical methods. Brown's (2014) analysis shows how hadith transmission combined oral and written elements within pedagogical relationships.

Indigenous traditions emphasize orality's relational and performative dimensions. Momaday's (1997) analysis highlights how oral transmission embeds knowledge within lived relationships rather than abstracting it into textual form.

13.4.2 Apostolic Succession and Transmission Lines

Religious traditions maintain authorized transmission through recognized lineages, ensuring doctrinal and spiritual authenticity across generations.

Catholic and Orthodox apostolic succession claims unbroken episcopal continuity from the apostles, guaranteeing teaching authority and sacramental validity. The Lima Document (World Council of Churches, 1982) represents ecumenical convergence while acknowledging interpretive differences.

Tibetan Buddhist lineage (brgyud pa) involves lung (textual transmission), tri (explanation), and wang (empowerment), ensuring texts receive proper interpretation and realization rather than merely academic study. The tulku system attempts to preserve spiritual realization across incarnations, reflecting convictions about consciousness continuity (Ray, 2001).

Sufi *silsilah* maintains spiritual genealogies transmitting *baraka* (blessing) and *ma'rifa* (gnosis) through personal relationships. Chittick (2000) emphasizes that authentic spiritual knowledge requires direct transmission beyond textual study.

13.4.3 The Role of Community

Religious communities serve as matrices for receiving, preserving, interpreting, and applying revelation, challenging individualistic assumptions about religious knowledge.

Jewish torah lishmah (study for its own sake) treats communal interpretation as continuing revelation. The Talmudic validation of machloket l'shem shamayim (argument for heaven's sake) preserves interpretive pluralism within unity (Hartman, 1997).

Catholic theology since Vatican II articulates a dynamic understanding through Dei Verbum's integration of scripture and tradition within the ecclesial community guided by the Spirit (Second Vatican Council, 1965). Orthodox sobornost emphasizes conciliar wisdom over hierarchical decree (Zizioulas, 1985).

Protestant communities function as interpretive authorities despite formal commitment to sola scriptura. Fish's (1980) concept of "interpretive communities" illuminates how communal practices shape textual meaning.

Islamic *ijma'* (consensus) makes community agreement authoritative alongside the Qur'an and sunnah. Jackson's (2002) analysis shows how consensus accommodates change while maintaining continuity.

13.5 NATURAL THEOLOGY: REASON'S REACH

13.5.1 Classical Arguments for Divine Existence

Natural theology attempts to establish religious truths through reason alone, potentially providing universal first principles about ultimate reality.

Aquinas's Five Ways argue from empirical observations to divine existence, with cumulative strength exceeding individual demonstrations. Davies (2004) clarifies that these establish philosophical conclusions about the universe's cause rather than proving the biblical God.

The kalām cosmological argument, revived by Craig (2009), argues from temporal beginning to personal creator. Contemporary cosmology provides empirical support through Big Bang theory and the Borde-Guth-Vilenkin theorem (2003), though multiverse theories offer alternative explanations.

Fine-tuning arguments employ Bayesian analysis, suggesting design over chance. Collins (2009) calculates vastly higher probability given theism than naturalism, though Stenger (2011) challenges specific calculations.

Swinburne's (2004) cumulative case uses Bayesian methodology to argue that total evidence makes theism more probable than naturalism, avoiding reliance on single arguments.

13.5.2 The Limits of Natural Reason

Natural theology faces fundamental criticisms questioning reason's capacity to reach transcendent reality.

Kant's (1781/1998) critical philosophy demonstrated that theoretical reason cannot legitimately apply phenomenal categories to noumenal reality, though practical reason requires God as a moral postulate. Contemporary neo-Kantian approaches continue to develop these insights through emphasis on theology's constructive character (Kaufman, 1993).

Kierkegaard's (1992) "infinite qualitative distinction" makes rational divine knowledge impossible rather than difficult, requiring passionate subjective appropriation transcending objective reasoning.

Al-Ghazali's (1095/2000) critique argued that philosophical reasoning produces contradictions when applied to ultimate questions, locating certainty in direct spiritual experience (*dhawq*) through contemplative practice.

Pascal's (1995) practical approach shifts from theoretical proof to decision under uncertainty, though religious diversity complicates the wager's application.

13.5.3 Reformed Epistemology

Plantinga's (2000) reformed epistemology argues that theistic belief can be properly basic—justified without inferential support—through the *sensus divinitatis*, an innate cognitive faculty for perceiving divine reality.

Critics raise the "Great Pumpkin objection" about arbitrary beliefs and religious diversity challenges. Plantinga responds that proper basicality requires appropriate circumstances, reliable faculties, and the absence of defeaters.

Wolterstorff (1976) extends this approach, arguing that religious believers are rationally justified without arguments for divine existence. Contemporary virtue epistemology provides additional support through emphasis on intellectual virtues enabling appropriate response to transcendent reality (Zagzebski, 2012).

13.6 REVEALED THEOLOGY: BEYOND REASON'S GRASP

13.6.1 The Content of Revelation

Revealed theology encompasses truths exceeding natural reason's capacity—Aquinas's *mysteria fidei* that transcend without contradicting rational understanding.

Christian doctrine includes the Trinity, the Incarnation, and eschatological fulfillment that stretch conceptual categories. Contemporary Trinitarian theology emphasizes divine relationality's implications for understanding personhood and community (Coakley, 2013; LaCugna, 1991).

Islamic distinction between rational (*'aql*) and revealed (*naql*) knowledge recognizes truths requiring prophetic disclosure. The Qur'an's inimitability (*i'jāz*) serves as a validating miracle while debates continue about reconciling revelation with modern knowledge (Nasr, 2015).

Hindu śruti discloses dharma unavailable through ordinary perception or inference. Different schools debate whether Vedic injunctions represent eternal truths or divine commands while agreeing on revelation's necessity (Clooney, 1990).

Rahner's (1978) "supernatural existential" explains how finite beings receive infinite truth through obediential potency actualized by grace rather than natural capacity.

13.6.2 The Grammar of Faith

Faith involves complex cognitive, volitional, and affective processes, distinguishing religious from theoretical knowledge.

Aquinas defined faith as intellectual assent commanded by will moved by grace, preserving rational character while acknowledging divine dependence. Newman's (1870) "illative sense" describes convergent probabilities producing certitude exceeding logical demonstration.

Contemporary virtue epistemology treats faith as an intellectual virtue enabling an appropriate response to transcendent reality. Zagzebski (1996) identifies constituent virtues including courage, perseverance, and humility.

Tillich's (1957) dynamic understanding treats doubt as faith's internal element rather than its opposite, recognizing faith's existential character as an ongoing relationship with mystery.

13.6.3 Miracles and Signs

Miracles serve as validating signs while raising complex questions about evidential value and natural law.

Hume's (1748/2007) critique establishes formidable evidential barriers through prior improbability arguments. Swinburne's (2003) Bayesian response shows that background beliefs significantly affect probability assessments.

Holland's (1965) distinction between violation and coincidence miracles preserves religious significance without requiring supernatural causation. Contemporary discussion engages quantum indeterminacy and chaos theory as potential frameworks for divine action (Russell, Murphy, & Peacocke, 1995).

Islamic *mu'jizāt* (prophetic miracles) differ from *karāmāt* (saintly miracles), with the Qur'an's literary miracle remaining perpetually accessible for evaluation (al-Baqillani, 1013/2003).

13.7 THE FAITH-REASON SYNTHESIS

13.7.1 Historical Approaches

Various synthetic approaches attempt to preserve both revelation's authority and rational inquiry's legitimacy.

Augustine's *fides quaerens intellectum* makes faith the starting point enabling rational exploration. His divine illumination theory explains eternal truth through participation in divine light (Augustine, 397/1991).

Aquinas distinguished naturally accessible truths (*praeambula fidei*) from revealed mysteries (*articuli fidei*), with grace perfecting rather than destroying nature. This enables natural and revealed theology without competitive conflict (Aquinas, 1265/1981).

Islamic tradition developed sophisticated approaches through Mu'tazila rationalism, Ash'ari synthesis, and al-Ghazali's integration of philosophy, theology, and mysticism. These debates continue shaping contemporary Islamic thought (Leaman, 2009).

Maimonides navigated Aristotelian philosophy while maintaining biblical authority, using negative theology to preserve divine transcendence within rational discourse (Maimonides, 1963).

13.7.2 Modern Challenges and Responses

The Enlightenment elevation of autonomous reason challenged traditional syntheses, generating new approaches.

Kant (1781/1998) restricted theoretical knowledge to phenomena while establishing practical foundations for rational faith through moral postulates. Neo-Kantian theology emphasizes religious language's regulative rather than constitutive character (Kaufman, 1993).

Liberal Protestant theology relocated religion's essence to experience—Schleiermacher's (1999) "feeling of absolute dependence"—avoiding conflict with scientific reason while risking subjectivization.

Neo-orthodox theology rejected anthropocentric starting points while maintaining sophisticated rational engagement. Barth (2004) insisted on revelation's priority while employing elaborate argumentation.

Process theology seeks comprehensive integration through metaphysical innovation, preserving divine action and natural causation through dipolar theism (Hartshorne, 1984).

13.7.3 Contemporary Integration

Current approaches seek new syntheses transcending traditional dichotomies.

Critical realism acknowledges reality's stratified character, requiring different methodologies. Barbour (1997) and McGrath (2004) apply this framework to theology, treating science and religion as complementary investigations.

Murphy's (1990) postfoundationalist approach treats religious traditions as research programs evaluable through criteria including coherence, scope, and fruitfulness.

Polkinghorne's (1998) "binocular vision" integrates scientific and religious perspectives through recognition of complementary questions. Recent developments in fine-tuning, information theory, and consciousness studies suggest areas for dialogue.

Panikkar's (1993) "cosmotheandric vision" attempts radical integration through "dialogical dialogue" that transforms participants while maintaining distinctive identities.

13.8 AUTHORITY AND INTERPRETATION

13.8.1 Institutional Authority

Religious institutions claim various interpretive authorities, generating ongoing controversies about foundation, scope, and limitations.

The Catholic magisterium claims infallibility when teaching *ex cathedra* on faith and morals through apostolic succession. Vatican II nuanced this through emphasis on *sensus fidei* and collegiality while preserving papal primacy (Second Vatican Council, 1964).

Orthodox sobornost locates authority in conciliar consensus guided by the Spirit rather than hierarchical decree, though facing practical challenges from nationalism and jurisdictional disputes (Ware, 1993).

Protestant *sola scriptura* formally locates authority in biblical text, though interpretive communities function as practical authorities. Gregory (2012) argues that the resulting fragmentation undermined intended scriptural authority.

Islamic authority operates through scholarly consensus and interpretive tradition rather than formal hierarchy, with contemporary debates about renewed *ijtihād* for modern contexts (Hallaq, 2009).

13.8.2 Charismatic Authority and Innovation

Charismatic individuals claim direct divine authorization, potentially challenging established structures.

Weber's (1978) analysis distinguishes charismatic from traditional and legal-rational authority, noting tendencies toward routinization. Prophetic authority throughout history involves direct divine communication, bypassing religious establishments.

Contemporary movements emphasize direct spiritual experience, challenging institutional authority. Evaluating claims remains problematic given the lack of agreed criteria and the possibility of genuine renewal appearing as deviation (Csordas, 1997).

13.8.3 Interpretive Pluralism and Authority

Contemporary hermeneutics reveals interpretation's political dimensions and social location's significance.

Feminist hermeneutics demonstrates patriarchal assumptions shaping interpretation. Schüssler Fiorenza's (1983) methodology combines critical suspicion with creative reconstruction.

Liberation theology reads scripture from oppressed perspectives, discovering overlooked justice themes. Gutiérrez (1988) argues for the poor's epistemological privilege in biblical interpretation.

Postcolonial criticism reveals colonial contexts shaping missionary interpretation and indigenous resistance (Sugirtharajah, 2001). African theologians develop contextual interpretation honoring both biblical authority and cultural wisdom (Bediako, 1995).

Tracy (1981) seeks correlation between texts and experience while acknowledging plurality. Frei (1974) defends traditional reading's normativity while recognizing other approaches' legitimacy.

13.9 SYNTHESIS: REVELATION AS FIRST PRINCIPLE

Systematic investigation yields several fundamental principles transcending particular traditions while respecting distinctive characteristics.

The Principle of Divine Communication suggests that ultimate reality possesses communicative capacity rather than remaining mute. Convergence across traditions indicates that meaning represents fundamental rather than accidental features of reality. Information-theoretic approaches in physics and biology provide potential scientific support (Davies & Gregersen, 2010).

The Principle of Epistemic Humility recognizes finite reason's limitations in comprehending ultimate reality, necessitating receptive openness while maintaining rational engagement. This tempers both rationalistic hubris and fideistic anti-intellectualism.

The Principle of Mediated Immediacy addresses how infinite truth accommodates finite reception through human mediation without compromising transcendent character. Incarnational logic appears across traditions, suggesting participatory communication.

The Principle of Transformative Knowledge indicates authentic religious knowledge produces existential transformation rather than merely theoretical information, explaining the emphasis on practice and community participation.

The Principle of Ongoing Disclosure recognizes that while foundational revelation may be complete, interpretive application continues generating new insights. This enables continuity and development within traditions.

The Principle of Communal Discernment emphasizes revelation's communal character for reception, preservation, and application. The dialectical relationship between the individual and community prevents both anarchic individualism and oppressive institutionalism.

These principles suggest that revelation addresses fundamental human conditions—finite beings seeking infinite truth, temporal creatures yearning for eternal meaning. Whether accepting specific claims, the phenomenon reveals important insights about human orientation toward transcendence and meaningful communication between finite and infinite reality dimensions.

Contemporary engagement with pluralism, secularization, and scientific worldviews makes revelation's role in providing foundational assumptions increasingly apparent. Investigation requires serious engagement with revelatory traditions' insights while maintaining a critical assessment of cognitive contents and practical implications.

CHAPTER 14: MORAL FIRST PRINCIPLES

14.1 THE MORAL DIMENSION OF REALITY: FOUNDATIONAL QUESTIONS

The ontological status of morality represents one of philosophy's most consequential inquiries, determining whether moral principles constitute genuine first principles about reality's fundamental structure or require reduction to non-moral phenomena. This investigation bears directly on the central thesis of this work: that first principles emerge through convergent insights across empirical, rational, and revelatory domains, revealing a participatory reality that transcends reductive materialism.

Religious traditions consistently maintain morality's objective grounding in transcendent sources. The Hebrew conception of humans created b'tselem Elohim establishes inherent dignity as ontologically basic rather than socially constructed (Genesis 1:27). As Levenson (2004) demonstrates, this theological anthropology grounds universal moral obligations that transcend cultural particularity. Islamic articulation of fitrah—the primordial human nature oriented toward moral truth—suggests innate moral knowledge susceptible to corruption through environmental factors (Mohamed, 2016). The Qur'anic declaration "We have honored the children of Adam" (17:70) establishes human dignity as divinely ordained rather than conventionally assigned.

Hindu dharma encompasses both eternal principles (sanatana dharma) and contextual applications (svadharma), suggesting moral truth that transcends circumstances while requiring practical wisdom (Sharma, 2000). As Perrett (2016) analyzes, this framework navigates between absolutism and relativism through a sophisticated understanding of moral complexity. Buddhist ethics locates moral requirements within pratityasamutpada (dependent origination), making ethical causation inseparable from metaphysical truth about reality's interconnected nature (Goodman, 2017).

Contemporary challenges emerge from multiple disciplinary perspectives. Evolutionary psychology interprets moral intuitions as fitness-enhancing adaptations rather than truth-tracking capacities (Joyce, 2006). Neuroscientific research localizes moral judgments in specific brain regions, suggesting neurobiological rather than metaphysical foundations (Greene, 2013). Cultural anthropology documents extensive moral diversity, from honor-based vendetta systems to pacific societies rejecting violence, challenging universal moral truth claims (Prinz, 2007).

This chapter examines whether objective moral values exist as genuine features of reality, analyzes diverse sources of moral knowledge, investigates cross-cultural moral patterns, and explores the relationship between agency and responsibility. The analysis reveals that morality's status as a first principle depends fundamentally on broader metaphysical commitments regarding consciousness, personhood, and reality's axiological structure.

14.2 THE OBJECTIVITY DEBATE: REALISM AND ITS CRITICS

14.2.1 The Case for Moral Realism

Moral realism maintains that moral facts exist independently of human beliefs, desires, or conventions—a position with profound implications for morality's status as a first principle. Contemporary defenses employ sophisticated philosophical arguments while engaging empirical challenges from evolutionary biology and neuroscience.

Shafer-Landau's (2003) systematic defense addresses standard objections through multiple argumentative strategies. The phenomenological argument emphasizes that moral experience presents itself as discovery rather than invention: "When we judge that slavery is wrong, we take ourselves to be recognizing a moral fact, not creating one". The categoricity of moral requirements—their application regardless of agent desires—

supports objectivist over subjectivist interpretations. Furthermore, moral progress appears conceptually coherent only given objective standards against which change can be measured.

Enoch's (2011) influential defense employs the deliberative indispensability argument. Rational deliberation presupposes that some alternatives are objectively better than others, making moral realism a precondition for practical reasoning itself. As Enoch argues, "The project of deliberation... commits us to there being facts that count in favor of some alternatives over others". This transcendental argument grounds moral realism in the structure of agency rather than controversial metaphysical claims.

Cuneo's (2007) companions-in-guilt strategy argues that moral and epistemic facts stand or fall together. Epistemic facts about what we ought to believe share the same problematic features as moral facts—categoricity, normativity, and stance-independence. Since epistemic anti-realism leads to self-refutation (claiming we ought not believe in oughts), we must accept both epistemic and moral realism or face global normative skepticism.

Contemporary naturalistic moral realism, developed by Boyd (1988), Brink (1989), and Sturgeon (1985), identifies moral properties with complex natural properties discoverable through empirical investigation. Moral properties supervene on natural properties with nomological necessity, avoiding Mackie's (1977) charge of metaphysical queerness. As Brink (1989) argues, "Moral facts are constituted by natural facts and moral properties are realized by natural properties".

14.2.2 Evolutionary and Neurobiological Challenges

Evolutionary debunking arguments pose fundamental challenges to moral realism by explaining moral beliefs through fitness-enhancing mechanisms rather than truth-tracking processes. These arguments have generated extensive philosophical debate about the relationship between genealogy and justification.

Street's (2006) Darwinian Dilemma presents the challenge starkly: either moral realists accept that evolutionary forces shaped moral beliefs (undermining their reliability) or deny evolutionary influence (contradicting scientific evidence). The coincidence of evolutionarily advantageous beliefs with independent moral truths would require extraordinary luck lacking principled explanation. As Street argues, "The realist must hold that an astonishing coincidence took place—that as a matter of sheer luck, evolutionary pressures... happened to shape our evaluative attitudes toward mind-independent truths".

Joyce's (2006) evolutionary error theory argues that natural selection produced moral beliefs because they enhanced cooperation and social cohesion, not because they tracked moral facts. The belief that moral requirements possess categorical force motivated compliance even when self-interest counseled otherwise. This genealogical explanation allegedly undermines moral beliefs' justification by revealing their non-truth-tracking origins.

Neuroscientific findings provide additional challenges. Greene's (2013) dual-process model, based on extensive neuroimaging studies, associates deontological judgments with emotional processing and utilitarian judgments with cognitive calculation. The trolley problem variations reveal that moral judgments depend heavily on morally irrelevant factors like physical proximity and causal directness. As Greene notes, "Deontological philosophy... is not espoused for its rigorous logical derivation from self-evident principles but rather as an elaborate rationalization of emotionally driven intuitions".

However, several responses limit these debunking arguments' scope. The third-factor response, developed by Enoch (2010) and Wielenberg (2010), suggests that the same properties making actions morally right also made believing them right evolutionarily advantageous. Parfit's (2011) convergence argument notes that evolutionary pressures might have selected for reliable moral beliefs because accurate moral knowledge enhanced cooperation.

Vavova's (2015) calibration response argues that evolutionary influence provides no reason to doubt moral beliefs unless we have independent reason to think evolution unreliable about morality specifically. Since evolution shaped all cognitive capacities, selective skepticism about morality requires special justification. As Vavova argues, "Learning about evolutionary influence gives us no reason to think that influence is distorting".

14.2.3 Constructivist and Expressivist Alternatives

Contemporary metaethics offers sophisticated alternatives to both robust realism and simple subjectivism, attempting to preserve moral discourse's objectivity without controversial metaphysical commitments.

Korsgaard's (2009) Kantian constructivism grounds moral truth in rational agency's constitutive features rather than mind-independent facts. The categorical imperative emerges from the logic of rational willing itself: to will an end commits one to willing necessary means, and consistency requires universalizability. As Korsgaard argues, "The normativity of moral values... springs from the fact that they are expressions of our autonomy". This approach preserves moral objectivity through rational necessity while avoiding metaphysical commitments to stance-independent moral facts.

Street's (2008) Humean constructivism takes a more modest approach, grounding moral truth in the logical entailments of agents' evaluative attitudes. What agents ought to do depends on what follows from their deepest values through means-end reasoning and coherence requirements. This metaethical constructivism preserves moral truth's agent-relativity while maintaining substantive objectivity within evaluative frameworks.

Gibbard's (2003) expressivist program explains moral discourse's cognitive appearance while maintaining non-cognitivist foundations. Sophisticated expressivism employs possible worlds semantics to explain moral discourse's logical structure without commitment to moral facts. Normative judgments express contingency plans for what to do and feel across possible circumstances. As Gibbard notes, "Normative thinking consists in contingency planning... planning what to do and what to feel in various contingencies".

Blackburn's (1998) quasi-realist project demonstrates how projectivist foundations support realist-sounding discourse through "semantic ascent." Through attitudes' projection and subsequent objectification, moral discourse acquires propositional surface grammar supporting theoretical reasoning. This preserves moral discourse's practical functionality while avoiding robust metaphysical commitments.

These alternatives face significant challenges. The Frege-Geach problem questions how non-cognitive states can figure in logically valid arguments. The problem of creeping minimalism suggests that quasi-realism ultimately collapses into genuine realism. As Dreier (2004) argues, if expressivists accept all realist-sounding claims, the distinction from realism becomes merely verbal.

14.3 Sources And Methods Of Moral Knowledge

14.3.1 Natural Law Theory: Reason and Human Nature

Natural law theory grounds moral knowledge in rational reflection on human nature and natural teleology, promising universal accessibility while remaining compatible with theological foundations. Contemporary versions address traditional objections while maintaining the approach's core insights.

Aquinas's classical formulation identifies practical reason's first principle: "Good is to be done and pursued, and evil avoided" (Summa Theologiae). From this foundation, reason apprehends basic human goods toward which humans naturally incline: life, procreation, knowledge, and society. As Murphy (2001) explicates, these goods are not inferred from human nature but directly apprehended through practical reason, avoiding naturalistic fallacy.

Finnis's (2011) new natural law theory identifies seven basic goods that are self-evidently valuable and incommensurable: life, knowledge, play, aesthetic experience, sociability, practical reasonableness, and religion. These goods provide reasons for action without requiring further justification. The master principle of morality requires choices compatible with integral human fulfillment—openness to all basic goods in all persons. As Finnis argues, "The basic human goods are not moral values... they are what moral values are values of".

Grisez, Boyle, and Finnis (1987) develop eight modes of responsibility specifying the master principle: fairness requirements, respect for goods in all acts, fidelity to commitments, and community-building choices. These specifications provide concrete guidance while maintaining a rational foundation. The Golden Rule emerges as a rational requirement of fairness in pursuing basic goods.

Critics raise several objections. The specification problem questions how human nature can be determined given evolutionary change and cultural variation. Nussbaum (2006) argues that natural law theory wrongly assumes a fixed human essence. However, Lee and George (2008) respond that natural law identifies capacities and fulfillments universal to rational animals, not statistical regularities.

The fact-value problem challenges deriving normative conclusions from natural facts. However, new natural law theorists argue that practical reason operates differently from theoretical reason, beginning with goods rather than facts. As Tollefsen (2008) explains, basic goods are grasped through practical insight, not derived from metaphysical biology.

14.3.2 Divine Command Theory: Theological Foundations

Divine command theory grounds moral obligations in God's will, providing a metaphysical foundation for morality's authority and categorical nature. Contemporary versions address classical objections while maintaining divine sovereignty's importance.

Adams's (1999) modified divine command theory avoids arbitrariness by grounding commands in God's essentially loving nature. God constitutes moral obligations through commands, but divine love constrains possible commands. As Adams argues, "The part of morality that I aim to analyze in terms of divine commands is... the system of moral obligation". This preserves divine sovereignty while explaining moral content through divine character.

Evans's (2013) divine command theory emphasizes obligations' distinctive deontic character—their binding force differing from mere values. Only personal authority can create genuine obligations, and only divine authority possesses sufficient scope and legitimacy. As Evans notes, "Moral obligations are constituted by the commands or will of a loving God".

Quinn's (1978) theological voluntarism argues that divine commands provide moral properties' metaphysical foundation rather than merely revealing independent moral facts. This strong position maintains complete divine sovereignty over morality while facing challenges about God's own moral status.

The Euthyphro dilemma poses the central challenge: arbitrariness on one horn, divine irrelevance on the other. Contemporary responses typically embrace modified versions identifying goodness with God's nature. Alston (2002) argues that God's nature provides the standard of goodness, while divine commands create obligations. This preserves both divine sovereignty and moral content's non-arbitrariness.

Islamic theological ethics navigates similar tensions. The Ash'ari school emphasizes the divine command's constitutive role, while Mu'tazila rationalism maintains reason's capacity for independent moral knowledge. Al-Attar's (2010) analysis shows how Ibn Rushd synthesized these positions through a sophisticated divine command theory compatible with rational ethics.

14.3.3 Moral Intuition and Rational Insight

Many traditions recognize immediate moral intuition as a knowledge source, though explaining intuition's nature and reliability remains controversial.

Ross's (1930) intuitionism identifies self-evident *prima facie* duties through mature moral reflection: promise-keeping, reparation, gratitude, justice, beneficence, self-improvement, and non-maleficence. These duties are known non-inferentially through intellectual perception analogous to mathematical intuition. As Ross argues, "The moral order... is just as much part of the fundamental nature of the universe... as is the spatial or numerical structure".

Audi's (2004) moderate intuitionism provides a sophisticated epistemological framework. Moral intuitions constitute non-inferential but defeasible justification, subject to defeat by conflicting evidence or debunking explanations. Self-evident moral propositions are knowable through adequate understanding, though actual knowledge requires sufficient reflection and maturity.

Huemer's (2005) phenomenal conservatism grounds moral knowledge in appearances: "It seems to S that p" provides prima facie justification for believing p. Moral intuitions provide defeasible justification absent defeaters. This approach treats moral and perceptual justification symmetrically, avoiding special skepticism about ethics.

Eastern traditions offer alternative frameworks. Hindu buddhi represents discriminating intelligence perceiving dharma when properly functioning (Prasad, 2008). The Bhagavad Gita analyzes how attachment distorts judgment, requiring spiritual practice for accurate moral perception. Confucian liangzhi—innate moral knowledge—recognizes good spontaneously when uncorrupted by selfish desires (Ivanhoe, 2002).

Contemporary psychological research reveals intuition's complexity. Haidt's (2012) social intuitionist model demonstrates that moral judgments typically occur through rapid automatic processes with post-hoc rationalization. However, Kennett and Fine (2009) argue that empirical findings about intuition's psychological mechanisms don't determine its epistemic status.

14.4 UNIVERSAL PATTERNS IN MORAL JUDGMENT

14.4.1 Cross-Cultural Convergence and Moral Foundations

Despite surface diversity, empirical research reveals striking universal patterns suggesting either common evolutionary heritage, functional convergence, or recognition of objective moral truths.

Haidt and Joseph's (2004) moral foundations theory, refined by Graham et al. (2013), identifies six universal domains based on extensive cross-cultural research: care/harm, fairness/cheating, loyalty/betrayal, authority/subversion, sanctity/degradation, and liberty/oppression. While cultures weigh these differently, all recognize their relevance. As Graham et al. (2013) demonstrate, "These foundations are best thought of as learning modules... that can be triggered by culturally variable inputs".

The Golden Rule's independent emergence across traditions separated geographically and historically suggests fundamental moral insight. Wattles's (1996) comprehensive study documents variations: Christianity's positive formulation (Matthew 7:12), Judaism's negative version (Talmud, Shabbat 31a), Buddhism's emphasis on avoiding harm (Udana-Varga 5:18), and Confucius's reciprocity principle (Analects 15:23). This convergence transcends cultural transmission, suggesting recognition of moral truth about reciprocal consideration.

Brown's (1991) human universals research identifies moral patterns across all documented cultures: prohibitions on in-group murder, sexual regulations, reciprocity norms, parental care obligations, and property concepts. These universals persist despite dramatic environmental and social variation, suggesting a deep moral structure.

Mikhail's (2011) universal moral grammar hypothesis, based on trolley problem research across cultures, reveals remarkable judgment consistency. Participants distinguish intended from merely foreseen harm, evaluate acts versus omissions differently, and consider causal proximity morally relevant. Many cannot articulate underlying principles, suggesting unconscious moral knowledge analogous to linguistic competence.

14.4.2 Evolutionary Psychology and Moral Universals

Evolutionary approaches explain moral universals through fitness-enhancing mechanisms, though their implications for moral truth remain contested.

Trivers's (1971) reciprocal altruism theory explains fairness intuitions through iterated cooperation dynamics. When individuals interact repeatedly, cooperation yields greater benefits than defection, selecting for psychological mechanisms supporting reciprocity: gratitude, sympathy, guilt, and moral anger. These emotions track cooperative value rather than moral facts, yet may reliably indicate objective moral truths about cooperation's value.

Hamilton's (1964) inclusive fitness theory explains special obligations toward kin through genetic selection. Helping relatives enhances inclusive fitness proportional to relatedness degree. Lieberman, Tooby, and Cosmides (2007) identify psychological mechanisms detecting kinship through co-residence and maternal perinatal association, generating incest aversion and altruistic motivation.

Multilevel selection theory, developed by Wilson and Wilson (2007), explains group-directed morality through between-group competition. Groups with stronger internal cooperation outcompete others, selecting for traits promoting solidarity: loyalty, conformity, and parochial altruism. Bowles's (2008) models demonstrate how intergroup conflict could drive the evolution of human hyper-cooperation.

These evolutionary accounts face explanatory limitations. Buchanan and Powell (2018) argue that human morality exhibits "open-ended normativity" transcending evolutionary constraints. The expansion of moral consideration to strangers, future generations, and other species exceeds biological fitness predictions. De Waal's (2006) research on primate morality reveals continuities while acknowledging human morality's unique features, including abstract principles and universal scope.

Cultural evolution provides additional explanatory resources. Henrich's (2016) theory of cumulative cultural evolution explains rapid moral change through cultural rather than genetic selection. Moral innovations spread through prestige-biased transmission and conformist learning, enabling moral progress exceeding biological evolution's pace.

14.5 MORAL AGENCY: FREE WILL AND RESPONSIBILITY

14.5.1 The Determinism Challenge

Moral responsibility appears to require freedom to do otherwise, yet scientific evidence increasingly suggests human action results from prior causes beyond ultimate control. This tension generates extensive philosophical debate about responsibility's nature and conditions.

Pereboom's (2014) hard incompatibilism argues that free will is incompatible with both determinism and indeterminism. Four-case manipulation argument demonstrates that causal determination undermines responsibility regardless of determination's source. Even agent causation cannot provide the ultimate origination required for basic desert. As Pereboom argues, "The kind of free will required for moral responsibility... is incompatible with the causal determination of our actions by factors beyond our control".

Strawson's (1994) basic argument demonstrates ultimate responsibility's impossibility through regress: to be ultimately responsible for actions requires being responsible for their causes, generating infinite regress. No one can be causa sui—cause of oneself—as ultimate responsibility requires.

Libertarian theories maintain genuine free will through various mechanisms. Kane's (1996) self-forming actions locate freedom in torn decisions where quantum indeterminacy enables genuine choice. O'Connor's (2000) agent-causal libertarianism posits irreducible agent causation transcending event causation. These theories face challenges about randomness and mysterious causation.

Contemporary neuroscience provides evidence for neural determination. Schurger and Uithol's (2015) review shows that readiness potentials precede conscious decisions, suggesting prior neural determination. However, Mele (2009) argues that neuroscientific evidence remains inconclusive about free will, as experimental paradigms involve trivial decisions unlike moral choices.

14.5.2 Compatibilist Responses

Compatibilism dominates contemporary philosophy, offering various strategies for preserving moral responsibility without libertarian free will.

Frankfurt's (1971) hierarchical theory locates freedom in harmony between first-order desires and higher-order volitions. The willing addict who endorses addiction acts freely, while the unwilling addict resisting addiction lacks freedom. Frankfurt cases—where agents act freely despite inability to do otherwise—challenge the principle of alternative possibilities. As Frankfurt argues, "A person's will is free only if he is free to have the will he wants".

Fischer and Ravizza's (1998) guidance control distinguishes regulative control (alternative possibilities) from guidance control (reasons-responsiveness). Moral responsibility requires only moderate reasons-responsiveness: recognizing moral reasons and reacting appropriately in some possible worlds. This preserves responsibility without alternative possibilities.

Wolf's (1990) Reason View creates asymmetry between praise and blame. Good actions require only the ability to recognize and respond to moral reasons, while bad actions require the ability to do otherwise. This captures the intuition that "I couldn't help doing the right thing" doesn't excuse virtue as "I couldn't help doing wrong" might excuse vice.

Scanlon's (2008) contractualist approach grounds responsibility in relationships rather than metaphysics. Moral responsibility consists in vulnerability to moral assessment based on judgment-sensitive attitudes. What matters is whether actions reflect judgments about reasons, not ultimate causal origination.

14.5.3 Strawsonian Responsibility and Moral Relationships

Strawson's (1962) "Freedom and Resentment" shifted focus from metaphysics to practices constituting moral responsibility. Reactive attitudes—resentment, gratitude, indignation—constitute rather than presuppose responsibility. As Strawson argues, "The participant reactive attitudes are essentially natural human reactions to the good or ill will or indifference of others".

Watson's (2004) development distinguishes accountability (liability to sanctions) from attributability (expression of deep self) and answerability (owing justification). These dimensions can dissociate: psychopaths may be attributively responsible without accountability; children are answerable without full attributability.

McGeer's (2019) scaffolding account treats responsibility practices as cultivating rather than recognizing agency. Holding people responsible helps develop moral capacities through expectation and support. As McGeer argues, "Our responsibility practices are not just about responding to responsible agents but about fostering and sustaining responsible agency".

Vargas's (2013) revisionism abandons desert-based responsibility for a forward-looking moral influence system. Responsibility practices are justified by cultivating moral agency rather than giving deserved treatment.

This preserves the importance while avoiding metaphysical controversies.

14.6 NEUROSCIENCE, PSYCHOLOGY, AND MORAL JUDGMENT

14.6.1 Neural Substrates of Moral Cognition

Neuroscientific research reveals moral judgment's complex neural bases, informing philosophical debates while raising new questions.

Greene et al.'s (2001, 2004) neuroimaging studies using trolley dilemmas identify distinct neural patterns. Personal moral violations activate emotional regions (medial prefrontal cortex, posterior cingulate), while impersonal dilemmas engage cognitive control areas (dorsolateral prefrontal cortex). This supports dual-process models distinguishing automatic emotional from controlled cognitive processing.

However, Kahane et al.'s (2015) process dissociation studies challenge simple emotion-deontology associations. Reduced empathic concern predicts both decreased deontological and increased utilitarian judgments in different contexts. As Kahane notes, "There is no evidence for a general factor of utilitarian judgment".

Studies of clinical populations provide additional insights. Koenigs et al. (2007) found that ventromedial prefrontal cortex lesions increase utilitarian judgments in personal dilemmas. Crockett et al. (2010) showed that serotonin enhancement reduces willingness to harm others for personal gain. These findings suggest specific neural systems' causal roles in moral judgment.

Decety and Cowell's (2018) developmental neuroscience reveals moral capacities' extended maturation. Empathy emerges early but requires prefrontal regulation for mature moral judgment. Theory of mind, essential for moral evaluation, develops through childhood with corresponding neural changes.

14.6.2 Psychopathy and Moral Agency

Psychopathy research illuminates moral agency's psychological prerequisites and raises questions about responsibility.

Blair's (2007) integrated emotion systems model identifies core psychopathic deficits: reduced amygdala response to distress cues, impaired stimulus-reinforcement learning, and abnormal ventromedial prefrontal function. These deficits impair moral socialization and empathy-based moral judgment.

Marsh's (2014) research reveals psychopaths' selective moral deficits. While understanding conventional rules, psychopaths show reduced moral-conventional distinction and impaired care-based moral reasoning. They exhibit normal reasoning about fairness and justice but deficient harm-based moral judgment.

These findings raise responsibility questions. Levy (2014) argues that psychopaths lack moral responsibility due to impaired moral understanding. Shoemaker's (2015) pluralistic approach suggests psychopaths may lack accountability while retaining answerability. Jalava and Griffiths (2017) challenge the psychopathy construct's validity, questioning implications for responsibility.

14.6.3 Moral Development and Neuroplasticity

Research reveals moral capacities' developmental trajectory and potential for enhancement.

Killen and Smetana's (2015) social domain theory identifies distinct developmental trajectories for moral, conventional, and personal domains. Young children distinguish moral from conventional violations, suggesting early-emerging moral capacity. Moral reasoning becomes increasingly sophisticated through recursive perspective-taking development.

Narvaez's (2014) neurobiological approach emphasizes early experience in shaping moral capacities. Secure attachment facilitates empathy development, while early adversity impairs moral functioning. The evolved developmental niche requires specific caregiving for optimal moral development.

Moral enhancement possibilities raise ethical questions. Persson and Savulescu (2012) argue for biomedical moral enhancement given existential risks. Critics like Harris (2011) argue that moral enhancement undermines freedom and authenticity. Empirical research on oxytocin, serotonin, and stimulation suggests limited enhancement potential with significant side effects.

14.7 SYNTHESIS: CONVERGENCE ACROSS TRADITIONS

14.7.1 Universal Moral Principles

Despite theoretical disagreements, several principles emerge as candidates for universal moral truths, suggesting recognition of objective moral reality.

The Principle of Inherent Dignity: Persons possess intrinsic worth irreducible to instrumental value. This principle grounds human rights and prohibitions on mere use. Religious traditions locate dignity in imago Dei (Christianity), fitrah (Islam), or Buddha-nature (Buddhism). Secular approaches ground dignity in autonomy (Kant), capabilities (Nussbaum), or sentience (Singer). Convergence suggests recognition of fundamental moral truth about persons' special moral status.

The Principle of Equal Consideration: Comparable interests deserve equal weight regardless of morally arbitrary characteristics. This principle underlies justice concepts across cultures, though its scope remains contested. Rawls's (1971) veil of ignorance, Singer's (1972) expanding circle, and Buddhist universal compassion represent variations on this theme.

The Principle of Compassion: Suffering generates moral reasons for amelioration. This appears across traditions: Christian agape, Buddhist karuna, Confucian ren, and secular beneficence. Convergence on suffering's moral significance suggests universal recognition of sentience's importance.

The Principle of Reciprocity: Moral requirements apply symmetrically across agents. The Golden Rule's cross-cultural emergence indicates widespread recognition of morality's impartial character. This principle grounds both negative duties (non-harm) and positive duties (assistance).

The Principle of Responsibility: Accountability scales with capacity, knowledge, and control. This principle appears in legal systems' mens rea requirements, religious concepts of sin requiring knowledge and will, and philosophical discussions of excuse and mitigation.

14.7.2 Toward Integration

These convergent principles don't resolve all moral questions but provide a framework transcending particular traditions. Their emergence across religious, philosophical, and empirical approaches using different methodologies suggests that morality represents a genuine first principle about reality's structure.

The relationship between moral principles and reality's fundamental nature admits various interpretations. Theistic approaches ground morality in divine nature or command. Natural law theories locate morality in rational nature's requirements. Kantian approaches identify morality with the practical reason's structure. Even naturalistic approaches increasingly recognize morality's objective features through moral functionalism and response-dependent realism.

The convergence thesis developed throughout this work finds strong support in morality's domain. Empirical sciences reveal moral judgment's psychological and neurobiological bases. Rational philosophy provides frameworks for understanding moral truth and knowledge. Religious traditions offer accounts of morality's ultimate ground and significance. These approaches converge on core principles while maintaining irreducible perspectives.

This convergence provides evidence that morality constitutes a genuine first principle about reality, requiring an integrated methodological approach. Just as mathematics reveals reality's quantitative structure and physics its dynamical laws, morality reveals reality's axiological dimension— objective values structuring rational action and relationship.

The implications extend beyond academic philosophy to practical questions about dignity, justice, and responsibility. If morality possesses objective reality grounded in reality's fundamental structure, moral requirements carry authority independent of preference, convention, or power. This grounds moral criticism and reform based on moral truth rather than mere preference.

The participatory understanding of reality developed throughout this work illuminates morality's nature. Moral truth emerges through participation in reality's axiological dimension, requiring integration of empirical understanding, rational reflection, and experiential wisdom. The ongoing quest for moral understanding exemplifies the broader pattern of human participation in reality's creative unfolding toward truth, goodness, and meaning.

PART V

CHAPTER 15: WHERE SCIENCE, PHILOSOPHY, AND RELIGION MEET

15.1 INTRODUCTION: THE CONVERGENCE HYPOTHESIS

The contemporary intellectual landscape frequently portrays science, philosophy, and religion as fundamentally incompatible approaches to understanding reality. This conflict narrative, popularized through works by evolutionary biologists and public intellectuals, obscures a more complex truth about the relationship between these domains of inquiry. Rather than representing mutually exclusive worldviews destined for perpetual conflict, these three approaches to understanding reality demonstrate remarkable convergence at the level of foundational commitments and first principles.

Barbour's (1997) influential typology identified four models of science-religion interaction: conflict, independence, dialogue, and integration. Each model represents different assumptions about epistemological and metaphysical relationships between domains. Stenmark's (2004) expanded framework demonstrates that relationships vary significantly across scientific disciplines and religious traditions, revealing the inadequacy of monolithic generalizations. As Stenmark argues, "The relationship between science and religion is not one thing but many things, varying with particular sciences, particular religions, and particular questions under consideration".

Harrison's (2015) historical analysis reveals that the conflict thesis itself represents a particular nineteenth-century construction rather than an inevitable logical relationship. The categories of "science" and "religion" have been socially constructed and continuously redefined across historical periods, with their perceived relationship shaped by broader cultural and political forces. Brooke's (1991) comprehensive investigation demonstrates that science-religion relationships have involved complex interactions between scientific, theological, political, and social factors that resist simple categorization.

Numbers's (2009) systematic examination of science-religion myths exposes how popular understanding relies on historically inaccurate portrayals. The Galileo affair, for instance, involved ecclesiastical politics and personal rivalries as much as cosmological disputes, while Darwin's theory of evolution found both religious supporters and scientific critics. These historical complexities suggest that contemporary assumptions about inevitable conflict may reflect cultural prejudices rather than logical necessities.

The convergence hypothesis examined in this chapter does not claim perfect harmony between all truth claims from these domains. Genuine tensions persist regarding specific historical assertions, methodological priorities, and metaphysical frameworks. Rosenberg's (2011) eliminative materialism argues that advancing neuroscience will ultimately eliminate folk psychological concepts, including religious experiences, through reductive explanation. Dennett's (2006) critique of religious epistemology challenges the compatibility of faith-based and evidence-based reasoning.

However, the convergence hypothesis proposes that at the level of first principles—those foundational commitments that make inquiry possible—science, philosophy, and religion share remarkable common ground deserving systematic examination. This convergence appears most clearly in shared epistemological foundations, assumptions about cosmic intelligibility, approaches to consciousness, responses to fine-tuning evidence, and recognition of reductive materialism's limitations.

15.2 SHARED EPISTEMOLOGICAL FOUNDATIONS

15.2.1 Commitment to Truth and Reality

All three domains begin with fundamental commitments that cannot be demonstrated without circularity, yet prove indispensable for rational inquiry. These commitments include the existence of truth, the reliability of human cognitive faculties, and the accessibility of reality to human understanding. Plantinga's (2000) analysis of proper basicality demonstrates that certain beliefs require no further justification while grounding other knowledge claims. As Plantinga argues, "There are certain beliefs that are properly basic—that is, beliefs it is entirely reasonable, rational, and proper to hold without having evidence or argument for them".

Scientists necessarily presuppose the reliability of sense perception, the validity of mathematical reasoning, and the legitimacy of inductive inference. These presuppositions cannot be empirically verified without circularity, as any verification would depend upon the very faculties being verified. Philosophers depend upon logical consistency, conceptual clarity, and argumentative validity—standards that themselves require philosophical justification. Religious thinkers across traditions affirm various forms of knowledge acquisition, from Aquinas's (1265/1981) natural reason to Al-Ghazali's (1095/2000) experiential validation to Śaṅkara's (8th century/1978) self-evident consciousness.

The commitment to objective reality represents another shared foundation. Bhaskar's (2008) critical realism provides a sophisticated framework for understanding how scientific investigation presupposes mind-independent reality while acknowledging epistemic fallibility. As Bhaskar argues, "Science... necessarily presupposes the existence, and action, of things independently of their being identified or of knowledge of them being produced". Psillos's (1999) defense of scientific realism demonstrates that mature scientific theories' predictive success provides compelling evidence for theoretical entities' reality.

Hacking's (1983) experimental realism offers a middle path between naive realism and anti-realist alternatives. The ability to manipulate theoretical entities experimentally—causing effects with electrons, genes, or quarks—provides particularly strong evidence for their mind-independent existence. As Hacking famously states, "If you can spray them, they are real".

Philosophers analyzing being and existence presuppose that their

249

concepts refer to genuine features of reality, even when that reality proves paradoxical or ineffable. From Aristotle's substance metaphysics to Nāgārjuna's dependent origination, philosophical analysis assumes correspondence between conceptual structures and reality's features. Religious traditions globally affirm transcendent realities—whether personal deity, impersonal absolute, or ultimate emptiness—existing independently of human recognition or understanding.

15.2.2 Critical Realism Across Domains

Polkinghorne (1998), a physicist-theologian, identifies this shared epistemic stance as critical realism—the recognition that while reality exists independently, human understanding remains fallible and requires continuous revision. This position avoids both naive realism's overconfidence and relativism's abandonment of objective truth. As Polkinghorne argues, "We have access to reality, but it is a limited access, yielding knowledge that is reliable but not absolute".

Scientific theories undergo continuous revision based on empirical evidence, as demonstrated in paradigmatic transitions from Newtonian to Einsteinian physics, steady-state to Big Bang cosmology, and classical to quantum mechanics. These revisions represent not the abandonment of realism but the refinement of understanding. Philosophical arguments develop through dialectical engagement, evident in centuries of refinement in epistemology, ethics, and metaphysics. Religious communities continuously reinterpret sacred texts and traditions through sophisticated hermeneutical methods, from Talmudic commentary to Buddhist abhidharma analysis to Christian theological development.

This shared epistemic humility acknowledges finite minds' partial grasp of reality, requiring multiple perspectives for comprehensive understanding. Putnam's (2002) analysis of the fact-value dichotomy's collapse demonstrates how descriptive and normative dimensions interpenetrate irreducibly. As Putnam argues, "Knowledge of facts presupposes knowledge of values", suggesting that comprehensive understanding requires integration of scientific, philosophical, and evaluative perspectives.

Critics like Dennett (2006) argue that religious faith fundamentally differs from scientific empiricism, representing belief without adequate evidence. This critique overlooks how all knowledge systems rest on unprovable foundational assumptions. The principle of induction cannot be inductively justified, the reliability of memory cannot be remembered to be reliable, and the correspondence between mathematics and physical reality cannot be empirically demonstrated without circularity. Quine's (1951) analysis of the "web of belief" demonstrates that even apparently foundational scientific principles prove revisable under sufficient empirical pressure.

15.3 THE INTELLIGIBILITY OF THE UNIVERSE

15.3.1 Mathematical Effectiveness and Cosmic Rationality

Wigner's (1960) observation about mathematics' "unreasonable effectiveness" in describing physical reality identifies a profound puzzle requiring explanation. Abstract mathematical structures conceived through pure thought correspond with extraordinary precision to natural phenomena. As Wigner notes, "The miracle of the appropriateness of the language of mathematics for the formulation of the laws of physics is a wonderful gift which we neither understand nor deserve".

Hamming's (1980) extension demonstrates that mathematical effectiveness operates across multiple levels: within mathematics itself, in physical sciences, and increasingly in biological and social sciences. This pervasive applicability suggests systematic rather than coincidental correspondence. Recent developments in theoretical physics intensify the puzzle—string theory's eleven-dimensional mathematics, gauge theory's abstract symmetries, and quantum field theory's infinite-dimensional spaces all prove indispensable for describing observable phenomena.

Tegmark's (2014) Mathematical Universe Hypothesis proposes that physical reality simply is mathematical structure, though this raises questions about consciousness and qualitative experience that resist mathematical formalization. Davies (2006) argues that pervasive rational structure suggests an underlying "cosmic blueprint" transcending particular phenomena. As Davies states, "The universe is not only queerer than we suppose, but queerer than we can suppose—except mathematically".

Weinberg's (1992) analysis reveals that mathematical beauty and elegance serve as genuine guides to truth rather than merely aesthetic preferences. The predictive success of theories chosen partly for mathematical elegance—general relativity's geometric beauty, quantum mechanics' Hilbert space formalism, gauge theory's symmetry principles—

supports the view that aesthetic criteria track objective features of reality.

15.3.2 Philosophical Analysis of Intelligibility

Philosophy contributes essential analysis of intelligibility's necessary conditions. Kant's (1781/1998) transcendental method demonstrates that experience presupposes certain necessary features of both consciousness and world. Contemporary developments of transcendental argumentation by Strawson (1966) and Stroud (1968) show how successful reference requires systematic correspondence between conceptual structures and reality's features.

Putnam's (1981) semantic externalism reveals that meaningful reference depends upon appropriate causal connections between mental representations and environmental features. Without assuming systematic correspondence between thought and reality, successful scientific theorizing becomes inexplicable. Davidson's (2001) principle of charity demonstrates that interpretation requires assuming massive truth in others' beliefs, implying that systematic error about reality's basic features proves impossible for rational agents.

Brandom's (1994) inferential semantics shows how conceptual content emerges through patterns of reasoning that must track objective logical relationships. As Brandom argues, "Grasping a concept is mastering the use of a word... in the game of giving and asking for reasons". This pragmatist approach grounds meaning in successful practice while maintaining realist commitments about logical structure.

15.3.3 Religious Perspectives on Cosmic Rationality

Religious and philosophical traditions globally have long affirmed that cosmic rationality derives from a transcendent intelligence or organizing principle. The Johannine logos concept presents divine reason as manifested in creation's order (John 1:1-3). The Quranic notion of ayat (signs) throughout nature points to divine wisdom accessible through investigation. The Daoist Dao represents the cosmic principle underlying natural patterns, while Vedantic sat-chit-ānanda identifies being, consciousness, and bliss as reality's fundamental nature.

Ibn Rushd (1179/1961) argued that studying nature through reason constitutes a religious obligation, as creation's rational structure reveals divine wisdom. As Ibn Rushd states, "It is a duty for those who study philosophy to study existing things so that they arrive at knowledge of the Creator". Al-Ghazali's (1095/2000) integration of rational demonstration and spiritual insight provided frameworks for understanding divine transcendence and cosmic intelligibility without contradiction.

Aquinas's (1265-1274/1947) synthesis demonstrates how natural reason discovers truth about God through investigating created reality, while revelation provides knowledge beyond reason's scope. This approach neither reduces religious truth to rational demonstration nor divorces faith from rational investigation. Contemporary process theologians like Griffin (2007) develop these themes through emphasis on divine persuasion operating through rather than against natural regularities.

Eliminative materialists contend that apparent intelligibility reflects evolutionary selection for pattern detection rather than genuine cosmic rationality. This naturalistic explanation faces self-referential difficulties—if cognitive faculties systematically mislead regarding truth, why trust reasoning supporting this conclusion? Moreover, mathematics' predictive success in domains far removed from evolutionary pressures—topology, number theory, abstract algebra—suggests cognitive capacities transcending survival utility.

15.4 CONSCIOUSNESS: THE INTERDISCIPLINARY CONVERGENCE POINT

15.4.1 The Hard Problem and Its Implications

Consciousness represents the clearest convergence point across disciplines, as no single domain provides an adequate explanation for subjective experience. Chalmers's (1995) formulation of the "hard problem" highlights consciousness as irreducibly mysterious within physicalist frameworks. As Chalmers argues, "Even when we have explained the performance of all the cognitive and behavioral functions in the vicinity of experience... there may still remain a further unanswered question: Why is there something it is like to be in these states?".

Contemporary neuroscience contributes crucial correlational data. Koch's (2019) research on neural correlates of consciousness identifies specific brain signatures associated with conscious states. Tononi's (2008) Integrated Information Theory attempts to quantify consciousness through measures of integrated information (Φ) in complex systems. These approaches yield testable predictions about which systems exhibit consciousness and to what degree.

Yet Koch (2019) acknowledges that complete neural description leaves unexplained why subjective experience exists at all—the "feeling of life itself" accompanying but seemingly irreducible to information processing. As Koch states, "The hard problem of consciousness will not be solved by more neuroscience data alone". Speculative theories like Penrose and Hameroff's (2014) Orchestrated Objective Reduction propose quantum mechanical explanations, though empirical support remains limited and controversial.

15.4.2 Philosophical Analysis of Consciousness

Philosophy provides an indispensable conceptual analysis revealing consciousness's unique status. Nagel's (1974) "what it is like" formulation demonstrates consciousness's irreducibly first-person character. Jackson's (1986) knowledge argument shows that complete physical knowledge omits qualitative aspects of experience—Mary, the color scientist, learns something new upon first seeing color despite knowing all physical facts about color vision.

Searle's (1992) analysis of intentionality demonstrates that consciousness exhibits intrinsic intentionality—genuine aboutness—while physical systems display only derived intentionality assigned by interpreters. This suggests consciousness cannot be eliminated without losing semantic properties essential to thought and language. As Searle argues, "Consciousness and intentionality are intrinsic, ineliminable features of certain biological systems".

Block's (1995) distinction between phenomenal consciousness (qualitative experience) and access consciousness (cognitive availability) reveals different aspects requiring different explanatory approaches. This pluralistic framework suggests consciousness research must address multiple phenomena rather than seeking unified reduction.

Hasker's (1999) emergent dualism offers a middle position between substance dualism and reductive physicalism, proposing that consciousness emerges from neural complexity while possessing irreducible causal powers. This approach acknowledges consciousness's dependence on brain function while preserving its distinctiveness and efficacy.

15.4.3 Contemplative Traditions and First-Person Investigation

Eastern philosophical traditions contribute sophisticated phenomenologies developed through systematic introspection. Buddhist abhidharma psychology analyzes consciousness into detailed taxonomies of mental factors (cetasika), distinguishing types of awareness, attention, and emotion through disciplined investigation. The Yogācāra school's eight-consciousness model provides frameworks paralleling contemporary discussions of conscious and unconscious processing.

Advaita Vedanta distinguishes witness consciousness (sākṣin) from mental modifications (vṛtti), proposing pure consciousness as a fundamental reality rather than an emergent property. This analysis offers alternative conceptual frameworks challenging materialist assumptions. As Śaṅkara (8th century/1978) argues, "Consciousness is the very nature of the Self, and not a quality or attribute".

These traditions offer rigorous methodologies—meditation, contemplative inquiry, mindfulness—for investigating consciousness empirically through first-person methods. Varela's (1996) neurophenomenology program explicitly combines neuroscientific investigation with disciplined introspection, demonstrating productive synthesis potential. Davidson and Lutz's (2008) research reveals that contemplative practices produce measurable changes in brain structure and function, including enhanced emotional regulation and attention.

The convergence suggests consciousness requires genuinely interdisciplinary investigation. Neuroscience maps neural correlates, philosophy analyzes conceptual structure, and contemplative traditions explore experiential dimensions. Each domain illuminates aspects invisible to others, with integration promising advances unavailable to single approaches.

15.5 FINE-TUNING AND THE ANTHROPIC PRINCIPLE

15.5.1 The Fine-Tuning Evidence

The observation that fundamental physical parameters appear precisely calibrated for life's possibility generates intense interdisciplinary debate. Multiple dimensionless constants fall within extremely narrow ranges permitting stellar nucleosynthesis, chemical complexity, and biological evolution. Barrow and Tipler's (1986) comprehensive analysis documented numerous apparent "coincidences" requiring explanation.

Rees's (1999) identification of six fundamental numbers whose precise values seem essential for a life-bearing universe provides specific focus. The cosmological constant, for instance, is approximately 10^{120} times smaller than quantum field theory predictions yet falls precisely within the narrow range allowing cosmic structure formation. As Rees notes, "The conditions in our universe really do seem to be uniquely suitable for life forms like ourselves".

Collins's (2009) Bayesian analysis calculates that life-permitting parameter values occupy an infinitesimally small region of theoretically possible parameter space. Collins argues, "The fine-tuning evidence provides significant confirmation of theism over the naturalistic single-universe hypothesis". Barnes's (2012) systematic review evaluates which parameters genuinely require explanation versus those reflecting selection effects or theoretical artifacts, confirming that several fine-tuning cases withstand critical scrutiny.

15.5.2 Scientific Responses and Multiverse Theories

Scientific responses divide into several camps. Multiverse hypotheses propose vast ensembles of universes with varying parameters, making observed values unremarkable through anthropic selection. Eternal inflation, string theory's landscape, and many-worlds quantum mechanics provide potential mechanisms for generating such ensembles.

However, multiverse theories face significant challenges. Ellis (2011) argues that multiverse hypotheses remain empirically untestable and potentially unfalsifiable, raising questions about scientific status. As Ellis states, "The multiverse proposal is not testable and should not be considered science". These theories shift fine-tuning questions to deeper levels—why does the multiverse-generating mechanism permit life-friendly universes?

Susskind's (2005) string theory landscape proposes 10^{500} possible vacuum states providing parameter variation. Yet this requires anthropic reasoning to explain why observers find themselves in life-permitting regions. Weinberg's (1987) successful anthropic prediction of the cosmological constant's value demonstrates the approach's potential utility while raising questions about its scope and limitations.

15.5.3 Philosophical and Theological Perspectives

Necessity arguments propose that apparently arbitrary parameters derive from deeper principles constraining possible values. Despite decades of research, such principles remain elusive. Even proposed "theories of everything" contain adjustable parameters requiring explanation.

Philosophical analysis reveals that fine-tuning arguments need not invoke supernatural intervention violating natural processes. Contemporary teleological naturalism offers frameworks where purpose emerges from reality's fundamental structure. Whitehead's (1929/1978) process philosophy and Nagel's (2012) natural teleology provide conceptual resources for understanding apparent design without external manipulation.

Craig and Sinclair's (2009) analysis demonstrates how fine-tuning evidence supports different interpretations depending on broader metaphysical commitments. Theistic interpretations understand fine-tuning as reflecting divine wisdom expressed through natural law. Sophisticated religious interpretations avoid "god-of-the-gaps" reasoning by understanding fine-tuning as revealing creation's inherent fertility and directedness. Peacocke's (2001) and Polkinghorne's (1994) theological approaches interpret fine-tuning as illuminating divine creativity operating through natural processes.

15.6 CHALLENGES TO REDUCTIVE MATERIALISM

15.6.1 Philosophical Problems with Physicalism

While methodological naturalism proves extraordinarily successful as a scientific strategy, philosophical materialism faces mounting challenges. Kim's (2005) rigorous analysis reveals persistent problems: the causal exclusion problem, mental causation difficulties, and property dualism challenges. As Kim argues, "Physicalism faces a stark choice: either embrace reductionism or give up mental causation".

Papineau's (2002) comprehensive defense acknowledges these challenges while maintaining physicalism's superiority to alternatives. Yet consistent physicalism may lead toward eliminativism rather than reductive identification. Strong emergence presents particular difficulties—complex systems exhibit irreducible causal powers unpredictable from complete knowledge of components. Biological organisms display goal-directed behavior, ecosystems self-organize, and social systems generate emergent norms that resist bottom-up reduction.

15.6.2 Information, Meaning, and Abstract Objects

Information and meaning resist straightforward physical reduction. Biosemiotic research reveals that living systems process semantic information irreducible to syntactic operations. DNA functions as a genuine code requiring interpretation beyond chemical interaction. Deacon's (2011) analysis of "absential" features—what is not present but could be—demonstrates how biological and mental processes involve causal relationships with merely possible states, challenging standard physical causation.

Abstract objects pose particular challenges for materialist ontology. Mathematical entities, logical principles, and values appear indispensable yet resist physical instantiation. Putnam's (1975) indispensability argument contends that science requires mathematical truth transcending physical processes. Colyvan's (2001) analysis demonstrates that theoretical physics requires a genuine commitment to abstract mathematical structures that appear to constrain rather than merely describe physical possibilities.

15.6.3 Alternative Metaphysical Frameworks

Sophisticated alternatives to reductive materialism accommodate scientific findings while addressing explanatory gaps. Dual-aspect monism proposes mental and physical as complementary descriptions of neutral reality. Contemporary versions develop this through information-theoretic and quantum frameworks.

Goff's (2017) cosmopsychist approach suggests consciousness exists at fundamental levels, becoming unified in special organizational contexts. This panpsychist solution addresses the hard problem by locating consciousness at reality's foundation. Nagel's (2012) critique argues that consciousness, cognition, and value require expanding naturalistic frameworks to include teleological principles. While controversial, Nagel's analysis highlights explanatory gaps that purely physicalist approaches struggle to address.

15.7 METHODOLOGICAL PLURALISM AND INTEGRATION

15.7.1 Complementarity Across Domains

The convergences examined reveal that science, philosophy, and religion function as complementary approaches to reality's multidimensional nature. Each domain contributes essential insights while acknowledging limitations requiring interdisciplinary collaboration.

Science excels at investigating efficient causation and empirically testable hypotheses, but cannot address ultimate purpose or value. Philosophy provides rigorous conceptual analysis and systematic integration but requires empirical grounding. Religion offers existential meaning and normative guidance but benefits from rational critique and empirical knowledge.

Habermas's (2008) analysis demonstrates how secular and religious perspectives can engage productively without reduction. His approach acknowledges both naturalistic explanations' legitimate scope and religious experience's irreducible dimensions. Bohr's (1958) complementarity principle provides a methodological model—apparently contradictory descriptions may both prove necessary for complete understanding, with contradiction resolved through recognizing different contexts revealing different aspects of reality.

15.7.2 Criteria for Evaluation

Convergences around truth-seeking, intelligibility, consciousness, fine-tuning, and materialism's limits provide evaluative criteria for assessing worldviews. Adequate worldviews must honor insights from all domains while maintaining consistency and empirical adequacy.

Worldviews that arbitrarily exclude entire dimensions of experience prove inadequate to reality's complexity. Pure scientism, dismissing philosophical analysis and religious experience, fails to account for science's own presuppositions. Religious fundamentalism, rejecting scientific findings, is intellectually untenable. Philosophical approaches that ignore empirical findings remain abstractly inadequate.

Successful integration requires discriminating between genuine insights and theoretical overextension. Not all religious claims prove compatible with scientific findings, not all scientific theories address philosophical questions, and not all philosophical arguments withstand empirical scrutiny.

15.7.3 Future Directions

Contemporary developments suggest increasing opportunities for productive integration. Consciousness studies increasingly require interdisciplinary collaboration. Environmental challenges demand integrating scientific understanding, ethical reflection, and spiritual wisdom. Artificial intelligence development raises questions requiring scientific expertise, philosophical analysis, and reflection on human values.

McGrath's (2004) scientific theology demonstrates how theological reflection can engage science constructively while maintaining integrity. The emergence of neurotheology, contemplative science, and empirical investigation of religious experience represents productive synthesis potential. While facing methodological challenges, these fields suggest possibilities for investigating phenomena traditionally considered beyond the scientific scope.

15.8 CONCLUSION: TOWARD COMPREHENSIVE UNDERSTANDING

The examination of convergence points reveals that science, philosophy, and religion can function as complementary approaches to reality's multidimensional character rather than inevitably conflicting worldviews. Their shared commitments to truth, objective reality, and human cognitive capacity provide common epistemological foundations. Cosmic intelligibility, consciousness, and fine-tuning represent phenomena requiring interdisciplinary investigation. The limitations of reductive materialism suggest the need for expanded frameworks accommodating the full range of human experience and scientific discovery.

This convergence does not eliminate genuine disagreements or reduce all domains to uniform methodology. Real tensions persist regarding specific truth claims, methodological priorities, and metaphysical commitments. The convergence hypothesis proposes that these tensions occur within broader frameworks of shared commitment to understanding reality's nature.

Methodological pluralism offers a path forward employing different investigative approaches appropriate to different aspects of reality while maintaining overall coherence. This approach neither reduces all knowledge to a single type nor accepts contradictory claims uncritically. Complex realities require multiple perspectives for adequate understanding.

The path toward integration requires intellectual virtues from all domains: scientific commitment to empirical rigor, philosophical dedication to logical consistency, and religious attention to meaning and transcendence. Each contributes essential elements for comprehensive understanding, with their convergence suggesting that reality's fundamental nature transcends any single domain's methodological scope.

As the examination turns to competing worldviews in subsequent analysis, these convergence points provide an evaluative framework. Worldviews integrating genuine insights from scientific investigation, philosophical reflection, and religious wisdom while maintaining logical coherence deserve serious consideration. Those arbitrarily excluding entire dimensions of understanding prove inadequate to existence's complexity. The quest for first principles ultimately requires recognizing the essential complementarity of science, philosophy, and religion in humanity's ongoing effort to comprehend reality's ultimate ground and meaning.

CHAPTER 16: COMPETING WORLDVIEWS

16.1 Introduction: The Interpretive Framework Of Reality

First principles do not exist within interpretive vacuums. Every observation, argument, and insight undergoes filtration through comprehensive frameworks that determine what phenomena receive attention, how events receive explanation, and what constitutes legitimate knowledge. These worldviews—systematic perspectives on reality's nature, knowledge sources, and value foundations—function as interpretive lenses through which first principles appear fundamentally different. Understanding these frameworks proves essential for navigating disagreements about reality's fundamental structure.

Thomas Kuhn's analysis of scientific paradigms revealed how theoretical commitments shape observation itself, making theory-neutral facts impossible (Kuhn, 1962/1996). What Kuhn demonstrated for scientific practice extends more broadly across intellectual domains: worldviews determine not merely answers but which questions merit investigation. Norwood Russell Hanson's earlier work on the theory-ladenness of observation showed how background assumptions permeate even basic perceptual reports, making pure empiricism untenable (Hanson, 1958). This insight has been further developed by Helen Longino, who demonstrates how background assumptions shape not only observation but also the standards of evidence and explanatory adequacy employed across scientific disciplines (Longino, 1990).

The concept of worldview (Weltanschauung) emerged from German Idealism, particularly through Wilhelm Dilthey's hermeneutical philosophy, which emphasized the historical and cultural embeddedness of all human understanding (Dilthey, 1976). David Naugle traces this conceptual genealogy through contemporary usage, demonstrating how pre-theoretical commitments shape all theoretical endeavors (Naugle, 2002). Rather than functioning as neutral recording devices, human minds operate through interpretive frameworks that organize experience into meaningful patterns. James W. Sire's systematic analysis identifies worldviews as comprehensive commitments addressing fundamental questions about reality's nature, human identity, moral foundations, and ultimate meaning (Sire, 2009).

Contemporary cognitive science supports this philosophical insight. Research in conceptual metaphor theory demonstrates that abstract reasoning depends upon embodied experiential structures that vary across cultures and linguistic communities (Lakoff & Johnson, 1999). Neuroscientific investigations reveal that prior beliefs literally shape neural processing of incoming information, with top-down predictions influencing perception at the earliest stages of sensory processing (Clark, 2013). These empirical findings underscore the impossibility of purely objective, framework-independent observation.

The worldviews examined here—naturalistic materialism, theistic realism, idealistic philosophies, process thought, Eastern non-dualism, and pragmatic approaches—represent fundamentally different approaches to construing reality's structure. Each provides a coherent interpretation of first principles explored throughout this investigation, yet reaches divergent conclusions about their significance and interrelationships. Ninian Smart observes that worldviews combine doctrinal, mythological, ethical, ritual, experiential, and social dimensions into comprehensive life-orientations shaping both theoretical understanding and practical engagement (Smart, 1989).

Michael Polanyi's concept of tacit knowledge illuminates how worldviews operate beneath explicit awareness, structuring perception and reasoning through subsidiary awareness that remains largely unarticulated (Polanyi, 1966). This tacit dimension explains why worldview disagreements prove so intractable—disputants often cannot articulate the fundamental assumptions generating their divergent interpretations. Charles Taylor's analysis of "social imaginaries" extends this insight, showing how shared background understandings constitute the conditions of possibility for both individual thought and collective practice (Taylor, 2004).

This examination does not attempt definitive adjudication between competing worldviews—such adjudication presupposes evaluative criteria that different worldviews themselves contest. Instead, we analyze how each framework interprets first principles, examine the strengths and challenges each confronts, and investigate how worldview commitments shape apparently factual claims. The objective involves informed understanding rather than premature closure, acknowledging that worldview evaluation represents philosophy's most challenging undertaking.16.2 Naturalistic Materialism: Reality As Physical Process

16.2.1 The Physicalist Framework

Naturalistic materialism—more precisely termed physicalism—represents the dominant worldview within contemporary science and substantial portions of academic philosophy. This framework maintains that reality consists entirely of physical entities and processes describable through physics, with all other phenomena emerging from or reducing to physical interactions. Mental states, values, and meanings either face elimination or require explanation through purely physical mechanisms. First principles, within this perspective, ultimately constitute physical laws governing matter-energy within spacetime.

Daniel Stoljar's comprehensive analysis reveals the complexity underlying apparently straightforward materialist claims (Stoljar, 2010). Contemporary physicalism confronts what Hempel called the dilemma of physicalism: if "physical" means what current physics describes, physicalism is likely false given physics' incompleteness; if "physical" means what future completed physics will describe, physicalism becomes vacuous since we cannot specify future physics' content (Hempel, 1980). This definitional challenge undermines physicalism's apparent clarity while revealing its promissory character.

Contemporary physicalism divides into type-A and type-B variants, following David Chalmers' taxonomy (Chalmers, 2010). Type-A physicalists, including Paul Churchland and Patricia Churchland, maintain that consciousness poses no special explanatory challenge beyond temporary ignorance. Paul Churchland's eliminative materialism advances the most radical position, arguing that folk psychological concepts, including beliefs, desires, and consciousness, will be eliminated by advancing neuroscience, just as vitalism was eliminated by biochemistry (Churchland, 1981). This approach does not merely reduce mental phenomena to physical processes but eliminates mental categories entirely as theoretical artifacts lacking referential content.

Patricia Churchland extends neuroscientific materialism to moral and social phenomena, contending that ethical intuitions reduce to neural mechanisms evolved for social cooperation (Churchland, 2011). Apparent objective values represent survival-enhancing behavioral dispositions embedded in neural architecture rather than responses to mind-independent moral facts. Love reduces to oxytocin and attachment systems, religious experience to temporal lobe activity, and aesthetic appreciation to reward circuit activation. This neuroethical approach has been criticized by Selim Berker for committing the "neuroscientific fallacy"—illegitimately inferring normative conclusions from descriptive neuroscientific premises (Berker, 2009).

16.2.2 Sophisticated Physicalist Responses

Type-B physicalists acknowledge an explanatory gap between physical and phenomenal properties while maintaining ontological physicalism. David Papineau argues that the explanatory gap reflects a conceptual rather than metaphysical divide—phenomenal concepts employ different modes of presentation than physical concepts while referring to identical states (Papineau, 2002). Joseph Levine, who introduced the explanatory gap concept, maintains that while subjective experience resists transparent reduction to physical processes, this epistemic limitation does not entail ontological dualism (Levine, 1983).

Alex Rosenberg pushes materialist implications to their logical conclusions through what he terms "nice nihilism" (Rosenberg, 2011). If physicalism proves correct, consciousness constitutes illusion, free will becomes impossible, moral facts remain non-existent, and meaning represents mere projection. This eliminative approach accepts that common sense and scientific materialism conflict fundamentally, then consistently endorses scientific conclusions over phenomenological appearances. Yet critics like Thomas Nagel argue that Rosenberg's position becomes self-refuting—if consciousness is illusory, who experiences the illusion? If reasoning lacks reliability, why trust arguments for physicalism? (Nagel,

2012).

Donald Davidson's anomalous monism proposes a non-reductive physicalism where mental events are physical events but resist reduction to physical descriptions due to the holistic nature of mental content (Davidson, 2001). Mental properties supervene on physical properties without strict psychophysical laws connecting them. This preserves mental causation without invoking substance dualism. Similarly, functionalist approaches argue that mental states constitute multiply realizable functional organizations rather than specific physical configurations, maintaining physicalism while acknowledging explanatory autonomy of mental descriptions (Putnam, 1975).

Jaegwon Kim's causal exclusion argument challenges non-reductive physicalism by demonstrating that mental causation becomes epiphenomenal if physical events have sufficient physical causes (Kim, 2005). Either mental properties reduce to physical properties, violating non-reductionism, or they lack genuine causal efficacy, rendering them explanatorily irrelevant. This dilemma forces physicalists toward either eliminativism or reductionism, both carrying significant costs.

16.2.3 Interpretive Implications

Materialists interpret scientific first principles as the only genuine first principles deserving recognition. Conservation laws, thermodynamics, and quantum mechanics describe reality's fundamental nature without remainder. Mathematical effectiveness reflects evolutionary selection for pattern detection rather than mysterious correspondence between abstract structures and physical reality. Eugene Wigner's "unreasonable effectiveness of mathematics" becomes reasonable through a naturalistic explanation (Wigner, 1960).

Fine-tuning requires no explanation beyond anthropic selection effects or multiverse scenarios generating numerous parameter combinations. Steven Weinberg calculates that anthropic reasoning successfully predicts the cosmological constant's order of magnitude, supporting naturalistic over design interpretations (Weinberg, 1987). Leonard Susskind's cosmic landscape proposal explains fine-tuning through selection effects across vast numbers of vacuum states without invoking design (Susskind, 2005).

Consciousness will eventually yield to neuroscientific explanation as vitalism yielded to biochemistry, according to this worldview. The apparent hard problem of consciousness reflects temporary ignorance rather than fundamental explanatory gaps. Daniel Dennett argues that consciousness consists of multiple drafts of information processing, lacking any central theater or qualitative properties requiring special explanation (Dennett, 1991). Moral realism, though psychologically compelling, lacks an ontological foundation—ethical claims express attitudes or describe evolutionary adaptations rather than stating objective facts about reality's evaluative structure.

Yet materialist worldviews face persistent challenges that resist resolution through additional empirical investigation. The hard problem of consciousness persists despite decades of neuroscientific advances. Frank Jackson's knowledge argument and David Chalmers' zombie argument suggest that complete physical information leaves out phenomenal properties (Jackson, 1982; Chalmers, 1996). Abstract objects—mathematical entities, logical principles, possible worlds—appear to exist independently of physical instantiation yet remain indispensable for scientific theorizing.

16.3 THEISTIC REALISM: REALITY AS DIVINE CREATION

16.3.1 Classical Theistic Arguments

Theistic realism interprets first principles through divine creation and providential governance. Reality exists as the purposeful creation of a transcendent, personal God whose necessary existence grounds contingent existence, whose intellect explains cosmic intelligibility, and whose moral nature provides objective standards for ethical evaluation. Rather than competing with scientific explanation at the level of efficient causation, theism addresses different explanatory levels—ultimate rather than proximate, formal and final rather than merely efficient.

Contemporary natural theology has undergone a significant revival through rigorous philosophical analysis. Richard Swinburne develops cumulative case arguments demonstrating that multiple phenomena together render theism more probable than naturalistic alternatives (Swinburne, 2004). The universe's existence, law-governed structure, fine-tuning for life, consciousness, moral awareness, religious experience, and historical testimony constitute converging evidence lines. While each phenomenon admits a naturalistic explanation individually, their conjunction points toward divine agency as the most economical explanation. Swinburne employs Bayesian confirmation theory to formalize this cumulative case, calculating that theism's prior probability combined with evidence yields a posterior probability exceeding 0.5.

William Lane Craig and J.P. Moreland advance sophisticated philosophical arguments interpreting first principles as indicating transcendent reality (Craig & Moreland, 2009). The Kalām cosmological argument, refined through engagement with contemporary cosmology and philosophy of time, infers transcendent causation from the universe's temporal beginning. Alexander Pruss and Joshua Rasmussen develop new modal cosmological arguments demonstrating that contingent reality requires a necessary foundation (Pruss & Rasmussen, 2018). Robert Koons presents a novel mereological argument from the impossibility of self-grounding composite entities (Koons, 1997).

Fine-tuning arguments have achieved unprecedented sophistication through engagement with contemporary physics. Robin Collins calculates that life-permitting parameter ranges occupy vanishingly small regions of theoretical parameter space, with some constants requiring precision exceeding one part in 10^{120} (Collins, 2009). Luke Barnes's comprehensive review demonstrates that fine-tuning extends across multiple independent parameters whose life-permitting ranges do not overlap, compounding improbability (Barnes, 2012). These arguments address multiverse objections by noting that universe-generating mechanisms themselves require fine-tuning, generating regress rather than explanation.

16.3.2 Epistemological Approaches

Alvin Plantinga's reformed epistemology challenges classical evidentialist assumptions requiring inferential support for religious beliefs (Plantinga, 2000). Just as agents trust perception and memory without argumentative justification, belief in God can arise from immediate awareness through sensus divinitatis—a cognitive faculty producing theistic belief in appropriate circumstances. This approach shifts the burden of proof from theistic believers to critics who must demonstrate that direct religious awareness lacks reliability. Plantinga's evolutionary argument against naturalism demonstrates that naturalistic evolution cannot guarantee cognitive reliability, undermining naturalistic critiques of religious belief (Plantinga, 2011).

Contemporary perfect being theology systematizes divine attribute analysis through conceptual investigation of maximal perfection. Katherin Rogers develops sophisticated analyses addressing classical problems regarding divine immutability, omniscience, and moral perfection through careful attention to logical relationships between perfections and their compatibility with creation and providence (Rogers, 2000). Brian Leftow's neoplatonic approach grounds abstract objects in divine intellect, resolving tensions between divine aseity and mathematical truth (Leftow, 2012).

Islamic philosophical theology contributes distinctive perspectives through classical and contemporary scholars. Al-Ghazali's occasionalism argues that efficient causation requires divine action—natural causes serve as occasions for divine creation of effects rather than possessing independent causal powers (Al-Ghazali, 1095/2000). Contemporary Islamic philosophers like Seyyed Hossein Nasr integrate traditional Islamic metaphysics with modern scientific understanding while maintaining theocentric orientation (Nasr, 1993). Ibn Rushd's harmonization of Aristotelian philosophy with Islamic theology demonstrates that investigating natural causation reveals divine wisdom, making scientific investigation a form of religious obligation rather than secular enterprise (Ibn Rushd, 1179/2001).

16.3.3 Contemporary Challenges

Graham Oppy's systematic critique reveals persistent difficulties confronting natural theology (Oppy, 2006). The logical problem of evil, while largely resolved through free will defenses, gives way to evidential arguments from gratuitous suffering. William Rowe's fawn argument and Paul Draper's hypothesis of indifference challenge theistic explanations of apparently pointless suffering (Rowe, 1979; Draper, 1989). Theodicies invoking soul-making, natural law, or divine hiddenness strain credibility when confronting horrific evils.

J.L. Schellenberg's hiddenness argument contends that perfect divine love would ensure universal accessibility to divine relationship, yet widespread non-resistant non-belief suggests divine absence (Schellenberg, 2015). The argument's force derives from connecting divine love with human analogies—loving parents do not hide from children seeking relationship. Responses invoking goods of divine hiddenness or denying non-resistant non-belief face empirical and conceptual challenges.

Religious diversity undermines specific theistic truth claims through conflicting revelatory traditions. John Hick's pluralistic hypothesis interprets diverse religions as culturally conditioned responses to ineffable Real, but this approach sacrifices traditional theistic claims about divine nature and action (Hick, 2004). The interaction problem questions how an immaterial deity affects material creation without violating causal closure. Divine action proposals invoking quantum indeterminacy or emergence face charges of god-of-the-gaps reasoning.

16.4 IDEALISTIC PHILOSOPHIES: CONSCIOUSNESS AS FUNDAMENTAL

16.4.1 Classical and Contemporary Idealism

Idealistic worldviews reverse materialist priorities by treating consciousness as metaphysically fundamental while explaining matter as mental construction, appearance, or phenomenal manifestation. From Berkeley's immaterialism through German Absolute Idealism to contemporary consciousness-first approaches, idealism interprets first principles as primarily experiential rather than physical. This orientation naturally accommodates consciousness, meaning, and value while confronting challenges regarding material regularity and intersubjective agreement.

George Berkeley's immaterialist philosophy argues that material substances lack coherent conception—all qualities attributed to matter prove mental in character (Berkeley, 1710/1965). Primary qualities like extension and solidity reduce to sensory experiences just as secondary qualities like color and taste. External objects consist of collections of ideas perceived by minds, with God's continuous perception maintaining objective reality between finite observations. This approach eliminates the interaction problem plaguing substance dualism while preserving empirical science through systematic correlation of experiential sequences.

Contemporary analytical idealism finds sophisticated expression in Timothy Sprigge's panpsychist idealism, which contends that reality consists entirely of experiential centers arranged hierarchically from simple occasions to cosmic consciousness (Sprigge, 1983). Physical laws describe external appearances of inner experiential processes rather than mind-independent structures. Human consciousness emerges through combining simpler experiences, though the combination problem—explaining how micro-experiences yield unified macro-consciousness—remains challenging. Sprigge addresses this through holistic emergence, where wholes possess irreducible properties transcending constituent summation.

Howard Robinson's contemporary defense of idealism employs updated versions of Berkeley's arguments while engaging modern physics and neuroscience (Robinson, 2016). The argument from perceptual relativity demonstrates that all perceived qualities depend upon observational perspective, undermining mind-independent material properties. The problem of matter's intrinsic nature reveals that physics describes only structural/relational properties, leaving matter's categorical base unspecified—idealism proposes experience as this categorical foundation.

16.4.2 Contemporary Developments

Bernardo Kastrup articulates analytical idealism, proposing consciousness as ontologically primitive (Kastrup, 2019). Matter consists of perceptual experiences within universal consciousness rather than possessing independent existence. The external world represents mental processes' extrinsic appearance, analogous to how brain states appear as experiences from within while displaying neural activity from external observation. Kastrup addresses the decomposition problem through dissociative boundaries, creating distinct experiential streams within universal consciousness.

Philip Goff's cosmopsychism posits universe-wide consciousness grounding individual minds rather than consciousness emerging from unconscious components (Goff, 2017). This approach reverses the hard problem by making unconscious matter rather than consciousness require explanation. Russellian monism, developed through engagement with Bertrand Russell's neutral monism, suggests that physics describes structural relationships while intrinsic nature may prove experiential throughout reality's fundamental levels (Russell, 1927). Galen Strawson's argument from non-emergence demonstrates that experiential properties cannot emerge from purely non-experiential foundations, necessitating panpsychism or idealism (Strawson, 2006).

Itay Shani's cosmopsychist idealism integrates Eastern philosophical insights with contemporary consciousness studies (Shani, 2015). Individual minds represent localized manifestations of cosmic consciousness, explaining both unity and multiplicity through field-theoretic models. This approach addresses combination problems through holistic determination, where cosmic consciousness grounds individual experiences without aggregation from components.

16.4.3 Explanatory Advantages and Difficulties

Idealism elegantly explains consciousness's epistemological immediacy—subjective experience requires no further explanation since it serves as the foundation for all other explanations. The knowledge argument's force dissipates if physical properties themselves prove mental. Values and meanings possess genuine rather than merely projected reality within fundamentally mental frameworks. Mathematical objects exist as constructs within the divine or absolute mind rather than abstract entities lacking causal powers. Nature's intelligibility reflects a pervasive mind-like structure rather than mysterious correspondence between rational thought and independent reality.

Donald Hoffman's interface theory of perception supports idealist interpretations by demonstrating that evolution selects for fitness rather than veridical perception—our experiences constitute user interfaces hiding reality's true nature (Hoffman, 2019). Quantum mechanics' observer-dependence supports idealist interpretations where measurement represents interaction between conscious systems rather than consciousness collapsing wave functions. Information-theoretic approaches to physics suggest that information rather than matter constitutes fundamental reality, with information requiring mental interpretation.

Nevertheless, idealism confronts serious empirical and conceptual challenges. Matter's recalcitrance to mental control suggests genuine external constraint transcending wishful thinking. Samuel Johnson's stone-kicking refutation, while philosophically naive, captures intuitive resistance to idealism. Physical causation operates independently of conscious observation in most contexts—radioactive decay proceeds unobserved, geological processes shaped Earth before consciousness emerged. Intersubjective agreement about external reality implies shared objective structures rather than purely subjective construction.

16.5 PROCESS PHILOSOPHY AND PANENTHEISTIC WORLDVIEWS

16.5.1 Whiteheadian Process Metaphysics

Process philosophy, initiated by Alfred North Whitehead and developed through various panentheistic approaches, emphasizes becoming over being, experience over substance, and relationship over isolation

(Whitehead, 1929). This framework interprets first principles dynamically—reality consists of events ("actual occasions") rather than enduring entities, with each occasion possessing both physical and mental poles through which it integrates influences from its environment into novel synthetic unities.

Whitehead's categorial scheme provides a systematic metaphysical framework addressing classical philosophical problems. The ontological principle states that actual occasions constitute final realities underlying apparent substances—"apart from things that are actual, there is nothing" (Whitehead, 1929). Each occasion emerges through "prehending" past occasions via conformal physical feelings while entertaining possibilities through conceptual feelings of eternal objects. This temporal process accounts for both continuity through causal inheritance and novelty through creative self-determination.

Nicholas Rescher's systematic process metaphysics demonstrates how this approach addresses perennial philosophical problems through temporal and relational categories (Rescher, 1996). Change becomes fundamental rather than derivative, emergence receives natural explanation through creative synthesis, and mind-body relationships dissolve into complementary aspects of the underlying process. Process coherence replaces substantial identity as the principle of individuation. Dispositional properties ground causal powers without requiring underlying substances.

Michel Weber's genetic interpretation emphasizes Whitehead's empirical methodology and phenomenological foundations (Weber, 2006). Process philosophy begins with the immediate experience of temporal passage, causal efficacy, and creative advance rather than abstract principles. This experiential grounding distinguishes process thought from purely speculative metaphysics while maintaining systematic comprehensiveness.

16.5.2 Process Theology and Panentheism

David Ray Griffin develops process theology, arguing for naturalistic theism, avoiding both supernatural interventionism and materialistic reductionism (Griffin, 2001). God acts through persuasion rather than coercion, offering possibilities ("initial aims") that creatures freely actualize according to their subjective aims. This explains natural evil through creaturely freedom extending throughout nature, religious diversity through partial divine responses to different cultural contexts, and evolutionary creativity through divine lure toward greater complexity and consciousness.

Charles Hartshorne's neoclassical theism proposes a dipolar deity possessing both eternal-abstract and temporal-concrete aspects (Hartshorne, 1984). The primordial nature contains eternal possibilities, while the consequent nature experiences and preserves worldly actualizations. Divine perfection includes supreme relativity—being optimally responsive to creation—rather than static immutability. God remains supremely excellent through surpassing all others, including prior divine states, yet genuinely affected by creaturely experiences.

Philip Clayton's emergentist panentheism connects process insights with contemporary scientific understanding of emergence and complexity (Clayton, 2004). God works through emergent dynamics without violating natural laws, utilizing quantum indeterminacy, chaotic sensitivity, and emergent downward causation. Strong emergence generates genuine novelty irreducible to component properties, providing loci for divine action without interventionism. This synthesis honors both scientific discoveries and religious insight without requiring either reductionism or supernaturalistic intervention.

Catherine Keller's process theology emphasizes creation from chaos (tehom) rather than ex nihilo, interpreting Genesis through Whitehead's cosmology (Keller, 2003). Divine creativity works with primordial potentiality rather than unilaterally determining outcomes. This addresses theodicy through divine limitation while maintaining religious adequacy through ultimate divine victory achieved through persuasive love rather than coercive power.

16.5.3 Process Interpretation of First Principles

Process thought interprets first principles relationally and temporally rather than as eternal static truths. Physical laws describe dominant patterns of occasions' habitual responses rather than external constraints imposed upon passive matter. Societies of occasions maintain structural patterns through inherited characteristics while allowing creative deviation. Mathematical relationships map event-structures and their formal possibilities (eternal objects) rather than abstract entities existing independently of temporal becoming.

Consciousness represents high-grade experience emerging from lower-grade experiential processes throughout nature rather than emerging discontinuously from purely unconscious matter. This addresses the hard problem through panexperientialism—all actual occasions possess experiential poles, though most lack consciousness's complex integration. Values possess objective reality as divine aims influencing creaturely decision-making, yet require subjective actualization through free responses.

Evolution expresses divine creativity channeled through creaturely freedom toward enhanced complexity, consciousness, and value-realization. Stuart Kauffman's investigations of self-organization and emergence complement process interpretations of evolutionary creativity (Kauffman, 1995). Terrence Deacon's work on emergent dynamics and absent phenomena resonates with process accounts of final causation (Deacon, 2011).

Critics challenge process philosophy's coherence and explanatory adequacy. Actual occasions remain conceptually obscure and potentially unfalsifiable through empirical investigation. The ontological principle generates regress—what actualizes eternal objects before first temporal occasions? Divine limitation conflicts with religious intuitions regarding omnipotence and providential control. Process theology's God appears insufficient for robust religious practice requiring divine reliability and ultimate triumph over evil.

16.6 EASTERN NON-DUALISTIC AND PRAGMATIC ALTERNATIVES

16.6.1 Buddhist Philosophy and Dependent Origination

Buddhist philosophical traditions, particularly Nāgārjuna's Madhyamaka analysis, demonstrate the emptiness (śūnyatā) of inherent existence through investigating dependent origination (pratītyasamutpāda) (Garfield, 1995). All phenomena arise interdependently without permanent essences or independent substances. Conventional entities represent useful designations rather than ultimate realities. First principles constitute pragmatic conventions facilitating successful navigation rather than descriptions of fundamental metaphysical structures.

Mark Siderits's systematic presentation reveals sophisticated analyses addressing classical philosophical problems through non-substantialist frameworks (Siderits, 2007). Personal identity dissolves into causal streams (santāna) of psychophysical processes without a permanent self (anātman). The five aggregates (skandhas) constitute conventional persons without substantial unity. Consciousness consists of a temporal series of mental factors (cetasika) arising through causes and conditions without a substantial agent.

The Yogācāra school develops consciousness-only (vijñaptimātra) idealism, where external objects represent consciousness transformations rather than independent realities. Vasubandhu's Twenty Verses demonstrates how apparently objective features result from karmic seeds (bīja) and conceptual construction (vikalpa) rather than representing genuine metaphysical structures (Vasubandhu, 1991). Yet this differs from Western idealism by denying substantial consciousness—awareness itself arises interdependently without a permanent nature.

Contemporary Buddhist philosophy engages Western philosophical problems while maintaining distinctive Buddhist commitments. Jan Westerhoff's analysis of Madhyamaka demonstrates its relevance to contemporary debates about realism, anti-realism, and metaphysical foundationalism (Westerhoff, 2009). Owen Flanagan explores naturalistic interpretations of Buddhist philosophy compatible with scientific worldviews while preserving ethical and soteriological dimensions (Flanagan, 2011).

16.6.2 Daoist and Advaitic Perspectives

Daoist philosophy articulates reality through complementary processes (yin-yang) and spontaneous emergence from ineffable Dao rather than static principles or substances. The Daodejing's opening verse—"The Dao that can be spoken is not the eternal Dao"—establishes limits of conceptual knowledge (Laozi, 2003). Chad Hansen's analysis demonstrates how Daoist thought challenges Western metaphysical assumptions about identity, causation, and knowledge through its distinctive semantic and metaphysical perspectives (Hansen, 1992).

Zhuangzi's philosophical skepticism questions conventional distinctions through transformation stories and perspective shifts (Zhuangzi, 2013). The butterfly dream raises questions about identity persistence and reality criteria. Relativism about usefulness (yong) undermines universal standards while preserving contextual appropriateness. This generates a therapeutic philosophy aimed at cognitive flexibility rather than doctrinal systems.

Advaita Vedanta, systematized by Śaṅkara and refined through subsequent commentary tradition, asserts non-dual consciousness

(Brahman) as the sole reality (Śaṅkara, 1992). Phenomenal diversity (māyā) constitutes neither pure illusion nor separate reality but Brahman appearing through limiting adjuncts (upādhi). Individual consciousness (ātman) equals universal consciousness, though ignorance (avidyā) creates apparent separation. Knowledge (jñāna) removes ignorance, revealing ever-present unity rather than achieving something absent.

Contemporary Advaita philosophy engages Western philosophical problems while maintaining non-dualist commitments. Eliot Deutsch's systematic presentation demonstrates Advaita's sophisticated analyses of consciousness, knowledge, and reality (Deutsch, 1969). Bina Gupta's work shows how Advaita addresses contemporary consciousness studies while maintaining its distinctive metaphysical framework (Gupta, 2003).

16.6.3 Pragmatic Approaches

William James's pragmatism interprets first principles through practical consequences rather than foundational metaphysics (James, 1907/1975). Truth constitutes successful action-guidance rather than correspondence to independent reality. Rather than asking what first principles are essentially, pragmatism investigates what practical differences they generate within experience. This approach dissolves pseudo-problems while focusing attention upon experiential "cash value."

John Dewey's naturalistic pragmatism reconstructs philosophical problems through analysis of inquiry processes rather than pursuing ultimate foundations (Dewey, 1929). Knowledge emerges through experimental interaction with the environment rather than passive reflection of independent structures. Intelligence evolved for problem-solving rather than metaphysical speculation. Values arise through intelligent reconstruction of problematic situations rather than discovery of objective moral facts.

Contemporary pragmatism continues evolving through engagement with analytic philosophy and continental thought. Hilary Putnam's pragmatic realism maintains that truth transcends verification while rejecting metaphysical realism's god's-eye view (Putnam, 1981). Robert Brandom's inferentialism grounds meaning in social practices of giving and asking for reasons rather than representation relations (Brandom, 1994). Huw Price's global expressivism extends pragmatic strategies across philosophical domains while maintaining a naturalistic orientation (Price,

2011).

Richard Rorty extends anti-foundationalist approaches by challenging the entire philosophical project of discovering first principles (Rorty, 1979). Philosophy should abandon representationalist assumptions and focus upon conversation and social practices rather than pursuing objective knowledge of reality's fundamental nature. This neo-pragmatic approach treats worldview debates as cultural conversations rather than disputes about metaphysical truth. Cheryl Misak's critical pragmatism preserves truth's normative force while maintaining fallibilism and experimental method (Misak, 2013).

16.7 THE HERMENEUTICAL STRUCTURE OF WORLDVIEW INTERPRETATION

16.7.1 Theory-Ladenness and Interpretive Frameworks

Worldviews fundamentally shape what phenomena count as factual, what constitutes adequate explanation, and what evidence proves relevant— making theory-neutral observation impossible. Understanding how interpretive frameworks determine observation proves crucial for evaluating first principles claims and adjudicating between competing worldview systems.

Hans-Georg Gadamer's philosophical hermeneutics demonstrates that understanding necessarily involves pre-understanding (Vorverständnis) that interpretation subsequently modifies through encounter with texts, traditions, and phenomena (Gadamer, 2004). The hermeneutical circle— interpretation requiring prior understanding which interpretation transforms—operates throughout human knowledge rather than representing mere methodological limitation. Prejudices (Vorurteile) enable rather than obstruct understanding when subjected to critical examination through dialogical encounter.

Paul Ricoeur extends hermeneutical insights through dialectic of explanation and understanding (Ricoeur, 1976). Scientific explanation provides necessary moment within interpretive arc but requires integration with understanding that grasps meaning and significance. This hermeneutical approach applies to natural as well as human sciences—even physical phenomena require interpretation through theoretical frameworks determining observational significance.

Imre Lakatos demonstrated how scientific research programs protect theoretical hard cores through auxiliary hypothesis modifications preserving central commitments while accommodating anomalous observations (Lakatos, 1978). Similarly, worldviews deflect challenges through protective belt adjustments maintaining core tenets. Materialists promise future neuroscientific explanations of consciousness; theists invoke divine hiddenness or greater good defenses; idealists appeal to universal mind or cosmic consciousness; pragmatists question the meaningfulness of disputed claims.

16.7.2 Tradition-Dependent Rationality

Alasdair MacIntyre's analysis reveals that rationality operates within tradition-dependent frameworks rather than through universal neutral standards (MacIntyre, 1988). Different worldviews employ distinct criteria for evaluating explanation adequacy, evidence relevance, and argumentative success. These differences reflect constitutive features rather than mere preferences, making neutral adjudication between comprehensive worldviews impossible through appeal to shared rational standards.

Consider fine-tuning evidence interpretation across worldview frameworks. Materialists perceive observer selection effects or multiverse scenarios eliminating design implications. Theists interpret precise parameter values as indicating divine wisdom and purposeful creation. Idealists understand apparent fine-tuning as mental self-organization within cosmic consciousness. Process philosophers view parameter values as expressing divine lure toward complexity and consciousness. Eastern non-dualists regard fine-tuning discussions as conceptual constructions lacking ultimate significance. Pragmatists focus on fine-tuning arguments' practical implications rather than metaphysical truth.

Each interpretation follows rationally from background commitments while appearing question-begging from alternative perspectives. This reflects what MacIntyre calls "conceptual incommensurability"— frameworks employ concepts lacking direct translation across worldview boundaries. Yet incommensurability does not entail incomparability. Worldviews can be evaluated through their ability to resolve internal crises, incorporate rivals' insights, and provide superior explanatory resources.

16.7.3 Phenomenological Variation

Worldviews shape not merely theoretical interpretation but experiential phenomenology itself—how reality appears within conscious awareness. Maurice Merleau-Ponty's phenomenology of perception demonstrates that embodied consciousness structures experience through acquired habits and cultural sedimentations rather than passively receiving sensory data (Merleau-Ponty, 1945/2012). Different worldviews generate distinct lived worlds (Lebenswelt) rather than different beliefs about identical experiences.

Contemporary enactive cognition research supports phenomenological insights about experience's worldview-dependence. Perception involves sensorimotor contingencies shaped by cultural practices and conceptual frameworks (Thompson, 2007). Meditation practices alter perceptual processing and self-experience in measurable ways (Lutz et al., 2004). Psychedelic experiences reveal perception's constructed character while potentially accessing alternative organizational modes (Carhart-Harris & Friston, 2019).

Charles Taylor's analysis reveals how worldviews constitute different forms of life rather than merely different theoretical positions (Taylor, 1989). Secular materialism generates disenchanted experience where nature appears as meaningless mechanism. Theistic frameworks produce providential awareness where events carry divine significance. Buddhist practice cultivates perception of impermanence and non-self. These represent genuinely different experiences rather than identical perceptions differently interpreted.

16.8 CRITERIA FOR WORLDVIEW EVALUATION

16.8.1 Internal Consistency and Logical Coherence

Despite worldviews' pervasive interpretive influence, rational evaluation remains possible through criteria emerging from comparative analysis of explanatory successes, internal tensions, and practical implications. While no absolutely neutral standpoint exists, evaluative criteria develop through critical examination, acknowledging situatedness while pursuing truth.

Internal consistency represents a minimal requirement—worldviews should avoid self-contradiction, though determining genuine contradiction requires careful analysis, distinguishing apparent from real logical conflicts.

Eliminative materialists face performative contradiction by presupposing consciousness while theoretically denying its existence. As Galen Strawson observes, denying consciousness's existence represents "the silliest claim ever made" given consciousness's indubitable givenness (Strawson, 2018). Theists confront logical tensions between divine attributes—can omniscience coexist with libertarian free will? Does divine immutability permit genuine responsiveness?

However, apparent contradictions may reflect inadequate formulations rather than fundamental incoherence. Sophisticated worldview development addresses tensions through conceptual refinement. Peter van Inwagen's consequence argument clarifies compatibilist and incompatibilist positions regarding free will and determinism (van Inwagen, 1983). Open theism modifies classical divine attributes to preserve genuine divine-human interaction (Pinnock et al., 1994). The presence of challenging problems does not automatically refute worldview systems.

16.8.2 Explanatory Scope and Depth

Comprehensive worldviews should illuminate rather than ignore significant phenomena within human experience and scientific investigation. Explanatory scope involves addressing the full range of considerations any adequate worldview must accommodate: consciousness, moral experience, scientific success, religious phenomena, aesthetic value, logical and mathematical knowledge, interpersonal relationships, and existential meaning.

Materialism excels at explaining physical regularities, technological success, and evolutionary development but struggles with consciousness, meaning, and objective value. The "explanatory gap" between neural processes and subjective experience persists despite neuroscientific advances (Levine, 2001). Theism accounts for cosmic purpose, moral objectivity, and religious experience while confronting evil, hiddenness, and religious diversity. Idealism accommodates mental phenomena, value, and meaning, but strains explaining material recalcitrance and intersubjective agreement.

Explanatory depth concerns whether worldviews address fundamental questions or merely postpone them. Multiverse explanations of fine-tuning may shift questions about parameter values to questions about multiverse-generating mechanisms. Divine command theories face questions about God's nature and reasons for commands. Pragmatic deflation may avoid rather than resolve genuine metaphysical problems requiring resolution.

16.8.3 Existential and Practical Adequacy

Worldviews must prove livable—adherents should act consistently according to theoretical implications without performative contradiction or systematic self-deception. This existential criterion reveals theory-practice tensions that purely theoretical analysis might overlook.

Thomas Nagel notes that eliminativists regarding consciousness cannot genuinely eliminate first-person experience from their lives—they continue acting as conscious agents while denying consciousness theoretically (Nagel, 1986). Determinists deliberate about choices while denying that genuine alternatives exist. Relativists argue for positions while denying objective truth. Idealists navigate material constraints while denying matter's independent existence.

Yet existential criteria require careful application. Truth may prove existentially challenging without being false. Evolutionary accounts of morality may undermine moral motivation without falsifying moral realism. Determinism may generate fatalism without being incorrect. The criterion concerns whether worldviews enable consistent practical engagement rather than whether they provide psychological comfort.

16.8.4 Empirical Fruitfulness and Research Productivity

Worldviews generating productive research programs and practical applications demonstrate vitality that stagnant alternatives lack. This pragmatic criterion evaluates frameworks through their capacity to stimulate discovery, solve problems, and enhance understanding.

Materialist worldviews have generated remarkable technological achievements and scientific discoveries. Neuroscience, evolutionary biology, and physics advance through methodological naturalism regardless of ultimate metaphysical truth. Contemplative traditions produce psychological insights validated through empirical research on meditation, mindfulness, and consciousness alteration. Process approaches illuminate ecological relationships and complex systems. Theistic frameworks motivate medical research, charitable work, and meaning-creation, enhancing human flourishing.

However, practical success within limited domains does not establish comprehensive truth. Effective techniques may operate through mechanisms different from those proposed by associated worldviews. Newtonian mechanics remains practically successful despite theoretical falsity. The pragmatic criterion supplements rather than replaces considerations of truth, coherence, and explanatory adequacy.

16.9 CONCLUSION: THE HERMENEUTICAL CHALLENGE OF FIRST PRINCIPLES

The examination of competing worldviews reveals that first principles appear fundamentally different when viewed through alternative interpretive lenses. Each comprehensive framework provides coherent accounts of reality's nature while generating distinct phenomenologies, explanatory priorities, and evaluative standards. This hermeneutical situation does not eliminate rational assessment but requires acknowledging perspectival limitations while pursuing truth through critical dialogue.

Rather than representing mere intellectual positions, worldviews constitute comprehensive orientations involving theoretical, practical, experiential, and existential dimensions. William James's concept of "will to believe" recognizes that worldview commitment necessarily exceeds conclusive evidence while remaining constrained by logical, empirical, and practical considerations (James, 1896). Underdetermination by evidence means that existential, aesthetic, and pragmatic factors legitimately influence worldview adoption without violating rational standards.

The convergences identified in previous chapters—shared epistemic commitments, cosmic intelligibility, consciousness phenomena, fine-tuning patterns—suggest that exclusive adherence to single worldviews may impoverish understanding. Perhaps wisdom involves recognizing how different frameworks illuminate complementary aspects of reality's complexity while remaining committed to truth-seeking through critical engagement.

Each worldview contributes genuine insights while facing distinctive limitations. John Hick's critical realism proposes that different worldviews represent varying responses to transcendent Reality that exceeds complete capture by any single framework (Hick, 1989). Yet this need not collapse into relativism. Some worldviews prove more adequate than others for particular explanatory tasks. The challenge involves integrating insights while maintaining critical standards.

The task for first principles investigation involves neither relativistic acceptance of all worldviews as equally valid nor dogmatic insistence upon single framework adequacy. Instead, it requires what Gadamer calls "fusion of horizons"—critical dialogue that remains open to truth while acknowledging interpretive situatedness (Gadamer, 2004). This approach maintains both truth-commitment and perspectival humility, recognizing that reality's complexity may exceed any single worldview's explanatory scope while preserving rational standards for evaluation and comparison.

As the investigation proceeds toward examining truth's unity amid this diversity of interpretive frameworks, these competing worldviews provide essential context for integration attempts while demonstrating that first principles investigation cannot bypass hermeneutical challenges through appeal to neutral objectivity. The quest requires intellectual rigor, existential engagement, theoretical sophistication, practical wisdom, and critical analysis combined with interpretive charity. Understanding first principles ultimately involves not choosing between comprehensive frameworks but learning from their insights while pursuing truth that transcends any single perspective's limitations.

CHAPTER 17: THE UNITY OF TRUTH

The pursuit of truth across scientific, philosophical, and religious domains frequently yields seemingly incompatible results. Contemporary neuroscience describes consciousness as emergent from neural networks, while phenomenological philosophy emphasizes the irreducible first-person character of experience. Evolutionary biology explains complex organisms through undirected natural selection, while theological traditions affirm purposive divine action in natural history. Quantum mechanics reveals fundamental indeterminacy at microscopic scales, while moral philosophy often presupposes objective normative truths. Yet if truth corresponds to reality, and reality possesses fundamental unity, these divergent accounts must ultimately cohere within a comprehensive framework. This chapter examines how truth functions as a unifying principle across different domains of inquiry, addresses substantive contradictions through hierarchical integration, and proposes methodological strategies for navigating epistemic diversity.

17.1 THE METAPHYSICS OF TRUTH

Before examining inter-domain relationships, we must establish a robust account of truth itself that can accommodate both diversity and unity. The correspondence theory, formalized by Alfred Tarski and refined by contemporary philosophers, holds that truth consists in correspondence between propositions and reality (Tarski, 1944). The T-schema—"Snow is white" is true if and only if snow is white—captures this intuition while avoiding semantic paradoxes. However, this apparently straightforward formulation conceals profound metaphysical and epistemological complexities that become acute when applied across fundamentally different types of inquiry.

Crispin Wright identifies several dimensions along which truth-apt discourse can vary: cognitive command (whether disagreement indicates error), width of cosmological role (whether truth transcends human practices), and evidence-transcendence (whether truth can outrun ideal verification) (Wright, 1992). These variations suggest that truth itself may be pluralistic while preserving minimal core conditions. Michael P. Lynch develops this insight into moderate alethic pluralism, arguing that different domains employ distinct truth properties—correspondence for empirical claims, coherence for mathematical statements, pragmatic success for moral judgments—while sharing formal logical properties like consistency and closure under logical consequence (Lynch, 2009).

The correspondence relation proves more complex than initial formulations suggest. Field argues that correspondence requires both linguistic-conceptual relations and word-world relations, with the latter presenting particular challenges for abstract domains (Field, 2001). Devitt's scientific realism maintains that correspondence obtains between theoretical terms and mind-independent entities, but this becomes problematic for mathematical and moral truths lacking obvious worldly correlates (Devitt, 1997). Armstrong's truthmaker theory requires that for every truth, something in the world makes it true, but identifying truthmakers for negative existentials, modal claims, and normative statements remains controversial (Armstrong, 2004).

Scientific truths paradigmatically involve correspondence relations between theoretical statements and observable phenomena, mediated by sophisticated instrumentation and mathematical modeling. The claim that "the cosmic microwave background exhibits near-perfect blackbody radiation at 2.7255 Kelvin" achieves truth through precise correspondence between theoretical predictions derived from Big Bang cosmology and spectroscopic measurements from the Wilkinson Microwave Anisotropy Probe (Fixsen, 2009). Yet even paradigmatic scientific truths involve idealization, approximation, and model-dependent interpretation that complicate simple correspondence accounts (Cartwright, 1983).

Mathematical truths achieve necessity through proof-theoretic derivation within formal systems, as Kurt Gödel's incompleteness theorems demonstrate for arithmetic (Gödel, 1931). Benacerraf's dilemma highlights the tension between mathematical truth and knowledge: if mathematical objects exist abstractly to serve as truthmakers, how can causally isolated humans know them? If mathematical truth reduces to provability in formal systems, how do we account for the apparent objectivity of mathematical facts? (Benacerraf, 1973). Structuralist approaches attempt resolution by identifying mathematical truth with structural relationships rather than object-correspondence (Shapiro, 1997).

Moral truths, if they exist, may require different criteria altogether. Rawls suggests that moral truths emerge through ideal rational endorsement under conditions of full information and impartial concern, as modeled by the original position thought experiment (Rawls, 1971). Street challenges moral realism by arguing that evolutionary forces shaped our evaluative attitudes without tracking attitude-independent moral facts, undermining justification for moral beliefs (Street, 2006). Cuneo responds that moral skepticism entails epistemic skepticism since both moral and epistemic facts are irreducibly normative, making global normative anti-realism self-defeating (Cuneo, 2007).

Religious truth claims present particular challenges for any unified account. Statements like "God is omniscient" or "ultimate reality is consciousness" invoke transcendent realities that appear to exceed both empirical verification and formal derivation. William Alston argues that mystical perception can generate justified religious beliefs through direct experiential acquaintance with divine reality, analogous to how sensory perception justifies beliefs about physical objects (Alston, 1991). However, the privacy and ineffability of mystical experience, combined with conflicting reports across traditions, complicates any straightforward epistemological assessment. Hick's religious pluralism interprets diverse religious experiences as culturally conditioned responses to the same ultimate Real, but this threatens the truth-evaluability of specific doctrinal claims (Hick, 2004).

Despite these differences, all legitimate truth claims share certain formal constraints that point toward underlying unity. The principle of non-contradiction requires that no statement and its negation can both be true in the same sense at the same time, regardless of the domain. The principle of explosion (ex contradictione quodlibet) dictates that from any contradiction, any statement follows—thus preserving logical consistency becomes essential for meaningful discourse. Graham Priest has argued for the coherence of true contradictions (dialetheias) in certain paradoxical contexts through paraconsistent logic, but even these systems typically preserve consistency for most statements while restricting explosion to local contexts (Priest, 2006).

Davidson's principle of charity demonstrates that successful interpretation presupposes mostly true beliefs about a shared world (Davidson, 2001). Even when discussing abstract mathematics or spiritual experiences, we employ concepts and linguistic frameworks that evolved through collective engagement with common reality. This suggests that different types of truth claims ultimately refer to aspects of a single, complex reality rather than entirely disparate realms. The principle of charity functions as a transcendental argument: the possibility of radical interpretation requires sufficient agreement about truth to establish reference.

17.2 THE CONVERGENCE THESIS AND ITS CRITICS

The convergence thesis maintains that genuine truths discovered through different methodological approaches must prove ultimately compatible, even if initially appearing contradictory. This thesis draws support from successful interdisciplinary syntheses and the explanatory power of unified theoretical frameworks. However, it faces significant challenges from paradigm incommensurability, theoretical underdetermination, and social construction arguments.

Contemporary cognitive science exemplifies successful convergence across traditionally distinct disciplines. Neuroscientific investigations using functional magnetic resonance imaging (fMRI) and electroencephalography (EEG) map neural correlates of cognitive processes, identifying specific brain regions associated with working memory in the dorsolateral prefrontal cortex, attention networks spanning frontal and parietal regions, and value-based decision-making in the ventromedial prefrontal cortex (Christoff et al., 2016). Ned Block's philosophical analysis clarifies conceptual structures underlying mental phenomena, distinguishing between access consciousness (information availability for use in reasoning and behavioral control) and phenomenal consciousness (subjective experiential qualities)

(Block, 1995).

Artificial intelligence research develops computational models that simulate cognitive functions through deep learning architectures, achieving human-level performance in pattern recognition, game playing, and natural language processing (LeCun et al., 2015). These successes suggest that mental processes admit computational description despite their subjective character. Contemplative science documents systematic changes in brain structure and function following meditation practice, with increased gray matter density in regions associated with attention regulation and emotional processing after eight weeks of mindfulness training (Hölzel et al., 2011).

Rather than competing, these approaches prove complementary and mutually constraining. Neuroscience provides mechanistic explanations for cognitive phenomena but cannot address normative questions about rational belief formation or moral responsibility without philosophical analysis. Philosophy clarifies conceptual foundations but requires empirical constraints to adjudicate between competing theories of mind. Computational modeling offers precise formalization but needs philosophical guidance regarding appropriate levels of abstraction and explanatory targets. Contemplative practices generate first-person data about consciousness but benefit from third-person verification through neuroscientific methods and critical philosophical assessment.

The Human Connectome Project demonstrates institutional commitment to interdisciplinary integration, mapping neural connectivity across multiple scales from synaptic to whole-brain networks (Van Essen et al., 2013). The project assumes that understanding consciousness requires coordinating insights from molecular neuroscience, systems neuroscience, cognitive psychology, and computational modeling rather than privileging any single approach. Early results reveal how structural connectivity constrains functional dynamics while allowing flexible reconfiguration for diverse cognitive demands (Sporns, 2013).

However, Thomas Kuhn's analysis of scientific revolutions reveals how paradigm shifts can render previously accepted theories not merely false but meaningless within new frameworks (Kuhn, 1962/1996). Newtonian absolute simultaneity did not translate into relativistic physics; phlogiston theory's combustion explanations became unintelligible after Lavoisier's oxygen paradigm; vitalist life-forces found no place in molecular biology. If paradigms determine what counts as meaningful questions, relevant evidence, and valid inference patterns, then convergence across paradigms may prove impossible in principle.

Paul Feyerabend's methodological anarchism pushes this criticism further, arguing that scientific progress requires the proliferation of mutually inconsistent alternatives rather than convergence toward consensus (Feyerabend, 1975). The history of science reveals how theoretical diversity stimulates innovation: heliocentric astronomy contradicted established physics; quantum mechanics violated classical determinism; continental drift challenged geological orthodoxy. From this perspective, premature convergence threatens intellectual progress by suppressing creative alternatives that might yield revolutionary insights.

The Duhem-Quine thesis of underdetermination argues that any finite set of observations remains compatible with indefinitely many theoretical frameworks (Duhem, 1906/1991; Quine, 1951). Empirical evidence cannot uniquely determine theory choice because auxiliary hypotheses can always be adjusted to accommodate recalcitrant data. If evidence never conclusively adjudicates between theories, apparent convergence may reflect social consensus rather than objective truth. Larry Laudan documents how scientific values like simplicity, scope, and fruitfulness vary across communities and historical periods, further complicating convergence claims (Laudan, 1984).

Social constructivists argue that scientific facts are constructed through laboratory practices, instrumental techniques, and rhetorical strategies rather than discovered through neutral observation (Latour & Woolgar, 1979). Ian Hacking's analysis of dynamic nominalism shows how human kinds like "multiple personality disorder" come into being through looping effects between classification and behavior (Hacking, 1995). If truth claims reflect social interests, power relations, and available conceptual resources, convergence across different communities seems unlikely absent coercive homogenization.

These challenges deserve serious consideration, but do not decisively refute convergence. Regarding incommensurability, careful historical analysis typically reveals sufficient conceptual continuity to enable rational comparison between paradigms. Einstein understood Newtonian mechanics well enough to identify its limitations and specify the conditions under which it provides an adequate approximation. The oxygen paradigm explained combustion phenomena that motivated phlogiston theory while resolving its anomalies. Complete incommensurability would make such a comparative evaluation impossible.

Hilary Putnam's causal theory of reference provides resources for preserving semantic continuity across theory change (Putnam, 1975). Natural kind terms like "water," "gold," and "electron" maintain reference to the same entities despite dramatic conceptual shifts. Water remains H_2O whether conceived as a classical element or molecular compound. This referential stability enables cumulative knowledge despite theoretical revolution.

The underdetermination thesis, while logically sound, overestimates the plasticity of theoretical alternatives. Theories must accommodate existing data, generate novel predictions, integrate with established knowledge from independent domains, and inspire fruitful research programs. These constraints significantly reduce viable options. As Wesley Salmon argues, scientific objectivity emerges from communal practices of empirical testing, critical scrutiny, and theoretical refinement rather than algorithmic theory selection (Salmon, 1990).

Social influences on knowledge production need not undermine objective truth. Helen Longino demonstrates how social diversity enhances objectivity by exposing hidden assumptions, challenging dominant paradigms, and expanding the range of investigated phenomena (Longino, 2002). Feminist standpoint epistemology reveals how marginalized perspectives can identify biases in mainstream science while contributing distinctive insights (Harding, 1991). Social embeddedness enables rather than prevents reliable knowledge when coupled with appropriate critical practices and institutional safeguards.

17.3 HIERARCHICAL INTEGRATION AND EMERGENT PROPERTIES

Resolving apparent contradictions between domains requires recognizing hierarchical relationships between different levels of reality and corresponding explanatory frameworks. Physical processes provide the substrate for chemical reactions, which enable biological functions, which support psychological phenomena, which make possible social institutions and cultural meanings. Each level exhibits distinctive regularities requiring autonomous explanatory principles while remaining constrained by lower-level processes.

Philip Anderson's seminal argument "More Is Different" demonstrates how broken symmetries and emergent properties arise at each organizational level that cannot be predicted from knowledge of constituent parts alone (Anderson, 1972). Superconductivity emerges from Cooper pair formation in certain materials below critical temperatures, but cannot be deduced from quantum mechanics applied to individual electrons. The BCS theory required new conceptual frameworks involving macroscopic quantum coherence and spontaneous symmetry breaking (Bardeen et al., 1957). Consciousness emerges from neural processes but exhibits properties—subjective experience, intentional content, rational agency— absent from neurochemical descriptions.

Contemporary emergence theory distinguishes between weak and strong variants. Weak emergence involves novel properties arising from complex interactions between lower-level components that remain, in principle, derivable from complete microphysical information plus composition principles (Bedau, 1997). Conway's Game of Life exemplifies weak emergence: gliders, oscillators, and other patterns emerge from simple rules but could be predicted by sufficient computation. Strong emergence involves genuinely novel causal powers that cannot be predicted from or reduced to lower-level phenomena even with complete information and unlimited computation (O'Connor & Wong, 2015).

Jaegwon Kim's causal exclusion argument challenges strong emergence by claiming that if physical events have sufficient physical causes, emergent properties cannot exercise genuine causal power without violating causal closure (Kim, 2005). Consider mental causation: if neural event N1 causes neural event N2, which fully determines behavior B, then mental state M appears causally impotent. Either M reduces to N1, violating irreducibility, or M lacks genuine efficacy, rendering it epiphenomenal.

However, this argument assumes problematic conceptions of causation and levels. George Ellis demonstrates how downward causation operates through configurational constraints that selectively realize lower-level possibilities without adding forces or violating conservation laws (Ellis, 2016). DNA sequences constrain protein folding through information rather than energy transfer; social institutions constrain individual behavior through normative expectations rather than physical coercion; mathematical proofs constrain acceptable reasoning through logical rather than causal necessity.

Christian List and Peter Menzies develop a sophisticated account preserving both higher-level causation and physical closure (List & Menzies, 2009). They argue that exclusion problems arise from conflating different grains of description rather than genuine metaphysical conflicts. Physical events have microphysical causes, but higher-level properties can be difference-makers for higher-level effects. Mental state M causes action A not by competing with neural mechanisms but by being the causally relevant property at the appropriate level of description.

Denis Noble's analysis of biological systems reveals how causation operates across multiple levels simultaneously (Noble, 2012). Heart rhythm emerges from ion channel dynamics, cellular electrophysiology, tissue architecture, and organ-level feedback loops. No single level provides complete explanation; understanding requires integration across scales. Downward causation from organ to cell operates through boundary conditions and rate constants rather than mysterious vital forces.

This hierarchical framework clarifies how different disciplines contribute complementary insights without mutual reduction. Consider moral responsibility for criminal behavior. Neuroscience reveals how prefrontal cortex lesions impair impulse control and moral reasoning, as demonstrated in patients with ventromedial prefrontal damage who show preserved moral knowledge but impaired moral behavior (Koenigs et al., 2007). Psychology identifies cognitive biases like fundamental attribution error that distort moral judgment (Ross, 1977). Sociology examines how poverty, discrimination, and institutional structures shape criminal behavior (Sampson & Laub, 1993). Philosophy analyzes conceptual requirements for moral agency and evaluates theories of punishment (Pereboom, 2014).

Each perspective contributes essential insights, but none alone provides adequate understanding. Neuroscientific explanations illuminate biological constraints on agency without eliminating responsibility. Psychological accounts identify cognitive mechanisms without reducing morality to psychology. Sociological analyses reveal structural influences without denying individual choice. Philosophical investigations clarify concepts and evaluate arguments without determining empirical facts. Integration requires recognizing both autonomy and constraint at each level.

The principle of organizational levels extends throughout nature. Physics describes fundamental particles and forces but cannot predict chemical bonding patterns without additional principles. Chemistry explains molecular interactions but cannot predict biological function without evolutionary context. Biology elucidates life processes but cannot explain consciousness without psychological concepts. Psychology analyzes individual minds but cannot explain cultural phenomena without social frameworks. Each level exhibits emergent regularities requiring distinctive explanatory resources.

Arthur Peacocke's concept of "consonance" captures how different levels relate harmoniously without reduction or competition (Peacocke, 2001). Physical laws constrain but do not determine biological evolution; evolutionary history constrains but does not determine cultural development; cultural context constrains but does not determine individual choice. The resulting picture resembles musical harmony where different voices contribute distinct melodies that combine into unified compositions exceeding any single part.

17.4 METHODOLOGICAL STRATEGIES FOR EPISTEMIC INTEGRATION

Achieving truth's unity requires sophisticated methodological strategies that acknowledge legitimate diversity while promoting integration across domains. These strategies must balance epistemic humility regarding human limitations with confidence in truth's accessibility, preserve disciplinary autonomy while encouraging interdisciplinary dialogue, and maintain critical rigor while remaining open to unexpected insights.

Methodological pluralism provides the foundational principle for integration. No single investigative approach can access all aspects of reality—each reveals certain features while concealing others (Kellert et al., 2006). Controlled experiments isolate causal relationships but sacrifice ecological validity; naturalistic observation preserves real-world complexity but confounds variables; mathematical modeling achieves precision but requires simplifying assumptions; phenomenological description captures lived experience but lacks intersubjective verification; contemplative practice may access subtle states but resists public confirmation.

Alvin Goldman's social epistemology recognizes how knowledge emerges through collective inquiry involving diverse perspectives and distributed expertise (Goldman, 1999). Individual knowers possess limited cognitive resources, observational access, and processing capacity, but communities can pool information, divide epistemic labor, and implement error-correction mechanisms. Wikipedia exemplifies successful knowledge aggregation through collaborative editing, citation requirements, and dispute resolution procedures, achieving accuracy comparable to traditional encyclopedias despite open participation (Giles, 2005).

Linda Zagzebski's epistemic authority theory provides resources for navigating expertise across domains (Zagzebski, 2012). We appropriately defer to recognized authorities within their competence while maintaining critical vigilance regarding boundary violations and ideological distortions. Physicists possess authority regarding quantum mechanics, neuroscientists regarding brain function, philosophers regarding conceptual analysis, theologians regarding scriptural interpretation—but these authorities remain fallible and domain-specific. The replication crisis in psychology and biomedicine reveals how uncritical deference to authority can perpetuate errors (Ioannidis, 2005).

Roy Bhaskar's critical realism offers a framework that maintains both confidence in objective truth and awareness of epistemic limitations (Bhaskar, 2008). Reality exists independently with a stratified structure and causal powers, but knowledge remains fallible, theory-laden, and historically conditioned. Scientific progress involves dialectical movement between theoretical development and empirical investigation, with each moment correcting the other's limitations. Truth emerges through ongoing dialogue rather than algorithmic procedure or immediate intuition.

Philip Kitcher's analysis of scientific progress provides a model for cumulative knowledge, acknowledging both continuity and revolution (Kitcher, 1993). Science advances not merely by accumulating isolated facts but by developing increasingly comprehensive frameworks integrating diverse phenomena while exposing new questions. Darwin's theory unified biogeography, embryology, paleontology, and artificial selection while generating research programs in genetics, ecology, and molecular evolution. This "explanatory unification" preserves past insights while enabling novel discoveries.

Donald Davidson's principle of charity proves essential for interdisciplinary dialogue (Davidson, 2001). When encountering apparently bizarre claims from other domains, we should seek maximally coherent interpretations consistent with speakers' rationality rather than attributing massive error. Buddhist claims about non-self need not be interpreted as denying obvious facts about personal continuity but as highlighting the constructed, impermanent nature of identity. This principle does not require accepting all claims uncritically but mandates serious engagement with sophisticated formulations.

Hans-Georg Gadamer's philosophical hermeneutics emphasizes how understanding emerges through dialogue between different horizons of interpretation (Gadamer, 2004). Each domain possesses interpretive frameworks shaped by historical development, methodological commitments, and practical interests. Scientific horizons emphasize prediction and control; philosophical horizons pursue conceptual clarity; religious horizons seek existential meaning. Genuine understanding requires neither abandoning one's horizon nor imposing it on others, but allowing "fusion of horizons" through sustained conversation.

These methodological principles find practical application in successful research programs. Climate science integrates atmospheric physics, ocean dynamics, ice sheet modeling, ecosystem ecology, and economic analysis to project future scenarios and evaluate policy interventions (IPCC, 2021). The interdisciplinary synthesis required developing new computational methods, data assimilation techniques, and uncertainty quantification frameworks that transcend individual disciplines.

Precision medicine combines genomics, proteomics, metabolomics, clinical phenotyping, and environmental exposure data to tailor treatments to individual patients (Collins & Varmus, 2015). This requires not just data integration but conceptual frameworks spanning molecular mechanisms, physiological systems, and population health. The All of Us Research Program exemplifies methodological pluralism by incorporating diverse populations, data types, and analytical approaches while maintaining scientific rigor.

The emerging field of contemplative science exemplifies sophisticated integration of first-person and third-person methodologies (Lutz et al., 2015). Experienced meditators provide detailed phenomenological reports calibrated through systematic training; neuroscientists measure neural correlates using neuroimaging and electrophysiology; psychologists assess behavioral and clinical outcomes through validated instruments; philosophers analyze conceptual frameworks and epistemic implications. This multi-methodological approach reveals how mental training induces neuroplastic changes associated with enhanced attention, emotional regulation, and well-being.

17.5 ADDRESSING PERSISTENT CHALLENGES

Despite theoretical frameworks and methodological strategies supporting unity, persistent challenges remain for any comprehensive account of truth across domains. These include irreducible value pluralism, the problem of evil for theistic worldviews, tensions between scientific determinism and moral responsibility, and apparent cosmic indifference to human meaning. Addressing these challenges requires sophisticated philosophical analysis combined with empirical investigation and practical wisdom.

The fact-value distinction, articulated by David Hume and developed by logical positivists, suggests an unbridgeable gap between descriptive and normative claims (Hume, 1739/2000). Science can describe how the world is, but cannot determine how it ought to be. This creates apparent incommensurability between scientific facts and moral values, threatening unified understanding. If values float free from facts, convergence seems impossible across the descriptive-normative divide.

However, this sharp distinction faces multiple challenges. Hilary Putnam argues that the fact-value dichotomy rests on untenable assumptions about language, reality, and objectivity (Putnam, 2002). Scientific practice presupposes epistemic values—coherence, simplicity, fruitfulness, empirical adequacy—that cannot be justified on purely factual grounds. Many apparently factual claims contain embedded evaluations: "normal" physiology presumes health norms; "invasive" species assumes ecological values; "genetic defect" implies standards of proper function.

Philippa Foot develops a neo-Aristotelian approach, grounding moral facts in facts about human flourishing and natural goodness (Foot, 2001). Just as biological science reveals what constitutes health for organisms based on species-typical functioning, moral philosophy can discover what constitutes virtue for humans based on our rational and social nature. Courage, honesty, and compassion prove objectively valuable for human life, not through divine command or social convention but through their contribution to individual and collective flourishing. This naturalistic approach preserves moral objectivity while maintaining continuity with scientific understanding.

The problem of evil presents formidable challenges for religious worldviews affirming divine omnipotence, omniscience, and perfect goodness. The logical problem—whether God and evil can coexist—has largely been resolved through free will defenses and soul-making theodicies (Plantinga, 1974). However, the evidential problem remains acute: the amount, distribution, and character of suffering seem incompatible with divine providence. Children dying from painful diseases, natural disasters destroying innocent lives, and predation throughout nature appear to serve no greater good.

Michael Bergmann develops skeptical theism, arguing that human cognitive limitations prevent us from assessing whether evils serve greater goods beyond our comprehension (Bergmann, 2001). Just as children cannot understand parents' painful medical decisions, humans cannot evaluate the divine permission of suffering. This preserves logical consistency but potentially undermines religious practice by making divine goodness epistemically inaccessible. If we cannot judge whether evils serve greater goods, how can we trust divine benevolence?

Marilyn McCord Adams proposes that horrendous evils—evils that *prima facie* destroy the possibility of meaningful life—require defeat through intimate divine participation rather than justification through greater goods (Adams, 1999). The crucifixion transforms rather than explains suffering by demonstrating divine solidarity with victims. This approach maintains religious viability while acknowledging evil's genuine horror, but requires specifically Christian commitments that limit general applicability.

The tension between scientific determinism and moral responsibility generates persistent philosophical controversy. If human behavior results from prior causes according to natural laws, praise and blame appear inappropriate. Benjamin Libet's experiments revealing unconscious neural activity preceding conscious decisions seem to support hard incompatibilism about free will (Libet, 1985). Recent neuroscience using machine learning can predict decisions from brain activity several seconds before conscious awareness (Schultze-Kraft et al., 2016).

However, sophisticated compatibilist theories argue that moral responsibility requires appropriate agency rather than ultimate origination. Harry Frankfurt's hierarchical theory locates freedom in harmony between first-order desires and higher-order volitions regardless of causal history (Frankfurt, 1971). Susan Wolf's Reason View requires that agents act in accordance with reason, where reason involves both cognitive and evaluative capacities shaped by but not reducible to causal history (Wolf, 1990). These accounts preserve moral responsibility within naturalistic frameworks.

The apparent silence of the universe regarding meaning and purpose challenges both religious and secular worldviews. Scientific cosmology reveals a universe vast beyond comprehension, ancient beyond imagination, and apparently indifferent to human concerns. We inhabit a tiny planet orbiting an ordinary star among hundreds of billions in one galaxy among trillions, existing for a cosmic instant before inevitable extinction. This "disenchantment" threatens existential meaning (Weber, 1946).

Yet demands for cosmic meaning may reflect anthropomorphic projection rather than genuine requirements. Terry Eagleton argues that meaning emerges through human practices, relationships, and projects rather than requiring cosmic endorsement (Eagleton, 2007). Viktor Frankl's logotherapy demonstrates how individuals create meaning even in concentration camps through choosing attitudes toward unavoidable suffering (Frankl, 1946/2006). Thomas Nagel's absurdism acknowledges the ultimate contingency of human projects while affirming their immediate significance (Nagel, 1971).

17.6 TOWARD COMPREHENSIVE UNDERSTANDING

The unity of truth emerges not as dogmatic assertion but as regulative ideal guiding inquiry across domains while respecting irreducible plurality. This unity consists neither in reductive monism eliminating legitimate diversity nor relativistic pluralism abandoning objective standards, but in systematic integration preserving hierarchy and emergence, objectivity and interpretation, universality and contextuality.

The hierarchical framework developed throughout this chapter provides scaffolding for comprehensive understanding while avoiding both eliminative reduction and dualistic separation. Physical processes provide necessary substrate for all natural phenomena, but emergent properties at higher levels exhibit genuine novelty requiring autonomous explanation. Biological evolution explains organismic complexity, but psychological and social phenomena transcend biological description. Scientific methods excel within proper scope, but philosophical analysis and religious reflection address questions exceeding empirical investigation.

This framework suggests that apparent contradictions between domains often signal opportunities for deeper integration rather than irreconcilable conflicts. When evolutionary biology seems to conflict with theological claims about divine providence, the tension may reveal inadequate formulations on both sides—evolution as purely random versus creation as divine micromanagement—rather than fundamental incompatibility. Process theology and evolutionary theodicy demonstrate how divine action through natural processes preserves both scientific integrity and religious meaning (Haught, 2000).

When neuroscience appears to eliminate moral responsibility, the conflict may expose problematic assumptions about freedom requiring exemption from causation rather than appropriate kinds of causation. Compatibilist theories and degrees of responsibility accommodate neuroscientific findings while preserving moral agency (McKenna & Pereboom, 2016). When physics suggests a purposeless mechanism, the inference may conflate the absence of evidence for teleology with evidence of absence, ignoring how purposes might emerge through rather than despite natural processes.

The practical implications extend beyond academic philosophy to education, public discourse, and personal development. Educational institutions should model integrative approaches by requiring engagement with multiple perspectives while developing critical thinking for evaluation. Harvard's General Education curriculum exemplifies this approach through courses examining complex topics from scientific, social scientific, and humanistic angles while emphasizing methodological sophistication over superficial coverage (Harvard University, 2016).

Public policy benefits from recognizing how empirical questions, normative principles, and practical constraints intersect without mutual reduction. Climate policy requires atmospheric science to project scenarios, economics to evaluate costs, ethics to address intergenerational justice, and politics to navigate competing interests. The Intergovernmental Panel on Climate Change integrates these perspectives through working groups addressing physical science, impacts and adaptation, and mitigation while maintaining disciplinary rigor (IPCC, 2021).

Personal worldview formation requires integrating insights from science, philosophy, and religion without premature closure. Science provides understanding of natural processes and technological capabilities; philosophy clarifies concepts and evaluates arguments; religion addresses ultimate questions and existential concerns. Mature worldviews incorporate all three while recognizing their distinctive contributions and limitations.

The Dalai Lama's engagement with neuroscience while maintaining Buddhist commitments exemplifies sophisticated integration respecting both empirical findings and contemplative wisdom (Dalai Lama, 2005).

The unity we seek is neither monolithic uniformity nor mere aggregation but dynamic coherence preserving reality's richness while maintaining logical consistency and empirical adequacy. This coherence emerges through ongoing dialogue between approaches, each contributing distinctive insights while remaining open to correction through encounter with others. Like jazz musicians improvising together, different disciplines contribute unique voices that harmonize through mutual listening and response rather than following predetermined scores.

As understanding deepens and perspectives mature, we approach—asymptotically rather than absolutely—a comprehensive vision doing justice to reality's complexity while preserving fundamental unity. This vision motivates continued inquiry across all domains, confident that genuine truths will ultimately harmonize in understanding transcending present limitations while remaining eternally open to deeper insight. The unity of truth thus functions not as a terminus but as a horizon guiding and inspiring the endless human quest for understanding.

17.7 CONCLUSION

The unity of truth represents both achievement and aspiration within human intellectual history. Through careful analysis of truth's nature, examination of convergence patterns across disciplines, development of hierarchical integration frameworks, and implementation of sophisticated methodological strategies, we have outlined how diverse approaches to knowledge can contribute to coherent understanding without sacrificing distinctive contributions.

This unity does not eliminate the legitimate plurality of methods, questions, and perspectives characterizing mature intellectual inquiry. Rather, it provides principled grounds for coordinating diverse approaches while maintaining critical standards distinguishing genuine insights from mere opinion or wishful thinking. The resulting vision preserves both truth's objectivity and knowledge's interpretive character, both logical principles' universality and particular investigations' contextuality.

The implications extend far beyond academic philosophy to practical challenges of living thoughtfully in a complex world. Recognition of truth's unity encourages intellectual courage and epistemic humility, promotes constructive dialogue across traditional boundaries, and provides resources for addressing deepest questions about reality, knowledge, and human purpose. As we continue the ancient human quest for understanding, we do so with confidence that reality itself rewards those who seek truth with sufficient patience, rigor, and openness to transcend any single perspective's limitations.

PART VI

CHAPTER 18: LIVING WITH FIRST PRINCIPLES

The interface between abstract philosophical commitments and concrete human experience constitutes a fundamental challenge in practical philosophy. While first principles might appear remote from quotidian concerns, they function as what Bourdieu (1990) termed the "habitus" of intellectual and moral life—deeply sedimented dispositions that structure perception, evaluation, and action across all domains of human existence. This chapter examines how scientific, philosophical, and religious first principles manifest in lived experience, shaping responses to fundamental human situations from routine decision-making to existential crisis. The analysis demonstrates that foundational metaphysical and epistemological commitments operate as invisible architectures that determine the quality and direction of human life in profound ways.

18.1 THE ONTOLOGICAL STRUCTURE OF LIVED EXPERIENCE

Every human being navigates existence through what Heidegger (1962) called a "fore-structure of understanding" (Vor-struktur des Verstehens)—a background framework of assumptions about being, knowledge, and value that makes meaningful experience possible. These first principles function not merely as propositional beliefs but as what Wittgenstein (1969) described as "hinge propositions"—foundational assumptions so basic they rarely surface for explicit examination yet determine the entire flow of conscious life (§341-343). Contemporary phenomenology has extended this insight, with Ratcliffe (2008) demonstrating how "existential feelings" constitute pre-intentional background orientations that shape all conscious experience.

Taylor's (2004) concept of the "social imaginary" captures how these frameworks operate collectively, creating shared background understandings that make social practices intelligible and legitimate. However, as Archer (2003) argues in her morphogenetic approach, individual appropriation of these collective frameworks varies considerably through processes of reflexive deliberation, creating what we might term "personal ontologies"—unique configurations of first principles that shape individual existence while remaining embedded in cultural contexts.

Consider how differing anthropological assumptions generate distinct approaches to human relationships. The mechanistic worldview emerging from seventeenth-century natural philosophy treats humans as complex biological machines operating according to deterministic physical laws (Descartes, 1637/1996). This framework, refined by contemporary eliminative materialists such as Churchland (1981) and further developed in computational theories of mind (Dennett, 1991), reduces consciousness to neural computation and interpersonal relationships to strategic interactions between biological agents maximizing inclusive fitness (Trivers, 1971).

Alternative anthropological frameworks generate fundamentally different relational ontologies. Personalist philosophy, developed by Buber (1923/1970) and Marcel (1949), grounds relationships in mutual recognition between irreducible centers of consciousness and value. The I-Thou encounter transcends subject-object relationships, creating what Levinas (1961/1969) describes as ethical space that precedes ontology itself. Religious frameworks often extend this further, with Christian theology understanding human relationships as participation in divine love (Zizioulas, 1985) and Buddhist philosophy emphasizing interdependent origination (pratītyasamutpāda) that dissolves boundaries between self and other (Garfield, 1995).

These competing frameworks generate measurably different patterns of social behavior. Empirical research by Vohs et al. (2006) demonstrates that priming deterministic beliefs reduces helping behavior and increases dishonesty, while studies by Shariff and Norenzayan (2007) show that

304

religious priming increases prosocial behavior even among non-believers. However, as Sarkissian (2010) notes, these effects are mediated by cultural context and individual differences in ways that complicate simple causal narratives.

The practical implications extend beyond interpersonal relationships to fundamental questions of identity and temporal existence. Linear time consciousness, dominant in Western contexts since Augustine's (397/1991) phenomenological analysis in Confessions XI, structures experience as narrative progression toward future goals. McTaggart's (1908) philosophical analysis distinguishes between A-series time (past-present-future) and B-series time (earlier-later relations), with profound implications for how individuals understand agency, responsibility, and meaning.

Cyclical time consciousness, analyzed extensively by Eliade (1954) and embodied in Hindu concepts of kalpa and Buddhist notions of saṃsāra, locates individual existence within eternal cosmic processes. As Collins (1982) demonstrates through textual analysis, these frameworks potentially reduce death anxiety while complicating notions of historical progress. Indigenous temporal frameworks often emphasize what Deloria (1973) calls "spatial thinking"—grounding meaning in place and relationship rather than historical progression, a perspective that Whitt et al. (2003) argue provides resources for environmental ethics unavailable within linear temporal frameworks.

18.2 DECISION-MAKING ARCHITECTURES AND PRACTICAL REASONING

The translation of first principles into concrete decisions occurs through what Simon (1955) originally termed "bounded rationality"—structured processes for evaluating options within cognitive and informational constraints. Contemporary research reveals these "decision-making architectures" as complex interactions between conscious deliberation and automatic processing systems that reflect underlying metaphysical and epistemological commitments (Evans & Stanovich, 2013).

Kahneman's (2011) dual-process theory, building on decades of empirical research, distinguishes between System 1 (fast, automatic, intuitive) and System 2 (slow, controlled, reflective) cognitive processes. However, as Osman (2004) argues, this dichotomous framework oversimplifies the continuous interaction between automatic and controlled processes. More fundamentally, the framework requires philosophical interpretation regarding the relationship between conscious agency and causal determination—questions that pure empirical research cannot resolve (Nahmias, 2014).

Rational choice theory, formalized by von Neumann and Morgenstern (1944) and extended by Savage (1954), assumes agents possess complete, transitive preference orderings and select actions maximizing expected utility. This framework embeds substantial philosophical commitments challenged by extensive empirical evidence. Kahneman and Tversky's (1979) prospect theory demonstrates systematic violations of expected utility theory, while Sen's (1977) philosophical critique reveals the framework's inability to accommodate commitment and sympathy as distinct from self-interest.

Practical wisdom (phronesis), as analyzed by Aristotle (Nicomachean Ethics, 384-322 BCE/1984) and developed by contemporary virtue ethicists (Hursthouse, 1999), offers an alternative decision-making architecture emphasizing contextual judgment. Dunne's (1993) careful analysis demonstrates how phronesis involves a non-algorithmic integration of universal principles with particular situations through what Gadamer (2004) describes as the "fusion of horizons"—a hermeneutical process irreducible to rule application.

This particularist approach finds support in Dancy's (2004) moral particularism, which argues that moral reasons are inherently context-dependent and resist codification into exceptionless principles. However, as McKeever and Ridge (2006) argue, extreme particularism faces challenges explaining moral learning and justification. A moderate position, defended by Väyrynen (2006), maintains that while moral principles exist, their application requires irreducibly contextual judgment.

Religious decision-making frameworks incorporate what Wainwright (1995) terms "mystical perception"—seeking guidance through prayer, meditation, or spiritual discernment. These practices presuppose controversial metaphysical frameworks about divine action and religious experience. However, empirical research by Luhrmann (2012) demonstrates that contemplative practices produce measurable changes in perception and decision-making regardless of their metaphysical interpretation. Studies by Schjoedt et al. (2009) using neuroimaging reveal that religious believers activate different neural networks during prayer-based decision-making compared to secular deliberation.

Career selection exemplifies how first principles structure major life decisions. The modern Western emphasis on self-actualization through work reflects what Taylor (1989) calls the "ethics of authenticity"—the moral imperative to discover and express one's true self. This framework, critiqued by MacIntyre (1984) as contributing to moral fragmentation, presupposes controversial metaphysical commitments about personal identity and autonomy challenged by Buddhist anatta doctrine (Harvey, 2013) and sociological demonstrations of habitus-structured choice (Bourdieu & Passeron, 1977).

18.3 MORAL PSYCHOLOGY AND THE FOUNDATIONS OF ETHICAL LIFE

Contemporary moral psychology has revolutionized the understanding of ethical judgment and behavior, revealing complex interactions between reasoning and intuition that challenge traditional philosophical approaches. Haidt's (2001) social intuitionist model, supported by extensive empirical research, demonstrates that moral judgments typically emerge from rapid intuitive evaluations subsequently rationalized through post-hoc reasoning. This finding raises what Kennett and Fine (2009) call the "normative challenge"—determining whether psychological descriptions of moral judgment have implications for moral epistemology.

Greene's (2013) dual-process theory attempts to bridge descriptive and normative domains through what he terms "deep pragmatism." His neuroimaging studies (Greene et al., 2001) show that deontological judgments correlate with increased activity in brain regions associated with emotion, while utilitarian judgments engage regions associated with abstract reasoning. However, as Kahane et al. (2012) demonstrate through refined experiments, utilitarian judgments often reflect reduced empathic concern rather than enhanced moral reasoning, complicating Greene's normative conclusions.

Critics argue this neuroscientific approach commits what Berker (2009) calls the "normative insignificance thesis"—empirical findings about judgment mechanisms cannot establish which judgments are morally correct. As Parfit (2011) argues, moral truths are irreducibly normative facts that cannot be reduced to or derived from natural facts. This position, defended through sophisticated arguments by Enoch (2011) and Huemer (2005), maintains that moral knowledge requires *a priori* rational insight rather than empirical investigation.

Virtue ethics provides an alternative framework that integrates psychological and normative dimensions. Rather than treating emotions and reasons as competing systems, Aristotelian virtue ethics understands properly cultivated emotions as perceptive capacities that reliably track moral salience (Hursthouse, 1999). Contemporary work by Annas (2011) develops this insight through the "skill analogy," arguing that virtues are acquired through practice like practical skills, integrating cognitive and affective dimensions.

This neo-Aristotelian approach faces challenges from situationist psychology. Doris (2002) marshals extensive evidence that behavior varies more with situational factors than character traits, challenging virtue ethics' empirical assumptions. However, as Miller (2013) argues in developing a position he terms "mixed traits," the empirical evidence is compatible with modest claims about character provided we abandon assumptions about global trait consistency.

Religious frameworks provide distinctive moral resources that secular approaches struggle to replicate. Adams' (1999) sophisticated divine command theory grounds moral obligations in the commands of a loving God, avoiding crude voluntarism through what he calls "social requirement theory." Evans (2013) extends this approach, arguing that divine commands create moral obligations while natural law provides their content. However, as Wielenberg (2005) argues, secular moral realism can ground robust moral obligations without theological assumptions through what he terms "brute ethical facts."

18.4 EXISTENTIAL MEANING AND THE ARCHITECTURE OF SIGNIFICANCE

The question of life's meaning represents the intersection between abstract philosophical commitments and lived experience. Frankl's (1946/2006) logotherapy, grounded in his Holocaust experience, demonstrates that humans require meaning for psychological survival. Contemporary philosophical analysis has refined the understanding of meaning's structure. Metz's (2013) comprehensive taxonomy distinguishes between supernatural theories (meaning requires a relationship with God), natural purpose theories (meaning emerges from objective natural purposes), and subjective theories (meaning depends on subjective attitudes).

Wolf's (2010) "fitting fulfillment" view attempts synthesis by requiring both subjective attraction and objective worth—one must care about something genuinely worth caring about. This hybrid approach preserves meaning's partial independence from psychology while acknowledging its subjective dimension. However, as Bramble (2015) argues, Wolf's view faces the problem of specifying objective worth without controversial metaphysical commitments.

The challenge becomes acute within naturalistic frameworks. If reality consists entirely of particles governed by physical laws, objective value becomes problematic. Rosenberg's (2011) "eliminative nihilism" embraces this conclusion, arguing that naturalism entails life's meaninglessness. However, as Nagel (2012) argues in his critique of neo-Darwinian naturalism, the conviction that life has meaning may itself constitute evidence against purely naturalistic worldviews.

Religious frameworks typically ground meaning in a transcendent purpose. Craig's (2013) philosophical theology argues that without God and immortality, life lacks ultimate significance. However, as Cottingham (2003) argues more subtly, religious frameworks provide not just metaphysical grounding but transformative practices that generate experienced meaning. Empirical research by Park (2013) confirms that religious meaning-making correlates with resilience and well-being, though causal direction remains disputed.

18.5 SUFFERING, MORTALITY, AND THE LIMITS OF HUMAN EXISTENCE

Human responses to suffering and mortality test worldviews' practical adequacy. Different first principles generate distinct frameworks for confronting these universal experiences. Scientific materialism treats death as the cessation of information-processing functions (Churchland, 2013). While potentially eliminating fears of post-mortem suffering, this framework offers limited resources for meaning-making in the face of loss.

The Epicurean argument that death cannot harm the non-existent subject faces sophisticated philosophical challenges. Feldman's (1991) deprivation theory argues that death harms by depriving one of life's goods, while Bradley's (2009) temporal analysis demonstrates how death can be evil for the person who dies even without post-mortem experience. These debates reveal deep metaphysical issues about personal identity and temporal existence explored by Parfit (1984) and developed by Schechtman (2014).

Religious frameworks offer distinctive resources. Christian belief in resurrection, philosophically defended by Swinburne (1997) and Wright (2003), grounds hope for personal continuity. Buddhist concepts of anatta (no-self) and anicca (impermanence) potentially reduce death anxiety through different mechanisms, as empirically demonstrated by Niemiec et al. (2010). Islamic frameworks emphasize divine justice and mercy, providing what Bowker (1991) calls "structural immortality" through incorporation into divine purpose.

The problem of evil challenges theistic frameworks. Rowe's (1979) evidential argument from evil contends that gratuitous suffering provides evidence against God's existence. Responses include Hick's (1966) soul-making theodicy, Plantinga's (1974) free will defense, and van Inwagen's (2006) "no minimum thesis." Skeptical theism, developed by Wykstra (1984) and Howard-Snyder and Bergmann (2004), argues that human cognitive limitations prevent assessment of whether apparently gratuitous evils serve greater goods.

18.6 TEMPORAL ORIENTATION AND THE QUESTION OF PROGRESS

First principles shape temporal orientation profoundly. The modern Western confidence in progress, analyzed by Bury (1920) and critiqued by Gray (2004), rests on Enlightenment assumptions about reason's capacity for cumulative improvement. Pinker's (2018) extensive documentation of improvements in health, wealth, and peace appears to vindicate progressive optimism.

However, as Kumar (2017) argues, progress narratives face philosophical and empirical challenges. Environmental degradation threatens long-term sustainability (Rockström et al., 2009), while psychometric evidence suggests declining mental health despite material improvements (Twenge et al., 2018). These debates reflect deeper disagreements about progress criteria and value weighting analyzed by Chang (1997) in her work on incommensurability.

Alternative temporal frameworks generate different orientations. Hindu cyclical cosmology, analyzed by Sharma (2000), understands time through vast cycles (kalpas) that relativize historical change. Mircea Eliade's (1954) phenomenology of religion demonstrates how cyclical time consciousness enables what he terms "eternal return"—regeneration through ritual participation in primordial time.

18.7 PRACTICAL INTEGRATION AND THE SYNTHESIS OF WORLDVIEWS

Living authentically with first principles requires navigating tensions between intellectual coherence and existential adequacy. MacIntyre's (1988) account of "traditions of rational enquiry" provides one framework for understanding how individuals navigate competing worldview claims. His analysis demonstrates that rational evaluation across traditions requires what he terms "dialectical encounter"—sustained engagement that may transform both traditions.

Habermas's (2008) "post-secular" consciousness suggests possibilities for mutual learning between religious and secular worldviews. This approach, developed by Cooke (2006) and critiqued by Calhoun et al. (2013), requires what Taylor (2011) calls "radical reflexivity"—acknowledgment of one's own tradition's limitations while remaining open to insights from others.

Contemporary neuroscience provides empirical support for worldview flexibility. Research on neuroplasticity by Davidson and Lutz (2008) demonstrates that contemplative practices produce measurable changes in brain structure and function. Studies of psychedelic-assisted psychotherapy by Carhart-Harris et al. (2016) reveal possibilities for rapid worldview transformation, though ethical and epistemological questions remain about chemically-induced belief change.

18.8 CONCLUSION

The examination of how first principles manifest in lived experience reveals their profound practical significance. Foundational philosophical commitments shape decision-making, moral psychology, meaning-making, responses to suffering, temporal orientation, and worldview integration in fundamental ways. These influences operate largely below conscious awareness yet determine life's quality and direction.

The analysis demonstrates that no single worldview tradition possesses complete resources for navigating existence's full complexity. This situation requires what might be termed "worldview wisdom"—the capacity to draw insights from multiple traditions while maintaining coherence and practical adequacy. Such wisdom demands both intellectual humility about understanding's limitations and existential courage to live by provisional commitments despite ultimate uncertainty.

Contemporary global challenges require resources from multiple worldview traditions. Climate change, technological disruption, and existential risks demand integration across scientific, philosophical, and religious perspectives. The path forward involves neither relativistic pluralism nor fundamentalist dogmatism but committed engagement with first principles combined with intellectual humility and practical wisdom.

Living with first principles proves not merely a philosophical exercise but an intensely practical endeavor affecting every aspect of human existence. Through understanding these relationships more clearly, individuals gain freedom to choose foundational commitments consciously rather than accepting them passively, opening possibilities for more authentic existence grounded in carefully examined convictions about reality's fundamental nature.

CHAPTER 19: THE ONGOING QUEST

The pursuit of first principles constitutes what Aristotle (384-322 BCE/1984) termed an "infinite regress," wherein each purported foundation reveals deeper substrata requiring further investigation. This recursive structure characterizes not merely philosophical speculation but empirical science and theological inquiry alike. After systematically examining the methodological approaches of natural science, philosophical analysis, and religious epistemology, this investigation arrives not at epistemic closure but at a critical reflexive juncture. This position enables a comprehensive assessment of both successfully mapped intellectual territories and the vast conceptual regions that resist current methodological frameworks. The present chapter analyzes three interrelated dimensions of this ongoing quest: first, the inherent incompleteness of foundational inquiry as a structural feature rather than a contingent limitation; second, the identification of emerging paradigms that promise fundamental reconceptualization of existing frameworks; and third, the cultivation of epistemic virtues that enable productive engagement with irreducible uncertainty while maintaining rigorous standards of inquiry.

19.1 THE DIALECTICAL STRUCTURE OF KNOWLEDGE EXPANSION

The expansion of human knowledge exhibits what Rescher (1978) characterized as "epistemic dialectics": the paradoxical phenomenon whereby increased understanding generates proportionally greater awareness of ignorance. This pattern transcends mere quantitative accumulation of information, revealing instead the fundamentally recursive architecture of systematic inquiry. Each resolution of existing problems exposes previously invisible dependencies, generating what Popper (1963) termed "the growth of ignorance"—not absolute ignorance but sophisticated recognition of increasingly subtle complexities.

Consider the trajectory of classical mechanics. Newton's (1687/1999) *Philosophiæ Naturalis Principia Mathematica* appeared to establish absolute foundations for mechanical description, providing a comprehensive mathematical formalization of motion through three fundamental laws and universal gravitation. This framework's extraordinary predictive success— calculating planetary orbits, explaining tidal phenomena, unifying terrestrial and celestial mechanics—suggested proximity to the final truth about physical reality (Westfall, 1980). Yet this very success created the conceptual space within which anomalies became visible: the perihelion precession of Mercury, the Michelson-Morley experiment's null result, and blackbody radiation's ultraviolet catastrophe (Pais, 1982). Einstein's (1915/2015) resolution through general relativity generated new foundational questions about spacetime singularities, quantum gravity, and the reconciliation of relativistic and quantum frameworks that remain unresolved despite century-long investigation (Rovelli, 2004; Smolin, 2006).

This dialectical pattern characterizes all domains of systematic inquiry. Gödel's (1931) incompleteness theorems demonstrated that any consistent formal system encompassing elementary arithmetic contains true statements unprovable within that system. Rather than representing failure, these theorems reveal what Franzén (2005) identifies as the "inexhaustible" character of mathematical truth—reality's formal structure exceeds any particular axiomatization while remaining rationally accessible through iterative refinement. Subsequent developments in mathematical logic, including Cohen's (1963) forcing technique and Paris and Harrington's (1977) concrete mathematical independence results, confirm that incompleteness represents a fundamental feature rather than a technical curiosity.

The phenomenon Wigner (1960) termed "the unreasonable effectiveness of mathematics in the natural sciences" exemplifies another dialectical tension. Mathematical structures developed through pure abstraction— complex analysis, Riemannian geometry, group theory—subsequently prove indispensable for physical description. Quantum mechanics requires Hilbert spaces, general relativity employs differential geometry, and particle physics depends on gauge theory (Penrose, 2004). This correspondence suggests profound connections between mathematical and physical reality, yet the nature of these connections remains contentious. Tegmark's (2014) mathematical universe hypothesis proposes complete identification, while constructivists like Balaguer (1998) maintain that mathematics represents human construction projected onto nature. Each position faces serious objections, suggesting that the relationship between mathematical and physical truth may require conceptual frameworks not yet developed.

Contemporary neuroscience exemplifies how empirical success paradoxically deepens conceptual puzzles. The Human Connectome Project has mapped neural connectivity with unprecedented resolution, identifying approximately 86 billion neurons and 100 trillion synapses in the human brain (Sporns, 2012). Functional neuroimaging reveals precise neural correlates for perception, emotion, and cognition (Poldrack & Farah, 2015). Yet what Chalmers (1995) designated the "hard problem of consciousness"— explaining how subjective experience emerges from objective neural processes—remains intractable. Levine's (1983) "explanatory gap" between physical and phenomenal properties resists closure despite accumulating neuroscientific detail. Indeed, Block (2007) argues that increased understanding of neural mechanisms makes the hard problem more, rather than less, acute by highlighting the conceptual chasm between mechanistic and experiential description.

The recursive character of inquiry appears most starkly in consciousness studies, where the investigating subject coincides with the investigated object. This reflexivity generates what Thompson (2007) terms "the problem of phenomenological self-reference": consciousness must employ its own resources to understand itself, creating inevitable blind spots and conceptual circularities. Varela, Thompson, and Rosch (1991) propose "enactive cognition" as a framework acknowledging this recursivity, wherein mind and world co-emerge through embodied interaction rather than existing as independent entities. However, Zahavi (2005) contends that this approach insufficiently addresses the transcendental conditions enabling phenomenological investigation itself.

Philosophy confronts analogous recursive challenges when examining its own foundations. Kant's (1781/1998) critical philosophy emerged from recognizing that dogmatic metaphysics had failed to establish secure foundations, yet his transcendental arguments presuppose the very rational capacities they purport to vindicate—what Stroud (1968) identified as the "transcendental circle." Contemporary metaepistemology grapples with what Fumerton (2001) calls "the problem of the criterion": establishing epistemic principles requires already possessing criteria for evaluating such principles, generating vicious circularity or infinite regress. Sosa's (2009) virtue epistemology attempts resolution through "epistemic circularity" that proves virtuous rather than vicious, though critics like Bergmann (2006) argue this merely displaces rather than solves the fundamental problem.

Religious and contemplative traditions encounter parallel recursive structures. The Christian mystical tradition's *via negativa*, exemplified by Pseudo-Dionysius (c. 500/1987), maintains that ultimate reality transcends all conceptual categories, knowable only through systematic negation of finite predicates. Similarly, Śaṅkara's (c. 800/1972) Advaita Vedanta employs *neti neti* ("not this, not that") to indicate Brahman's trans-conceptual nature, while Nāgārjuna's (c. 200/1995) Madhyamaka demonstrates the emptiness (*śūnyatā*) of all conceptual constructs including emptiness itself. These approaches generate what Sells (1994) terms "mystical languages of unsaying"—discourses that systematically undermine their own propositions to gesture toward ineffable realities. Yet articulating the ineffable creates performative contradictions that resist logical resolution, suggesting limits to propositional knowledge that contemplative practice may transcend but cannot eliminate.

19.2 THE HISTORICAL CONTINGENCY OF FOUNDATIONAL FRAMEWORKS

Historical analysis reveals that seemingly necessary first principles emerge from specific cultural matrices and undergo radical transformation across epochs. Foucault's (1966/1994) archaeological investigations uncovered discontinuous "epistemes"—fundamental ordering structures that determine what counts as knowledge within particular periods. These epistemes shift through ruptures rather than evolution, transforming not merely knowledge's content but its basic categories and validation criteria. Hacking (1982) extends this analysis through "historical ontology," demonstrating how fundamental categories like probability, chance, and normality emerged at specific historical junctures rather than representing timeless features of reality.

The transition from Aristotelian to modern science exemplifies such an epistemic transformation. Medieval natural philosophy, grounded in Aristotle's (384-322 BCE/1984) framework, organized explanation around four causes—material, efficient, formal, and final—seeking to understand substances through essential natures and teleological purposes. The scientific revolution, initiated by figures like Galileo (1632/2001) and culminating in Newton (1687/1999), restricted legitimate explanation to efficient causation operating according to mathematical laws, eliminating formal and final causes as explanatory principles (Dear, 2006). This shift, analyzed comprehensively by Koyré (1957), represented not empirical progress within a stable framework but a fundamental reconceptualization of nature, knowledge, and explanation themselves.

The emergence of probability theory illustrates how new conceptual resources create previously impossible forms of knowledge. Before the seventeenth century, Hacking (1975) demonstrates, the concept of probability in its modern dual sense—both statistical frequency and degree of belief—did not exist. The correspondence between Pascal and Fermat in 1654 inaugurated probability theory, enabling quantitative treatment of uncertainty, risk assessment, and statistical inference (Daston, 1988). Contemporary quantum mechanics employs probability as fundamental rather than epistemic, suggesting that reality itself may be inherently probabilistic rather than deterministic—a possibility conceptually unavailable before probability's invention (Gleason, 1957).

Kuhn's (1962/1996) analysis of scientific revolutions challenged cumulative progress narratives by demonstrating that paradigm shifts involve "incommensurable" frameworks. The transition from Newtonian to Einsteinian physics altered the meaning of fundamental terms: "mass" shifts from an invariant quantity to an energy-dependent variable, "space" and "time" transform from absolute containers to relative dimensions of spacetime, and "simultaneity" becomes frame-dependent rather than absolute (Friedman, 2001). Scientists operating within different paradigms, Kuhn argued, inhabit different worlds—not metaphorically but literally, as their observational categories and explanatory resources generate divergent empirical experiences. Critics like Laudan (1984) contest strong incommensurability, arguing for continuity across paradigm shifts, yet even moderate versions acknowledge fundamental conceptual discontinuities.

This historical contingency extends beyond empirical science to philosophical frameworks themselves. The emergence of analytic philosophy through Frege (1892/1952), Russell and Whitehead (1910-1913), and early Wittgenstein (1921/2001) privileged logical analysis, linguistic precision, and scientific methodology. Continental philosophy, developing through Husserl (1913/2014), Heidegger (1927/1962), and Merleau-Ponty (1945/2012), emphasized phenomenological description, existential analysis, and embodied experience. These traditions address similar fundamental questions through such divergent methodologies that translation requires extensive hermeneutical work, as Ricoeur (1974) demonstrated. Contemporary efforts at rapprochement, exemplified by McDowell (1994) and Brandom (1994), remain controversial within both traditions.

Religious and theological frameworks exhibit comparable historical transformation. Christianity's encounter with Greek philosophy, initiated by Justin Martyr (c. 150/2003) and culminating in Aquinas (1265/1981), produced a scholastic synthesis unimaginable to apostolic communities. Islamic philosophy's engagement with Aristotelian thought through Al-Fārābī (c. 950/1985), Ibn Sīnā (Avicenna). (c. 1020/2005), and Ibn Rushd (c. 1180/1986) generated systematic theological frameworks quite different from the Quranic revelation's original context. Buddhist philosophy evolved from the Buddha's practical teachings, preserved in the Pāli Canon (c. 100 BCE/1995), into sophisticated metaphysical systems like Yogācāra and Tathāgatagarbha thought through centuries of scholastic development (Williams, 2009). These transformations raise questions about whether contemporary formulations preserve or distort original insights.

Yet historical contingency need not entail relativism. Putnam (1981) argues persuasively that conceptual relativity—the fact that multiple conceptual schemes can describe the same reality—differs from relativism about truth. Certain discoveries exhibit robustness across paradigm shifts: conservation principles persist despite theoretical revolutions, logical laws maintain validity across cultural contexts, and mathematical theorems proved by ancient Greeks remain demonstrable today (Shapiro, 1997). The challenge involves distinguishing genuinely invariant principles from those appearing necessary due to cultural universality or cognitive bias.

Kitcher (1993) provides a sophisticated account of scientific progress that acknowledges historical contingency while maintaining realist commitments. Scientific communities preserve "cognitive resources"—problem-solving techniques, experimental methods, mathematical tools—

while remaining open to revolutionary innovations when anomalies accumulate. This process involves neither simple accumulation nor complete discontinuity but what he terms "progressive problemshift": new frameworks must solve their predecessors' problems plus additional ones. Progress occurs not toward final truth but away from error, through increasingly adequate representations of reality's structure.

Contemporary historiography of science, exemplified by Galison (1997) and Daston and Galison (2007), reveals how epistemic virtues themselves undergo historical transformation. "Objectivity" as currently understood— mechanical reproduction, elimination of subjective judgment, statistical analysis—emerged only in the mid-nineteenth century, replacing earlier ideals like "truth-to-nature" that required expert judgment to identify essential features. These shifting epistemic virtues shape what counts as legitimate knowledge, suggesting that even methodological principles considered foundational may prove historically contingent.

19.3 CONTEMPORARY FRONTIERS AND EMERGING PARADIGMS

Current research frontiers suggest impending paradigm shifts that may fundamentally reconceptualize existing first principles. Information theory increasingly appears foundational across multiple domains, with theorists proposing information-theoretic reformulations of physics, biology, and consciousness. Wheeler's (1990) "it from bit" hypothesis proposes that physical entities derive from binary information choices, suggesting information rather than matter or energy constitutes reality's fundamental level. This perspective gained support through Bekenstein's (1973) discovery that black hole entropy proportionally relates to surface area rather than volume, suggesting that spacetime regions' information content faces fundamental limits described by the holographic principle (Susskind, 1995; Bousso, 2002).

Lloyd's (2006) work on quantum computation extends information-theoretic approaches by demonstrating that the universe's evolution can be understood as quantum information processing. If reality fundamentally consists of quantum computational processes, traditional distinctions between physical and computational collapse. This perspective potentially unifies quantum mechanics with cosmology while providing new approaches to persistent puzzles. Deutsch's (1997) constructor theory attempts to reformulate physics entirely in terms of which transformations are possible versus impossible, with information and computation as primitive concepts rather than emergent phenomena. Critics like Timpson (2013) argue that information-theoretic approaches merely redescribe rather than explain physical phenomena, though proponents contend that information provides a more fundamental ontological category than traditional physical properties.

The study of consciousness represents another frontier where first principles remain fundamentally contested. Integrated Information Theory (IIT), developed by Tononi (2008) and refined by Tononi and Koch (2015), proposes quantitative measures of consciousness based on systems' integrated information (Φ). This mathematical framework suggests that any system with non-zero integrated information possesses some degree of consciousness, extending phenomenal experience beyond biological organisms to potentially include artificial systems and even protons. While IIT provides precise mathematical formalism and generates testable predictions, critics like Searle (2013) argue it conflates information processing with genuine consciousness, while Bayne (2018) questions whether integrated information constitutes consciousness's necessary and sufficient conditions.

Panpsychist theories have gained renewed philosophical respectability through rigorous formulations by Strawson (2006), who argues that the emergence of consciousness from non-conscious components violates the principle that emergence requires proto-phenomenal properties in substrates. Goff (2017) develops "cosmopsychism"—the view that the universe itself instantiates consciousness from which individual minds derive. These positions address the hard problem by denying that consciousness emerges from purely physical processes, though they face the "combination problem" of explaining how micro-experiences unite into macro-consciousness (Chalmers, 2016). Russellian monism, defended by Alter and Nagasawa (2015), offers a middle path wherein consciousness emerges from intrinsic properties of physical entities that themselves are neither mental nor physical in conventional senses.

The extended mind thesis, formulated by Clark and Chalmers (1998) and developed by Clark (2008), challenges traditional boundaries between cognitive agents and environmental resources. If cognitive processes extend beyond biological boundaries to encompass tools, technologies, and social institutions, conventional assumptions about mind, knowledge, and personal identity require fundamental revision. Contemporary developments in brain-computer interfaces, reviewed by Wolpaw and Wolpaw (2012), make these questions increasingly practical: neural implants enabling direct thought-controlled computation blur the distinction between internal cognition and external processing. Critics like Adams and Aizawa (2008) defend "brainbound" cognition, arguing that genuine cognitive processes possess distinctive marks absent from external resources, though extended mind proponents argue such marks reflect prejudice rather than principled distinctions.

Artificial intelligence development raises profound questions requiring potential revision of fundamental philosophical principles. Large language models demonstrate sophisticated linguistic competence, reasoning abilities, and apparent creativity that challenge assumptions about understanding, intentionality, and consciousness (Brown et al., 2020). Whether such systems genuinely understand or merely simulate understanding remains contested. Searle's (1980) Chinese Room argument maintains that syntax cannot generate semantics, while computationalists like Dennett (1991) argue that sufficiently complex information processing constitutes genuine understanding. The prospect of artificial general intelligence (AGI) surpassing human capabilities, analyzed comprehensively by Bostrom (2014), may require entirely new frameworks for understanding intelligence, agency, and moral status.

Contemporary physics continues to generate paradoxes suggesting the need for foundational revision. The black hole information paradox, crystallized by Hawking (1976), challenges quantum mechanics' unitarity principle by suggesting that information falling into black holes gets destroyed when they evaporate. Proposed resolutions—including complementarity (Susskind, Thorlacius, & Uglum, 1993), firewalls (Almheiri, Marolf, Polchinski, & Sully, 2013), and ER=EPR correspondence (Maldacena & Susskind, 2013)—require abandoning cherished principles about locality, unitarity, or spacetime structure. String theory and loop quantum gravity propose radically different foundational structures, each implying different first principles about reality's fundamental constituents (Green, Schwarz, & Witten, 2012; Rovelli & Vidotto, 2014).

Religious and contemplative traditions contribute evolving frontiers through systematic investigation of consciousness and human flourishing.

The emerging field of contemplative science, pioneered by researchers like Davidson and Lutz (2008), studies meditation's effects on brain structure and function using rigorous neuroscientific methods. Long-term meditation practitioners exhibit altered brain activity patterns, increased gray matter density, and enhanced emotional regulation compared to controls (Lutz, Slagter, Dunne, & Davidson, 2004). These findings suggest that contemplative practices may access dimensions of consciousness unavailable to ordinary introspection, though interpreting such results requires careful distinction between neural correlates and phenomenological claims (Thompson, 2020).

19.4 EPISTEMIC VIRTUES AND THE METHODOLOGY OF INQUIRY

The provisional character of first principles demands cultivating specific intellectual virtues enabling productive inquiry while avoiding both dogmatism and skeptical paralysis. These epistemic virtues function as methodological principles essential for knowledge advancement rather than mere psychological dispositions. Zagzebski's (1996) virtue epistemology provides a systematic framework wherein intellectual virtues like open-mindedness, intellectual courage, and epistemic humility constitute knowledge's necessary conditions alongside truth and justification.

Intellectual humility emerges as perhaps the most fundamental epistemic virtue. Roberts and Wood (2007) analyze intellectual humility as proper attentiveness to one's epistemic limitations combined with appropriate confidence within one's competence domains. This disposition proves crucial for scientific discovery, where premature theoretical commitment can blind researchers to anomalous data signaling revolutionary discoveries. The history of science provides numerous examples: Planck's (1950) observation that new scientific truths triumph not through convincing opponents but through generational replacement illustrates how intellectual pride impedes progress.

Contemporary empirical research confirms intellectual humility's epistemic value. The Dunning-Kruger effect, documented extensively by Kruger and Dunning (1999) and replicated cross-culturally, demonstrates that cognitive incompetence correlates with overconfidence while genuine expertise increases awareness of knowledge limitations. Individuals scoring in the bottom quartile on tests of humor, grammar, and logic overestimate their performance by approximately 50%, while top performers slightly underestimate their abilities. This metacognitive deficit—inability to recognize one's own incompetence—suggests that intellectual humility requires sufficient knowledge to appreciate knowledge's limits. Subsequent research by Pennycook, Ross, Koehler, and Fugelsang (2017) links intellectual humility with resistance to misinformation and conspiracy theories, suggesting its broader epistemic benefits.

However, intellectual humility must be distinguished from epistemic paralysis or excessive deference. James's (1896) analysis of "the will to believe" remains philosophically significant: when facing what he termed "genuine options"—living, forced, and momentous choices—suspension of judgment itself constitutes a choice with practical consequences. Contemporary discussions of transformative experiences by Paul (2014) extend this insight: certain knowledge comes only through experience that fundamentally alters one's epistemic position, making fully informed rational choice impossible. The decision to pursue a scientific career, undergo religious conversion, or have children involves epistemic leaps that intellectual humility must accommodate rather than preclude.

Polanyi's (1958) analysis of tacit knowledge reveals another dimension requiring epistemic humility. Much expert knowledge resists explicit articulation—practitioners "know more than they can tell." This tacit dimension underlies scientific practice, skilled performance, and contemplative realization. Collins (2010) demonstrates through sociological studies that transmitting scientific expertise requires extended apprenticeship precisely because crucial knowledge remains tacit. Master practitioners access knowledge forms that resist complete propositional formulation, suggesting that first principles may be partially grasped through embodied practice rather than theoretical comprehension alone.

Intellectual courage complements humility by enabling investigators to pursue inquiry despite social pressure, institutional resistance, or psychological discomfort. Galileo's telescopic observations, Darwin's evolutionary theory, and Wegener's continental drift hypothesis all required intellectual courage to advance despite fierce opposition (Thagard, 1992). Contemporary cases include Marshall and Warren's (1984) bacterial theory of ulcers, initially ridiculed but eventually Nobel Prize-winning, and Prusiner's (1998) prion hypothesis, which violated the central dogma that pathogens require nucleic acids. Code (1987) argues that intellectual courage involves not mere contrarianism but principled commitment to following evidence despite personal costs.

Epistemic justice, analyzed comprehensively by Fricker (2007), highlights how social factors systematically distort knowledge production. "Testimonial injustice" occurs when speakers receive deficient credibility due to identity prejudice, while "hermeneutical injustice" arises when marginalized groups lack interpretive resources to articulate their experiences. The historical exclusion of women from science, documented by Schiebinger (1989), represents not merely social injustice but epistemic impoverishment—loss of perspectives, questions, and insights that would enrich collective understanding. Anderson's (2012) analysis of diversity in science demonstrates that including researchers from varied backgrounds improves problem-solving and error detection, suggesting that epistemic justice serves truth rather than merely political goals.

19.5 THE HERMENEUTICS OF CROSS-DOMAIN INTEGRATION

Integrating insights from science, philosophy, and religion requires sophisticated hermeneutical strategies honoring each domain's integrity while enabling productive dialogue. This cannot proceed through crude reduction or superficial synthesis but requires what Gadamer (2004) termed "fusion of horizons"—transformation of understanding through encounter with alternative perspectives. The hermeneutical challenge involves neither abandoning one's framework nor assimilating others' insights without modification, but allowing genuinely new understanding to emerge through sustained engagement.

Contemporary philosophy of science increasingly recognizes science's hermeneutical dimensions. Heelan (1983) argues that scientific observation involves interpretation comparable to textual reading, requiring background knowledge and theoretical frameworks to render phenomena intelligible. Laboratory instruments do not provide transparent access to nature but require skilled interpretation informed by theoretical understanding—what Baird (2004) terms "thing knowledge" embodied in material culture. Even mathematical formalism requires interpretation to connect with empirical phenomena, as Morrison (1999) demonstrates through case studies in physics.

The dialogue between scientific and religious worldviews presents acute hermeneutical challenges. Barbour's (1997) typology identifies four relationships: conflict (incompatible truth claims), independence (separate domains), dialogue (methodological parallels), and integration (unified understanding). Each model presupposes different assumptions about truth, reality, and knowledge that themselves require examination. Polkinghorne (1998), a physicist-theologian, argues for "critical realism," acknowledging both domains' truth claims while recognizing their distinct methodologies and evidential bases. Critics like Dawkins (2006) maintain that scientific and religious claims inevitably conflict when addressing empirical questions, while others like Gould (1997) defend "non-overlapping magisteria" wherein science addresses factual questions while religion treats meaning and values.

Process theology, developed from Whitehead's (1929) philosophy by Hartshorne (1948) and contemporary theologians like Clayton (2004), represents a sophisticated integration attempting to honor both scientific and religious insights. By understanding God and world as involved in temporal becoming rather than static being, process theology addresses traditional puzzles about divine action while maintaining theological content. Griffin (2000) argues that process thought provides resources for science-religion dialogue by offering a metaphysical framework compatible with scientific findings while preserving religious meaning. Critics from both scientific and religious perspectives question whether such integration succeeds: scientific naturalists argue it introduces unnecessary metaphysical commitments, while traditional theists contend it compromises essential divine attributes like omnipotence and immutability.

19.6 FUTURE TRAJECTORIES AND EMERGING SYNTHESES

Projecting future developments in foundational inquiry requires acknowledging both accelerating change and persistent patterns. The convergence of artificial intelligence, neuroscience, and contemplative studies promises unprecedented insights into consciousness while potentially requiring fundamental conceptual revision. Brain-computer interfaces enabling direct neural control of external devices, reviewed comprehensively by Lebedev and Nicolelis (2017), challenge conventional boundaries between mind and world. If cognitive processes seamlessly extend through technological augmentation, traditional assumptions about personal identity, moral agency, and epistemic responsibility require reconsideration.

Quantum computing's development may reveal computational principles more fundamental than classical logic. Quantum algorithms demonstrating exponential speedup over classical computation for certain problems suggest that quantum logic might capture reality's structure more accurately than Boolean logic (Nielsen & Chuang, 2010). However, quantum mechanics' interpretation remains contested after a century of debate, with competing interpretations—Copenhagen, many-worlds, QBism, relational—implying different ontologies and epistemologies (Schlosshauer, 2007). Quantum computing's practical success might force theoretical resolution, though it could equally deepen interpretive puzzles.

Climate change and ecological crisis demand reconceptualizing relationships between human flourishing and natural systems. The Anthropocene epoch, wherein human activity constitutes a geological force, requires what Latour (2017) terms "terrestrial politics"—frameworks integrating human society within planetary boundaries. Traditional ethical theories developed assuming unlimited natural resources prove inadequate for addressing intergenerational justice, species extinction, and ecosystem integrity. Norton's (2005) "convergence hypothesis" suggests that anthropocentric and ecocentric ethics may converge on practical policies despite theoretical differences, though fundamental questions about nature's moral status remain unresolved.

19.7 CONCLUSION: THE QUEST AS CONSTITUTIVE PRINCIPLE

This investigation's trajectory suggests that the quest for first principles itself represents the most fundamental principle—not as a final answer awaiting discovery but as the constitutive activity through which rational consciousness engages reality. This reflexive insight transforms the enterprise: rather than seeking external foundations existing independently of inquiry, we recognize that foundations emerge through the inquiring process itself. The quest continues not from failure to achieve closure but from the inexhaustible richness of reality that always exceeds any framework's comprehension.

The dialogical character of this quest—requiring communities of inquiry spanning disciplinary, cultural, and temporal boundaries—ensures its ongoing nature. Each generation must appropriate inherited wisdom while confronting novel challenges that reveal previously hidden dimensions of perennial questions. Historical transmission involves creative transformation rather than passive reception, as new contexts illuminate aspects invisible to predecessors while obscuring others that were previously clear.

Understanding this quest as a constitutive principle reframes the relationship between epistemic humility and confident action. Recognizing knowledge's provisional character need not paralyze decision-making but can inform what Dewey (1929) termed "intelligent action"—experimental engagement that treats beliefs as hypotheses tested through consequences rather than dogmas demanding defense. This pragmatic orientation proves especially crucial as emerging technologies force practical decisions about artificial intelligence, genetic engineering, and planetary stewardship that presuppose answers to foundational questions.

As we transition to this inquiry's final synthesis, we carry forward both achievements and limitations: genuine insights accumulated through millennia of investigation across multiple traditions, and humble recognition of vast territories remaining unexplored. The ongoing quest for first principles emerges not as a problem requiring solution but as the fundamental orientation that defines rational consciousness—the commitment to understanding that makes all other knowledge possible. This understanding frames our concluding task: not providing definitive answers but synthesizing insights while indicating directions for future inquiry, recognizing that wisdom lies not in possessing final truths but in learning to pose ever-better questions.

CHAPTER 20: CONCLUSIONS – THE GROUND OF REALITY

The culmination of this systematic investigation into first principles across the domains of science, philosophy, and religion reveals a fundamental paradox that structures all human inquiry: the pursuit of absolute foundations has paradoxically disclosed the provisional nature of all foundational claims. This concluding synthesis articulates the convergent insights emerging from our analysis while maintaining intellectual honesty about irreducible tensions, establishes provisional affirmations that command reasonable confidence despite ongoing contestation, and delineates implications for continued investigation. Rather than imposing artificial closure on inherently open questions, this analysis articulates what Kuhn (1962/1996) identified as the "essential tension" between tradition and innovation that characterizes productive intellectual engagement across all domains of inquiry.

20.1 THE ARCHITECTURE OF INQUIRY

The investigation commenced with Aristotle's (384-322 BCE/1984) classical formulation of first principles as "the first basis from which a thing is known"—those foundational truths that cannot be deduced from more basic premises. However, comprehensive analysis reveals that the relationship between foundation and superstructure exhibits greater complexity than Aristotelian metaphors suggest. Following Lakatos's (1978) sophisticated analysis of scientific research programmes, apparent foundational principles often function as protective belts surrounding deeper theoretical cores that themselves undergo historical transformation through what he terms "progressive" and "degenerative" problemshifts.

Contemporary philosophy of science has substantially complicated traditional foundationalist assumptions. Laudan's (1984) detailed historical analysis demonstrates that even science's most fundamental commitments—empirical adequacy, predictive success, theoretical simplicity, explanatory scope—undergo significant evolution across historical periods. This historical variability challenges assumptions about permanent methodological foundations. Wigner's (1960) influential observation regarding the "unreasonable effectiveness of mathematics in the natural sciences" points toward an even deeper epistemological puzzle: the relationship between formal mathematical structures and physical reality remains fundamentally mysterious despite centuries of successful application.

The anti-realist challenge mounted by van Fraassen (2002) in *The Empirical Stance* argues that empirical adequacy rather than truth should constitute science's primary goal, suggesting that successful scientific theories need not reveal metaphysical truths about reality's fundamental structure. This constructive empiricism maintains that scientific principles, however predictively successful, may function as useful instruments rather than accurate descriptions of mind-independent reality. In response, scientific realists like Psillos (1999) deploy the "no miracles" argument, contending that science's predictive success would constitute an inexplicable miracle unless our best theories approximated truth. Boyd's (1983) influential formulation argues that scientific methodology exhibits a virtuous circle wherein approximately true theories generate successful predictions that justify continued confidence in theoretical frameworks.

The emergence of complexity science introduces additional challenges to reductionist approaches seeking simple foundations. Anderson's (1972) seminal article "More Is Different" demonstrates that each level of complexity exhibits emergent properties irreducible to lower-level descriptions. This thesis gained empirical support through Ellis's (2016) comprehensive analysis of top-down causation in biological and psychological systems, which documents numerous cases where higher-level organizational principles constrain lower-level processes in ways that cannot be captured through bottom-up analysis alone. Laughlin and Pines (2000) extend this argument by proposing that many fundamental physical principles themselves emerge from collective phenomena rather than representing truly basic features of reality.

Within philosophy proper, the quest for foundational certainty has generated both systematic insights and sustained critiques of foundationalism itself. Descartes's (1637/1996) methodological skepticism, while establishing the cogito as an allegedly indubitable foundation, generated rather than resolved fundamental questions about mind-world relations. Kant's (1781/1998) critical philosophy revealed the mind's constitutive role in structuring experience while simultaneously restricting knowledge to phenomenal appearances, leaving noumenal reality permanently inaccessible. Hegel's (1807/1977) dialectical response challenged both Cartesian and Kantian frameworks by arguing that absolute knowledge emerges through historical development rather than from fixed foundations.

Contemporary epistemology has largely abandoned classical foundationalist ambitions. BonJour's (2010) systematic analysis demonstrates that both traditional foundationalism and its coherentist alternative face insurmountable objections, leading many epistemologists toward more modest goals. Zagzebski's (1996) virtue epistemology shifts focus from belief properties to the intellectual virtues of epistemic agents, while Goldman's (1999) social epistemology emphasizes the irreducibly communal nature of knowledge production. These approaches suggest that knowledge emerges through complex social processes rather than from indubitable individual foundations.

Feminist epistemology has mounted particularly significant challenges to traditional foundationalism. Code's (2006) ecological thinking reveals how claims to universal rationality often mask particular perspectives embedded in power relations. Haraway's (1988) concept of "situated knowledges" argues that all knowledge claims emerge from specific social locations that both enable and constrain understanding. Fricker's (2007) analysis of epistemic injustice demonstrates how marginalized voices are systematically excluded from knowledge production, challenging assumptions about the neutrality of supposedly universal principles. These critiques do not advocate relativism but rather what Harding (1993) terms "strong objectivity"—enhanced rigor through incorporation of previously excluded perspectives.

Religious traditions contribute distinctive first principles emerging not from empirical observation or logical deduction but from reported encounters with transcendent reality. These revelatory insights—whether

Moses's theophany at Sinai, Buddha's awakening under the Bodhi tree, or Muhammad's reception of the Qur'an—establish comprehensive frameworks for understanding reality's ultimate nature. Hick's (1989) pluralist hypothesis attempts to reconcile religious diversity by proposing that different traditions represent culturally conditioned responses to the same ultimate reality. However, critics like Plantinga (2000) argue that genuine religious diversity involves incompatible truth claims that resist harmonization through inclusivist or pluralist strategies.

The hermeneutical complexity of religious knowledge parallels science's theory-ladenness. Gadamer's (2004) philosophical hermeneutics demonstrates that understanding always occurs within historically specific horizons that shape interpretation. Religious understanding involves what Ricoeur (1976) terms a "surplus of meaning" that exceeds propositional formulation, requiring ongoing interpretive engagement. This hermeneutical dimension does not undermine religious knowledge but reveals its distinctive epistemological structure.

20.2 CONVERGENT PATTERNS ACROSS DOMAINS

Despite profound methodological differences and cultural variations, certain structural principles recur across diverse approaches to understanding reality. These convergences merit careful analysis while acknowledging that apparent agreement may mask deeper disagreements about meaning and application.

The assumption of reality's fundamental intelligibility appears across most intellectual traditions, though interpreted through different frameworks. Scientific practice presupposes that nature follows discoverable regularities; philosophical inquiry depends on reason's capacity to grasp truth; religious traditions frequently proclaim a cosmos structured by logos, dharma, or divine wisdom. Davies's (1992) analysis in *The Mind of God* argues that the universe's rational comprehensibility represents a brute fact requiring explanation that transcends scientific methodology. Einstein's (1936) famous declaration that "the eternal mystery of the world is its comprehensibility" articulates this puzzle that continues to perplex physicists and philosophers.

However, postmodern critiques fundamentally challenge intelligibility assumptions. Lyotard's (1984) analysis of the "postmodern condition" argues that grand narratives about rational progress have lost credibility, replaced by local language games with incommensurable criteria. Derrida's (1976) deconstruction reveals how meaning emerges through différance—endless deferral and differentiation that resists final determination. These critiques suggest that intelligibility may be constructed through interpretive communities rather than discovered in mind-independent reality. Rorty's (1979) neo-pragmatism extends this critique by arguing that truth represents compliments we pay to sentences that work rather than correspondence with reality.

Smart's (1989) comprehensive cross-cultural analysis reveals that different traditions construct intelligibility through distinct categorical frameworks and narratives. What appears self-evidently rational within one conceptual scheme may seem arbitrary or incoherent within another. Needham's (1969) monumental study of Chinese science demonstrates that alternative frameworks can generate sophisticated understanding while operating with fundamentally different assumptions about causation, matter, and method. This cultural variability challenges claims about universal principles while not necessarily undermining the possibility of trans-cultural understanding.

The persistence of irreducible phenomena despite centuries of reductionist success suggests fundamental limits to decomposition strategies. Chalmers's (1995) formulation of consciousness's "hard problem" exemplifies this challenge: complete knowledge of neural processes appears insufficient to explain subjective experience. Block's (1995) distinction between access consciousness and phenomenal consciousness suggests that different aspects of mentality require distinct explanatory approaches, with phenomenal consciousness potentially requiring new fundamental principles.

Contemporary consciousness research increasingly acknowledges these explanatory limits. Koch's (2019) recent work argues that subjective experience represents an intrinsic feature of certain physical systems that cannot be reduced to functional or computational properties. Tononi and Koch's (2015) Integrated Information Theory proposes mathematical measures of consciousness corresponding to integrated information (Φ) in physical systems. Critics including Searle (2013) argue that such approaches either fail to address the hard problem or inadvertently embrace panpsychism. The persistence of this debate after decades of neuroscientific progress suggests that consciousness may require fundamentally new conceptual frameworks.

Similar irreducibility characterizes other domains. The origin of life from non-living matter remains poorly understood despite advances in prebiotic chemistry and synthetic biology (Luisi, 2016). The emergence of meaningful symbols from physical processes poses what Deacon (2011) calls the "zero transition" problem. In ethics, the fact-value gap identified by Hume (1739/2000) persists despite numerous naturalization attempts. Moore's (1903) open question argument—that questions about the good remain open even given complete natural facts—continues to challenge naturalistic ethics. These persistent explanatory gaps suggest either methodological limitations or genuinely emergent properties requiring autonomous principles.

Contemporary physics increasingly reveals matter's fundamentally relational character. Quantum entanglement demonstrates non-local correlations that challenge assumptions about independent existence (Aspect, Dalibard, & Roger, 1982). Rovelli's (2021) relational quantum mechanics proposes that physical properties exist only relative to observing systems rather than absolutely. Quantum field theory describes particles as excitations in fields rather than independent entities (Weinberg, 1995). These developments challenge substance-based metaphysics inherited from Aristotelian and Cartesian traditions.

Philosophy exhibits parallel developments toward relational ontologies. Husserl's (1913/2014) phenomenology reveals consciousness as inherently intentional—always directed toward objects. Heidegger's (1927/1962) fundamental ontology replaces subject-object dualism with Dasein's being-in-the-world. Levinas's (1969) ethics locates the foundation of meaning in the face-to-face encounter with the Other. These approaches suggest that relationality rather than substance may be ontologically primary.

Religious and indigenous traditions have long emphasized relational ontologies. Buddhism's pratītyasamutpāda (dependent origination) denies independent existence to all phenomena (Garfield, 1995). The Lakota concept of Mitákuye Oyás'iŋ ("all my relations") expresses fundamental interconnection (Deloria, 1973). Ubuntu philosophy's principle that "a person is a person through other persons" emphasizes communal rather than individual identity (Mbiti, 1990). These frameworks offer sophisticated alternatives to Western substantialism.

Yet substantialist metaphysics retains serious philosophical defenders. Lowe's (2006) four-category ontology argues that relations require relata—entities that stand in relations. Armstrong's (1997) combinatorial theory grounds reality in states of affairs combining particulars and universals. Schaffer's (2010) priority monism argues for one fundamental object (the cosmos) with derivative parts. These positions suggest that complete abandonment of substance concepts may be premature.

20.3 IRREDUCIBLE TENSIONS AND COMPLEMENTARITY

Certain conflicts between domains appear to involve genuinely incompatible first principles rather than complementary perspectives addressing different aspects of reality. Acknowledging these tensions maintains intellectual integrity while avoiding premature synthesis that obscures real disagreements.

The conflict between scientific naturalism and religious supernaturalism involves fundamental disagreements about reality's ultimate constitution. Methodological naturalism—science's self-imposed restriction to natural causes—has proven extraordinarily successful in generating reliable knowledge about physical processes (Boudry, Blancke, & Braeckman, 2010). However, metaphysical naturalism—the philosophical claim that only natural entities exist—directly contradicts religious worldviews affirming divine action, miracles, or transcendent realities.

Gould's (1997) proposal of "non-overlapping magisteria" (NOMA) attempts reconciliation by restricting science to empirical facts while assigning religion to values and meaning. However, this solution satisfies neither committed naturalists who view values as natural phenomena (Flanagan, 2007) nor religious believers making factual claims about divine action in history (Plantinga, 2011). McGrath's (2004) "scientific theology" proposes integration while respecting domain autonomy, but critics question whether such synthesis avoids reducing one domain to another.

The determinism-agency tension reflects fundamental disagreements about human nature. Physics describes causally closed systems operating according to deterministic or probabilistic laws that appear to leave no room for libertarian free will (Laplace, 1814/1951). Contemporary neuroscience reinforces this challenge: Libet's (1985) experiments demonstrating unconscious neural activity preceding conscious decisions have been extended and refined by Schurger and colleagues (2012), suggesting that conscious will may be epiphenomenal rather than causally efficacious.

Hard incompatibilists like Pereboom (2001) argue that free will is impossible, whether determinism or indeterminism obtains. Their argument has gained support from Caruso (2012), who argues that consciousness lacks the causal power required for moral responsibility. Compatibilists respond with increasingly sophisticated analyses. Dennett's (2003) multiple drafts model locates freedom in the capacity for rational reflection rather than ultimate origination. Frankfurt's (1971) hierarchical theory grounds free will in the capacity to form second-order desires about one's first-order desires. Kane's (1996) libertarian approach proposes that quantum indeterminacy creates space for self-forming actions. The persistence of this debate suggests genuinely incompatible intuitions about human agency.

The fact-value distinction articulated by Hume (1739/2000) continues to generate philosophical controversy. Science aspires to a value-neutral description of how things are, while ethics concerns normative prescriptions about how things ought to be. This gap between descriptive and evaluative claims challenges naturalistic approaches to ethics that seek to ground moral facts in natural facts.

Street's (2006) "Darwinian dilemma" poses a powerful challenge to moral realism by arguing that evolutionary forces shaped our moral beliefs for reproductive success rather than truth-tracking. If our moral intuitions result from evolutionary pressures unrelated to moral truth, their reliability becomes questionable. Shafer-Landau's (2003) robust moral realism responds by arguing that evolution may have equipped us to track moral facts just as it equipped us to track physical facts. Korsgaard's (1996) constructivist approach grounds normativity in the constitutive standards of rational agency itself, avoiding commitment to mind-independent moral facts.

Putnam's (2002) later work argues for the "entanglement of fact and value," claiming that even scientific observation involves evaluative judgments about relevance, simplicity, and coherence. However, critics maintain that this entanglement does not eliminate the logical distinction between descriptive and prescriptive claims (Blackburn, 2013). The persistence of this debate suggests that the fact-value gap may reflect a fundamental feature of human cognition rather than a philosophical confusion.

20.4 PROVISIONAL AFFIRMATIONS

Despite persistent disagreements and historical evolution of first principles, certain commitments command reasonable confidence while acknowledging their provisional and contested status. These affirmations emerge from convergent evidence across domains rather than from indubitable foundations.

The convergence of intersubjective agreement, nature's resistance to arbitrary manipulation, and the discovery of previously unimagined phenomena strongly suggests reality's mind-independent existence. Even anti-realist philosophers typically acknowledge objective constraints on experience, whether through social construction (Hacking, 1999), empirical adequacy (van Fraassen, 2002), or pragmatic success (Rorty, 1979). The discovery of phenomena like radioactivity, DNA, and cosmic microwave background radiation—completely unexpected from prior theoretical frameworks—provides strong evidence for reality's independent structure (Hacking, 1983).

This minimal realism does not entail naive correspondence theories or commitment to particular metaphysical frameworks. Chakravartty's (2007) structural realism offers a sophisticated position affirming the reality of mathematical structures and relations while remaining agnostic about the intrinsic nature of relata. This approach acknowledges scientific success while accommodating anti-realist insights about the theory-ladenness of observation and the underdetermination of theory by evidence.

The persistence of explanatory gaps across multiple domains suggests fundamental limits to reductive explanation. Levine's (1983) analysis of the "explanatory gap" between physical and phenomenal properties has proven remarkably durable despite advances in neuroscience. Similar gaps appear between chemistry and life, syntax and semantics, mechanism and meaning, nature and normativity. While future science may close these gaps, their persistence across diverse domains suggests something significant about the architecture of explanation itself.

Nagel's (2012) controversial argument in *Mind and Cosmos* that materialist neo-Darwinism is "almost certainly false" reflects the seriousness of these challenges. While most philosophers reject Nagel's specific proposals for teleological principles, the problems he identifies—consciousness, cognition, value—remain genuine puzzles. The explanatory gaps may indicate emergent properties requiring autonomous principles rather than mere temporary ignorance.

The cross-cultural convergence on mathematical truths, mathematics' effectiveness in physical science, and the apparent constraint mathematical reasoning places on mathematical imagination collectively suggest some form of mathematical objectivity. Benacerraf's (1973) influential dilemma highlights the epistemological puzzle: if mathematical objects exist independently, how do we gain knowledge of them without causal contact? Various responses have been proposed, including Field's (1980) nominalist program eliminating mathematical ontology, Maddy's (1997) naturalistic approach grounding mathematics in set-theoretic practice, and Linnebo's (2017) thin objects account. Each position captures important insights while facing objections, suggesting that mathematical objectivity may require novel metaphysical categories.

The phenomenology of moral experience involves apparent perception of objective requirements transcending individual preference. Empirical research reveals both universal patterns—prohibitions on unprovoked harm, requirements of fairness, care for vulnerable individuals—and significant cultural variation in moral systems (Haidt, 2012). This pattern suggests that while moral experience may track objective features of reality, moral knowledge is inevitably mediated through cultural frameworks.

Prinz's (2007) sentimentalist approach argues that emotional responses constitute rather than detect moral properties. However, this view faces difficulty explaining the apparent objectivity of moral discourse and the possibility of moral error. A more promising approach may be Wiggins's (1987) sensible subjectivism, which grounds moral properties in the responses of idealized observers while maintaining their reality. This position acknowledges both the subjective basis of moral experience and its objective pretensions.

20.5 THE PARTICIPATORY UNIVERSE

Recent developments across physics, philosophy, and religious studies converge on recognizing knowledge and reality's fundamentally participatory character. Wheeler's (1990) concept of the "participatory universe" suggests that observation plays a constitutive role in determining physical properties rather than merely revealing pre-existing facts. This participatory dimension appears across multiple domains, suggesting a fundamental feature of the knowledge-reality relationship.

Quantum mechanics reveals measurement's fundamental role in determining physical properties. While interpretations differ substantially, most acknowledge that the classical separation between observer and observed cannot be maintained at quantum scales (Schlosshauer, 2007). The Copenhagen interpretation's emphasis on measurement's role in collapsing wave functions, though controversial, highlights how observation partially constitutes rather than merely reveals physical facts. QBism (Quantum Bayesianism), developed by Fuchs and Peres (2000), takes this further, treating quantum states as subjective degrees of belief rather than objective features of reality.

These developments challenge assumptions about scientific knowledge, providing what Nagel (1986) termed a "view from nowhere." Instead, scientific knowledge emerges through particular interactions between knowing subjects and physical systems, mediated by theoretical frameworks and experimental apparatuses. Barad's (2007) agential realism argues that properties emerge through "intra-action" within phenomena rather than pre-existing interaction. This participatory dimension does not undermine objectivity but reveals its complex, emergent character.

Gadamer's (2004) philosophical hermeneutics demonstrates that understanding always occurs within historically specific horizons that both enable and constrain interpretation. We cannot transcend our historical situation to achieve a neutral perspective; instead, understanding emerges through the "fusion of horizons" between interpreter and interpreted. This hermeneutical insight extends beyond textual interpretation to encompass all knowledge forms. Scientific observation requires theoretical interpretation, philosophical analysis employs inherited conceptual frameworks, and religious understanding occurs within traditional communities of practice.

Process theology, developed from Whitehead's (1929) metaphysics by Hartshorne (1948) and contemporary theologians like Griffin (2001), proposes that God and world exist in relations of mutual influence rather than unilateral determination. This vision challenges classical theism's emphasis on divine sovereignty while maintaining genuine divine influence in cosmic processes. Similar participatory themes appear across religious traditions. Panikkar's (1993) "cosmotheandric" vision emphasizes the mutual interpenetration of cosmic, human, and divine dimensions. Jewish mysticism's concept of tikkun olam suggests human responsibility for completing divine creation (Scholem, 1941). These perspectives emphasize participation rather than passive observation in religious understanding.

20.6 TOWARD INTEGRAL METHODOLOGY

Contemporary global challenges—climate change, artificial intelligence, biotechnology, economic inequality—require integrated approaches that honor insights from multiple domains while maintaining rigorous standards. Wilber's (2000) integral theory offers one framework, though alternative approaches deserve equal consideration. The key insight involves recognizing that different aspects of reality become visible through different investigative methods.

Rather than privileging any single methodology, integral approaches acknowledge what Kellert, Longino, and Waters (2006) term "pluralistic stance"—the view that complex phenomena require multiple perspectives for adequate understanding. Taylor's (1989) analysis demonstrates how different moral frameworks illuminate distinct dimensions of ethical life. Bhaskar's (2008) critical realism argues that reality's stratified nature—with physical, biological, psychological, and social levels—requires corresponding methodological diversity.

This methodological pluralism avoids relativism through what Haack (2003) calls "innocent realism"—recognition that reality's objective structure constrains while not fully determining human interpretation. Different methods suit different investigative purposes: controlled experiments for causal relationships, hermeneutical analysis for meaning, contemplative practice for consciousness, and mathematical modeling for structural relationships. Mitchell's (2009) "integrative pluralism" provides detailed guidelines for combining insights from different methodological approaches while maintaining scientific rigor.

20.7 THE RECURSIVE NATURE OF INQUIRY

The investigation of first principles exhibits what Hofstadter (1979) termed "strange loops"—self-referential structures generating complexity through recursion. We employ consciousness to study consciousness, reason to examine reason's foundations, and language to analyze linguistic structures. This reflexivity represents not a methodological defect but an essential feature of self-aware inquiry.

Gödel's (1931) incompleteness theorems demonstrate that formal systems complex enough to express arithmetic cannot prove their own consistency, revealing fundamental limits to self-referential reasoning. Yet these limitations generate rather than eliminate creative possibilities. Smith's (2013) analysis shows how Gödel's results open space for genuine mathematical discovery beyond formal derivation. Similarly, consciousness's self-awareness enables new experiential and cognitive possibilities. Damasio's (2010) neuroscientific research reveals how self-referential processes create the autobiographical self, enabling complex cognition and emotion.

Campbell's (1974) evolutionary epistemology proposes that knowledge-seeking processes undergo selection pressures favoring cognitive strategies that track environmental regularities. This process operates across biological, cultural, and individual levels, creating nested hierarchies of adaptive learning. However, Plantinga's (2011) evolutionary argument against naturalism highlights a crucial tension: if cognitive faculties evolved for reproductive success rather than truth, their reliability becomes questionable. While responses have been offered (Sober, 2011), this challenge reveals deep questions about the relationship between evolutionary success and epistemic virtue.

20.8 LIVING GROUND: PROCESS AND EMERGENCE

After traversing scientific, philosophical, and religious approaches to first principles, we discover not static bedrock but what Bohm (1980) termed "holomovement"—dynamic wholeness from which apparent stability emerges. Reality's ground exhibits what Whitehead (1929) identified as creativity—"the universal of universals characterizing ultimate matter of fact".

Process philosophy challenges substance metaphysics by treating becoming rather than being as ontologically primary. Whitehead's (1929) philosophy of organism proposes that reality consists of "actual occasions of experience" achieving temporary stability through creative synthesis of past influences. Contemporary developments in physics and biology increasingly support process ontologies. Quantum field theory describes particles as temporary stabilizations in field fluctuations rather than permanent entities (Weinberg, 1995). Biological systems exhibit what Kauffman (1993) terms "order for free"—self-organization emerging from dynamic interactions rather than imposed from external sources.

Clayton's (2004) analysis of strong emergence argues that complex systems generate genuinely novel causal powers irreducible to their components. Ellis's (2016) detailed examination provides numerous examples of top-down causation in biological and psychological systems. While controversial, these analyses suggest that reality exhibits hierarchical organization with emergent properties at each level requiring autonomous explanatory principles.

20.9 IMPLICATIONS FOR CONTINUED INQUIRY

This investigation yields several implications for future research into first principles and their applications to contemporary challenges.

All identified principles should be held with what Peirce (1877) termed "fallibilistic" commitment—firmly enough to guide inquiry while remaining revisable based on new evidence or arguments. This fallibilistic stance, elaborated by Haack (1993), avoids both dogmatic certainty and paralyzing skepticism. Popper's (1963) emphasis on falsifiability provides methodological guidance, though Kuhn's (1962/1996) analysis of paradigmatic science and Lakatos's (1978) research programme methodology reveal that theoretical commitments require protection from premature falsification.

Reality's complexity demands both specialized expertise and integrative synthesis. Snow's (1959) analysis of "two cultures" remains relevant as disciplinary boundaries often impede necessary collaboration. Wilson's (1998) concept of "consilience" offers one integration model, though critics worry about reductionist implications (Dupré, 1993). Alternative approaches emphasizing dialogue and mutual enrichment rather than unification may prove more fruitful.

Indigenous scholars demonstrate how Western knowledge systems have marginalized alternative ways of knowing. Smith's (2012) decolonizing methodologies reveal sophisticated Indigenous knowledge systems offering valuable insights for contemporary challenges. Whyte's (2017) work on Indigenous climate science provides concrete examples of how traditional ecological knowledge contributes to environmental understanding. These perspectives challenge universal claims about first principles while enriching our collective intellectual resources.

20.10 CONCLUSION: THE CONTINUING QUEST

The search for first principles across science, philosophy, and religion reveals both convergent insights and irreducible tensions that resist final resolution. Rather than providing definitive answers, this investigation establishes frameworks for continued inquiry while acknowledging the provisional nature of all human knowledge. The principles identified— intelligibility, emergence, mathematical objectivity, moral phenomenology, participatory knowledge—function as what Kauffman (2008) calls "enabling constraints" that simultaneously limit and create possibilities for understanding.

These principles prove sufficiently robust to guide inquiry and action while remaining open to revision through continued investigation. They provide orientation without determining destination, establishing grammar without dictating content, and offering foundations without preventing creative construction. In Lonergan's (1957) formulation, they express the "pure, unrestricted desire to know" that drives human inquiry across all domains of experience and reflection.

The ultimate insight may be that reality's ground is neither purely objective nor purely subjective but emerges through dynamic interaction between inquiring consciousness and the world it inhabits. This participatory universe requires neither passive reception of given truths nor arbitrary construction of meaning but active engagement honoring both reality's constraints and consciousness's creative contributions. As we face unprecedented global challenges, the first principles identified in this investigation provide resources for integration without reduction, dialogue without relativism, and commitment without dogmatism.

The quest for first principles continues because reality itself continues— creating, evolving, emerging through processes we partially understand and partially constitute. We participate in this ongoing process not as external observers but as conscious agents contributing to the very reality we seek to comprehend. In this participation, the search for first principles finds both its ground and its ultimate justification, not as a completed achievement but as an ongoing commitment to understanding that defines human consciousness at its most fundamental level.

GLOSSARY OF KEY TERMS

A

Abstract Objects A class of entities, including numbers, sets, propositions, and logical principles, that are defined by their non-spatiotemporal, causally inert, and non-mental nature. Their existence is affirmed by mathematical realists and poses a significant challenge to naturalist and physicalist worldviews, which struggle to account for entities that exist outside the physical nexus of cause and effect. The monograph treats the existence of abstract objects as a key piece of evidence against reductive materialism. The indispensability of mathematical entities for our best scientific theories—a position known as the Quine-Putnam indispensability argument—suggests that reality contains more than just physical entities. This supports the book's broader thesis that a purely scientific worldview is incomplete, as the very success of physics appears to depend on a non-physical, abstract reality. The challenge of abstract objects illustrates the Convergence Hypothesis by showing how a philosophical problem (the ontology of mathematics) arises directly from scientific practice and points toward a reality that transcends physicalism.

Actual Occasions of Experience The fundamental units of reality in Alfred North Whitehead's process philosophy. These are not enduring substances but momentary events of "becoming" that achieve concrete actuality before "perishing" into "objective immortality," becoming data for subsequent occasions. Each occasion possesses both a physical pole (its reception of the past) and a mental pole (its subjective aim and integration of data), making experience (panexperientialism) a universal feature of reality. This concept is central to the monograph's exploration of dynamic and relational ontologies as alternatives to classical substance metaphysics. Process philosophy, with its foundation in actual occasions, offers a framework for resolving long-standing philosophical problems. It addresses Zeno's paradoxes by treating motion as a succession of discrete events and reconceives the mind-body problem as an issue of different types of occasions rather than the interaction of two different substances.

Advaita Vedanta An influential school of Hindu philosophy that asserts non-dual consciousness (Brahman) as the sole ultimate reality. In this worldview, the phenomenal diversity of the world (māyā) is neither a pure illusion nor a separate reality but is the appearance of Brahman through limiting adjuncts. The individual self or consciousness (ātman) is held to be identical to the universal consciousness (Brahman), though ignorance (avidyā) creates the appearance of separation. Advaita Vedanta serves as a primary example of an idealistic worldview and an Eastern non-dualistic alternative to Western metaphysics. It challenges the foundational assumptions of both materialism and substance dualism by positing consciousness as metaphysically primary. The tradition's use of systematic negation (neti neti, "not this, not that") to point toward a trans-conceptual reality provides a powerful parallel to the apophatic theology of the West.

Agrippa's Trilemma A foundational skeptical argument, also known as the Münchhausen Trilemma, which asserts that any attempt to justify a belief must terminate in one of three equally problematic outcomes: an infinite regress of reasons, circular reasoning, or a dogmatic, unproven assumption. This trilemma is introduced in Chapter 2 to frame the "Problem of Foundation" that motivates the entire inquiry into first principles. It establishes the central epistemological challenge that any theory of knowledge must confront. The monograph presents the major epistemological architectures—foundationalism, coherentism, and infinitism—as distinct responses to this single, powerful problem. The trilemma reveals the inherent difficulty in securing knowledge on an unshakeable ground, forcing a deeper investigation into what can count as a legitimate starting point for reason.

Anomalous Monism A sophisticated philosophical position on the mind-body problem, developed by Donald Davidson, which attempts to reconcile mental causation with the causal closure of the physical world. It holds that while every individual mental event is identical to some physical event (token identity), there are no strict, law-like connections between types of mental events and types of physical events (the "anomalous" part). This preserves the autonomy of psychological explanation while maintaining an overall physicalist ontology. Anomalous monism is presented as a key development in the evolution of materialist metaphysics, moving beyond the simplistic claims of early type identity theory to accommodate the complexities of mental life. However, the monograph also notes its significant weakness: by denying strict psychophysical laws, it risks making mental properties causally irrelevant (epiphenomenal), since it is the event's physical properties, not its mental ones, that feature in physical laws.

Apophatic Theology (Via Negativa) A theological method, prominent in mystical and philosophical traditions, that approaches the ultimate ground of reality by systematically negating all finite concepts and attributes. It asserts that ultimate reality transcends all conceptual categories and is known more accurately by what it is not than by what it is. This method is exemplified by figures like Pseudo-Dionysius in Christianity and is paralleled by Śaṅkara's neti neti ("not this, not that") in Advaita Vedanta and Nāgārjuna's systematic negations in Buddhist philosophy. This concept is crucial to the author's argument for epistemic humility and the limits of rationalism. It serves as a key example of how the "revelatory path" acknowledges the limitations of language and reason when confronting the transcendent. Apophatic theology is presented not as an anti-rational stance but as a form of "meta-rationality" that uses reason to demonstrate reason's own limits.

Arche The Greek term, meaning "beginning" or "origin," used by pre-Socratic philosophers to denote the fundamental substance or principle from which all of reality is derived. Thinkers like Thales (water), Anaximander (apeiron, the boundless), and Heraclitus (logos, perpetual flux) were engaged in a search for the arche. The search for the arche represents the historical starting point in the Western tradition for the investigation of first principles. It established the intellectual pattern of seeking a single, irreducible explanatory principle beneath the diversity of phenomena. This ancient quest is the direct ancestor of modern physics' search for a unified theory and metaphysics' search for the ultimate ground of being.

Axioms Explicitly stated first principles within a formal or mathematical system that are accepted without proof and from which all other theorems are derived. Euclid's geometry, with its axioms such as "things equal to the same thing are equal to each other," provides the paradigmatic example. The monograph uses mathematical axioms to illustrate the function of first principles in their clearest form. The development of non-Euclidean geometries in the 19th century demonstrated a crucial insight: axioms are not necessarily self-evident truths about physical reality but are foundational assumptions that define a conceptual framework. Different sets of axioms can generate different, internally consistent systems (e.g., Euclidean vs. Riemannian geometry), showing that first principles can be both necessary for reasoning within a system and contingent from a wider perspective.

B

Bell's Theorem A theorem in quantum physics, developed by John Stewart Bell, which demonstrates that no physical theory based on the principle of local realism can reproduce all the predictions of quantum mechanics. Experiments have consistently violated the inequalities derived from the theorem, confirming that the universe is non-local, non-realist, or both. This forces a radical revision of classical assumptions about the nature of physical reality. Bell's Theorem is cited as a prime example of how scientific inquiry can compel a revision of deeply ingrained first principles. The classical principles of locality (causes must be contiguous) and realism (properties exist independently of measurement) were once considered self-evident. The theorem and its experimental confirmation show that empirical evidence can overturn what previously seemed to be necessary truths.

Big Bang Model The prevailing cosmological model describing the universe's evolution from an extremely hot, dense initial state approximately 13.8 billion years ago. The model is supported by a wide range of empirical evidence, including the expansion of the universe (Hubble's Law), the existence of the cosmic microwave background radiation, and the observed abundances of light elements (Big Bang nucleosynthesis). While celebrated as a major achievement of modern science, the Big Bang model is also used to illustrate the inherent limits of scientific explanation. The model successfully describes cosmic evolution from the Planck era forward but cannot explain the initial singularity itself or the origin of the laws and conditions that governed it. This explanatory boundary, where science points to a beginning it cannot explain, is a key point of convergence where scientific inquiry opens onto philosophical and theological questions about ultimate origins.

Bootstrapping Problem A term for the recursive, self-referential challenge inherent in any attempt to justify foundational principles. The problem manifests when one must use the very faculty or system being justified in the process of justification. For example, one must use logic to argue for the validity of logic, or use reason to demonstrate the reliability of reason. This concept is central to the monograph's theme of the recursive nature of inquiry. It is the most general formulation of the foundational limit that appears in various domains: as the Problem of the Criterion in epistemology, as the challenge of proving consistency in logic (Gödel's Incompleteness Theorems), and as the problem of self-reference in consciousness studies. Recognizing this inescapable circularity fosters epistemic humility and suggests that ultimate foundations cannot be secured from a neutral, external standpoint but must be accepted as pragmatically necessary or self-verifying from within our cognitive practices.

Brahman In Hindu philosophy, particularly in the Upanishads and Advaita Vedanta, Brahman is the ultimate, non-dual reality that is the ground of all being, consciousness, and bliss (saccidānanda). It is the single, indivisible reality of which the entire universe of diverse phenomena is an appearance (māyā). Brahman is presented as a sophisticated conception of ultimate reality that contrasts with the personal God of Western theistic realism. It represents a form of idealism or cosmopsychism where consciousness is not a property of some beings but is the fundamental nature of reality itself. The concept challenges the substance-based ontologies of the West and illustrates how the "revelatory path" can lead to a radically different, yet philosophically rigorous, understanding of the ultimate first principle.

C

Catuṣkoṭi (Tetralemma) A logical framework prominent in Buddhist philosophy, particularly in the Madhyamaka school of Nāgārjuna, that considers four possibilities for any proposition: that it is true, that it is false, that it is both true and false, or that it is neither true nor false. This stands in stark contrast to the bivalent logic of the Western tradition, which is based on the Law of Excluded Middle. The catuṣkoṭi is used to demonstrate the limits of conceptual thought and to deconstruct metaphysical claims about the ultimate nature of reality. By showing that all four possibilities lead to contradiction or incoherence when applied to ultimate reality, Nāgārjuna argues that reality is empty (śūnyatā) of any inherent, definable nature. This serves as a powerful example of an alternative logical tradition that challenges the universality of classical Western logic and supports the author's argument for logical pluralism.

Cogito (Cogito ergo sum) The foundational principle of Cartesian philosophy ("I think, therefore I am"), established through the method of systematic doubt as the one indubitable certainty: the act of doubting one's own existence proves the existence of a thinking self. In Chapter 7, the cogito serves as the "Archimedean point" for the entire epistemological investigation. It is the first positive answer to the skeptical challenges raised by Agrippa's Trilemma. From this single point of certainty about the existence of consciousness, the author builds his case for the irreducibility of mind and the inadequacy of purely materialist ontologies. The author establishes a crucial argumentative chain: The cogito proves the certainty of consciousness. The certainty and unique properties of consciousness lead to the Hard Problem of Consciousness. The Hard Problem serves as the primary empirical and philosophical defeater for Naturalistic Materialism.

Coherentism An epistemological theory that stands as an alternative to foundationalism. It argues that a belief is justified not by resting on a foundation of basic, non-inferential beliefs, but by being part of a coherent system of mutually supporting beliefs. In this view, "first principles" are simply the most central and interconnected beliefs in the web of belief. Coherentism is presented as one of the major responses to Agrippa's Trilemma. While the author ultimately leans towards a form of pluralistic, modest foundationalism, coherentism is treated as a serious framework that correctly highlights the holistic and systematic nature of knowledge. The author subtly connects the logic of coherentism to the evaluation of scientific paradigms and competing worldviews.

Complementarity A principle, first developed by Niels Bohr in quantum physics to account for wave-particle duality, which holds that a complete understanding of a phenomenon may require multiple, mutually exclusive descriptions. For example, an electron may exhibit properties of a wave or a particle depending on the experimental context, but never both simultaneously. Both descriptions are necessary for a full account, yet they cannot be applied at the same time. The author elevates complementarity from a principle in physics to a general methodological principle for integrating science, philosophy, and religion. It serves as a key plank in the Convergence Hypothesis. Just as wave and particle descriptions are complementary aspects of quantum reality, the author argues that scientific, philosophical, and religious descriptions are complementary ways of knowing that reveal different, non-competing aspects of a single, unified reality.

Conservation Laws Principles in physics which state that certain physical quantities (e.g., energy, momentum, electric charge) remain constant in an isolated system over time. These laws are not mere empirical generalizations but are understood, via Noether's Theorem, to be the necessary mathematical consequences of underlying symmetries in nature. Conservation laws are presented as a paradigmatic example of first principles within the scientific domain. Their stability across revolutionary changes in physical theory (from Newton to Einstein to quantum mechanics) suggests they reflect deep, structural features of reality. They function as absolute constraints that any viable physical theory must respect, providing a clear example of how first principles thinking operates in modern science.

Convergence Hypothesis The central thesis of the monograph, which proposes that science, philosophy, and religion, when pursued with intellectual rigor and humility, are not conflicting but are complementary paths that converge toward a unified, albeit incomplete, understanding of reality's fundamental principles. This hypothesis, explicitly articulated in Chapter 15, serves as the interpretive key to the entire book. It reframes the relationship between the "three paths" from one of conflict (the "warfare metaphor") to one of mutual enrichment and complementarity. The author's purpose in drawing parallels between disparate fields—such as linking the fine-tuning problem in cosmology to theological design arguments, or Gödel's Incompleteness Theorems to apophatic theology—is to provide evidence for this convergence.

Cosmic Inflation A theoretical modification to the standard Big Bang model which posits a period of extremely rapid, exponential expansion of the universe in the first fraction of a second after its origin. Inflation was proposed to solve several major puzzles in cosmology, including the horizon problem (why the cosmic microwave background is so uniform) and the flatness problem (why the universe's geometry is so close to flat). While inflation is a successful explanatory model, the author uses it to illustrate the recursive nature of foundational questions in science. Inflation solves certain problems with the Big Bang model, but it introduces its own set of unexplained initial conditions (e.g., the existence and properties of the "inflaton" field). Furthermore, the Borde-Guth-Vilenkin theorem shows that even an inflationary spacetime cannot be past-eternal, meaning inflation itself requires a beginning.

Cosmopsychism A form of idealism or panpsychism which posits that the universe as a whole is conscious, and that the consciousness of individual beings is derived from or is a fragment of this cosmic consciousness. This view reverses the standard materialist assumption that consciousness emerges from complex arrangements of non-conscious matter. Cosmopsychism is presented as a serious contemporary worldview that offers a potential solution to the hard problem of consciousness. By making consciousness fundamental to the cosmos, it avoids the problem of explaining its emergence. The author connects this modern philosophical position to ancient non-dual traditions like Advaita Vedanta, which also posits a universal consciousness (Brahman) as the ultimate reality.

Creatio ex nihilo The theological doctrine, central to the Abrahamic religions (Judaism, Christianity, and Islam), that God created the universe "out of nothing," with no pre-existing matter or substrate. This doctrine establishes a radical ontological distinction between the necessary being of the Creator and the contingent being of creation, which depends on God for its existence at every moment. This concept is presented as the primary model of creation within theistic realism. It is contrasted with the emanationist and cyclical models of Hindu cosmology and the acosmic view of Buddhist philosophy. The author notes how the doctrine gained philosophical support from the kalām cosmological argument and, in modern times, from the evidence for a temporal beginning of the universe provided by the Big Bang model.

D

Dao (Tao) The central concept of Daoist philosophy, representing the ineffable, natural source, pattern, and process of the cosmos. The Dao is not a personal creator God but an impersonal, dynamic principle of reality that is both transcendent (the "nameless" source) and immanent (the pattern within all things). The Dao is a key example of a first principle from a non-Western tradition that challenges the categories of Western metaphysics. It is neither a substance nor a set of laws but a "way" or "process." This aligns with the monograph's broader shift in emphasis from static, substance-based ontologies to dynamic, relational ones, finding resonance with modern process philosophy and even some interpretations of quantum physics. The Daoist emphasis on the limits of language ("The Dao that can be spoken is not the eternal Dao") also parallels the apophatic traditions of the West.

Dependent Origination (Pratītyasamutpāda) The core metaphysical principle of Buddhist philosophy, which holds that all phenomena arise in dependence upon other phenomena in a web of interconnected causes and conditions. Nothing possesses svabhāva (inherent, independent existence).

This principle provides the foundation for the doctrine of śūnyatā (emptiness). Dependent origination is the central first principle of the Buddhist worldview and provides the most radical alternative to the substance-based metaphysics of the West. It dissolves the "origin problem" by denying the existence of a first cause, instead positing an endless, beginningless network of causal relationships. The author presents this as a sophisticated relational ontology that resonates with insights from modern physics (e.g., quantum entanglement) and ecology, again supporting the Convergence Hypothesis.

Dialectical Understanding A mode of understanding that recognizes the interplay of opposing or complementary forces and concepts, resolving them into a higher synthesis. In the context of the monograph, it refers to the view that first principles (such as physical laws) emerge from a dialectical interaction between the constraints of reality and the creative constructs of the human mind. This concept offers a middle path between naive realism (the view that we simply "discover" laws that exist independently) and social constructivism (the view that laws are purely human inventions). It captures the dynamic, interactive nature of inquiry that is a central theme of the book. This dialectical process is also reflected in the hermeneutical circle of interpretation and in the Hegelian logic of thesis-antithesis-synthesis.

E

Eliminative Materialism The most radical form of naturalistic materialism, which argues that our common-sense understanding of the mind ("folk psychology")—including concepts like belief, desire, and consciousness itself—is a deeply flawed theory that will eventually be eliminated and replaced by a mature neuroscience. This worldview is presented as the most extreme and consistent expression of the materialist research program. The author uses it to highlight the profound stakes of the mind-body problem. If eliminative materialism is correct, then the very foundation of the author's epistemological starting point—the certainty of consciousness from the cogito—is an illusion. The position is critiqued for its performative contradictions, as its proponents must use the concepts of belief and reason to argue that belief and reason do not exist.

Emergence The arising of novel properties and behaviors in a system that are not present in its component parts and cannot be straightforwardly predicted from them. The monograph distinguishes between weak emergence (novel but reducible in principle) and strong emergence

352

(irreducible, with new causal powers). Emergence is a crucial concept for the author's argument for a hierarchically structured reality and against reductive materialism. Phenomena like life, consciousness, and meaning are presented as strongly emergent properties. The concept of top-down causation is invoked to explain how these higher-level properties can exert genuine causal influence on their lower-level physical substrates. This allows for a non-reductive naturalism that is open to the insights of philosophy and religion without violating the principles of physics.

Epistemic Humility An intellectual virtue characterized by an attentive awareness of one's own cognitive limitations and the fallibility of one's beliefs. It is not a form of skepticism but a realistic assessment of the human epistemic condition, which fosters openness to revision, attentiveness to counter-evidence, and respect for alternative perspectives. Epistemic humility is presented as a necessary virtue for the quest for first principles. The author argues that the discoveries of inherent limits in our most rigorous domains—Gödel's Incompleteness Theorems in logic, the measurement problem in physics, and the paradoxes of self-reference in philosophy—mandate this stance. It is the antidote to the dogmatism that can afflict science, philosophy, and religion alike, and it is the necessary precondition for the kind of open, integrative dialogue required by the Convergence Hypothesis.

Epistemic Injustice A form of injustice, analyzed by Miranda Fricker, that harms individuals specifically in their capacity as knowers. It includes testimonial injustice (where a speaker's credibility is unfairly deflated due to prejudice) and hermeneutical injustice (where a collective lack of interpretive resources prevents someone from making sense of their own social experiences). This concept is vital to the monograph's argument that the quest for first principles is an irreducibly social and political enterprise. It shows that claims to universal, objective knowledge can mask the perspectives of dominant groups and silence marginalized voices. Achieving genuine understanding requires not just logical rigor and empirical evidence but also social justice. The author argues that incorporating insights from standpoint theory and attending to epistemic injustice leads to a "stronger objectivity" by correcting for systemic biases.

Equivalence Principle The foundational principle of Albert Einstein's General Relativity, which states that there is no local experiment that can distinguish between the effects of gravity and the effects of acceleration. This principle is cited as a powerful example of how a shift in first principles can lead to a scientific revolution. By treating the long-observed equality of gravitational and inertial mass not as a coincidence but as a fundamental principle, Einstein was led to reconceive gravity not as a force, but as the curvature of spacetime. This illustrates the transformative power of first principles thinking in science.

F

Falsifiability The criterion, proposed by Karl Popper, that for a theory to be considered scientific, it must be possible to conceive of an observation or experiment that could prove it false. Falsifiability is presented as a key epistemic virtue of the scientific path to truth, ensuring that scientific knowledge remains provisional, self-correcting, and grounded in empirical reality. The author contrasts this with some metaphysical or religious claims that may be unfalsifiable. However, the author also uses this criterion to question the scientific status of some contemporary physical theories, such as certain versions of string theory and the multiverse hypothesis, which may not make unique, testable predictions.

Fine-Tuning Problem The observation in contemporary cosmology that the fundamental constants and initial conditions of the universe are balanced within an extraordinarily narrow range to permit the emergence of complex, intelligent life. Fine-tuning is a critical piece of data used to support the Convergence Hypothesis. It is a scientific discovery that demands a philosophical or theological explanation, as science alone struggles to account for it. The author uses it as a primary example of where the three paths of inquiry meet, analyzing the competing explanations offered by different worldviews (e.g., the multiverse, theistic realism). The discovery of fine-tuning has had a causal effect on the landscape of contemporary metaphysics, weakening the explanatory power of simple naturalistic materialism while providing new, scientifically-grounded data for modern versions of the teleological argument.

First Principles (Archai) The foundational truths, bases, or origins (archai) from which all other knowledge is derived. In a technical philosophical sense, a first principle is a proposition that cannot be deduced from any other and serves as a necessary starting point for reasoning, thereby halting an infinite regress. This is the central concept of the entire monograph. The author explores how first principles function differently across domains: as axioms in mathematics, as conservation laws and symmetries in physics, as indubitable experiences (the cogito) in epistemology, as logical laws in reasoning, and as revealed truths or ultimate realities in religion. The overarching goal of the book is to investigate, compare, and seek convergence among the first principles identified by these different paths of inquiry.

Foundationalism The epistemological theory that knowledge is structured like a building, resting on a foundation of "properly basic beliefs" that are justified without reference to other beliefs (e.g., through self-evidence or direct experience). This structure is intended to halt the infinite regress threatened by Agrippa's Trilemma. This is the primary epistemological architecture explored in the book. The author traces its history from Aristotle and Descartes to contemporary forms like moderate foundationalism and virtue epistemology. The entire quest for first principles is, in essence, a foundationalist project. The monograph subtly traces the evolution of foundationalism from a quest for absolute, infallible certainty (strong foundationalism) to a more modest, fallibilist, and pluralistic model that seeks a network of reliable, though revisable, starting points drawn from multiple domains of experience.

G

General Relativity Albert Einstein's theory of gravitation, which describes gravity not as a force but as a consequence of the curvature of spacetime caused by the distribution of mass and energy. Its foundational principle is the equivalence principle. General Relativity is presented as a triumph of first principles reasoning in science. It also illustrates the dynamic and relational nature of reality that the author sees as a convergent theme across disciplines. In this theory, spacetime is not a static background but a dynamic entity that interacts with matter and energy, dissolving the classical distinction between container and content. The ongoing challenge of unifying General Relativity with quantum mechanics represents the current frontier of physics and highlights the incompleteness of our current understanding of physical first principles.

Gödel's Incompleteness Theorems A pair of theorems in mathematical logic proven by Kurt Gödel which demonstrate inherent limitations of formal axiomatic systems. The first theorem states that any consistent formal system powerful enough to do basic arithmetic contains true statements that cannot be proven within the system. The second theorem states that such a system cannot prove its own consistency. These theorems are of profound importance to the monograph's central argument. They represent a definitive limit to the power of formal, rational inquiry, demonstrating that truth necessarily transcends provability. The author repeatedly draws a parallel between this limit in logic and the limits found in other domains: the measurement problem in physics, the initial singularity in cosmology, and the need for apophatic theology in religion. This recurring pattern of "limitation disclosing a deeper reality" is a cornerstone of the Convergence Hypothesis.

H

Hard Problem of Consciousness The term coined by philosopher David Chalmers to distinguish the problem of explaining the functional and behavioral aspects of consciousness (the "easy problems") from the problem of explaining its qualitative, subjective, experiential character (phenomenal consciousness or qualia). The Hard Problem is arguably the single most important piece of evidence the author deploys against naturalistic materialism. It serves as a central node in the Convergence Hypothesis, as it is a problem that arises from scientific and philosophical inquiry but seems to point toward a reality that physicalism cannot accommodate. The author argues that the immediacy and certainty of phenomenal experience (grounded in the cogito) makes consciousness an undeniable datum that any complete worldview must explain. The failure of materialism to do so opens the door to alternative ontologies like idealism, panpsychism, or some form of dualism.

Hermeneutical Circle The principle of philosophical hermeneutics which states that understanding a whole requires understanding its parts, but understanding the parts requires a preliminary understanding of the whole. This creates a circular, or spiral, process of interpretation where understanding is gradually deepened through a back-and-forth movement between part and whole. This concept is used to describe the interpretive structure of worldviews. It explains why it is so difficult to adjudicate between competing worldviews from a neutral standpoint. Each worldview interprets evidence and arguments through its own pre-existing set of commitments (its "fore-structure of understanding"). This doesn't lead to relativism, but it does mean that worldview evaluation is a complex, holistic process rather than a simple matter of checking facts.

Hylomorphism The Aristotelian metaphysical theory that all natural substances are a composite of matter (hyle) and form (morphe). Matter is the potential principle, the "stuff" of which a thing is made, while form is the actualizing principle that gives the thing its specific nature and structure. Hylomorphism is presented as the foundational framework of classical Western substance ontology. It offered a powerful solution to the problem of change and persistence. The monograph contrasts this substance-based view with the process philosophy of Whitehead and the relational ontologies of Buddhism and modern physics, tracing a major thematic shift in metaphysics from a focus on static substances to dynamic processes and relationships.

I

Idealism A class of metaphysical worldviews that hold that reality is fundamentally mental or of the nature of consciousness. In this view, matter is either an appearance in consciousness, a construct of mind, or a phenomenal manifestation of a deeper mental reality. Idealism is presented as a major competitor to naturalistic materialism and theistic realism. It offers a straightforward solution to the hard problem of consciousness by making mind, rather than matter, the primary stuff of reality. The author explores various forms, from Berkeley's theistic idealism to contemporary versions like panpsychism and cosmopsychism, and notes its deep resonances with non-dual traditions like Advaita Vedanta.

Indispensability Argument An argument for the reality of abstract objects (like numbers and sets), most famously associated with W.V.O. Quine and Hilary Putnam. The argument states that because our best scientific theories make indispensable reference to mathematical entities, and we ought to be ontologically committed to the entities posited by our best scientific theories, we ought to be committed to the existence of mathematical entities. This argument is a key tool the author uses to challenge naturalistic materialism from within. It demonstrates that the practice of science itself seems to commit us to the existence of non-physical entities, thereby undermining the physicalist claim that reality is exhausted by the physical. This creates a powerful tension that motivates the search for a more comprehensive metaphysical framework.

Initial Singularity The state of infinite density and temperature at the beginning of the universe, as predicted by the standard Big Bang model when extrapolating the laws of General Relativity backward in time. The initial singularity represents a fundamental boundary to scientific explanation. It is a point where the known laws of physics break down, meaning science can describe what happened after the singularity but cannot explain its origin or nature. This "explanatory limit" is a crucial point of contact between cosmology, philosophy, and theology, as it raises ultimate questions about existence that science by itself is unequipped to answer.

Integrated Information Theory (IIT) A scientific and philosophical theory of consciousness, developed by Giulio Tononi, which proposes that consciousness is identical to a system's capacity for "integrated information" (quantified as Φ, or phi). A system is conscious to the degree that it is composed of differentiated, yet highly integrated, parts. IIT is presented as one of the most promising contemporary scientific theories of consciousness, attempting to bridge the gap between physical processes and subjective experience. However, the author also notes its radical implications, such as its leaning toward panpsychism (attributing some degree of consciousness to any system with non-zero Φ). It serves as an example of how cutting-edge science is pushing beyond simple materialism and engaging with questions traditionally reserved for philosophy.

K

Kalām Cosmological Argument A philosophical argument for the existence of God, prominent in medieval Islamic theology (kalām), which argues that (1) whatever begins to exist has a cause, (2) the universe began to exist, and therefore (3) the universe has a cause. This argument is presented as a key rational tool within theistic realism for grounding the doctrine of creatio ex nihilo. The author notes that the argument's second premise has received unexpected support from modern Big Bang cosmology, which provides scientific evidence for a temporal beginning of the universe. This is another prime example of the Convergence Hypothesis, where a conclusion from one path (theology/philosophy) is supported by findings from another (science).

L

Law of Non-Contradiction The classical law of logic which states that a proposition and its negation cannot both be true at the same time and in the same respect. Aristotle considered it the "most certain principle of all." This law is presented as one of the most fundamental first principles of reason. Its indispensability for coherent thought and discourse makes it a candidate for a necessary truth about the structure of reality itself. However, the author also explores challenges to its universal applicability from quantum superposition, semantic paradoxes, and non-Western logical traditions like the Buddhist catuṣkoṭi, suggesting the need for a nuanced view that may involve logical pluralism.

Local Realism The conjunction of two classical principles in physics: locality (objects are influenced only by their immediate surroundings) and realism (objects have definite properties independent of observation). This concept is crucial for understanding the philosophical revolution brought about by quantum mechanics. Bell's Theorem and subsequent experiments have shown that local realism is incompatible with the observed universe. Nature violates at least one of these seemingly common-sense principles. This forces a revision of our fundamental ontology and serves as a powerful example of how empirical science can overturn metaphysical first principles.

M

Many-Worlds Interpretation (MWI) An interpretation of quantum mechanics which proposes that the universal wave function never collapses. Instead, every quantum measurement causes the universe to "branch" into a multitude of parallel universes, one for each possible outcome of the measurement. MWI is discussed as a prominent scientific response to both the measurement problem in quantum mechanics and the fine-tuning problem in cosmology (as a type of multiverse). It avoids the conceptual difficulties of wave function collapse but does so at the cost of a vastly inflated ontology of unobservable worlds. The author presents it as a key example of how different choices of first principles (in this case, preserving the unitary evolution of the wave function at all costs) lead to radically different pictures of reality.

Mathematical Realism The philosophical view that mathematical entities (such as numbers, sets, and functions) and truths exist objectively and independently of the human mind. This position is also known as Platonism. This view is supported by the "unreasonable effectiveness of mathematics" in describing the physical world, which would be a miracle unless mathematics were tracking some objective structure of reality. It is challenged by the epistemological problem of how humans could have access to a causally inert, abstract realm. The debate over mathematical realism is central to the monograph's investigation of abstract objects and their challenge to naturalistic materialism.

Measurement Problem The unresolved problem in quantum mechanics of how or why wave function collapse occurs during the act of measurement, leading to a single definite outcome from a superposition of multiple possibilities. The measurement problem is another key example of a limit-point in science that opens onto deeper philosophical questions. The various interpretations of quantum mechanics (Copenhagen, Many-Worlds, spontaneous collapse) are different proposed solutions to this single problem, each with radically different ontological implications. This demonstrates that even our most successful scientific theory is foundationally incomplete and that empirical adequacy underdetermines our choice of first principles.

Methodological Naturalism The principle that science should seek explanations only in terms of natural causes and mechanisms, without invoking supernatural or transcendent entities. The author carefully distinguishes methodological naturalism, which is a procedural rule for doing science, from metaphysical naturalism (or naturalistic materialism), which is the philosophical claim that only natural entities exist. The success of methodological naturalism within science is undeniable, but the author argues it is a category mistake to assume this success proves the truth of metaphysical naturalism. Science's self-imposed limitation is precisely what creates the space for philosophical and theological inquiry into questions that lie beyond its methodological scope.

Multiverse Hypothesis A theoretical proposal in cosmology and physics which posits the existence of a vast, perhaps infinite, number of universes, collectively known as the multiverse. These universes may have different physical laws, constants, or initial conditions. The multiverse is presented primarily as a scientific response to the fine-tuning problem. By postulating a cosmic lottery with enough universes to realize all possibilities, our own life-permitting universe becomes statistically inevitable via an anthropic selection effect. However, the author highlights the profound philosophical and methodological problems with this hypothesis, including its potential unfalsifiability, the unsolved "measure problem," and the problem of "meta-fine-tuning" (the multiverse-generating mechanism may itself need to be fine-tuned).

N

Naturalistic Materialism (Physicalism) The metaphysical worldview which holds that reality consists entirely of physical entities, properties, and processes as described by the natural sciences, particularly physics. In this view, all phenomena, including life, mind, and consciousness, are either reducible to or emergent from this physical base. This worldview is presented as one of the major competing frameworks for understanding reality. Its strengths lie in its coherence with the methods and successes of modern science. However, the author argues that it faces severe challenges that it cannot adequately explain, most notably the hard problem of consciousness, the existence of abstract objects, objective moral value, and the fine-tuning problem. The inability of materialism to account for these phenomena is a primary motivation for the monograph's search for a more comprehensive, integrated worldview.

Noether's Theorem A fundamental theorem in mathematical physics which establishes a one-to-one correspondence between continuous symmetries in a physical system and conserved quantities. For example, the symmetry of physical laws with respect to time translation implies the conservation of energy. This theorem is a paradigmatic example of a first principle in physics. It elevates conservation laws from mere empirical observations to necessary mathematical consequences of fundamental symmetries. It demonstrates the profound connection between the mathematical structure of our theories and the physical behavior of the universe, highlighting the "unreasonable effectiveness of mathematics" and providing strong support for a rational order inherent in the cosmos.

Numinous A term coined by the theologian Rudolf Otto to describe the unique, irreducible experience of the sacred or holy. It is characterized by the dual qualities of mysterium tremendum (an awe-inspiring mystery that evokes a sense of creatureliness and dread) and fascinans (an attractive, compelling, and fascinating mystery). The numinous experience is the foundational datum for the "revelatory path" to truth. The author treats it as a genuine phenomenological category that, while subject to naturalistic explanations from cognitive science, cannot be dismissed out of hand. The persistence and cross-cultural nature of such experiences suggest they may provide epistemic access to a transcendent dimension of reality, a possibility that a purely materialist worldview excludes by fiat.

O

Ontology The branch of metaphysics concerned with the study of being, existence, and the fundamental categories of reality. It asks the question, "What is there?" and seeks to provide a systematic account of the most general features of what exists. The entire monograph is an exercise in ontology, an "inquiry into first principles" that seeks to understand the nature of being. Chapter 8 is specifically dedicated to exploring competing ontological frameworks, from Aristotelian substance metaphysics to modern process philosophy and relational ontologies. The author argues that our ontological commitments are not abstract academic matters but have profound implications for how we understand ourselves and live our lives.

P

Panentheism The theological and metaphysical view that God is in the world and the world is in God, but God is also more than the world. It differs from pantheism (which identifies God with the world) by maintaining God's transcendence, and from classical theism by positing a more intimate, dynamic, and reciprocal relationship between God and the cosmos. Panentheism, particularly as developed in process philosophy, is presented as a sophisticated worldview that attempts to integrate scientific insights (like evolution and quantum indeterminacy) with religious intuitions about divine action and immanence. It offers a model of divine action as persuasion rather than coercion, which avoids conflicts with scientific accounts of natural causation. It represents a creative synthesis that seeks to overcome the traditional dichotomies between naturalism and supernaturalism.

Participatory Universe A concept, associated with physicist John Archibald Wheeler, which suggests that the observer plays a constitutive role in bringing physical reality into being. This interpretation of quantum mechanics challenges the classical view of a detached observer passively recording a pre-existing, independent reality. The author adopts this concept and broadens it into a general metaphysical principle that undergirds the Convergence Hypothesis. The idea is that reality is not a static "thing" to be observed but a dynamic process that is co-created through the "intra-action" (a term from Karen Barad) of consciousness and the cosmos. This view helps to explain why different modes of inquiry (scientific, philosophical, religious) can reveal genuinely different, yet equally valid, aspects of reality.

Past Hypothesis The hypothesis in cosmology and the philosophy of physics which states that the universe began in a state of extraordinarily low entropy. This special initial condition is posited as the ultimate explanation for the arrow of time and the second law of thermodynamics (the tendency of entropy to increase). The Past Hypothesis is a clear example of a first principle that is required by science but cannot be explained by science. It is an un-explained initial condition that must be put in "by hand" to make the rest of physics work. This highlights the limits of scientific explanation and points toward deeper questions about why the universe had such an improbable beginning—a question that directly engages the fine-tuning problem and the broader "origin problem."

Phenomenal Consciousness (Qualia) The subjective, qualitative, experiential character of conscious states; what it is like to see red, feel pain, or taste a lemon. This is distinguished from access consciousness, which refers to the availability of information for cognitive processing. Phenomenal consciousness is the epistemological bedrock of the author's argument. Its existence is established as indubitable via the cogito. Its nature gives rise to the hard problem of consciousness, which serves as the primary challenge to naturalistic materialism. The author argues that any adequate worldview must take the reality of phenomenal consciousness seriously, and that its existence points toward a reality in which mind is a fundamental, rather than derivative, feature.

Physical Laws The fundamental, mathematically expressible regularities that govern the behavior of matter and energy. The monograph explores their epistemic status, debating whether they are discovered features of reality (mathematical realism) or human constructs that effectively model phenomena (constructivism), ultimately favoring a dialectical understanding. Physical laws, particularly conservation laws, are the paradigmatic first principles of the scientific path to truth. Their universality, precision, and predictive power are a primary source of evidence for the intelligibility of the cosmos. However, the book also emphasizes their limitations: they are incomplete (lacking a theory of quantum gravity), they require unexplained initial conditions (the Past Hypothesis), and they seem to be fine-tuned for life.

Process Philosophy A metaphysical tradition, most prominently associated with Alfred North Whitehead, that takes process, change, and becoming as ontologically primary, rather than static substance. Reality is composed of momentary events (actual occasions) rather than enduring objects. Process philosophy is presented as a major alternative to classical substance-based metaphysics and as a worldview that is particularly well-suited to integrating the insights of modern science (e.g., relativity, quantum mechanics, evolution) with philosophical and religious concerns. Its relational and dynamic ontology resonates with the book's overarching theme of a shift away from substance toward relation as the fundamental category of being.

Properly Basic Beliefs In Reformed Epistemology, a belief that can be rationally held without being based on evidence or argument from other beliefs. Proponents like Alvin Plantinga argue that belief in God can be properly basic, grounded in a direct experience or awareness via a *sensus divinitatis*, much like the belief in other minds or the external world. This concept is a key epistemological tool for defending the rationality of theistic realism. It challenges the "evidentialist" assumption that all rational beliefs must be supported by propositional evidence. It provides a way of understanding how the "revelatory path" can provide genuine knowledge through a non-inferential mode of awareness.

Q

Quantum Entanglement A quantum mechanical phenomenon in which two or more quantum particles become linked in such a way that their fates are intertwined, regardless of the distance separating them. A measurement on one particle instantaneously influences the state of the other(s). Entanglement is the most dramatic confirmation of the failure of local realism and the strangeness of the quantum world. The author presents it as a profound scientific discovery that supports a relational ontology. It suggests that, at a fundamental level, reality is not composed of separate, independent objects, but of interconnected systems where relationship is primary. This scientific insight converges with similar principles found in process philosophy and Buddhist dependent origination.

Quantum Gravity The theoretical field of physics that seeks to unify quantum mechanics with General Relativity into a single, coherent theory. Such a theory is needed to describe phenomena where both quantum effects and strong gravitational effects are important, such as at the initial singularity or inside black holes. The absence of a successful theory of quantum gravity represents the single biggest gap in our current understanding of physical first principles. The leading candidates, such as string theory and loop quantum gravity, have radically different ontological implications, demonstrating that the fundamental nature of space, time, and matter remains an open question at the frontiers of science.

Quantum Mechanics The fundamental theory of physics that describes the behavior of matter and energy at the atomic and subatomic levels. Its core principles include quantization, wave-particle duality, superposition, and indeterminacy. Quantum mechanics represents a radical break with the first principles of classical physics. It replaced determinism with irreducible probability and challenged our common-sense notions of reality, locality, and objectivity. The philosophical puzzles it raises, such as the measurement problem and the implications of quantum entanglement, are central to the monograph's argument that science does not provide a complete or easily interpretable picture of reality, but instead opens up deep metaphysical questions.

R

Reformed Epistemology An approach to the epistemology of religious belief, championed by Alvin Plantinga, which argues that belief in God does not need to be supported by evidence to be rational. Instead, it can be a properly basic belief grounded in a cognitive faculty called the sensus divinitatis. This is a major epistemological framework within the worldview of theistic realism. It provides a sophisticated defense against the evidentialist challenge that there is insufficient evidence for God's existence. By treating religious awareness as a basic cognitive faculty, it places religious knowledge on a similar footing to perceptual or memorial knowledge.

Relational Ontology A metaphysical view that holds that relationships, processes, and interactions are ontologically primary, and that entities or "things" are derivative of these relations. This is one of the most important convergent themes in the monograph. The author argues that a shift from substance-based ontologies to relational ones is supported by insights from multiple domains: quantum entanglement in physics, process philosophy in metaphysics, Buddhist dependent origination, and African ubuntu philosophy. This convergence suggests that a relational view of reality may be a more adequate first principle than the classical substance-property model.

S

Saccidānanda A term from Hindu philosophy, particularly Advaita Vedanta, used to describe the nature of Brahman, the ultimate reality. It is a compound of three Sanskrit words: sat (being, existence), cit (consciousness, awareness), and ānanda (bliss, fullness). This concept represents a sophisticated philosophical conclusion about the nature of the ultimate ground of being. It posits that ultimate reality is not unconscious matter or an impersonal force, but is of the nature of existence-consciousness-bliss. It is a central tenet of the idealistic and non-dual worldviews explored in the book.

Scientific Naturalism See Naturalistic Materialism. The monograph uses the terms largely interchangeably to refer to the worldview that reality is exhausted by the entities and laws described by the natural sciences. A careful distinction is made, however, between this metaphysical position and methodological naturalism.

Standpoint Theory A feminist epistemological theory which argues that knowledge is socially situated, and that the perspectives of marginalized and oppressed groups can provide a more complete and objective understanding of reality than the perspectives of dominant groups. This theory is a key component of the author's argument for the social and political dimensions of knowledge. It challenges the idea of a "view from nowhere" and shows how claims to universal objectivity can mask a partial and privileged perspective. It supports the need for methodological pluralism and the inclusion of diverse voices in the quest for first principles, not merely for ethical reasons, but for epistemic ones: doing so leads to better, more objective knowledge.

String Theory A theoretical framework in physics that attempts to provide a unified description of all fundamental forces and particles by modeling them as tiny, vibrating strings in a higher-dimensional spacetime. String theory is a leading candidate for a theory of quantum gravity. However, the author also uses it to illustrate the challenges and potential pitfalls of modern theoretical physics. The theory's requirement for extra dimensions and its prediction of a vast "landscape" of some 10^{500} possible universes have led it to become a primary motivation for the multiverse hypothesis. This has also led to criticism that the theory may be unfalsifiable, blurring the line between science and metaphysics.

Substance (Ousia) In classical Aristotelian and Cartesian metaphysics, substance is the fundamental category of being. A substance is an individual thing that can exist independently and which serves as the bearer of properties but is not itself a property of anything else. The concept of substance is the cornerstone of the classical Western ontology that the author argues is being challenged from multiple directions. The monograph traces a major thematic shift from this substance-based metaphysics to the relational ontologies suggested by modern physics, process philosophy, and non-Western traditions.

Śūnyatā (Emptiness) The central doctrine of Nāgārjuna's Madhyamaka school of Buddhist philosophy, which asserts that all phenomena are "empty" (śūnya) of any intrinsic, independent existence or self-nature (svabhāva). This emptiness is a consequence of dependent origination. Śūnyatā is not a nihilistic denial of existence, but a radical critique of substantialist metaphysics. It is presented as a sophisticated philosophical position that deconstructs our conceptual categories to point toward a reality that transcends them. The author draws parallels between this Buddhist concept and the apophatic traditions of the West, as both use reason and language to point to the limits of reason and language.

T

Theistic Realism The worldview which holds that reality is the purposeful creation of a transcendent, personal, and good God who is the ultimate ground of all existence, knowledge, and value. This is one of the major competing worldviews analyzed in the monograph. Its first principles include the existence of God, the doctrine of creatio ex nihilo, and the possibility of divine revelation. The author argues that this worldview offers powerful explanations for the intelligibility of the universe, the fine-tuning problem, and the existence of objective moral values, while acknowledging that it faces significant challenges, such as the problem of evil.

Tradition-Dependent Rationality A concept, developed by Alasdair MacIntyre, which holds that standards of rationality and justification are not universal and neutral, but are internal to and dependent upon specific historical and conceptual traditions of inquiry. This concept is crucial for the author's analysis of competing worldviews. It explains why debates between, for example, a naturalistic materialist and a theistic realist are so intractable. They are not simply disagreeing about facts, but are operating with different fundamental assumptions about what counts as a good explanation or sufficient evidence. This does not imply relativism, but it does mean that worldview comparison requires a deep, hermeneutical engagement with the internal logic of each tradition.

U

Ubuntu A philosophical concept from southern African traditions, often summarized by the phrase "a person is a person through other persons." It expresses a deeply relational ontology where individual identity and personhood are constituted through community and relationships. Ubuntu is cited as a powerful example of a non-Western first principle that offers an alternative to Western individualism. It is a key piece of evidence for the convergent theme that relationality is a more fundamental category of being than substance. It provides a framework where ethics and ontology are inseparable.

V

Virtue Epistemology An approach to epistemology that focuses on the intellectual character and virtues of the cognitive agent (e.g., intellectual courage, humility, open-mindedness) rather than on the properties of individual beliefs or belief-forming processes. This approach is presented as a valuable contemporary development that enriches our understanding of knowledge. It provides a more holistic and naturalistic account of inquiry, grounding justification in the excellent functioning of the knower. The author emphasizes its ability to integrate the normative and descriptive dimensions of epistemology and its importance for navigating the practical and social challenges of the quest for first principles.

W

Worldviews (Weltanschauung) Systematic and comprehensive perspectives on the nature of reality, the sources of knowledge, and the foundations of value. They function as the ultimate interpretive frameworks through which first principles are understood and organized. The monograph analyzes five major competing worldviews: Naturalistic Materialism, Theistic Realism, Idealism/Panpsychism, Process Philosophy/Panentheism, and Eastern Non-Dualism. The concept of a worldview is central to the hermeneutical structure of the book's argument. The author argues that first principles are not evaluated in isolation but as parts of these larger, coherent systems of thought. The final part of the book is dedicated to comparing these worldviews based on criteria such as logical consistency, explanatory scope and depth, and existential adequacy, in order to assess which provides the most comprehensive and plausible account of reality.

REFERENCES

A

Aaronson, S. (2014). *Why I am not an integrated information theorist.* MIT Press.

Abbott, B. P., Abbott, R., Abbott, T. D., et al. (2016). Observation of gravitational waves from a binary black hole merger. *Physical Review Letters*, 116.

Abimbola, W. (1976). *Ifa: An exposition of Ifa literary corpus.* Oxford University Press.

Abramsky, S., & Coecke, B. (2004). A categorical semantics of quantum protocols. *Proceedings of the 19th Annual IEEE Symposium on Logic in Computer Science* (pp. 415-425).

Adams, F., & Aizawa, K. (2008). *The bounds of cognition.* Blackwell Publishing.

Adams, M. M. (1999). *Horrendous evils and the goodness of God.* Cornell University Press.

Adams, R. M. (1974). Theories of actuality. *Noûs*, 8, 211-231.

Adams, R. M. (1987). *The virtue of faith and other essays in philosophical theology.* Oxford University Press.

Adams, R. M. (1999). *Finite and infinite goods: A framework for ethics.* Oxford University Press.

Aikin, S. F. (2011). *Epistemology and the regress problem.* Routledge.

Al-Attar, A. M. (2010). *Islamic ethics: Divine command theory in Arabo-Islamic thought.* Routledge.

Al-Bāqillānī, A. B. (2003). *I'jāz al-Qur'ān* (M. A. Sallabi, Ed.). Dar Ihya' al-'Ulum. (Original work published c. 1013)

Al-Ghazali. (2000). *The incoherence of the philosophers* (M. E. Marmura, Trans.). Brigham Young University Press. (Original work published 1095).

Al-Ghazali (2014). *The revival of the religious sciences.* Islamic Texts Society. (Original work published 1106).

Albert, D. (2012, March 23). On the origin of everything: A universe from nothing. *The New York Times Sunday Book Review.*

Albert, D. Z. (1992). *Quantum mechanics and experience.* Harvard University Press.

Albrecht, A., & Sorbo, L. (2004). Can the universe afford inflation? *Physical Review D*, 70(6), 063528.

Al-Fārābī. (c. 950/1985). *Al-Farabi on the perfect state* (R. Walzer, Trans.). Oxford University Press.

Alles, G. D. (2001). Toward a genealogy of the holy: Rudolf Otto and the apologetics of religion. *Journal of the American Academy of Religion*, 69, 323-341.

Allison, H. E. (2004). *Kant's transcendental idealism: An interpretation and defense* (Revised ed.). Yale University Press.

Almheiri, A., Marolf, D., Polchinski, J., et al. (2013). Black holes: Complementarity or firewalls? *Journal of High Energy Physics*, 2013(2), Article 62.

Alpher, R. A., Bethe, H., & Gamow, G. (1948). The origin of chemical elements. *Physical Review*, 73, 803-804.

Alston, W. P. (1991). *Perceiving God: The epistemology of religious experience.* Cornell University Press.

Alston, W. P. (2002). *What Euthyphro should have said.* Edinburgh University Press.

Alter, T., & Nagasawa, Y. (2015). *Consciousness in the physical world: Perspectives on Russellian monism.* Oxford University Press.

Ames, R. T., & Hall, D. L. (2003). *Dao de jing: A philosophical translation.* Ballantine Books.

Anderson, A. R., & Belnap, N. D. (1975). *Entailment: The logic of relevance and necessity* (Vol. 1). Princeton University Press.

Anderson, E. (2012). Epistemic justice as a virtue of social institutions. *Social Epistemology*, 26, 163-173.

Anderson, E. (2020). Feminist epistemology and philosophy of science. *Stanford Encyclopedia of Philosophy.*

Anderson, P. W. (1972). More is different: Broken symmetry and the nature of the hierarchical structure of science. *Science*, 177, 393-396.

Angle, S. C. (2018). *Growing moral: A Confucian guide to life*. Oxford University Press.

Annas, J. (2011). *Intelligent virtue*. Oxford University Press.

Anselm. (2007). *Proslogion* (T. Williams, Trans.). Hackett Publishing.

Aquinas, T. (1981). *Summa theologiae* (Fathers of the English Dominican Province, Trans.). Christian Classics (Original work published 1265-1274).

Archer, M. S. (2003). *Structure, agency and the internal conversation*. Cambridge University Press.

Ariew, R. (2014). Pierre Duhem. *Stanford Encyclopedia of Philosophy*.

Aristotle. (1984). *The complete works of Aristotle* (J. Barnes, Ed.). Princeton University Press.

Armstrong, D. M. (1997). *A world of states of affairs*. Cambridge University Press.

Armstrong, D. M. (2004). *Truth and truthmakers*. Cambridge University Press.

Arnold, D. (2005). *Buddhists, Brahmins, and belief: Epistemology in South Asian philosophy of religion*. Columbia University Press.

Arnold, D. (2012). *Brains, Buddhas, and believing: The problem of intentionality in classical Buddhist and cognitive-scientific philosophy of mind*. Columbia University Press.

Ascher, M. (1991). *Ethnomathematics: A multicultural view of mathematical ideas*. Brooks/Cole.

Aspect, A., Clauser, J. F., & Zeilinger, A. (2022). *Nobel Prize in Physics 2022: For experiments with entangled photons, establishing the violation of Bell inequalities and pioneering quantum information science*. Nobel Prize Committee Press Release.

Aspect, A., Dalibard, J., & Roger, G. (1982). Experimental test of Bell's inequalities using time-varying analyzers. *Physical Review Letters*, 49, 1804-1807.

Atkins, P. (2010). *The laws of thermodynamics: A very short introduction*. Oxford University Press.

Aubert, B., Boutigny, D., Gaillard, J. M., et al. (2001). Observation of CP violation in the B^0 meson system. *Physical Review Letters*, 87.

Audi, R. (2004). *The good in the right: A theory of intuition and intrinsic value*. Princeton University Press.

Audi, R. (2011). *Epistemology: A contemporary introduction to the theory of knowledge* (3rd ed.). Routledge.

Audi, R. (2011). *Rationality and religious commitment*. Oxford University Press.

Augustine. (1991). *Confessions* (H. Chadwick, Trans.). Oxford University Press. (Original work published 397).

Aurobindo, S. (2005). *The life divine*. Sri Aurobindo Ashram Publication Department. (Original work published 1939).

Avigad, J. (2008). Understanding proofs. *Cambridge University Press*.

Avigad, J., & Harrison, J. (2014). Formally verified mathematics. *Communications of the ACM*, 57, 66-75.

Awodey, S. (2010). *Category theory* (2nd ed.). Oxford University Press.

Ayer, A. J. (1936). *Language, truth and logic*. Victor Gollancz.

Ayer, A. J. (1954). Can there be a private language? *Proceedings of the Aristotelian Society*, 54, 63-94.

Azzouni, J. (2004). *Deflating existential consequence: A case for nominalism*. Oxford University Press.

B

Baden, J. S. (2012). *The composition of the Pentateuch: Renewing the documentary hypothesis*. Yale University Press.

Baehr, J. (2011). *The inquiring mind: On intellectual virtues and virtue epistemology*. Oxford University Press.

Baird, D. (2004). *Thing knowledge: A philosophy of scientific instruments*. University of California Press.

Baker, A. (2005). Are there genuine mathematical explanations of physical phenomena? *Mind*, 114(454), 223-238.

Baker, A. (2009). Mathematical explanation in science. *British Journal for the Philosophy of Science*, 60, 611-633.

Baker, L. R. (2000). *Persons and bodies: A constitution view*. Cambridge University Press.

Balaguer, M. (1998). *Platonism and anti-platonism in mathematics.* Oxford University Press.

Baldwin, T. (1990). *G. E. Moore.* Routledge.

Banach, S., & Tarski, A. (1924). Sur la décomposition des ensembles de points en parties respectivement congruentes. *Fundamenta Mathematicae,* 6, 244-277.

Bangu, S. (2012). *The applicability of mathematics in science: Indispensability and ontology.* Palgrave Macmillan.

Barad, K. (2007). *Meeting the universe halfway: Quantum physics and the entanglement of matter and meaning.* Duke University Press.

Barbour, I. G. (1997). *Religion and science: Historical and contemporary issues.* HarperCollins.

Bardeen, J., Cooper, L. N., & Schrieffer, J. R. (1957). Theory of superconductivity. *Physical Review,* 108, 1175-1204.

Barnes, J. (1990). *The toils of scepticism.* Cambridge University Press.

Barnes, J. (1994). *Aristotle: Posterior analytics* (2nd ed.). Oxford University Press.

Barnes, L. A. (2012). The fine-tuning of the universe for intelligent life. *Publications of the Astronomical Society of Australia,* 29, 529-564.

Barr, J. (1977). *Fundamentalism.* Westminster Press.

Barreira, L. (2006). Poincaré recurrence: Old and new. *Journal of Dynamics and Differential Equations,* 18, 415-422.

Barrett, J. L. (2004). *Why would anyone believe in God?* AltaMira Press.

Barrow, J. D. (1992). *Pi in the sky: Counting, thinking, and being.* Oxford University Press.

Barrow, J. D., & Tipler, F. J. (1986). *The anthropic cosmological principle.* Oxford University Press.

Barth, K. (2004). *Church dogmatics* (G. W. Bromiley & T. F. Torrance, Eds.). T&T Clark.

Bartley, W. W., III. (1984). *The retreat to commitment* (2nd ed.). Open Court.

Bassi, A., Lochan, K., Satin, S., et al. (2013). Models of wave-function collapse, underlying theories, and experimental tests. *Reviews of Modern Physics,* 85, 471-527.

Battaly, H. (2019). *The Routledge handbook of virtue epistemology.* Routledge.

Batterman, R. W. (2002). *The devil in the details: Asymptotic reasoning in explanation, reduction, and emergence.* Oxford University Press.

Batterman, R. W. (2010). On the explanatory role of mathematics in empirical science. *British Journal for the Philosophy of Science,* 61, 1-25.

Bayne, T. (2010). *The unity of consciousness.* Oxford University Press.

Bayne, T. (2018). On the axiomatic foundations of the integrated information theory of consciousness. *Neuroscience of Consciousness,* 2018.

Bealer, G. (2002). Modal epistemology and the rationalist renaissance. *Oxford University Press.*

Beall, J. C. (2009). *Spandrels of truth.* Oxford University Press.

Beall, J. C., & Restall, G. (2006). *Logical pluralism.* Oxford University Press.

Bedau, M. A. (1997). Weak emergence. *Philosophical Perspectives,* 11, 375-399.

Bediako, K. (1995). *Christianity in Africa: The renewal of a non-Western religion.* Edinburgh University Press.

Beebee, H. (2011). Necessary connections and the problem of induction. *Noûs,* 45, 504-527.

Beebee, H. (2016). *Hume on causation.* Routledge.

Beilby, J. K. (2005). *Naturalism defeated? Essays on Plantinga's evolutionary argument against naturalism.* Cornell University Press.

Bekenstein, J. D. (1973). Black holes and entropy. *Physical Review D,* 7, 2333-2346.

Bell, J. L. (2011). *Set theory: Boolean-valued models and independence proofs* (3rd ed.). Oxford University Press.

Bell, J. S. (1964). On the Einstein Podolsky Rosen paradox. *Physics,* 1, 195-200.

Bell, J. S. (1987). *Speakable and unspeakable in quantum mechanics.* Cambridge University Press.

Bell, J. S. (2004). *Speakable and unspeakable in quantum mechanics* (2nd ed.). Cambridge University Press.

Belnap, N., & Green, M. (1994). Indeterminism and the thin red line. *Philosophical Perspectives*, 8, 365-388.

Benacerraf, P. (1973). Mathematical truth. *Journal of Philosophy*, 70, 661-679.

Bender, E. M., & Koller, A. (2020). Climbing towards NLU: On meaning, form, and understanding in the age of data. *Proceedings of the 58th Annual Meeting of the Association for Computational Linguistics* (pp. 5185-5198).

Bennett, C. H. (1982). The thermodynamics of computation—a review. *International Journal of Theoretical Physics*, 21, 905-940.

Bennett, C. H., Brassard, G., Crépeau, C., et al. (1993). Teleporting an unknown quantum state via dual classical and Einstein-Podolsky-Rosen channels. *Physical Review Letters*, 70, 1895-1899.

Bennett, C. L., Larson, D., Weiland, J. L., et al. (2013). Nine-year Wilkinson Microwave Anisotropy Probe (WMAP) observations: Final maps and results. *The Astrophysical Journal Supplement Series*, 208.

Berger, P. L., & Luckmann, T. (1966). *The social construction of reality*. Doubleday.

Bergmann, M. (2001). Skeptical theism and Rowe's new evidential argument from evil. *Noûs*, 35, 278-296.

Bergmann, M. (2004). Epistemic circularity: Malignant and benign. *Philosophy and Phenomenological Research*, 69, 709-727.

Bergmann, M. (2006). *Justification without awareness*. Oxford University Press.

Bergmann, M. (2015). Religious disagreement and epistemic intuitions. *Royal Institute of Philosophy Supplement*, 76, 19-47.

Berkeley, G. (1710/1965). *A treatise concerning the principles of human knowledge*. Bobbs-Merrill. (Original work published 1710).

Berkeley, G. (1965). *Principles, dialogues, and philosophical correspondence* (C. M. Turbayne, Ed.). Bobbs-Merrill.

Berker, S. (2009). The normative insignificance of neuroscience. *Philosophy & Public Affairs*, 37, 293-329.

Berkes, F. (2012). *Sacred ecology* (3rd ed.). Routledge.

Berto, F., & Restall, G. (2019). Negation on the Australian plan. *Journal of Philosophical Logic*, 48, 1119-1144.

Bertone, G., & Hooper, D. (2018). History of dark matter. *Reviews of Modern Physics*, 90.

Bérut, A., Arakelyan, A., Petrosyan, A., et al. (2012). Experimental verification of Landauer's principle linking information and thermodynamics. *Nature*, 483, 187-189.

Bhaskar, R. (2008). *A realist theory of science*. Routledge.

Bhattacharyya, K. (1956). *Studies in philosophy*. Progressive Publishers.

Birkhoff, G., & von Neumann, J. (1936). The logic of quantum mechanics. *Annals of Mathematics*, 37, 823-843.

Bishop, E. (1967). *Foundations of constructive analysis*. McGraw-Hill.

Bishop, E., & Bridges, D. (1985). *Constructive analysis*. Springer-Verlag.

Bitbol, M. (2019). *Consciousness and the philosophy of signs*. Springer.

Blackburn, P., de Rijke, M., & Venema, Y. (2001). *Modal logic*. Cambridge University Press.

Blackburn, S. (1998). *Ruling passions: A theory of practical reasoning*. Oxford University Press.

Blackburn, S. (2013). *Essays in quasi-realism*. Oxford University Press.

Blair, R. J. R. (2007). The amygdala and ventromedial prefrontal cortex in morality and psychopathy. *Trends in Cognitive Sciences*, 11, 387-392.

Block, N. (1978). Troubles with functionalism. *Minnesota Studies in the Philosophy of Science*, 9, 261-325.

Block, N. (1995). On a confusion about a function of consciousness. *Behavioral and Brain Sciences*, 18(2), 227-247.

Block, N. (2007). Consciousness, accessibility, and the mesh between psychology and neuroscience. *Behavioral and Brain Sciences*, 30(5-6), 481-548.

Boghossian, P. (2000). Knowledge of logic. *Oxford University Press.*

Boghossian, P. (2006). *Fear of knowledge: Against relativism and constructivism.* Oxford University Press.

Bohm, D. (1980). *Wholeness and the implicate order.* Routledge.

Bohr, N. (1935). Can quantum-mechanical description of physical reality be considered complete? *Physical Review,* 48(8), 696-702.

Bohr, N. (1958). *Atomic physics and human knowledge.* John Wiley & Sons.

Bojowald, M. (2008). Loop quantum cosmology. *Living Reviews in Relativity,* 11.

Boltzmann, L. (1896). *Vorlesungen über Gastheorie.* J. A. Barth.

BonJour, L. (1985). *The structure of empirical knowledge.* Harvard University Press.

BonJour, L. (1998). *In defense of pure reason: A rationalist account of a priori justification.* Cambridge University Press.

BonJour, L. (2010). *Epistemology: Classic problems and contemporary responses* (2nd ed.). Rowman & Littlefield.

Boolos, G., Burgess, J. P., & Jeffrey, R. C. (2007). *Computability and logic* (5th ed.). Cambridge University Press.

Borde, A., Guth, A. H., & Vilenkin, A. (2003). Inflationary spacetimes are incomplete in past directions. *Physical Review Letters,* 90.

Born, M. (1926). Zur Quantenmechanik der Stoßvorgänge. *Zeitschrift für Physik,* 37, 863-867.

Borwein, J., & Bailey, D. (2004). *Mathematics by experiment: Plausible reasoning in the 21st century.* A K Peters.

Bostrom, N. (2003). Are we living in a computer simulation? *The Philosophical Quarterly,* 53(211), 243-255.

Bostrom, N. (2014). *Superintelligence: Paths, dangers, strategies.* Oxford University Press.

Bothwell, T., Kennedy, C. J., Aeppli, A., et al. (2022). Resolving the gravitational redshift across a millimetre-scale atomic sample. *Nature,* 602, 420-424.

Boudry, M., Blancke, S., & Braeckman, J. (2010). How not to attack intelligent design creationism: Philosophical misconceptions about methodological naturalism. *Foundations of Science,* 15, 227-244.

Bourdieu, P. (1990). *The logic of practice* (R. Nice, Trans.). Stanford University Press.

Bourdieu, P., & Passeron, J. C. (1977). *Reproduction in education, society and culture.* Sage Publications.

Bousso, R. (2002). The holographic principle. *Reviews of Modern Physics,* 74, 825-874.

Bowker, J. (1991). *The meanings of death.* Cambridge University Press.

Bowler, P. J. (2001). *Reconciling science and religion: The debate in early-twentieth-century Britain.* University of Chicago Press.

Bowles, S. (2008). Being human: Conflict: Altruism's midwife. *Nature,* 456, 326-327.

Boyd, R. (1983). On the current status of the issue of scientific realism. *Erkenntnis,* 19, 45-90.

Boyd, R. (1988). *How to be a moral realist.* Cornell University Press.

Boyer, P. (2001). *Religion explained: The evolutionary origins of religious thought.* Basic Books.

Brading, K., & Brown, H. R. (2003). Symmetries and Noether's theorems. *Cambridge University Press.*

Brading, K., & Castellani, E. (2003). *Symmetries in physics: Philosophical reflections.* Cambridge University Press.

Bradley, B. (2009). *Well-being and death.* Oxford University Press.

Bramble, B. (2015). Consequentialism about meaning in life. *Utilitas,* 27, 445-459.

Brandom, R. (1994). *Making it explicit: Reasoning, representing, and discursive commitment.* Harvard University Press.

Brandom, R. (2000). *Articulating reasons: An introduction to inferentialism.* Harvard University Press.

Bridges, D. (1999). Constructive mathematics: A foundation for computable analysis. *Theoretical Computer Science,* 219(1-2), 95-109.

Bridges, D., & Richman, F. (1987). *Varieties of constructive mathematics.* Cambridge University Press.

Bridges, D., & Vîță, L. (2006). *Techniques of constructive analysis.* Springer.

Brink, D. O. (1989). *Moral realism and the foundations of ethics*. Cambridge University Press.

Brooke, J. H. (1991). *Science and religion: Some historical perspectives*. Cambridge University Press.

Brouwer, L. E. J. (1907). *Over de grondslagen der wiskunde*. Maas & van Suchtelen.

Brouwer, L. E. J. (1912). Intuitionism and formalism. *Bulletin of the American Mathematical Society*, 20, 81-96.

Brouwer, L. E. J. (1975). *Collected works* (A. Heyting, Ed.). North-Holland.

Brown, D. E. (1991). *Human universals*. McGraw-Hill.

Brown, J. R. (2008). *Philosophy of mathematics: A contemporary introduction to the world of proofs and pictures* (2nd ed.). Routledge.

Brown, J. A. C. (2014). *Hadith: Muhammad's legacy in the medieval and modern world* (2nd ed.). Oneworld Publications.

Brown, T. B., Mann, B., Ryder, N., et al. (2020). Language models are few-shot learners. *Advances in Neural Information Processing Systems*, 33, 1877-1901.

Brunner, N., Cavalcanti, D., Pironio, S., et al. (2014). Bell nonlocality. *Reviews of Modern Physics*, 86, 419-478.

Buber, M. (1970). *I and thou* (W. Kaufmann, Trans.). Charles Scribner's Sons. (Original work published 1923).

Buchanan, A., & Powell, R. (2018). *The evolution of moral progress: A biocultural theory*. Oxford University Press.

Buchwald, J. Z. (1985). *From Maxwell to microphysics*. University of Chicago Press.

Bueno, O., & French, S. (2018). *Applying mathematics: Immersion, inference, interpretation*. Oxford University Press.

Bulkeley, K. (2008). *Dreaming in the world's religions: A comparative history*. New York University Press.

Burge, T. (1996). Our entitlement to self-knowledge. *Proceedings of the Aristotelian Society*, 96, 91-116.

Burge, T. (2005). Disjunctivism and perceptual psychology. *Philosophical Topics*, 33, 1-78.

Burgess, J. P. (2005). *Fixing Frege*. Princeton University Press.

Burgess, J. P. (2009). *Philosophical logic*. Princeton University Press.

Burrell, D. B. (2004). *Faith and freedom: An interfaith perspective*. Blackwell.

Bury, J. B. (1920). *The idea of progress: An inquiry into its origin and growth*. Macmillan.

Busch, P., Heinonen, T., & Lahti, P. (2007). Heisenberg's uncertainty principle. *Physics Reports*, 452, 155-176.

Butterfield, J., & Bouatta, N. (2014). Renormalization for philosophers. *The Ashgate companion to contemporary philosophy of physics*, 437-485.

Butterfield, J., & Earman, J. (2007). *Philosophy of physics*. Elsevier.

Butterfield, J., & Isham, C. (2001). Spacetime and the philosophical challenge of quantum gravity. *Cambridge University Press*.

Butterworth, B. (1999). *The mathematical brain*. Macmillan.

C

Cajete, G. (1994). *Native science: Natural laws of interdependence*. Clear Light Publishers.

Calhoun, C., Juergensmeyer, M., & VanAntwerpen, J. (2013). *Rethinking secularism*. Oxford University Press.

Callen, H. B. (1985). *Thermodynamics and an introduction to thermostatistics* (2nd ed.). John Wiley & Sons.

Calude, C. S. (2002). *Information and randomness: An algorithmic perspective* (2nd ed.). Springer.

Campbell, D. T. (1974). Evolutionary epistemology. *The philosophy of Karl Popper*, 413-463.

Cantor, G. (1874). Über eine Eigenschaft des Inbegriffs aller reellen algebraischen Zahlen. *Journal für die reine und angewandte Mathematik*, 77, 258-262.

Cantor, G. (1891). Über eine elementare Frage der Mannigfaltigkeitslehre. *Jahresbericht der Deutschen Mathematiker-Vereinigung*, 1, 75-78.

Cao, C., Carroll, S. M., & Michalakis, S. (2017). Space from Hilbert space: Recovering geometry from bulk entanglement. *Physical Review D*, 95.

Cardano, G. (1545). *Ars magna*. Johann Petreius.

Caret, C. R. (2017). The collapse of logical pluralism has been greatly exaggerated. *Erkenntnis*, 82, 739-760.

Carey, S. (2009). *The origin of concepts*. Oxford University Press.

Carhart-Harris, R. L., Bolstridge, M., Rucker, J., et al. (2016). Psilocybin with psychological support for treatment-resistant depression. *The Lancet Psychiatry*, 3, 619-627.

Carhart-Harris, R. L., & Friston, K. J. (2019). REBUS and the anarchic brain: Toward a unified model of the brain action of psychedelics. *Pharmacological Reviews*, 71, 316-344.

Carman, J. B. (1974). *The theology of Rāmānuja*. Yale University Press.

Carnap, R. (1937). *The logical syntax of language*. Kegan Paul.

Carnap, R. (1950). Empiricism, semantics, and ontology. *Revue Internationale de Philosophie*, 4, 20-40.

Carr, B. (2007). *Universe or multiverse?* Cambridge University Press.

Carroll, S. (2004). *Spacetime and geometry: An introduction to general relativity*. Addison Wesley.

Carroll, S. (2010). *From eternity to here: The quest for the ultimate theory of time*. Dutton.

Carroll, S. (2016). *The big picture: On the origins of life, meaning, and the universe itself*. Dutton.

Carruthers, P. (2019). *Human and animal minds: The consciousness questions laid to rest*. Oxford University Press.

Carter, B. (1974). Large number coincidences and the anthropic principle in cosmology. *IAU Symposium 63*, 291-298.

Cartwright, N. (1983). *How the laws of physics lie*. Oxford University Press.

Cartwright, N. (1999). *The dappled world: A study of the boundaries of science*. Cambridge University Press.

Cartwright, N. (2019). *Nature, the artful modeler: Lectures on laws, science, how nature arranges the world and how we can arrange it better*. Open Court.

Caruso, G. D. (2012). *Free will and consciousness: A determinist account of the illusion of free will*. Lexington Books.

Cassam, Q. (1987). Transcendental arguments, transcendental synthesis and transcendental idealism. *The Philosophical Quarterly*, 37, 355-378.

Cassam, Q. (1997). *Self and world*. Oxford University Press.

Chaitin, G. J. (1987). *Algorithmic information theory*. Cambridge University Press.

Chaitin, G. J. (2005). *Meta math! The quest for omega*. Pantheon Books.

Chakravartty, A. (2007). *A metaphysics for scientific realism: Knowing the unobservable*. Cambridge University Press.

Chakravartty, A. (2017). *Scientific ontology: Integrating naturalized metaphysics and voluntarist epistemology*. Oxford University Press.

Chalmers, D. J. (1995). Facing up to the problem of consciousness. *Journal of Consciousness Studies*, 2, 200-219.

Chalmers, D. J. (1996). *The conscious mind: In search of a fundamental theory*. Oxford University Press.

Chalmers, D. J. (2002). Does conceivability entail possibility? In T. S. Gendler & J. Hawthorne (Eds.), *Conceivability and possibility*. Oxford University Press.

Chalmers, D. J. (2006). The foundations of two-dimensional semantics. *Oxford University Press*.

Chalmers, D. J. (2007). Phenomenal concepts and the explanatory gap. *Oxford University Press*.

Chalmers, D. J. (2010). *The character of consciousness*. Oxford University Press.

Chalmers, D. J. (2016). The combination problem for panpsychism. *Oxford University Press*.

Chalmers, D. J. (2017). The combination problem for panpsychism. In G. Brüntrup & L. Jaskolla (Eds.), *Panpsychism: Contemporary perspectives*. Oxford University Press.

Chang, H. (2012). *Is water H$_2$O? Evidence, realism and pluralism*. Springer.

Chang, H. (2022). *Realism for realistic people: A new pragmatist philosophy of science*. Cambridge

University Press.

Chang, R. (1997). *Incommensurability, incomparability, and practical reason.* Harvard University Press.

Chisholm, R. M. (1982). *The foundations of knowing.* University of Minnesota Press.

Chittick, W. C. (2000). *Sufism: A beginner's guide.* Oneworld Publications.

Christensen, C. M. (2016). *The innovator's dilemma: When new technologies cause great firms to fail* (Reprint ed.). Harvard Business Review Press.

Christenson, J. H., Cronin, J. W., Fitch, V. L., et al. (1964). Evidence for the 2π decay of the $K^0{}_2$ meson. *Physical Review Letters*, 13, 138-140.

Christoff, K., Irving, Z. C., Fox, K. C., et al. (2016). Mind-wandering as spontaneous thought: A dynamic framework. *Nature Reviews Neuroscience*, 17, 718-731.

Churchland, P. M. (1981). Eliminative materialism and the propositional attitudes. *Journal of Philosophy*, 78, 67-90.

Churchland, P. M. (2013). *Touching a nerve: The self as brain.* W. W. Norton.

Churchland, P. S. (2002). *Brain-wise: Studies in neurophilosophy.* MIT Press.

Churchland, P. S. (2011). *Braintrust: What neuroscience tells us about morality.* Princeton University Press.

Clark, A. (2008). *Supersizing the mind: Embodiment, action, and cognitive extension.* Oxford University Press.

Clark, A. (2013). Whatever next? Predictive brains, situated agents, and the future of cognitive science. *Behavioral and Brain Sciences*, 36, 181-204.

Clark, A., & Chalmers, D. (1998). The extended mind. *Analysis*, 58, 7-19.

Clayton, P. (2004). *Mind and emergence: From quantum to consciousness.* Oxford University Press.

Clayton, P., & Davies, P. (2006). *The re-emergence of emergence: The emergentist hypothesis from science to religion.* Oxford University Press.

Clayton, P., & Simpson, Z. (2006). *The Oxford handbook of religion and science.* Oxford University Press.

Cling, A. D. (2009). The epistemic regress problem. *Philosophical Studies*, 140, 401-421.

Clooney, F. X. (1990). *Thinking ritually: Rediscovering the Purva Mimamsa of Jaimini.* De Nobili Research Library.

Coady, C. A. J. (1992). *Testimony: A philosophical study.* Oxford University Press.

Coakley, S. (2013). *God, sexuality, and the self: An essay 'on the Trinity'.* Cambridge University Press.

Code, L. (1987). *Epistemic responsibility.* Brown University Press.

Code, L. (2006). *Ecological thinking: The politics of epistemic location.* Oxford University Press.

Cohen, P. J. (1963). The independence of the continuum hypothesis. *Proceedings of the National Academy of Sciences*, 50, 1143-1148.

Cohen, P. J. (1966). *Set theory and the continuum hypothesis.* W. A. Benjamin.

Collins, F. S., & Varmus, H. (2015). A new initiative on precision medicine. *New England Journal of Medicine*, 372, 793-795.

Collins, H. (2010). *Tacit and explicit knowledge.* University of Chicago Press.

Collins, R. (2009). The teleological argument: An exploration of the fine-tuning of the universe. *Wiley-Blackwell.*

Collins, S. (1982). *Selfless persons: Imagery and thought in Theravāda Buddhism.* Cambridge University Press.

Colyvan, M. (2001). *The indispensability of mathematics.* Oxford University Press.

Colyvan, M. (2010). There is no easy road to nominalism. *Mind*, 119, 285-306.

Comesaña, J. (2005). Unsafe knowledge. *Synthese*, 146, 395-404.

Cooke, M. (2006). *Re-presenting the good society.* MIT Press.

Copeland, B. J. (2015). The Church-Turing thesis. *Stanford Encyclopedia of Philosophy.*

Corcoran, J. (2009). Aristotle's demonstrative logic. *History and Philosophy of Logic*, 30, 1-20.

Corfield, D. (2003). *Towards a philosophy of real mathematics.* Cambridge University Press.

Correia, F., & Skiles, A. (2019). Grounding, essence, and identity. *Philosophy Compass*, 14.

Cotnoir, A. J. (2018). Logical nihilism. *Oxford University Press*.

Cottingham, J. (2003). *On the meaning of life*. Routledge.

Cottingham, J. (2005). *The spiritual dimension: Religion, philosophy and human value*. Cambridge University Press.

Cottingham, J. (2008). *Cartesian reflections: Essays on Descartes's philosophy*. Oxford University Press.

Craig, W. L. (2008). *Reasonable faith: Christian truth and apologetics* (3rd ed.). Crossway Books.

Craig, W. L. (2009). The kalām cosmological argument. *Wiley-Blackwell*.

Craig, W. L. (2013). The absurdity of life without God. *Wiley-Blackwell*.

Craig, W. L., & Moreland, J. P. (2009). *The Blackwell companion to natural theology*. Wiley-Blackwell.

Craig, W. L., & Sinclair, J. D. (2009). The kalam cosmological argument. *Wiley-Blackwell*.

Crockett, M. J., Clark, L., Hauser, M. D., et al. (2010). Serotonin selectively influences moral judgment and behavior through effects on harm aversion. *Proceedings of the National Academy of Sciences*, 107, 17433-17438.

Csordas, T. J. (1997). *Language, charisma, and creativity: The ritual life of a religious movement*. University of California Press.

Cuneo, T. (2007). *The normative web: An argument for moral realism*. Oxford University Press.

Curley, E. M. (1978). *Descartes against the skeptics*. Harvard University Press.

Cusanus, N. (1997). *Nicholas of Cusa: Selected spiritual writings* (H. L. Bond, Trans.). Paulist Press. (Original work published 1453).

Cyburt, R. H., Fields, B. D., Olive, K. A., et al. (2016). Big bang nucleosynthesis: Present status. *Reviews of Modern Physics*, 88.

D

da Costa, N. C. A. (1974). On the theory of inconsistent formal systems. *Notre Dame Journal of Formal Logic*, 15(4), 497–510.

Dalai Lama. (2005). *The universe in a single atom: The convergence of science and spirituality*. Morgan Road Books.

Damasio, A. (2010). *Self comes to mind: Constructing the conscious brain*. Pantheon Books.

Dancy, J. (2004). *Ethics without principles*. Oxford University Press.

Daniels, N. (2020). Reflective equilibrium. *Stanford Encyclopedia of Philosophy*.

Daston, L. (1988). *Classical probability in the Enlightenment*. Princeton University Press.

Daston, L., & Galison, P. (2007). *Objectivity*. Zone Books.

Dauben, J. W. (1979). *Georg Cantor: His mathematics and philosophy of the infinite*. Harvard University Press.

Davidson, D. (1970). Mental events. *Humanities Press*.

Davidson, D. (2001). *Essays on actions and events* (2nd ed.). Clarendon Press.

Davidson, D. (2001). *Inquiries into truth and interpretation* (2nd ed.). Oxford University Press.

Davidson, D. (2001). *Subjective, intersubjective, objective*. Oxford University Press.

Davidson, R. J., & Lutz, A. (2008). Buddha's brain: Neuroplasticity and meditation. *IEEE Signal Processing Magazine*, 25, 176-174.

Davies, B. (2004). *An introduction to the philosophy of religion* (3rd ed.). Oxford University Press.

Davies, P. (1992). *The mind of God: The scientific basis for a rational world*. Simon & Schuster.

Davies, P. (2006). *The Goldilocks enigma: Why is the universe just right for life?* Penguin Books.

Davies, P., & Gregersen, N. H. (2010). *Information and the nature of reality: From physics to metaphysics*. Cambridge University Press.

Davis, C. F. (1989). *The evidential force of religious experience*. Oxford University Press.

Dawid, R. (2013). *String theory and the scientific method*. Cambridge University Press.

Dawkins, R. (2006). *The God delusion*. Houghton Mifflin.

D'Costa, G. (1990). *John Hick's theology of religions: A critical evaluation*. University Press of America.

da Costa, N. C. A. (1974). "On the theory of inconsistent formal systems." *Notre Dame Journal of*

Formal Logic, 15(4), 497–510.

De Jaegher, H., & Di Paolo, E. (2007). Participatory sense-making. *Phenomenology and the Cognitive Sciences*, 6, 485-507.

de Lubac, H. (1998). *Medieval exegesis: The four senses of scripture* (M. Sebanc, Trans.). Eerdmans.

de Moura, L., Kong, S., Avigad, J., et al. (2015). The Lean theorem prover. *Proceedings of the 25th International Conference on Automated Deduction*, 378-388.

de Waal, F. (2006). *Primates and philosophers: How morality evolved.* Princeton University Press.

Deacon, T. W. (2011). *Incomplete nature: How mind emerged from matter.* W. W. Norton.

Dear, P. (2006). *The intelligibility of nature: How science makes sense of the world.* University of Chicago Press.

Decety, J., & Cowell, J. M. (2018). Interpersonal harm aversion as a necessary foundation for morality: A developmental neuroscience perspective. *Development and Psychopathology*, 30, 153-164.

DeGrazia, D. (2005). *Human identity and bioethics.* Cambridge University Press.

Dehaene, S. (1997). *The Number Sense: How the Mind Creates Mathematics.* New York: Oxford University Press.

Dehaene, S. (2011). *The number sense: How the mind creates mathematics.* Oxford University Press.

Dehaene, S. (2014). *Consciousness and the brain: Deciphering how the brain codes our thoughts.* Viking.

Della Rocca, M. (2010). PSR. *Philosophers' Imprint*, 10, 1-13.

Deloria, V. Jr. (1973). *God is red: A native view of religion.* Grosset & Dunlap.

Deloria, V., Jr. (1999). *Spirit and reason: The Vine Deloria Jr. reader.* Fulcrum Publishing.

Dennett, D. C. (1991). *Consciousness explained.* Little, Brown and Company.

Dennett, D. C. (2003). *Freedom evolves.* Viking Press.

Dennett, D. C. (2006). *Breaking the spell: Religion as a natural phenomenon.* Viking.

DeRose, K. (1995). Solving the skeptical problem. *The Philosophical Review*, 104, 1-52.

DeRose, K. (1999). Responding to skepticism. *Oxford University Press.*

Derrida, J. (1976). *Of grammatology* (G. C. Spivak, Trans.). Johns Hopkins University Press.

Descartes, R. (1996). *Meditations on first philosophy* (J. Cottingham, Trans.). Cambridge University Press. (Original work published 1641).

Descartes, R. (1996). *Discourse on method and meditations on first philosophy* (J. Cottingham, Trans.). Cambridge University Press. (Original works published 1637 and 1641).

Detlefsen, M. (1986). *Hilbert's program: An essay on mathematical instrumentalism.* Reidel.

Deutsch, D. (1997). *The fabric of reality.* Penguin Books.

Deutsch, E. (1969). *Advaita Vedanta: A philosophical reconstruction.* University of Hawaii Press.

Deutsch, E., & Dalvi, R. (2004). *The essential Vedanta: A new source book of Advaita Vedanta.* World Wisdom.

Devitt, M. (1997). *Realism and truth* (2nd ed.). Princeton University Press.

deVries, W. A. (2005). *Wilfrid Sellars.* McGill-Queen's University Press.

Dewey, J. (1916). *Democracy and education.* Macmillan.

Dewey, J. (1929). *Experience and nature.* Open Court Publishing.

DeWitt, B. S. (1967). Quantum theory of gravity. I. The canonical theory. *Physical Review*, 160, 1113-1148.

Dilthey, W. (1976). *Selected writings* (H. P. Rickman, Ed. & Trans.). Cambridge University Press.

Dirac, P. A. M. (1928). The quantum theory of the electron. *Proceedings of the Royal Society A*, 117, 610-624.

DiSalle, R. (2006). *Understanding space-time: The philosophical development of physics from Newton to Einstein.* Cambridge University Press.

Dodelson, S. (2003). *Modern cosmology.* Academic Press.

Doerig, A., Schurger, A., Hess, K., et al. (2019). The unfolding argument: Why IIT and other causal structure theories cannot explain consciousness. *Consciousness and Cognition*, 72, 49-59.

Doniger, W. (1981). *The Rig Veda.* Penguin Books.

Doris, J. M. (2002). *Lack of character: Personality and moral behavior*. Cambridge University Press.

Dotson, K. (2014). Conceptualizing epistemic oppression. *Social Epistemology*, 28, 115-138.

Douglas, M. R. (2003). The statistics of string/M theory vacua. *Journal of High Energy Physics*, 2003.

Draper, P. (1989). Pain and pleasure: An evidential problem for theists. *Noûs*, 23, 331-350.

Dreier, J. (2004). Meta-ethics and the problem of creeping minimalism. *Philosophical Perspectives*, 18, 23-44.

Dreyfus, H. L. (1991). *Being-in-the-world: A commentary on Heidegger's Being and Time, Division I*. MIT Press.

Dreyfus, H. L. (1992). *What computers still can't do: A critique of artificial reason*. MIT Press.

Duhem, P. (1991). *The aim and structure of physical theory* (P. P. Wiener, Trans.). Princeton University Press. (Original work published 1906).

Dummett, M. (1977). *Elements of intuitionism*. Oxford University Press.

Dummett, M. (1991). *The logical basis of metaphysics*. Harvard University Press.

Dunn, J. M., & Restall, G. (2002). Relevance logic. *Handbook of philosophical logic*, 1-128.

Dunne, J. (1993). *Back to the rough ground: Practical judgment and the lure of technique*. University of Notre Dame Press.

Dupré, J. (1993). *The disorder of things: Metaphysical foundations of the disunity of science*. Harvard University Press.

Dutilh Novaes, C. (2015). A dialogical, multi-agent account of the normativity of logic. *Dialectica*, 69, 587-609.

Dutilh Novaes, C. (2020). *The dialogical roots of deduction*. Cambridge University Press.

E

Eagleton, T. (2007). *The meaning of life: A very short introduction*. Oxford University Press.

Earman, J. (1992). *Bayes or bust? A critical examination of Bayesian confirmation theory*. MIT Press.

Earman, J. (2003). Tracking down gauge: An ode to the constrained Hamiltonian formalism. *Cambridge University Press*.

Ebbs, G. (2017). *Carnap, Quine, and Putnam on methods of inquiry*. Cambridge University Press.

Einstein, A. (1905). Zur Elektrodynamik bewegter Körper. *Annalen der Physik*, 17, 891-921.

Einstein, A. (1916). Die Grundlage der allgemeinen Relativitätstheorie. *Annalen der Physik*, 49, 769-822.

Einstein, A. (2015). *Relativity: The special and the general theory* (100th anniversary ed.). Princeton University Press.

Einstein, A., Podolsky, B., & Rosen, N. (1935). Can quantum-mechanical description of physical reality be considered complete? *Physical Review*, 47(10), 777-780.

Eklund, M. (2009). Carnap and ontological pluralism. *Oxford University Press*.

Elgin, C. Z. (2017). *True enough*. MIT Press.

Eliade, M. (1954). *The myth of the eternal return* (W. R. Trask, Trans.). Pantheon Books.

Eliade, M. (1987). *The sacred and the profane* (W. R. Trask, Trans.). Harcourt. (Original work published 1957).

Ellis, B. (2001). *Scientific essentialism*. Cambridge University Press.

Ellis, G. (2016). *How can physics underlie the mind? Top-down causation in the human context*. Springer.

Ellis, G., & Silk, J. (2014). Scientific method: Defend the integrity of physics. *Nature*, 516, 321-323.

Ellis, G. F. R. (2005). Physics, complexity and causality. *Nature*, 435.

Ellis, G. F.R. (2007). "Issues in the Philosophy of Cosmology." In Jeremy Butterfield & John Earman (eds.), *Philosophy of Physics, Part B* (Handbook of the Philosophy of Science). Elsevier.

Ellis, G. F. R. (2011). Does the multiverse really exist? *Scientific American*, 305(2), 38-43.

Enderton, H. B. (2001). *A mathematical introduction to logic* (2nd ed.). Academic Press.

Enoch, D. (2010). The epistemological challenge to metanormative realism: How best to understand it, and how to cope with it. *Philosophical Studies*, 148, 413-438.

Enoch, D. (2011). *Taking morality seriously: A defense of robust realism.* Oxford University Press.

Esack, F. (2005). *The Qur'an: A user's guide.* Oneworld Publications.

Evans, C. S. (2013). *God and moral obligation.* Oxford University Press.

Evans, J. St. B., & Stanovich, K. E. (2013). Dual-process theories of higher cognition: Advancing the debate. *Perspectives on Psychological Science,* 8, 223-241.

Everett, H. (1957). "Relative state" formulation of quantum mechanics. *Reviews of Modern Physics,* 29, 454-462.

F

Faulkner, P. (2011). *Knowledge on trust.* Oxford University Press.

Faye, J. (2019). Copenhagen interpretation of quantum mechanics. *Stanford Encyclopedia of Philosophy.*

Feferman, S. (1998). *In the light of logic.* Oxford University Press.

Feferman, S. (2000). Does mathematics need new axioms? *American Mathematical Monthly,* 106(2), 99-111.

Feldman, F. (1991). Some puzzles about the evil of death. *The Philosophical Review,* 100, 205-227.

Ferrari, F., & Moruzzi, S. (2020). Logical pluralism, indeterminacy and the normativity of logic. *Inquiry,* 63(3-4), 271-290.

Ferreira, M. J. (1986). *Doubt and religious commitment: The role of the will in Newman's thought.* Oxford University Press.

Ferreirós, J. (2007). *Labyrinth of thought: A history of set theory and its role in modern mathematics* (2nd ed.). Birkhäuser.

Ferreirós, J. (2016). *Mathematical knowledge and the interplay of practices.* Princeton University Press.

Feser, E. (2014). *Scholastic metaphysics: A contemporary introduction.* Editiones Scholasticae.

Feyerabend, P. (1975). *Against method: Outline of an anarchistic theory of knowledge.* New Left Books.

Feynman, R. P. (1985). *QED: The strange theory of light and matter.* Princeton University Press.

Field, H. (1980). *Science without numbers.* Princeton University Press.

Field, H. (1989). *Realism, mathematics and modality.* Blackwell.

Field, H. (2001). *Truth and the absence of fact.* Oxford University Press.

Field, H. (2008). *Saving truth from paradox.* Oxford University Press.

Field, H. (2009). Pluralism in logic. *Review of Symbolic Logic,* 2, 342-359.

Field, H. (2016). *Science without numbers* (2nd ed.). Oxford University Press.

Fields, B. D. (2011). The primordial lithium problem. *Annual Review of Nuclear and Particle Science,* 61, 47-68.

Fine, G. (2019). *Plato on knowledge and forms: Selected essays.* Oxford University Press.

Fine, K. (1994). Essence and modality. *Philosophical Perspectives,* 8, 1-16.

Fine, K. (2001). The question of realism. *Philosophers' Imprint,* 1, 1-30.

Fine, K. (2002). The varieties of necessity. *Oxford University Press.*

Fine, K. (2005). *Modality and tense: Philosophical papers.* Oxford University Press.

Fine, K. (2009). The question of ontology. *Oxford University Press.*

Fine, K. (2012). Guide to ground. In F. Correia & B. Schnieder (Eds.), *Metaphysical grounding* (pp. 37-80). Cambridge University Press.

Fine, K. (2016). Identity criteria and ground. *Philosophical Studies,* 173, 1-19.

Finnis, J. (2011). *Natural law and natural rights* (2nd ed.). Oxford University Press.

Finocchiaro, M. A. (1989). *The Galileo affair: A documentary history.* University of California Press.

Fischer, J. M., & Ravizza, M. (1998). *Responsibility and control: A theory of moral responsibility.* Cambridge University Press.

Fish, S. (1980). *Is there a text in this class? The authority of interpretive communities.* Harvard University Press.

Fixsen, D. J. (2009). The temperature of the cosmic microwave background. *Astrophysical Journal,* 707, 916-920.

Flanagan, O. (2007). *The really hard problem: Meaning in a material world.* MIT Press.

Flanagan, O. (2011). *The bodhisattva's brain: Buddhism naturalized.* MIT Press.

Flint, T., & Freddoso, A. (1983). Maximal power. *University of Notre Dame Press.*

Flood, G. (1996). *An introduction to Hinduism.* Cambridge University Press.

Floridi, L. (2008). A defence of informational structural realism. *Synthese,* 161, 219-253.

Floridi, L. (2011). *The philosophy of information.* Oxford University Press.

Floridi, L. (2014). *The fourth revolution: How the infosphere is reshaping human reality.* Oxford University Press.

Foot, P. (2001). *Natural goodness.* Oxford University Press.

Forman, R. K. C. (1990). *The problem of pure consciousness.* Oxford University Press.

Forrest, P. (2010). The identity of indiscernibles. *Stanford Encyclopedia of Philosophy.*

Foster, J. (1985). Berkeley on the physical world. *Oxford University Press.*

Foucault, M. (1994). *The order of things: An archaeology of the human sciences* (A. Sheridan, Trans.). Vintage Books. (Original work published 1966)

Fraenkel, A. (1922). Zu den Grundlagen der Cantor-Zermeloschen Mengenlehre. *Mathematische Annalen,* 86, 230-237.

Frances, B. (2018). *Disagreement.* Polity Press.

Frankfurt, H. G. (1970). *Demons, dreamers, and madmen: The defense of reason in Descartes's Meditations.* Bobbs-Merrill.

Frankfurt, H. G. (1971). Freedom of the will and the concept of a person. *Journal of Philosophy,* 68, 5-20.

Frankl, V. E. (2006). *Man's search for meaning.* Beacon Press. (Original work published 1946).

Franklin, A. (1986). *The neglect of experiment.* Cambridge University Press.

Franks, C. (2009). *The autonomy of mathematical knowledge.* Cambridge University Press.

Franzén, T. (2005). *Gödel's theorem: An incomplete guide to its use and abuse.* A K Peters.

Frege, G. (1952). On sense and reference. In P. Geach & M. Black (Trans. & Eds.), *Translations from the philosophical writings of Gottlob Frege.* Basil Blackwell. (Original work published 1892).

Frege, G. (1879). *Begriffsschrift.* Louis Nebert.

Frege, G. (2013). *The foundations of arithmetic* (J. L. Austin, Trans.). Northwestern University Press. (Original work published 1884).

Frege, G. (2013). *Basic laws of arithmetic* (P. A. Ebert & M. Rossberg, Trans.). Oxford University Press.

Frei, H. W. (1974). *The eclipse of biblical narrative: A study in eighteenth and nineteenth century hermeneutics.* Yale University Press.

French, S., & Krause, D. (2006). *Identity in physics: A historical, philosophical, and formal analysis.* Oxford University Press.

French, S., & Ladyman, J. (2003). Remodelling structural realism: Quantum physics and the metaphysics of structure. *Synthese,* 136, 31-56.

Fricker, E. (2006). Testimony and epistemic autonomy. *Oxford University Press.*

Fricker, M. (2007). *Epistemic injustice: Power and the ethics of knowing.* Oxford University Press.

Friedman, H. (1998). Finite functions and the necessary use of large cardinals. *Annals of Mathematics,* 148, 803-893.

Friedman, M. (1983). *Foundations of space-time theories: Relativistic physics and philosophy of science.* Princeton University Press.

Friedman, M. (1999). *Reconsidering logical positivism.* Cambridge University Press.

Friedman, M. (2001). *Dynamics of reason.* CSLI Publications.

Friedman, M. (2013). *Kant's construction of nature: A reading of the metaphysical foundations of natural science.* Cambridge University Press.

Frigg, R., & Votsis, I. (2011). Everything you always wanted to know about structural realism but were afraid to ask. *European Journal for Philosophy of Science,* 1, 227-276.

Fuchs, C. A., Mermin, N. D., & Schack, R. (2014). An introduction to QBism with an application to the locality of quantum mechanics. *American Journal of Physics,* 82, 749-754.

Fuchs, C. A., & Peres, A. (2000). Quantum theory needs no 'interpretation'. *Physics Today*, 53, 70-71.

Fuchs, C. A., & Schack, R. (2013). Quantum-Bayesian coherence. *Reviews of Modern Physics*, 85, 1693-1715.

Fumerton, R. (1995). *Metaepistemology and skepticism*. Rowman & Littlefield.

Fumerton, R. (2001). Classical foundationalism. *Blackwell*.

Fumerton, R. (2001). Epistemic justification and normativity. *Oxford University Press*.

Fyfe, S. (2023). Epistemic exploitation. *Ergo*, 10, 123-145.

G

Gabrielse, G., Bowden, N. S., Oxley, P., et al. (1999). Precision mass spectroscopy of the antiproton and proton using simultaneously trapped particles. *Physical Review Letters*, 82, 3198-3201.

Gabrielse, G., Hanneke, D., Kinoshita, T., et al. (2006). New determination of the fine structure constant from the electron g value and QED. *Physical Review Letters*, 97.

Gadamer, H.-G. (2004). *Truth and method* (J. Weinsheimer & D. G. Marshall, Trans., 2nd rev. ed.). Continuum. (Original work published 1960)

Gale, R. M. (1991). *On the nature and existence of God*. Cambridge University Press.

Galilei, G. (2001). Dialogue concerning the two chief world systems: Ptolemaic and Copernican (S. Drake, Trans.). Modern Library. (Original work published 1632)

Galison, P. (1987). *How experiments end*. University of Chicago Press.

Galison, P. (1997). *Image and logic: A material culture of microphysics*. University of Chicago Press.

Gallagher, S. (2001). The practice of mind: Theory, simulation or primary interaction? *Journal of Consciousness Studies*, 8(5-7), 83-108.

Gallagher, S. (2008). Direct perception in the intersubjective context. *Consciousness and Cognition*, 17, 535-543.

Gallese, V. (2001). The 'shared manifold' hypothesis: From mirror neurons to empathy. *Journal of Consciousness Studies*, 8(5-7), 33-50.

Ganeri, J. (2001). *Philosophy in classical India: The proper work of reason*. Routledge.

Ganeri, J. (2012). *The self: Naturalism, consciousness, and the first-person stance*. Oxford University Press.

Garber, D. (1983). Old evidence and logical omniscience in Bayesian confirmation theory. *University of Minnesota Press*.

Garfield, J. L. (1995). *The fundamental wisdom of the middle way: Nagarjuna's Mulamadhyamakakarika*. Oxford University Press.

Garfield, J. L. (2015). *Engaging Buddhism: Why it matters to philosophy*. Oxford University Press.

Gazzaniga, M. S. (2005). Forty-five years of split-brain research and still going strong. *Nature Reviews Neuroscience*, 6, 653-659.

Gellman, J. I. (1997). *Experience of God and the rationality of theistic belief*. Cornell University Press.

Gentzen, G. (1936). Die Widerspruchsfreiheit der reinen Zahlentheorie. *Mathematische Annalen*, 112, 493-565.

Georgi, H. (1999). Grand unified theories. *Cambridge University Press*.

Gethin, R. (1998). *The foundations of Buddhism*. Oxford University Press.

Gettier, E. L. (1963). Is justified true belief knowledge? *Analysis*, 23(6), 121-123.

Ghirardi, G. C., Rimini, A., & Weber, T. (1986). Unified dynamics for microscopic and macroscopic systems. *Physical Review D*, 34, 470-491.

Giaquinto, M. (2007). *Visual thinking in mathematics*. Oxford University Press.

Gibbard, A. (2003). *Thinking how to live*. Harvard University Press.

Giere, R. N. (2006). *Scientific perspectivism*. University of Chicago Press.

Giles, J. (2005). Internet encyclopaedias go head to head. *Nature*, 438, 900-901.

Gilkey, L. (1959). *Maker of heaven and earth: A study of the Christian doctrine of creation*. Anchor Books.

Gilson, E. (1952). *Being and some philosophers*. Pontifical Institute of Mediaeval Studies.

Ginet, C. (2005). Infinitism is not the solution to the regress problem. *Blackwell.*

Ginsborg, H. (2015). *The normativity of nature: Essays on Kant's critique of judgement.* Oxford University Press.

Girard, J.-Y. (1987). Linear logic. *Theoretical Computer Science, 50,* 1-101.

Gisin, N., Ribordy, G., Tittel, W., et al. (2002). Quantum cryptography. *Reviews of Modern Physics, 74,* 145-195.

Gleason, A. M. (1957). Measures on the closed subspaces of a Hilbert space. *Journal of Mathematics and Mechanics, 6,* 885-893.

Gödel, K. (1931). Über formal unentscheidbare Sätze der Principia Mathematica und verwandter Systeme I. *Monatshefte für Mathematik, 38,* 173-198.

Gödel, K. (1933). Zur intuitionistischen Arithmetik und Zahlentheorie. *Ergebnisse eines mathematischen Kolloquiums, 4,* 34-38.

Gödel, K. (1940). *The consistency of the axiom of choice and of the generalized continuum hypothesis.* Princeton University Press.

Gödel, K. (1992). *On formally undecidable propositions of Principia Mathematica and related systems* (B. Meltzer, Trans.). Dover Publications.

Gödel, K. (1995). Some basic theorems on the foundations. *Oxford University Press.*

Godfrey-Smith, P. (2003). *Theory and reality: An introduction to the philosophy of science.* University of Chicago Press.

Goff, P. (2017). *Consciousness and fundamental reality.* Oxford University Press.

Goff, P. (2019). *Galileo's error: Foundations for a new science of consciousness.* Pantheon Books.

Goldberg, S. C. (2010). *Relying on others: An essay in epistemology.* Oxford University Press.

Goldberg, S. C. (2018). *To the best of our knowledge: Social expectations and epistemic normativity.* Oxford University Press.

Goldblatt, R. (2014). *Topoi: The categorial analysis of logic* (Rev. ed.). Dover.

Goldman, A. I. (1988). Strong and weak justification. *Philosophical Perspectives, 2,* 51-69.

Goldman, A. I. (1999). *Knowledge in a social world.* Oxford University Press.

Goldman, A. I. (2006). *Simulating minds: The philosophy, psychology, and neuroscience of mindreading.* Oxford University Press.

Goldman, A. I. (2008). Immediate justification and process reliabilism. *Oxford University Press.*

Goldman, A. I. (2012). *Reliabilism and contemporary epistemology: Essays.* Oxford University Press.

Goldman, A. I., & Blanchard, T. (2018). Social epistemology. *Stanford Encyclopedia of Philosophy.*

Goldstein, H., Poole, C., & Safko, J. (2002). *Classical mechanics* (3rd ed.). Addison-Wesley.

Gombrich, R. F. (2009). *What the Buddha thought.* Equinox Publishing.

Gonthier, G. (2008). Formal proof—the four-color theorem. *Notices of the AMS, 55,* 1382-1393.

Gonthier, G., Asperti, A., Avigad, J., et al. (2013). A machine-checked proof of the odd order theorem. *Interactive Theorem Proving,* 163-179.

Goodenough, U. (1998). *The sacred depths of nature.* Oxford University Press.

Goodfellow, I., Bengio, Y., & Courville, A. (2016). *Deep learning.* MIT Press.

Goodman, C. (2017). Ethics in Indian and Tibetan Buddhism. *Stanford Encyclopedia of Philosophy.*

Goodman, N. (1955). *Fact, fiction, and forecast.* Harvard University Press.

Gopnik, A., & Wellman, H. M. (1992). Why the child's theory of mind really is a theory. *Mind & Language,* 7(1-2), 145-171.

Gorenstein, D., Lyons, R., & Solomon, R. (1994). *The classification of the finite simple groups.* American Mathematical Society.

Gottlieb, R. S. (2006). *The Oxford handbook of religion and ecology.* Oxford University Press.

Gould, S. J. (1997). Nonoverlapping magisteria. *Natural History, 106,* 16-22.

Govier, T. (1987). *Problems in argument analysis and evaluation.* Foris Publications.

Graham, A. C. (2010). *Disputers of the Tao: Philosophical argument in ancient China.* Open Court.

Graham, A. C. (2010). *The way and its power: Lao Tzu's Tao te ching and its place in Chinese thought.*

Hackett Publishing.

Graham, J., Haidt, J., Koleva, S., et al. (2013). Moral foundations theory: The pragmatic validity of moral pluralism. *Advances in Experimental Social Psychology*, 47, 55-130.

Grant, E. (2004). *Science and religion, 400 B.C. to A.D. 1550: From Aristotle to Copernicus*. Johns Hopkins University Press.

Gray, J. (2004). *Heresies: Against progress and other illusions*. Granta Books.

Gray, J. (2007). *Worlds out of nothing: A course in the history of geometry in the 19th century*. Springer.

Greco, J. (2010). *Achieving knowledge: A virtue-theoretic account of epistemic normativity*. Cambridge University Press.

Green, M. B., Schwarz, J. H., & Witten, E. (2012). *Superstring theory* (25th anniversary ed., 2 vols.). Cambridge University Press.

Greene, B. (2011). *The hidden reality: Parallel universes and the deep laws of the cosmos*. Knopf.

Greene, J. D. (2013). *Moral tribes: Emotion, reason, and the gap between us and them*. Penguin Press.

Greene, J. D., Nystrom, L. E., Engell, A. D., et al. (2004). The neural bases of cognitive conflict and control in moral judgment. *Neuron*, 44, 389-400.

Greene, J. D., Sommerville, R. B., Nystrom, L. E., et al. (2001). An fMRI investigation of emotional engagement in moral judgment. *Science*, 293, 2105-2108.

Gregory, B. S. (2012). *The unintended Reformation: How a religious revolution secularized society*. Harvard University Press.

Grice, P. (1989). *Studies in the way of words*. Harvard University Press.

Griffel, F. (2009). *Al-Ghazali's philosophical theology*. Oxford University Press.

Griffin, D. R. (2000). *Religion and scientific naturalism: Overcoming the conflicts*. State University of New York Press.

Griffin, D. R. (2001). *Reenchantment without supernaturalism: A process philosophy of religion*. Cornell University Press.

Griffin, D. R. (2007). *Whitehead's radically different postmodern philosophy*. SUNY Press.

Griffiths, D. J. (2008). *Introduction to elementary particles* (2nd ed.). Wiley-VCH.

Griffiths, D. J. (2018). *Introduction to quantum mechanics* (3rd ed.). Cambridge University Press.

Griffiths, R. B. (2002). *Consistent quantum theory*. Cambridge University Press.

Griffiths, R. R., Richards, W. A., McCann, U., et al. (2006). Psilocybin can occasion mystical-type experiences having substantial and sustained personal meaning and spiritual significance. *Psychopharmacology*, 187, 268-283.

Grisez, G., Boyle, J., & Finnis, J. (1987). Practical principles, moral truth, and ultimate ends. *American Journal of Jurisprudence*, 32, 99-151.

Gross, D. J. (1996). The role of symmetry in fundamental physics. *Proceedings of the National Academy of Sciences*, 93, 14256-14259.

Grünbaum, A. (1989). The pseudo-problem of creation in physical cosmology. *Philosophy of Science*, 56, 373-394.

Grünbaum, A. (2009). Why is there a world at all, rather than just nothing? *Ontology Studies*, 9, 7-19.

Gupta, B. (2003). *Cit: Consciousness*. Oxford University Press.

Gutas, D. (2016). Ibn Rushd on demonstration and dialectic. *Cambridge University Press*.

Guth, A. H. (1981). Inflationary universe: A possible solution to the horizon and flatness problems. *Physical Review D*, 23, 347-356.

Guth, A. H. (1997). *The inflationary universe: The quest for a new theory of cosmic origins*. Perseus Books.

Guth, A. H. (2007). Eternal inflation and its implications. *Journal of Physics A: Mathematical and Theoretical*, 40, 6811-6826.

Gutiérrez, G. (1988). *A theology of liberation: History, politics, and salvation* (C. Inda & J. Eagleson, Trans.; Rev. ed.). Orbis Books.

Guyer, P. (2006). *Kant*. Routledge.

Gyekye, K. (1995). *An essay on African philosophical thought: The Akan conceptual scheme.* Temple University Press.

H

Haack, S. (1993). *Evidence and inquiry: Towards reconstruction in epistemology.* Blackwell.

Haack, S. (1996). *Deviant logic, fuzzy logic.* University of Chicago Press.

Haack, S. (2003). *Defending science—within reason: Between scientism and cynicism.* Prometheus Books.

Haack, S. (2009). *Evidence and inquiry: A pragmatist reconstruction of epistemology* (2nd ed.). Prometheus Books.

Habermas, J. (2008). *Between naturalism and religion: Philosophical essays.* Polity Press.

Hacker, P. (1995). *Philology and confrontation: Paul Hacker on traditional and modern Vedanta.* SUNY Press.

Hacking, I. (1975). *The emergence of probability.* Cambridge University Press.

Hacking, I. (1982). Historical ontology. Harvard University Press.

Hacking, I. (1983). *Representing and intervening: Introductory topics in the philosophy of natural science.* Cambridge University Press.

Hacking, I. (1995). *Rewriting the soul: Multiple personality and the sciences of memory.* Princeton University Press.

Hacking, I. (1999). *The social construction of what?* Harvard University Press.

Haidt, J. (2001). The emotional dog and its rational tail: A social intuitionist approach to moral judgment. *Psychological Review,* 108, 814-834.

Haidt, J. (2012). *The righteous mind: Why good people are divided by politics and religion.* Pantheon Books.

Haidt, J., & Joseph, C. (2004). Intuitive ethics: How innately prepared intuitions generate culturally variable virtues. *Daedalus,* 133, 55-66.

Halbertal, M. (1997). *People of the book: Canon, meaning, and authority.* Harvard University Press.

Hale, B., & Wright, C. (2001). *The reason's proper study: Essays towards a neo-Fregean philosophy of mathematics.* Oxford University Press.

Hall, D. L., & Ames, R. T. (1987). *Thinking through Confucius.* State University of New York Press.

Hallaq, W. B. (1999). The authenticity of prophetic ḥadîth: A pseudo-problem. *Studia Islamica,* 89, 75-90.

Hallaq, W. B. (2009). *Sharī'a: Theory, practice, transformations.* Cambridge University Press.

Hallett, M. (1984). *Cantorian set theory and limitation of size.* Oxford University Press.

Hamilton, W. D. (1964). The genetical evolution of social behaviour. *Journal of Theoretical Biology,* 7, 1-16.

Hamkins, J. D. (2012). The set-theoretic multiverse. *Review of Symbolic Logic,* 5, 416-449.

Hamming, R. W. (1980). The unreasonable effectiveness of mathematics. *American Mathematical Monthly,* 87, 81-90.

Hanna, R. (2018). *The fate of analysis: Analytic philosophy from Frege to the ash-heap of history.* Mad Duck Coalition.

Hansen, C. (1992). *A Daoist Theory of Chinese Thought: A Philosophical Interpretation.* Oxford University Press.

Hansen, C. (2000). *A Daoist theory of Chinese thought: A philosophical interpretation.* Oxford University Press.

Hansen, C. (2014). Daoism. *Stanford Encyclopedia of Philosophy.*

Hanson, N. R. (1958). *Patterns of discovery: An inquiry into the conceptual foundations of science.* Cambridge University Press.

Haraway, D. (1988). Situated knowledges: The science question in feminism and the privilege of partial perspective. *Feminist Studies,* 14, 575-599.

Harding, S. (1991). *Whose science? Whose knowledge? Thinking from women's lives.* Cornell University Press.

Harding, S. (1993). Rethinking standpoint epistemology: What is "strong objectivity"? In L. Alcoff & E. Potter (Eds.), *Feminist epistemologies*. Routledge.

Harding, S. (2015). *Objectivity and diversity: Another logic of scientific research*. University of Chicago Press.

Hardwig, J. (1991). The role of trust in knowledge. *The Journal of Philosophy*, 88, 693-708.

Hardy, G. H. (1940). *A mathematician's apology*. Cambridge University Press.

Harris, J. (2011). Moral enhancement and freedom. *Bioethics*, 25, 102-111.

Harrison, P. (2007). *The fall of man and the foundations of science*. Cambridge University Press.

Harrison, P. (2015). *The territories of science and religion*. University of Chicago Press.

Hartle, J. B. (2003). *Gravity: An introduction to Einstein's general relativity*. Addison-Wesley.

Hartle, J. B., & Hawking, S. W. (1983). Wave function of the universe. *Physical Review D*, 28, 2960-2975.

Hartman, D. (1997). *A living covenant: The innovative spirit in traditional Judaism*. Jewish Lights Publishing.

Hartmann, S. (2001). Effective field theories, reductionism and scientific explanation. *Studies in History and Philosophy of Science Part B*, 32, 267-304.

Hartshorne, C. (1948). *The divine relativity: A social conception of God*. Yale University Press.

Hartshorne, C. (1984). *Omnipotence and other theological mistakes*. State University of New York Press.

Harvard University. (2016). *Report of the task force on general education*. Harvard University Faculty of Arts and Sciences.

Harvey, P. (2013). *An introduction to Buddhism: Teachings, history and practices* (2nd ed.). Cambridge University Press.

Hasan, A. (2013). Phenomenal conservatism, classical foundationalism, and internalist justification. *Philosophical Studies*, 162, 119-141.

Hasker, W. (1999). *The emergent self*. Cornell University Press.

Hatfield, G. (2014). *The Routledge guidebook to Descartes' meditations*. Routledge.

Haught, J. F. (2000). *God after Darwin: A theology of evolution*. Westview Press.

Haught, J. F. (2006). *Is nature enough? Meaning and truth in the age of science*. Cambridge University Press.

Hauser, M. (2006). *Moral minds*. HarperCollins.

Hawking, S., & Mlodinow, L. (2010). *The grand design*. Bantam Books.

Hawking, S. W. (1975). Particle creation by black holes. *Communications in Mathematical Physics*, 43, 199-220.

Hawking, S. W. (1976). Breakdown of predictability in gravitational collapse. *Physical Review D*, 14, 2460-2473.

Hawley, K. (2001). *How things persist*. Oxford University Press.

Healey, R. (2017). *The quantum revolution in philosophy*. Oxford University Press.

Heelan, P. A. (1983). *Space-perception and the philosophy of science*. University of California Press.

Hegel, G. W. F. (1977). *Phenomenology of spirit* (A. V. Miller, Trans.). Oxford University Press. (Original work published 1807)

Hegel, G. W. F. (2010). *The science of logic* (G. di Giovanni, Trans.). Cambridge University Press.

Heidegger, M. (1962). *Being and time* (J. Macquarrie & E. Robinson, Trans.). Harper & Row. (Original work published 1927)

Heim, S. M. (1995). *Salvations: Truth and difference in religion*. Orbis Books.

Heintz, B. (2000). *Die Innenwelt der Mathematik*. Springer.

Heisenberg, W. (1927). Über den anschaulichen Inhalt der quantentheoretischen Kinematik und Mechanik. *Zeitschrift für Physik*, 43(3-4), 172-198.

Heisenberg, W. (1983). *Physics and philosophy: The revolution in modern science*. Harper & Row.

Heller, M. (2016). *The ontology of physical objects*. Cambridge University Press.

Hellman, G. (1989). *Mathematics without numbers*. Oxford University Press.

Hellman, G. (2001). Three varieties of mathematical structuralism. *Philosophia Mathematica*, 9, 184-211.

Helm, P. (2000). *Faith with reason*. Oxford University Press.

Hempel, C. G. (1966). *Philosophy of natural science*. Prentice-Hall.

Hempel, C. G. (1980). Comments on Goodman's Ways of Worldmaking. *Synthese*, 45, 193-199.

Henrich, J. (2016). *The secret of our success: How culture is driving human evolution, domesticating our species, and making us smarter*. Princeton University Press.

Hensen, B., Bernien, H., Dréau, A. E., et al. (2015). Loophole-free Bell inequality violation using electron spins separated by 1.3 kilometres. *Nature*, 526, 682-686.

Herzfeld, N. L. (2002). *In our image: Artificial intelligence and the human spirit*. Fortress Press.

Heyting, A. (1956). *Intuitionism: An introduction*. North-Holland.

Hick, J. (1966). *Evil and the God of love*. Harper & Row.

Hick, J. (1989). *An Interpretation of Religion: Human Responses to the Transcendent*. New Haven: Yale University Press.

Hick, J. (2004). *An interpretation of religion: Human responses to the transcendent* (2nd ed.). Yale University Press.

Hickman, L. A. (2007). *Pragmatism as post-postmodernism: Lessons from John Dewey*. Fordham University Press.

Hickok, G. (2014). *The myth of mirror neurons*. W. W. Norton.

Higgs, P. W. (1964). Broken symmetries and the masses of gauge bosons. *Physical Review Letters*, 13, 508-509.

Hilbert, D. (1971). *Foundations of Geometry* (L. Unger, Trans.). Open Court Publishing. (Original work published 1899)

Hintikka, J. (1962). Cogito, ergo sum: Inference or performance? *The Philosophical Review*, 71(1), 3-32.

Hirsch, E. (2011). *Quantifier variance and realism: Essays in metaontology*. Oxford University Press.

Hjortland, O. T. (2017). Anti-exceptionalism about logic. *Philosophical Studies*, 174, 631-658.

Hobson, J. A. (2009). REM sleep and dreaming: Towards a theory of protoconsciousness. *Nature Reviews Neuroscience*, 10, 803-813.

Hoffman, D. D. (2019). *The case against reality: Why evolution hid the truth from our eyes*. W. W. Norton.

Hofstadter, D. R. (1979). *Gödel, Escher, Bach: An eternal golden braid*. Basic Books.

Hofstadter, D. R. (2007). *I am a strange loop*. Basic Books.

Hohwy, J. (2013). *The predictive mind*. Oxford University Press.

Holland, J. H. (1995). *Hidden order: How adaptation builds complexity*. Perseus Books.

Holland, J. H. (2014). *Complexity: A very short introduction*. Oxford University Press.

Holland, R. F. (1965). The miraculous. *American Philosophical Quarterly*, 2, 43-51.

Hölzel, B. K., Carmody, J., Vangel, M., et al. (2011). Mindfulness practice leads to increases in regional brain gray matter density. *Psychiatry Research: Neuroimaging*, 191, 36-43.

Homotopy Type Theory Univalent Foundations Program. (2013). *Homotopy type theory: Univalent foundations of mathematics*. Institute for Advanced Study.

Hood, R. W., Jr., Hill, P. C., & Spilka, B. (2009). *The psychology of religion: An empirical approach* (4th ed.). Guilford Press.

Horgan, T., & Woodward, J. (1985). Folk psychology is here to stay. *Philosophical Review*, 94, 197-226.

Horsten, L. (2015). Philosophy of mathematics. *Stanford Encyclopedia of Philosophy*.

Hountondji, P. J. (1983). *African philosophy: Myth and reality*. Indiana University Press.

Howard, S. D. (2013). *The evidential argument from evil*. Indiana University Press.

Howard, S. D., & Bergmann, M. (2004). Evil does not make atheism more reasonable than theism. *Blackwell*.

Howson, C., & Urbach, P. (2006). *Scientific reasoning: The Bayesian approach* (3rd ed.). Open Court.

Hubble, E. (1929). A relation between distance and radial velocity among extra-galactic nebulae.

Proceedings of the National Academy of Sciences, 15, 168-173.

Huemer, M. (2001). *Skepticism and the veil of perception*. Rowman & Littlefield.

Huemer, M. (2005). *Ethical intuitionism*. Palgrave Macmillan.

Huemer, M. (2007). Compassionate phenomenal conservatism. *Philosophy and Phenomenological Research*, 74, 30-55.

Hume, D. (2000). *A treatise of human nature* (D. F. Norton & M. J. Norton, Eds.). Oxford University Press. (Original work published 1739).

Hume, D. (2007). *An enquiry concerning human understanding* (P. Millican, Ed.). Oxford University Press. (Original work published 1748).

Hursthouse, R. (1999). *On virtue ethics*. Oxford University Press.

Husserl, E. (2014). *Ideas: General introduction to pure phenomenology* (W. R. Boyce Gibson, Trans.). Routledge. (Original work published 1913)

Husserl, E. (1983). *Ideas Pertaining to a Pure Phenomenology and to a Phenomenological Philosophy, First Book: General Introduction to Pure Phenomenology*. Translated by F. Kersten. Dordrecht and Boston: Kluwer Academic Publishers.

Husserl, E. (2001). *Logical investigations* (J. N. Findlay, Trans.). Routledge.

Husserl, E. (2014). *Ideas: General introduction to pure phenomenology* (D. Dahlstrom, Trans.). Hackett Publishing. (Original work published 1913)

Hut, P., Alford, M., & Tegmark, M. (2006). On math, matter and mind. *Foundations of Physics*, 36, 765-794.

Huxley, A. (1945). *The perennial philosophy*. Harper & Brothers.

Hylton, P. (2007). *Quine*. Routledge.

Hyslop, A. (1995). *Other minds*. Kluwer Academic Publishers.

I

Ibn Rushd (Averroes). (1961). *On the harmony of religion and philosophy* (G. F. Hourani, Trans.). Luzac & Co. (Original work published 1179).

Ibn Rushd (Averroes). (2001). *The decisive treatise* (C. E. Butterworth, Trans.). Brigham Young University Press. (Original work published 1179).

Ibn Rushd (Averroes). (1986). *Ibn Rushd's metaphysics: A translation with introduction of Ibn Rushd's commentary on Aristotle's Metaphysics, Book Lām* (C. Genequand, Trans.). E. J. Brill. (Original work published c. 1180).

Ibn Sīnā (Avicenna). (2005). *The metaphysics of The healing* (M. E. Marmura, Trans.). Brigham Young University Press. (Original work published c. 1020)

Ilyenkov, E. V. (1977). *Dialectical logic*. Progress Publishers.

Indich, W. M. (1980). *Consciousness in Advaita Vedanta*. Motilal Banarsidass.

Ioannidis, J. P. A. (2005). Why most published research findings are false. *PLoS Medicine*, 2.

IPCC. (2021). *Climate change 2021: The physical science basis*. Cambridge University Press.

Irwin, T. (1988). *Aristotle's first principles*. Oxford University Press.

Ivanhoe, P. J. (2002). *Ethics in the Confucian tradition: The thought of Mengzi and Wang Yangming*. Hackett Publishing.

Ivanhoe, P. J., & Van Norden, B. W. (2005). *Readings in classical Chinese philosophy* (2nd ed.). Hackett Publishing.

J

Jackson, F. (1982). Epiphenomenal qualia. *Philosophical Quarterly*, 32, 127-136.

Jackson, F. (1986). What Mary didn't know. *Journal of Philosophy*, 83, 291-295.

Jackson, F. (2012). On Gettier holdouts. *Mind and Language*, 27, 468-481.

Jackson, S. A. (2002). *On the boundaries of theological tolerance in Islam*. Oxford University Press

Jalava, J., & Griffiths, S. (2017). Philosophers on psychopaths: A cautionary tale in interdisciplinarity. *Philosophy Compass*, 12.

James, W. (1896). The will to believe. *The New World*, 5, 327-347.

James, W. (1975). *Pragmatism: A new name for some old ways of thinking.* Harvard University Press. (Original work published 1907).

James, W. (2002). *The varieties of religious experience: A study in human nature.* Dover Publications. (Original work published 1902).

Jantzen, G. M. (1995). *Power, gender and Christian mysticism.* Cambridge University Press.

Jaynes, E. T. (1965). Gibbs vs Boltzmann entropies. *American Journal of Physics*, 33, 391-398.

Jech, T. (2003). *Set theory* (3rd millennium ed.). Springer.

Jeffrey, R. C. (1983). *The logic of decision* (2nd ed.). University of Chicago Press.

Jinpa, T. (2002). *Self, reality and reason in Tibetan philosophy.* RoutledgeCurzon.

Johnson, R. H. (2000). *Manifest rationality.* Lawrence Erlbaum.

Johnston, M. (2006). Hylomorphism. *Journal of Philosophy*, 103, 652-698.

Jolley, N. (2015). *Locke: His philosophical thought.* Oxford University Press.

Joseph, G. G. (2011). *The crest of the peacock: Non-European roots of mathematics* (3rd ed.). Princeton University Press.

Joyce, J. M. (1998). A nonpragmatic vindication of probabilism. *Philosophy of Science*, 65, 575-603.

Joyce, J. M. (2009). Accuracy and coherence: Prospects for an alethic epistemology of partial belief. *Springer.*

Joyce, R. (2006). *The evolution of morality.* MIT Press.

Justin Martyr. (c. 150/2003). *The first and second apologies* (L. W. Barnard, Trans.). Paulist Press.

K

Kagame, A. (1976). *La philosophie bantu comparée.* Présence Africaine.

Kahane, G., Wiech, K., Shackel, N., Farias, M., Savulescu, J., & Tracey, I. (2012). The neural basis of intuitive and counterintuitive moral judgment. *Social Cognitive and Affective Neuroscience*, 7(4), 393-402

Kahane, G., Everett, J. A., Earp, B. D., et al. (2015). 'Utilitarian' judgments in sacrificial moral dilemmas do not reflect impartial concern for the greater good. *Cognition*, 134, 193-209.

Kahneman, D. (2011). *Thinking, fast and slow.* Farrar, Straus and Giroux.

Kahneman, D., & Tversky, A. (1979). Prospect theory: An analysis of decision under risk. *Econometrica*, 47, 263-291.

Kaiser, C. B. (1992). Quantum complementarity and theological duality. *Theology and Science*, 1, 45-62.

Kanamori, A. (2003). *The higher infinite* (2nd ed.). Springer.

Kane, R. (1996). *The significance of free will.* Oxford University Press.

Kant, I. (1998). *Critique of pure reason* (P. Guyer & A. W. Wood, Trans.). Cambridge University Press. (Original work published 1781/1787).

Karatas, T. L., & Kowalski, K. L. (1990). Noether's theorem for local gauge transformations. *American Journal of Physics*, 58, 123-131.

Kastrup, B. (2019). *The idea of the world: A multi-disciplinary argument for the mental nature of reality.* iff Books.

Katz, S. T. (1978). *Mysticism and philosophical analysis.* Oxford University Press.

Katz, V. J. (1998). *A history of mathematics: An introduction* (2nd ed.). Addison-Wesley.

Kauffman, S. (2016). *Humanity in a creative universe.* Oxford University Press.

Kauffman, S. (1993). *The origins of order: Self-organization and selection in evolution.* Oxford University Press.

Kauffman, S. (1995). *At home in the universe: The search for laws of self-organization and complexity.* Oxford University Press.

Kauffman, S. (2008). *Reinventing the sacred: A new view of science, reason and religion.* Basic Books.

Kaufman, G. D. (1993). *In face of mystery: A constructive theology.* Harvard University Press.

Keats, J. (1817). *Letter to George and Tom Keats, December 21, 1817.* Harvard University Press.

Keefe, R. (2000). *Theories of vagueness.* Cambridge University Press.

Keefe, R., & Smith, P. (1996). *Vagueness: A reader.* MIT Press.

Keller, C. (2003). *Face of the deep: A theology of becoming*. Routledge.

Kellert, S. H. (1993). *In the wake of chaos: Unpredictable order in dynamical systems*. University of Chicago Press.

Kellert, S. H., Longino, H. E., & Waters, C. K. (2006). *Scientific pluralism*. University of Minnesota Press.

Kennett, J., & Fine, C. (2009). Will the real moral judgment please stand up? *Ethical Theory and Moral Practice*, 12(1), 77-96.

Kiefer, C. (2007). *Quantum gravity* (2nd ed.). Oxford University Press.

Kierkegaard, S. (1992). *Concluding unscientific postscript to philosophical fragments* (H. V. Hong & E. H. Hong, Trans.). Princeton University Press.

Killen, M., & Smetana, J. G. (2015). Origins and development of morality. *Wiley*.

Kim, H. J. (2004). *Eihei Dōgen: Mystical realist*. Wisdom Publications.

Kim, J. (1998). *Mind in a physical world: An essay on the mind-body problem and mental causation*. MIT Press.

Kim, J. (2005). *Physicalism, or something near enough*. Princeton University Press.

Kim, J. (2006). Emergence: Core ideas and issues. *Synthese*, 151, 547-559.

Kimmerer, R. W. (2013). *Braiding Sweetgrass: Indigenous Wisdom, Scientific Knowledge, and the Teachings of Plants*. Milkweed Editions.

Kirk, G. S., Raven, J. E., & Schofield, M. (2007). *The presocratic philosophers: A critical history with a selection of texts* (2nd ed.). Cambridge University Press.

Kitcher, P. (1984). *The nature of mathematical knowledge*. Oxford University Press.

Kitcher, P. (1992). The naturalists return. *The Philosophical Review*, 101, 53-114.

Kitcher, P. (1993). *The advancement of science: Science without legend, objectivity without illusions*. Oxford University Press.

Kitcher, P. (2011). *Science in a democratic society*. Prometheus Books.

Kitcher, P. (2012). *Preludes to pragmatism: Toward a reconstruction of philosophy*. Oxford University Press.

Kleban, M. (2012). Cosmic bubble collisions. *Classical and Quantum Gravity*, 29.

Kleene, S. C. (1945). On the interpretation of intuitionistic number theory. *Journal of Symbolic Logic*, 10, 109-124.

Klein, P. (1999). Human knowledge and the infinite regress of reasons. *Philosophical Perspectives*, 13, 297-325.

Klein, P. (2008). Contemporary responses to Agrippa's trilemma. *Oxford University Press*.

Klein, P. (2014). Infinitism is the solution to the regress problem. *Wiley-Blackwell*.

Koch, C. (2004). *The quest for consciousness: A neurobiological approach*. Roberts & Company.

Koch, C. (2019). *The feeling of life itself: Why consciousness is widespread but can't be computed*. MIT Press.

Koellner, P. (2010). Independence and large cardinals. *Stanford Encyclopedia of Philosophy*.

Koenigs, M., Young, L., Adolphs, R., et al. (2007). Damage to the prefrontal cortex increases utilitarian moral judgements. *Nature*, 446, 908-911.

Koons, R. C. (1997). A new look at the cosmological argument. *American Philosophical Quarterly*, 34, 193-211.

Kornblith, H. (2002). *Knowledge and its place in nature*. Oxford University Press.

Korsgaard, C. M. (1996). *The sources of normativity*. Cambridge University Press.

Korsgaard, C. M. (2009). *Self-constitution: Agency, identity, and integrity*. Oxford University Press.

Koslicki, K. (2008). *The structure of objects*. Oxford University Press.

Kosmann-Schwarzbach, Y. (2011). *The Noether theorems: Invariance and conservation laws in the twentieth century*. Springer.

Koyré, A. (1957). *From the closed world to the infinite universe*. Johns Hopkins University Press.

Kragh, H. (1996). *Cosmology and controversy: The historical development of two theories of the universe.*

Princeton University Press.

Krauss, L. M. (2012). *A universe from nothing: Why there is something rather than nothing.* Free Press.

Kraut, R. (2018). *The quality of life: Aristotle revised.* Oxford University Press.

Kretzmann, N. (1997). *The metaphysics of theism: Aquinas's natural theology in Summa contra gentiles I.* Oxford University Press.

Kripke, S. A. (1963). Semantical considerations on modal logic. *Acta Philosophica Fennica*, 16, 83-94.

Kripke, S. A. (1980). *Naming and necessity.* Harvard University Press.

Kruger, J., & Dunning, D. (1999). Unskilled and unaware of it: How difficulties in recognizing one's own incompetence lead to inflated self-assessments. *Journal of Personality and Social Psychology*, 77, 1121-1134.

Kugel, J. L. (2007). *How to read the Bible: A guide to scripture, then and now.* Free Press.

Kuhn, T. S. (1996). *The structure of scientific revolutions.* University of Chicago Press. (Original work published 1962).

Kumar, K. (2017). The idea of progress. *Blackwell.*

Kunen, K. (2011). *Set theory* (Studies in Logic ed.). College Publications.

Kusch, M. (2002). *Knowledge by agreement: The programme of communitarian epistemology.* Oxford University Press.

L

Lackey, J. (2008). *Learning from words: Testimony as a source of knowledge.* Oxford University Press.

Lackey, J. (2021). *The epistemology of groups.* Oxford University Press.

LaCugna, C. M. (1991). *God for us: The Trinity and Christian life.* HarperSanFrancisco.

Ladyman, J. (2002). *Understanding philosophy of science.* Routledge.

Ladyman, J. (2018). Structural realism. *Stanford Encyclopedia of Philosophy.*

Ladyman, J., & Ross, D. (2007). *Every thing must go: Metaphysics naturalized.* Oxford University Press.

Lai, K. (2017). *An introduction to Chinese philosophy* (2nd ed.). Cambridge University Press.

Lakatos, I. (1976). *Proofs and refutations.* Cambridge University Press.

Lakatos, I. (1978). *The methodology of scientific research programmes.* Cambridge University Press.

Lakoff, G., & Johnson, M. (1999). *Philosophy in the flesh: The embodied mind and its challenge to Western thought.* Basic Books.

Lakoff, G., & Núñez, R. (2000). *Where mathematics comes from.* Basic Books.

Lange, M. (2007). Laws and meta-laws of nature: Conservation laws and symmetries. *Studies in History and Philosophy of Modern Physics*, 38, 457-481.

Lange, M. (2013). What makes a scientific explanation distinctively mathematical? *British Journal for the Philosophy of Science*, 64(3), 485-511.

Lange, M. (2017). *Because without cause: Non-causal explanation in science and mathematics.* Oxford University Press.

Laozi. (2003). *Daodejing* (E. Slingerland, Trans.). Hackett Publishing.

Laplace, P. S. (1951). *A philosophical essay on probabilities* (F. W. Truscott & F. L. Emory, Trans.). Dover Publications. (Original work published 1814)

Larson, G. J. (1979). *Classical Sāṃkhya: An interpretation of its history and meaning.* Motilal Banarsidass.

Larson, G. J., & Bhattacharya, R. S. (1987). *Sāṃkhya: A dualist tradition in Indian philosophy.* Princeton University Press.

Latour, B. (2017). *Facing Gaia: Eight lectures on the new climatic regime.* Polity Press.

Latour, B., & Woolgar, S. (1979). *Laboratory life: The construction of scientific facts.* Sage Publications.

Laudan, L. (1977). *Progress and its problems: Towards a theory of scientific growth.* University of California Press.

Laudan, L. (1981). A confutation of convergent realism. *Philosophy of Science*, 48, 19-49.

Laudan, L. (1984). *Science and values: The aims of science and their role in scientific debate.* University of California Press.

Laughlin, R. B., & Pines, D. (2000). The theory of everything. *Proceedings of the National Academy of Sciences, 97*, 28-31.

Lawvere, F. W., & Rosebrugh, R. (2003). *Sets for mathematics.* Cambridge University Press.

Leaman, O. (2009). *The biographical encyclopedia of Islamic philosophy.* Continuum.

Leaman, O. (2009). *Islamic philosophy: An introduction* (2nd ed.). Polity Press.

Lear, J. (1984). The disappearing 'we'. *Proceedings of the Aristotelian Society, Supplementary Volume, 58*, 219-242.

Lebedev, M. A., & Nicolelis, M. A. (2017). Brain-machine interfaces: From basic science to neuroprostheses and neurorehabilitation. *Physiological Reviews, 97*, 767-837.

Lebowitz, J. L. (1993). Boltzmann's entropy and time's arrow. *Physics Today, 46*, 32-38.

LeCun, Y., Bengio, Y., & Hinton, G. (2015). Deep learning. *Nature, 521*, 436-444.

Lee, P., & George, R. P. (2008). *Body-self dualism in contemporary ethics and politics.* Cambridge University Press.

Leftow, B. (2012). *God and necessity.* Oxford University Press.

Lehrer, K. (2000). *Theory of knowledge* (2nd ed.). Westview Press.

Lehrer, K., & Paxson, T., Jr. (1969). Knowledge: Undefeated justified true belief. *The Journal of Philosophy, 66*, 225-237.

Leibniz, G. W. (1989). *Philosophical essays* (R. Ariew & D. Garber, Trans.). Hackett Publishing. (Original work published 1714).

Leifer, M. S. (2014). Is the quantum state real? An extended review of ψ-ontology theorems. *Quanta, 3*, 67-155.

Leng, M. (2010). *Mathematics and reality.* Oxford University Press.

Lennox, J. G. (2017). Aristotle's biology. *Stanford Encyclopedia of Philosophy.*

Lepore, E., & Ludwig, K. (2005). *Donald Davidson: Meaning, truth, language, and reality.* Oxford University Press.

Levenson, J. D. (1988). *Creation and the persistence of evil.* Harper & Row.

Levenson, J. D. (1993). *The Hebrew Bible, the Old Testament, and historical criticism.* Westminster John Knox Press.

Levenson, J. D. (2004). *Resurrection and the restoration of Israel: The ultimate victory of the God of life.* Yale University Press.

Levi, I. (1991). *The fixation of belief and its undoing.* Cambridge University Press.

Levinas, E. (1969). *Totality and infinity* (A. Lingis, Trans.). Duquesne University Press. (Original work published 1961).

Levine, J. (1983). Materialism and qualia: The explanatory gap. *Pacific Philosophical Quarterly, 64*, 354-361.

Levine, J. (2001). *Purple haze: The puzzle of consciousness.* Oxford University Press.

Levy, N. (2014). *Consciousness and moral responsibility.* Oxford University Press.

Lewis, C. I., & Langford, C. H. (1932). *Symbolic logic.* Century Company.

Lewis, D. (1972). Psychophysical and theoretical identifications. *Australasian Journal of Philosophy, 50*, 249-258.

Lewis, D. (1986). *On the plurality of worlds.* Blackwell.

Lewis, G. F., & Barnes, L. A. (2016). *A fortunate universe: Life in a finely tuned cosmos.* Cambridge University Press.

Libet, B. (1985). Unconscious cerebral initiative and the role of conscious will in voluntary action. *Behavioral and Brain Sciences, 8*, 529-539.

Liddle, A. R., & Lyth, D. H. (2000). *Cosmological inflation and large-scale structure.* Cambridge University Press.

Lieberman, D., Tooby, J., & Cosmides, L. (2007). The architecture of human kin detection. *Nature, 445*, 727-731.

Linde, A. (1986). Eternal chaotic inflation. *Modern Physics Letters A, 1*, 81-85.

Lindström, P. (2001). Penrose's new argument. *Journal of Philosophical Logic*, 30, 241-250.

Linnebo, Ø. (2017). *Philosophy of mathematics*. Princeton University Press.

List, C., & Menzies, P. (2009). Nonreductive physicalism and the limits of the exclusion principle. *Journal of Philosophy*, 106, 475-502.

Lloyd, G. E. R. (1970). *Early Greek science: Thales to Aristotle*. W. W. Norton.

Lloyd, S. (2006). *Programming the universe: A quantum computer scientist takes on the cosmos*. Knopf.

Loar, B. (1997). Phenomenal states. *MIT Press*.

Locke, J. (1975). *An essay concerning human understanding* (P. H. Nidditch, Ed.). Oxford University Press. (Original work published 1689).

Longino, H. E. (1990). *Science as social knowledge: Values and objectivity in scientific inquiry*. Princeton University Press.

Lonergan, B. J.F. (1957). *Insight: A Study of Human Understanding*. London: Longmans, Green and Co.

Longino, H. E. (2002). *The fate of knowledge*. Princeton University Press.

Longino, H. E. (2013). *Studying human behavior: How scientists investigate aggression and sexuality*. University of Chicago Press.

Longley, J., & Normann, D. (2015). *Higher-order computability*. Springer.

Look, B. C. (2021). Gottfried Wilhelm Leibniz. *Stanford Encyclopedia of Philosophy*.

Lossky, V. (1957). *The mystical theology of the Eastern Church*. James Clarke & Co.

Lowe, E. J. (2006). *The four-category ontology: A metaphysical foundation for natural science*. Oxford University Press.

Lowe, E. J. (2013). *Forms of thought*. Cambridge University Press.

Lucas, J. R. (1961). Minds, machines and Gödel. *Philosophy*, 36, 112-127.

Lüders, G. (1954). On the equivalence of invariance under time reversal and under particle-antiparticle conjugation for relativistic field theories. *Kongelige Danske Videnskabernes Selskab, Matematisk-Fysiske Meddelelser*, 28, 1-17.

Luhrmann, T. M. (2012). *When God talks back: Understanding the American evangelical relationship with God*. Knopf.

Luisi, P. L. (2016). *The emergence of life: From chemical origins to synthetic biology* (2nd ed.). Cambridge University Press.

Łukasiewicz, J. (1971). On the principle of contradiction in Aristotle. *Review of Metaphysics*, 24, 485-509.

Lusthaus, D. (2002). *Buddhist phenomenology: A philosophical investigation of Yogācāra Buddhism and the Ch'eng Wei-shih lun*. RoutledgeCurzon.

Lutz, A., Slagter, H. A., Dunne, J. D., & Davidson, R. J. (2004). Attention regulation and monitoring in meditation. *Trends in Cognitive Sciences*, 8(4), 163-169.

Lutz, A., Greischar, L. L., Rawlings, N. B., et al. (2004). Long-term meditators self-induce high-amplitude gamma synchrony during mental practice. *Proceedings of the National Academy of Sciences*, 101, 16369-16373.

Lutz, A., Jha, A. P., Dunne, J. D., et al. (2015). Investigating the phenomenological matrix of mindfulness-related practices from a neurocognitive perspective. *American Psychologist*, 70, 632-658.

Lynch, M. P. (2009). *Truth as one and many*. Oxford University Press.

Lyon, A., & Colyvan, M. (2008). The explanatory power of phase spaces. *Philosophia Mathematica*, 16, 227-243.

Lyotard, J.-F. (1984). *The postmodern condition: A report on knowledge* (G. Bennington & B. Massumi, Trans.). University of Minnesota Press.

M

Mac Lane, S. (1998). *Categories for the working mathematician* (2nd ed.). Springer.

MacDonald, J., & Mullan, D. J. (2009). Big bang nucleosynthesis: The strong nuclear force meets the weak anthropic principle. *Physical Review D*, 80.

MacFarlane, J. (2003). Future contingents and relative truth. *Philosophical Quarterly*, 53, 321-336.

Machery, E. (2017). *Philosophy within its proper bounds*. Oxford University Press.

Machery, E., Stich, S., Rose, D., et al. (2017). Gettier across cultures. *Noûs*, 51, 645-664.

Machina, K. F. (1976). Truth, belief and vagueness. *Journal of Philosophical Logic*, 5, 47-78.

MacIntyre, A. (1984). *After virtue* (2nd ed.). University of Notre Dame Press.

MacIntyre, A. (1988). *Whose justice? Which rationality?* University of Notre Dame Press.

MacKenzie, D. (2001). *Mechanizing proof: Computing, risk, and trust*. MIT Press.

Mackie, J. L. (1977). *Ethics: Inventing right and wrong*. Penguin Books.

Mackie, J. L. (1982). *The miracle of theism*. Oxford University Press.

Maddy, P. (1990). *Realism in mathematics*. Oxford University Press.

Maddy, P. (1997). *Naturalism in mathematics*. Oxford University Press.

Maddy, P. (2007). *Second philosophy: A naturalistic method*. Oxford University Press.

Maddy, P. (2014). *The logical must: Wittgenstein on logic*. Oxford University Press.

Maimonides, M. (1963). *The guide of the perplexed* (S. Pines, Trans.). University of Chicago Press. (Original work published 1190).

Malcolm, N. (1954). Wittgenstein's philosophical investigations. *Philosophical Review*, 63, 530-559.

Maldacena, J. (1999). The large N limit of superconformal field theories and supergravity. *International Journal of Theoretical Physics*, 38, 1113-1133.

Maldacena, J., & Susskind, L. (2013). Cool horizons for entangled black holes. *Fortschritte der Physik*, 61, 781-811.

Maimonides, M. (1963). *The Guide of the Perplexed*. Translated with an introduction and notes by Shlomo Pines. With an introductory essay by Leo Strauss. Chicago: University of Chicago Press.

Mancosu, P. (2008). *The philosophy of mathematical practice*. Oxford University Press.

Marcel, G. (1949). *The philosophy of existence*. Philosophical Library.

Marcus, G., & Davis, E. (2019). *Rebooting AI: Building artificial intelligence we can trust*. Pantheon Books.

Mares, E. (2020). Relevance logic. *Stanford Encyclopedia of Philosophy*.

Mares, E. D. (2004). *Relevant logic: A philosophical interpretation*. Cambridge University Press.

Markie, P. (1992). The cogito and its importance. *Cambridge University Press*.

Marsh, A. A. (2014). Understanding psychopathy: The cognitive side. *Wiley-Blackwell*.

Marshall, B. J., & Warren, J. R. (1984). Unidentified curved bacilli in the stomach of patients with gastritis and peptic ulceration. *The Lancet*, 323, 1311-1315.

Martin, M. G. F. (2004). The limits of self-awareness. *Philosophical Studies*, 120(1-3), 37-89.

Martin-Löf, P. (1984). *Intuitionistic type theory*. Bibliopolis.

Matilal, B. K. (1986). *Perception: An essay on classical Indian theories of knowledge*. Oxford University Press.

Maudlin, T. (2011). *Quantum non-locality and relativity* (3rd ed.). Wiley-Blackwell.

Maudlin, T. (2019). *Philosophy of physics: Quantum theory*. Princeton University Press.

Mavrodes, G. I. (1963). Some puzzles concerning omnipotence. *Philosophical Review*, 72, 221-223.

Maxwell, J. C. (1865). A dynamical theory of the electromagnetic field. *Philosophical Transactions of the Royal Society of London*, 155, 459-512.

May, G. (1994). *Creatio ex nihilo: The doctrine of 'creation out of nothing' in early Christian thought*. T&T Clark.

Mbiti, J. S. (1990). *African religions and philosophy* (2nd ed.). Heinemann.

McDaniel, K. (2017). *The fragmentation of being*. Oxford University Press.

McDowell, J. (1994). *Mind and world*. Harvard University Press.

McGeer, V. (2019). Scaffolding agency: A proleptic account of the reactive attitudes. *European Journal of Philosophy*, 27, 301-323.

McGinn, C. (1989). Can we solve the mind-body problem? *Mind*, 98(391), 349-366.

McGinnis, J. (2010). *Avicenna*. Oxford University Press.

McGinnis, J., & Reisman, D. C. (2007). *Classical Arabic philosophy*. Hackett.

McGrath, A. E. (2001). *A scientific theology: Volume 1, Nature*. Eerdmans.

McGrath, A. E. (2004). *The science of God: An introduction to scientific theology*. Eerdmans.

McGrath, A. E. (2011). *Christian theology: An introduction* (5th ed.). Wiley-Blackwell.

McGrath, A. E. (2019). *The territories of human reason: Science and theology in the image of God*. Oxford University Press.

McGrath, M. (2013). Phenomenal conservatism and cognitive penetration. *Oxford University Press*.

McKeever, S., & Ridge, M. (2006). *Principled ethics: Generalism as a regulative ideal*. Oxford University Press.

McKenna, M., & Pereboom, D. (2016). *Free will: A contemporary introduction*. Routledge.

McLarty, C. (2007). The rising sea: Grothendieck on simplicity and generality. *Journal of Logic & Analysis*, 301-322.

McLaughlin, B. P. (1985). Anomalous monism and the irreducibility of the mental. *Blackwell*.

McMahan, J. (2002). *The ethics of killing: Problems at the margins of life*. Oxford University Press.

McTaggart, J. E. (1908). The unreality of time. *Mind*, 17, 457-474.

Medina, J. (2013). *The epistemology of resistance: Gender and racial oppression, epistemic injustice, and resistant imaginations*. Oxford University Press.

Mele, A. R. (2009). *Effective intentions: The power of conscious will*. Oxford University Press.

Melia, J. (2000). Weaseling away the indispensability argument. *Mind*, 109, 455-479.

Melnyk, A. (2003). *A physicalist manifesto: Thoroughly modern materialism*. Cambridge University Press.

Mercier, H., & Sperber, D. (2017). *The enigma of reason*. Harvard University Press.

Merleau-Ponty, M. (2012). *Phenomenology of perception* (D. A. Landes, Trans.). Routledge. (Original work published 1945).

Mermin, N. D. (1985). Is the moon there when nobody looks? Reality and the quantum theory. *Physics Today*, 38, 38-47.

Metz, T. (2013). *Meaning in life: An analytic study*. Oxford University Press.

Metzger, B. M. (1987). *The canon of the New Testament: Its origin, development, and significance*. Clarendon Press.

Midgley, M. (2014). *Are you an illusion?* Routledge.

Mikhail, J. (2011). *Elements of moral cognition: Rawls' linguistic analogy and the cognitive science of moral and legal judgment*. Cambridge University Press.

Mill, J. S. (1865). *An examination of Sir William Hamilton's philosophy*. Longmans, Green.

Mill, J. S. (2002). *A system of logic, ratiocinative and inductive* (J. M. Robson, Ed.). Routledge. (Original work published 1843).

Miller, C. B. (2013). *Moral character: An empirical theory*. Oxford University Press.

Miller, D. (1994). *Critical rationalism: A restatement and defence*. Open Court.

Millican, P. (2017). Hume's fork, and his theory of relations. *Philosophy Compass*, 12.

Millikan, R. G. (2004). *Varieties of meaning*. MIT Press.

Millikan, R. G. (2017). *Beyond concepts: Unicepts, language, and natural information*. Oxford University Press.

Mills, C. W. (2017). *Black rights/white wrongs: The critique of racial liberalism*. Oxford University Press.

Minkowski, H. (1908). Raum und Zeit. *Physikalische Zeitschrift*, 10, 104-111.

Misak, C. (2013). *The American pragmatists*. Oxford University Press.

Misner, C. W., Thorne, K. S., & Wheeler, J. A. (1973). *Gravitation*. W. H. Freeman.

Mitchell, S. D. (2009). *Unsimple truths: Science, complexity, and policy*. University of Chicago Press.

Mohamed, Y. (2016). *The human being in Islamic philosophy and theology*. Cambridge University Press.

Mohanty, J. N. (1992). *Reason and tradition in Indian thought: An essay on the nature of Indian philosophical thinking*. Oxford University Press.

Momaday, N. S. (1997). *The man made of words: Essays, stories, passages*. St. Martin's Press.

Moore, G. E. (1903). *Principia ethica*. Cambridge University Press.

Moore, G. E. (1925). A defence of common sense. *Contemporary British Philosophy*, 193-223.

Moore, G. E. (1939). Proof of an external world. *Proceedings of the British Academy*, 25, 273-300.

Moore, G. H. (1982). *Zermelo's axiom of choice*. Springer.

Morganti, M., & Tahko, T. E. (2017). Moderately naturalistic metaphysics. *Synthese*, 194, 2557-2580.

Morin, E. (2008). *On complexity*. Hampton Press.

Morrison, M. (1999). Models as autonomous agents. In M. Morrison & M. S. Morgan (Eds.), *Models as Mediators: Perspectives on Natural and Social Science* (pp. 38-65). Cambridge University Press.

Morrison, M. (2000). *Unifying scientific theories: Physical concepts and mathematical structures*. Cambridge University Press.

Morrison, M. (2015). *Reconstructing reality: Models, mathematics, and simulations*. Oxford University Press.

Moser, P. K. (1989). *Knowledge and evidence*. Cambridge University Press.

Moser, P. K. (2008). *The elusive God: Reorienting religious epistemology*. Cambridge University Press.

Moyal-Sharrock, D. (2004). *Understanding Wittgenstein's On Certainty*. Palgrave Macmillan.

Mueller, I. (1981). *Philosophy of Mathematics and Deductive Structure in Euclid's Elements*. MIT Press.

Müller, F. M. (1899). *The six systems of Indian philosophy*. Longmans, Green and Co.

Mumford, S. (2004). *Laws in nature*. Routledge.

Mumford, S., & Anjum, R. L. (2011). *Getting causes from powers*. Oxford University Press.

Munn, N. D. (1973). *Walbiri iconography: Graphic representation and cultural symbolism in a Central Australian society*. Cornell University Press.

Murphy, M. C. (2001). *Natural law and practical rationality*. Cambridge University Press.

Murphy, N. (1990). *Theology in the age of scientific reasoning*. Cornell University Press.

Musgrave, A. (1985). Realism versus constructive empiricism. *University of Chicago Press*.

Myhill, J. (1952). Some philosophical implications of mathematical logic. *Review of Metaphysics*, 6, 165-198.

N

Nāgārjuna. (1995). *The fundamental wisdom of the middle way: Nāgārjuna's Mūlamadhyamakakārikā* (J. L. Garfield, Trans.). Oxford University Press. (Original work composed c. 200)

Nagasawa, Y. (2017). *Maximal God*. Oxford University Press.

Nagel, E., & Newman, J. R. (2001). *Gödel's proof* (Rev. ed.). New York University Press.

Nagel, T. (1970). Death. *Noûs*, 4, 73-80.

Nagel, T. (1971). The absurd. *Journal of Philosophy*, 68, 716-727.

Nagel, T. (1974). What is it like to be a bat? *The Philosophical Review*, 83(4), 435-450

Nagel, T. (1986). *The view from nowhere*. Oxford University Press.

Nagel, T. (2012). *Mind and cosmos: Why the materialist neo-Darwinian conception of nature is almost certainly false*. Oxford University Press.

Nagel, Thomas. *Mind and Cosmos: Why the Materialist Neo-Darwinian Conception of Nature Is Almost Certainly False*. Oxford University Press, 2012.

Nahmias, E. (2014). Is free will an illusion? Confronting challenges from the modern mind sciences. *MIT Press*.

Ñāṇamoli, B., & Bodhi, B. (1995). *The middle length discourses of the Buddha*. Wisdom Publications.

Narvaez, D. (2014). *Neurobiology and the development of human morality: Evolution, culture, and wisdom*. W. W. Norton.

Nasr, S. H. (1989). *Knowledge and the sacred*. State University of New York Press.

Nasr, S. H. (1993). *The need for a sacred science*. State University of New York Press.

Nasr, S. H. (2015). *The study Quran: A new translation and commentary*. HarperOne.

Naugle, D. K. (2002). *Worldview: The history of a concept*. Eerdmans.

Needham, J. (1969). *The grand titration: Science and society in East and West*. University of Toronto Press.

Neuwirth, A. (2010). *Der Koran als Text der Spätantike: Ein europäischer Zugang*. Verlag der

Weltreligionen.

Newberg, A. B., & d'Aquili, E. G. (2001). *Why God won't go away: Brain science and the biology of belief.* Ballantine Books.

Newman, J. H. (1870). *An essay in aid of a grammar of assent.* Burns, Oates, & Co.

Newton, I. (1999). *The Principia: Mathematical principles of natural philosophy* (I. B. Cohen & A. Whitman, Trans.). University of California Press. (Original work published 1687)

Nickerson, R. S. (1998). Confirmation bias: A ubiquitous phenomenon in many guises. *Review of General Psychology*, 2, 175-220.

Nielsen, M. A., & Chuang, I. L. (2010). *Quantum computation and quantum information* (10th anniversary ed.). Cambridge University Press.

Niemiec, C. P., Brown, K. W., Kashdan, T. B., et al. (2010). Being present in the face of existential threat: The role of trait mindfulness in reducing defensive responses to mortality salience. *Journal of Personality and Social Psychology*, 99, 344-365.

Noble, D. (2012). A theory of biological relativity: No privileged level of causation. *Interface Focus*, 2, 55-64.

Noë, A. (2004). *Action in perception.* MIT Press.

Noether, E. (1971). Invariant variation problems. *Transport Theory and Statistical Physics*, 1, 186-207.

Nordström, B., Petersson, K., & Smith, J. M. (1990). *Programming in Martin-Löf's type theory.* Oxford University Press.

Norell, U. (2007). *Towards a practical programming language based on dependent type theory* [PhD dissertation, Chalmers University of Technology].

North, J. (2009). The "structure" of physics: A case study. *Journal of Philosophy*, 106, 57-88.

Northcott, M. S. (2007). *A moral climate: The ethics of global warming.* Orbis Books.

Norton, B. G. (2005). *Toward unity among environmentalists.* Oxford University Press.

Norton, J. (1985). What was Einstein's principle of equivalence? *Studies in History and Philosophy of Science*, 16(3), 203-246.

Norton, J. D. (2021). *The material theory of induction.* BSPS Open.

Novak, D. (1998). *Natural law in Judaism.* Cambridge University Press.

Nozick, R. (1981). *Philosophical explanations.* Harvard University Press.

Numbers, R. L. (2006). *The creationists: From scientific creationism to intelligent design* (Expanded ed.). Harvard University Press.

Numbers, R. L. (2009). *Galileo goes to jail and other myths about science and religion.* Harvard University Press.

Nussbaum, M. C. (2006). *Frontiers of justice: Disability, nationality, species membership.* Harvard University Press.

Nussbaum, M. C. (2011). *Creating capabilities: The human development approach.* Harvard University Press.

O

O'Connor, T. (2000). *Persons and causes: The metaphysics of free will.* Oxford University Press.

O'Connor, T., & Wong, H. Y. (2015). Emergent properties. *Stanford Encyclopedia of Philosophy*.

Olivelle, P. (1998). *The early Upanishads: Annotated text and translation.* Oxford University Press.

Olson, E. T. (1997). *The human animal: Personal identity without psychology.* Oxford University Press.

Olsson, E. J. (2005). *Against coherence: Truth, probability, and justification.* Oxford University Press.

Oppy, G. (1995). *Ontological arguments and belief in God.* Cambridge University Press.

Oppy, G. (2006). *Arguing about gods.* Cambridge University Press.

Oppy, G. (2018). *Ontological arguments.* Cambridge University Press.

Oreskes, N. (1999). *The rejection of continental drift: Theory and method in American earth science.* Oxford University Press.

Ortiz, A. (1969). *The Tewa world: Space, time, being, and becoming in a Pueblo society.* University of Chicago Press.

Osman, M. (2004). An evaluation of dual-process theories of reasoning. *Psychonomic Bulletin & Review*, 11, 988-1010.

Otto, R. (1958). *The idea of the holy* (J. W. Harvey, Trans.). Oxford University Press. (Original work published 1917).

P

Page, D. N. (2008). Return of the Boltzmann brains. *Physical Review D*, 78.

Pais, A. (1982). *Subtle is the Lord: The science and the life of Albert Einstein*. Oxford University Press.

Pais, A. (1986). *Inward bound: Of matter and forces in the physical world*. Oxford University Press.

Pali Canon. (1995). (Various translators). Pali Text Society. (Original work compiled c. 100 BCE)

Panikkar, R. (1993). *The cosmotheandric experience: Emerging religious consciousness*. Orbis Books.

Paoli, F. (2002). *Substructural logics: A primer*. Kluwer.

Papineau, D. (2002). *Thinking about consciousness*. Oxford University Press.

Papineau, D. (2007). Phenomenal and perceptual concepts. *Oxford University Press*.

Pappas, G. S. (2000). *Berkeley's thought*. Cornell University Press.

Parfit, D. (1984). *Reasons and persons*. Oxford University Press.

Parfit, D. (2011). *On what matters* (Vols. 1-2). Oxford University Press.

Paris, J., & Harrington, L. (1977). A mathematical incompleteness in Peano arithmetic. *Handbook of mathematical logic*, 1133-1142.

Park, C. L. (2013). Religion and meaning. *Guilford Press*.

Parsons, C. (2008). *Mathematical thought and its objects*. Cambridge University Press.

Pascal, B. (1995). *Pensées* (A. J. Krailsheimer, Trans.). Penguin Books.

Pati, A. K., & Braunstein, S. L. (2000). Impossibility of deleting an unknown quantum state. *Nature*, 404, 164-165.

Paul, L. A. (2012). Metaphysics as modeling: The handmaiden's tale. *Philosophical Studies*, 160, 1-29.

Paul, L. A. (2014). *Transformative experience*. Oxford University Press.

Pauli, W. (1955). Exclusion principle, Lorentz group and reflection of space-time and charge. *McGraw-Hill*.

Peacocke, A. (2001). *Paths from science towards God*. Oneworld.

Peacocke, A. (2004). *Evolution: The disguised friend of faith?* Templeton Foundation Press.

Peacocke, C. (2012). Descartes defended. *Proceedings of the Aristotelian Society Supplementary Volume*, 86, 109-125.

Pearle, P. (2015). Collapse models. *Cambridge University Press*.

Peirce, C. S. (1877). The fixation of belief. *Popular Science Monthly*, 12, 1-15.

Pennycook, G., Ross, R. M., Koehler, D. J., et al. (2017). Dunning-Kruger effects in reasoning: Theoretical implications of the failure to recognize incompetence. *Psychonomic Bulletin & Review*, 24, 1774-1784.

Penrose, R. (1989). *The emperor's new mind*. Oxford University Press.

Penrose, R. (1994). *Shadows of the mind*. Oxford University Press.

Penrose, R. (2004). *The Road to Reality: A Complete Guide to the Laws of the Universe*. Jonathan Cape.

Penrose, R. (2010). *Cycles of time: An extraordinary new view of the universe*. Bodley Head.

Penrose, R., & Hameroff, S. (2014). Consciousness in the universe: A review of the 'Orch OR' theory. *Physics of Life Reviews*, 11, 39-78.

Penzias, A. A., & Wilson, R. W. (1965). A measurement of excess antenna temperature at 4080 Mc/s. *The Astrophysical Journal*, 142, 419-421.

Pereboom, D. (2001). *Living without free will*. Cambridge University Press.

Pereboom, D. (2014). *Free will, agency, and meaning in life*. Oxford University Press.

Peregrin, J. (2014). *Inferentialism*. Cambridge University Press.

Perlmutter, S., Aldering, G., Goldhaber, G., et al. (1999). Measurements of Ω and Λ from 42 high-redshift supernovae. *The Astrophysical Journal*, 517, 565-586.

Perrett, R. W. (2016). *An introduction to Indian philosophy*. Cambridge University Press.

Persson, I., & Savulescu, J. (2012). *Unfit for the future: The need for moral enhancement.* Oxford University Press.

Peskin, M. E., & Schroeder, D. V. (1995). *An introduction to quantum field theory.* Addison-Wesley.

Peters, T., Russell, R. J., & Welker, M. (2002). *Resurrection: Theological and scientific assessments.* Eerdmans.

Phillips, S. H. (2012). *Epistemology in classical India: The knowledge sources of the Nyāya school.* Routledge.

Pich, A. (2017). CP violation. *Cambridge University Press.*

Pickover, C. A. (2009). *The math book.* Sterling.

Pienaar, J. (2020). QBism and relational quantum mechanics compared. *Foundations of Physics,* 51.

Pike, N. (1992). *Mystic union: An essay in the phenomenology of mysticism.* Cornell University Press.

Pincock, C. (2012). *Mathematics and scientific representation.* Oxford University Press.

Pinker, S. (2018). *Enlightenment now: The case for reason, science, humanism, and progress.* Viking.

Pinnock, C., Rice, R., Sanders, J., et al. (1994). *The openness of God: A biblical challenge to the traditional understanding of God.* InterVarsity Press.

Planck, M. (1950). *Scientific autobiography and other papers* (F. Gaynor, Trans.). Williams & Norgate.

Planck Collaboration. (2020). Planck 2018 results VI. Cosmological parameters. *Astronomy & Astrophysics,* 641, A6.

Plantinga, A. (1974). *The nature of necessity.* Oxford University Press.

Plantinga, A. (1993). *Warrant and proper function.* Oxford University Press.

Plantinga, A. (2000). *Warranted Christian belief.* Oxford University Press.

Plantinga, A. (2011). *Where the conflict really lies: Science, religion, and naturalism.* Oxford University Press.

Plato. (1997). *Complete works* (J. M. Cooper, Ed.). Hackett Publishing.

Pnueli, A. (1977). The temporal logic of programs. *Proceedings of the 18th annual symposium on foundations of computer science,* 46-57.

Pohlhaus, G., Jr. (2012). Relational knowing and epistemic injustice: Toward a theory of willful hermeneutical ignorance. *Hypatia,* 27, 715-735.

Polanyi, M. (1958). *Personal knowledge: Towards a post-critical philosophy.* University of Chicago Press.

Polanyi, M. (1966). *The tacit dimension.* Doubleday.

Poldrack, R. A., & Farah, M. J. (2015). Progress and challenges in probing the human brain. *Nature,* 526, 371-379.

Polkinghorne, J. (1994). *The faith of a physicist.* Princeton University Press.

Polkinghorne, J. (1998). *Belief in God in an age of science.* Yale University Press.

Polkinghorne, J. (2007). *Quantum physics and theology: An unexpected kinship.* Yale University Press.

Polkinghorne, J., & Beale, N. (2009). *Questions of truth: Fifty-one responses to questions about God, science, and belief.* Westminster John Knox Press.

Popkin, R. H. (2003). *The history of scepticism: From Savonarola to Bayle* (Rev. ed.). Oxford University Press.

Popper, K. R. (1963). *Conjectures and refutations: The growth of scientific knowledge.* Routledge.

Porter, M. E. (1985). *Competitive advantage: Creating and sustaining superior performance.* Free Press.

Posy, C. (2020). *Mathematical intuitionism.* Cambridge University Press.

Prasad, R. (2008). *A conceptual-analytic study of classical Indian philosophy of morals.* Centre for Studies in Civilizations.

Price, H. (1996). *Time's arrow and Archimedes' point.* Oxford University Press.

Price, H. (2009). Metaphysics after Carnap: The ghost who walks? In D. J. Chalmers, D. Manley, & R. Wasserman (Eds.), *Metametaphysics.* Oxford University Press.

Price, H. (2011). *Naturalism without mirrors.* Oxford University Press.

Priest, G. (2006). *In contradiction: A study of the transconsistent* (2nd ed.). Oxford University Press.

Priest, G. (2018). The fifth corner of four. *Springer.*

Priest, G., Graham, J., & Tanaka, K. (2013). Paraconsistent logic. *Stanford Encyclopedia of Philosophy*.

Prinz, J. J. (2007). *The emotional construction of morals*. Oxford University Press.

Prior, A. N. (1967). *Past, present and future*. Oxford University Press.

Pritchard, D. (2005). *Epistemic luck*. Oxford University Press.

Pritchard, D. (2012). *Epistemological disjunctivism*. Oxford University Press.

Proudfoot, W. (1985). *Religious experience*. University of California Press.

Prusiner, S. B. (1998). Prions. *Proceedings of the National Academy of Sciences*, 95, 13363-13383.

Pruss, A. R. (2006). *The principle of sufficient reason: A reassessment*. Cambridge University Press.

Pruss, A. R. (2018). *Infinity, causation, and paradox*. Oxford University Press.

Pruss, A. R., & Rasmussen, J. L. (2018). *Necessary existence*. Oxford University Press.

Pryor, J. (2000). The skeptic and the dogmatist. *Noûs*, 34, 517-549.

Pryor, J. (2004). What's wrong with Moore's argument? *Philosophical Issues*, 14, 349-378.

Pseudo-Dionysius. (1987). *Pseudo-Dionysius: The complete works* (C. Luibheid, Trans.). Paulist Press. (Original work published c. 500)

Psillos, S. (1999). *Scientific realism: How science tracks truth*. Routledge.

Psillos, S. (2009). *Knowing the structure of nature: Essays on realism and explanation*. Palgrave Macmillan.

Putnam, H. (1960). Minds and machines. *New York University Press*.

Putnam, H. (1967). Psychological predicates. *University of Pittsburgh Press*.

Putnam, H. (1968). Is logic empirical? In R. S. Cohen & M. W. Wartofsky (Eds.), *Boston studies in the philosophy of science* (Vol. 5, pp. 216-241). D. Reidel.

Putnam, H. (1975). The meaning of 'meaning'. In *Mind, language and reality: Philosophical papers*. Cambridge University Press.

Putnam, H. (1975). What is mathematical truth? *Historia Mathematica*, 2(4), 529-543.

Putnam, H. (1981). *Reason, truth and history*. Cambridge University Press.

Putnam, H. (2002). *The collapse of the fact/value dichotomy and other essays*. Harvard University Press.

Q

Quigg, C. (2013). *Gauge theories of the strong, weak, and electromagnetic interactions* (2nd ed.). Princeton University Press.

Quine, W. V. (1951). Two dogmas of empiricism. *The Philosophical Review*, 60, 20-43.

Quine, W. V. (1969). Epistemology naturalized. *Columbia University Press*.

Quine, W. V., & Ullian, J. S. (1978). *The web of belief* (2nd ed.). Random House.

Quine, W. V. O. (1948). On what there is. *Review of Metaphysics*, 2, 21-38.

Quine, W. V. O. (1986). *Philosophy of logic* (2nd ed.). Harvard University Press.

Quinn, P. L. (1978). *Divine commands and moral requirements*. Clarendon Press.

Quinn, P. L. (2006). Theological voluntarism. *Oxford University Press*.

R

Raatikainen, P. (2015). Gödel's incompleteness theorems. *Stanford Encyclopedia of Philosophy*.

Radder, H. (2003). *The philosophy of scientific experimentation*. University of Pittsburgh Press.

Rahman, F. (1979). *Islam* (2nd ed.). University of Chicago Press.

Rahner, K. (1978). *Foundations of Christian faith: An introduction to the idea of Christianity* (W. V. Dych, Trans.). Seabury Press.

Rainville, S., Thompson, J. K., Myers, E. G., et al. (2005). A direct test of $E = mc^2$. *Nature*, 438, 1096-1097.

Ram-Prasad, C. (2007). *Indian philosophy and the consequences of knowledge*. Ashgate.

Rambachan, A. (2006). *The Advaita worldview: God, world, and humanity*. SUNY Press.

Ramose, M. B. (2002). *African philosophy through ubuntu*. Mond Books.

Ramsey, I. T. (1957). *Religious language: An empirical placing of theological phrases*. SCM Press.

Ratcliffe, M. (2008). *Feelings of being: Phenomenology, psychiatry and the sense of reality*. Oxford University Press.

Rathjen, M. (2005). The constructive Hilbert program and the limits of Martin-Löf type theory. *Synthese*, 147, 81-120.

Rawls, J. (1971). *A theory of justice*. Harvard University Press.

Ray, R. A. (2001). *Secret of the vajra world: The tantric Buddhism of Tibet*. Shambhala.

Redding, P. (2007). *Analytic philosophy and the return of Hegelian thought*. Cambridge University Press.

Rees, G., Wojciulik, E., Clarke, K., et al. (2002). Neural correlates of conscious and unconscious vision in parietal extinction. *Neurocase*, 8, 387-393.

Rees, M. (1999). *Just six numbers: The deep forces that shape the universe*. Basic Books.

Reichenbach, H. (1938). *Experience and prediction*. University of Chicago Press.

Rescher, N. (1978). *Scientific progress: A philosophical essay on the economics of research in natural science*. University of Pittsburgh Press.

Rescher, N. (1996). *Process metaphysics: An introduction to process philosophy*. SUNY Press.

Rescher, N. (2000). *Nature and understanding: The metaphysics and method of science*. Oxford University Press.

Rescher, N. (2003). *Epistemology: An introduction to the theory of knowledge*. State University of New York Press.

Rescher, N. (2005). *Epistemic logic: A survey of the logic of knowledge*. University of Pittsburgh Press.

Rescher, N. (2009). *Unknowability: An inquiry into the limits of knowledge*. Lexington Books.

Rescher, N. (2010). *Axiogenesis: An essay in metaphysical optimalism*. Lexington Books.

Resnik, M. (1996). Ought there to be but one logic? In B. J. Copeland (Ed.), *Logic and reality: Essays on the legacy of Arthur Prior*. Oxford University Press.

Resnik, M. (1997). *Mathematics as a science of patterns*. Oxford University Press.

Restall, G. (2000). *An introduction to substructural logics*. Routledge.

Richman, F. (1990). Intuitionism as generalization. *Philosophia Mathematica*, 5, 124-128.

Rickles, D. (2016). *The philosophy of physics*. Polity Press.

Ricoeur, P. (1969). *The symbolism of evil*. Beacon Press.

Ricoeur, P. (1974). *The conflict of interpretations: Essays in hermeneutics*. Northwestern University Press.

Ricoeur, P. (1976). *Interpretation theory: Discourse and the surplus of meaning*. Texas Christian University Press.

Ries, E. (2011). *The lean startup: How today's entrepreneurs use continuous innovation to create radically successful businesses*. Crown Business.

Riess, A. G., Filippenko, A. V., Challis, P., et al. (1998). Observational evidence from supernovae for an accelerating universe and a cosmological constant. *The Astronomical Journal*, 116, 1009-1038.

Rindler, W. (2006). *Relativity: Special, general, and cosmological* (2nd ed.). Oxford University Press.

Rizzolatti, G., & Craighero, L. (2004). The mirror-neuron system. *Annual Review of Neuroscience*, 27, 169-192.

Roberts, R. C., & Wood, W. J. (2007). *Intellectual virtues: An essay in regulative epistemology*. Oxford University Press.

Robinson, H. (1994). *Perception*. Routledge.

Robinson, H. (2016). *From the knowledge argument to mental substance: Resurrecting the mind*. Cambridge University Press.

Rocca, G. P. (2004). *Speaking the incomprehensible God: Thomas Aquinas on the interplay of positive and negative theology*. Catholic University of America Press.

Rockström, J., Steffen, W., Noone, K., et al. (2009). A safe operating space for humanity. *Nature*, 461, 472-475.

Rogers, K. A. (2000). *Perfect being theology*. Edinburgh University Press.

Rorty, R. (1979). *Philosophy and the mirror of nature*. Princeton University Press.

Rosen, G. (2006). The limits of contingency. *Oxford University Press*.

Rosen, G. (2010). Metaphysical dependence: Grounding and reduction. *Oxford University Press.*

Rosenberg, A. (2011). *The atheist's guide to reality: Enjoying life without illusions.* W. W. Norton.

Ross, L. (1977). The intuitive psychologist and his shortcomings: Distortions in the attribution process. *Advances in Experimental Social Psychology,* 10, 173-220.

Ross, W. D. (1930). *The right and the good.* Oxford University Press.

Rosser, J. B. (1936). Extensions of some theorems of Gödel and Church. *Journal of Symbolic Logic,* 1, 87-91.

Rossman, J. (2019). *Think like Amazon: 50 1/2 ideas to become a digital leader.* McGraw-Hill.

Rovane, C. (1998). *The bounds of agency.* Princeton University Press.

Rovelli, C. (1996). Relational quantum mechanics. *International Journal of Theoretical Physics,* 35, 1637-1678.

Rovelli, C. (2004). *Quantum gravity.* Cambridge University Press.

Rovelli, C. (2018). *The order of time.* Riverhead Books.

Rovelli, C. (2021). *Helgoland: Making sense of the quantum revolution.* Riverhead Books.

Rovelli, C., & Vidotto, F. (2014). *Covariant loop quantum gravity.* Cambridge University Press.

Rowe, W. L. (1979). The problem of evil and some varieties of atheism. *American Philosophical Quarterly,* 16, 335-341.

Rozemond, M. (1998). *Descartes's dualism.* Harvard University Press.

Rubin, H., & Rubin, J. E. (1985). *Equivalents of the axiom of choice II.* North-Holland.

Ruse, M. (1982). *Darwinism defended: A guide to the evolution controversies.* Addison-Wesley.

Ruse, M. (2010). *Science and spirituality: Making room for faith in the age of science.* Cambridge University Press.

Russell, B. (1903). *The principles of mathematics.* Cambridge University Press.

Russell, B. (1912). *The problems of philosophy.* Williams and Norgate.

Russell, B. (1927). *The analysis of matter.* Kegan Paul.

Russell, B. (1948). *Human knowledge: Its scope and limits.* Simon and Schuster.

Russell, B., & Whitehead, A. N. (1910-1913). *Principia mathematica* (3 vols.). Cambridge University Press.

Russell, G. (2018). Logical nihilism: Could there be no logic? *Philosophical Issues,* 28(1), 308-324.

Russell, R. J., Murphy, N., & Peacocke, A. R. (1995). *Chaos and complexity: Scientific perspectives on divine action.* Vatican Observatory Publications.

S

Sakharov, A. D. (1967). Violation of CP invariance, C asymmetry, and baryon asymmetry of the universe. *JETP Letters,* 5, 24-27.

Salmon, W. C. (1990). *Four decades of scientific explanation.* University of Minnesota Press.

Sampson, R. J., & Laub, J. H. (1993). *Crime in the making: Pathways and turning points through life.* Harvard University Press.

Śaṅkara. (1972). *The Bṛhadāraṇyaka Upaniṣad: With the commentary of Śaṅkarācārya* (Swami Madhavananda, Trans.). Advaita Ashrama. (Original work composed c. 800)

Śaṅkara. (1978). *Upadēśasāhasrī* [A Thousand Teachings] (Swami Jagadananda, Trans.). Sri Ramakrishna Math. (Original work composed 8th century)

Śaṅkara. (1992). *The Brahma Sūtra Bhāṣya* (S. Gambhirananda, Trans.). Advaita Ashrama.

Santos, B. de S. (2014). *Epistemologies of the South: Justice against epistemicide.* Paradigm Publishers.

Sarkissian, H. (2010). Minor tweaks, major payoffs: The problems and promise of situationism in moral philosophy. *Philosophers' Imprint,* 10, 1-15.

Saunders, S., Barrett, J., Kent, A., et al. (2010). *Many worlds? Everett, quantum theory, and reality.* Oxford University Press.

Savage, L. J. (1954). *The foundations of statistics.* John Wiley & Sons.

Scanlon, T. M. (2008). *Moral dimensions: Permissibility, meaning, blame.* Harvard University Press.

Scarre, G. (2020). *Mill: A guide for the perplexed.* Bloomsbury Academic.

Schaffer, J. (2009). On what grounds what. In D. Chalmers, D. Manley, & R. Wasserman (Eds.), *Metametaphysics: New Essays on the Foundations of Ontology.* Oxford University Press.

Schaffer, J. (2010). Monism: The priority of the whole. *Philosophical Review*, 119, 31-76.

Scharfe, H. (2002). *Education in ancient India.* Brill.

Schechtman, M. (1996). *The constitution of selves.* Cornell University Press.

Schechtman, M. (2014). *Staying alive: Personal identity, practical concerns, and the unity of a life.* Oxford University Press.

Schellenberg, J. L. (2015). *The hiddenness argument: Philosophy's new challenge to belief in God.* Oxford University Press.

Schiebinger, L. (1989). *The mind has no sex? Women in the origins of modern science.* Harvard University Press.

Schjoedt, U., Stødkilde-Jørgensen, H., Geertz, A. W., & Roepstorff, A. (2009). Highly religious participants recruit areas of social cognition in personal prayer. *Social Cognitive and Affective Neuroscience*, 4, 199-207.

Schleiermacher, F. (1999). *The Christian faith* (H. R. Mackintosh & J. S. Stewart, Eds.). T&T Clark.

Schlosshauer, M. (2007). *Decoherence and the quantum-to-classical transition.* Springer.

Schlosshauer, M., Kofler, J., & Zeilinger, A. (2013). A snapshot of foundational attitudes toward quantum mechanics. *Studies in History and Philosophy of Science Part B*, 44, 222-230.

Scholem, G. (1941). *Major trends in Jewish mysticism.* Schocken Books.

Schrödinger, E. (1935). Die gegenwärtige Situation in der Quantenmechanik. *Naturwissenschaften*, 23, 807-812.

Schulman, L. S. (1997). *Time's arrows and quantum measurement.* Cambridge University Press.

Schultze-Kraft, M., Birman, D., Rusconi, M., et al. (2016). The point of no return in vetoing self-initiated movements. *Proceedings of the National Academy of Sciences*, 113, 1080-1085.

Schurger, A., Sitt, J. D., & Dehaene, S. (2012). An accumulator model for spontaneous neural activity prior to self-initiated movement. *Proceedings of the National Academy of Sciences*, 109.

Schurger, A., & Uithol, S. (2015). Nowhere and everywhere: The causal origin of voluntary action. *Review of Philosophy and Psychology*, 6, 761-778.

Schüssler Fiorenza, E. (1983). *In memory of her: A feminist theological reconstruction of Christian origins.* Crossroad.

Schwartz, J. M., & Begley, S. (2002). *The mind and the brain: Neuroplasticity and the power of mental force.* Regan Books.

Schwitzgebel, E. (2008). The unreliability of naive introspection. *Philosophical Review*, 117, 245-273.

Searle, J. R. (1980). Minds, brains, and programs. *Behavioral and Brain Sciences*, 3, 417-424.

Searle, J. R. (1992). *The rediscovery of the mind.* MIT Press.

Searle, J. R. (1995). *The construction of social reality.* Free Press.

Searle, J. R. (2013). Can information theory explain consciousness? *New York Review of Books*, 60(1), 54-58.

Second Vatican Council. (1964). *Lumen gentium* [Dogmatic Constitution on the Church].

Second Vatican Council. (1965). *Dei verbum* [Dogmatic Constitution on Divine Revelation].

Seeskin, K. (2005). *Maimonides on the origin of the world.* Cambridge University Press.

Sellars, W. (1956). Empiricism and the philosophy of mind. University of Minnesota Press.

Sells, M. A. (1994). *Mystical languages of unsaying.* University of Chicago Press.

Sen, A. (1977). Rational fools: A critique of the behavioral foundations of economic theory. *Philosophy & Public Affairs*, 6, 317-344.

Sen, A. (2009). *The idea of justice.* Harvard University Press.

Seth, A. (2021). *Being you: A new science of consciousness.* Dutton.

Sextus Empiricus. (2000). *Outlines of scepticism* (J. Annas & J. Barnes, Trans.). Cambridge University Press.

Shafer-Landau, R. (2003). *Moral realism: A defence.* Oxford University Press.

Shani, I. (2015). Cosmopsychism: A holistic approach to the metaphysics of experience. *Philosophical Papers*, 44, 389-437.

Shapiro, L. (2007). *The correspondence between Princess Elisabeth of Bohemia and René Descartes.* University of Chicago Press.

Shapiro, S. (1997). *Philosophy of mathematics: Structure and ontology.* Oxford University Press.

Shapiro, S. (2000). *Thinking about mathematics: The philosophy of mathematics.* Oxford University Press.

Shapiro, S. (2003). Mechanism, truth, and Penrose's new argument. *Journal of Philosophical Logic*, 32, 19-42.

Shapiro, S. (2014). *Varieties of logic.* Oxford University Press.

Shariff, A. F., & Norenzayan, A. (2007). God is watching you: Priming God concepts increases prosocial behavior in an anonymous economic game. *Psychological Science*, 18, 803-809.

Sharma, A. (2000). *Classical Hindu thought: An introduction.* Oxford University Press.

Shelah, S. (1974). Infinite abelian groups, Whitehead problem and some constructions. *Israel Journal of Mathematics*, 18, 243-256.

Sher, G. (2016). *Epistemic friction.* Oxford University Press.

Shields, C. (2016). *Aristotle* (2nd ed.). Routledge.

Shimony, A. (1993). *Search for a naturalistic world view* (2 vols.). Cambridge University Press.

Shoemaker, D. (2015). *Responsibility from the margins.* Oxford University Press.

Shoemaker, S. (1996). *The first-person perspective and other essays.* Cambridge University Press.

Shoemaker, S. (2011). On what we are. In S. Gallagher (Ed.), *The Oxford handbook of the self.* Oxford University Press.

Shoemaker, S. (2012). Persons, animals, and identity. *Synthese*, 162, 313-324.

Shor, P. W. (1997). Polynomial-time algorithms for prime factorization and discrete logarithms on a quantum computer. *SIAM Journal on Computing*, 26, 1484-1509.

Sider, T. (2001). *Four-dimensionalism: An ontology of persistence and time.* Oxford University Press.

Sider, T. (2011). *Writing the book of the world.* Oxford University Press.

Siderits, M. (2003). *Personal identity and Buddhist philosophy: Empty persons.* Ashgate.

Siderits, M. (2007). *Buddhism as philosophy: An introduction.* Hackett Publishing.

Sieg, W. (2013). *Hilbert's programs and beyond.* Oxford University Press.

Simon, H. A. (1955). A behavioral model of rational choice. *The Quarterly Journal of Economics*, 69, 99-118.

Simons, D. J., & Rensink, R. A. (2005). Change blindness: Past, present, and future. *Trends in Cognitive Sciences*, 9, 16-20.

Simonton, D. K. (2004). *Creativity in science: Chance, logic, genius, and zeitgeist.* Cambridge University Press.

Simpson, L. B. (2017). *As we have always done: Indigenous freedom through radical resistance.* University of Minnesota Press.

Simpson, S. G. (2009). *Subsystems of second order arithmetic* (2nd ed.). Cambridge University Press.

Singer, P. (1972). Famine, affluence, and morality. *Philosophy & Public Affairs*, 1, 229-243.

Sire, J. W. (2009). *The universe next door: A basic worldview catalog* (5th ed.). InterVarsity Press.

Slingerland, E. (2003). *Effortless action: Wu-wei as conceptual metaphor and spiritual ideal in early China.* Oxford University Press.

Smart, J. J. C. (1959). Sensations and brain processes. *Philosophical Review*, 68, 141-156.

Smart, N. (1969). *The religious experience of mankind.* Charles Scribner's Sons.

Smart, N. (1983). *Worldviews: Crosscultural explorations of human beliefs.* Scribner.

Smart, N. (1989). *The world's religions.* Cambridge University Press.

Smith, J. Z. (1987). *To take place: Toward theory in ritual.* University of Chicago Press.

Smith, L. T. (2012). *Decolonizing methodologies: Research and indigenous peoples* (2nd ed.). Zed Books.

Smith, P. (2013). *An introduction to Gödel's theorems* (2nd ed.). Cambridge University Press.

Smith, Q. (1988). The uncaused beginning of the universe. *Philosophy of Science*, 55, 39-57.

Smith, R. (2019). Aristotle's logic. *Stanford Encyclopedia of Philosophy*.

Smith, W. C. (1993). *What is scripture? A comparative approach*. Fortress Press.

Smith, W. C. (2012). *Patterns of faith around the world*. Oneworld.

Smolin, L. (2006). *The trouble with physics: The rise of string theory, the fall of a science, and what comes next*. Houghton Mifflin.

Smullyan, R. M. (1992). *Gödel's incompleteness theorems*. Oxford University Press.

Snow, C. P. (1959). *The two cultures*. Cambridge University Press.

Soames, S. (2003). *Philosophical analysis in the twentieth century* (Vol. 2). Princeton University Press.

Sober, E. (2011). Evolution without naturalism. *Oxford University Press*.

Sobrino, J. (1988). *Spirituality of liberation: Toward political holiness*. Orbis Books.

Sokolowski, R. (2000). *Introduction to phenomenology*. Cambridge University Press.

Sørensen, M. H., & Urzyczyn, P. (2006). *Lectures on the Curry-Howard isomorphism*. Elsevier.

Sorkin, R. D. (2003). Causal sets: Discrete gravity. *Springer*.

Sosa, E. (1991). *Knowledge in perspective: Selected essays in epistemology*. Cambridge University Press.

Sosa, E. (2007). *A virtue epistemology: Apt belief and reflective knowledge* (Vol. 1). Oxford University Press.

Sosa, E. (2009). *Reflective knowledge: Apt belief and reflective knowledge* (Vol. 2). Oxford University Press.

Sosa, E. (2017). *Epistemology*. Princeton University Press.

Sozzi, M. S. (2008). *Discrete symmetries and CP violation*. Oxford University Press.

Speaks, J. (2018). *The greatest possible being*. Oxford University Press.

Sporns, O. (2012). *Discovering the human connectome*. MIT Press.

Sporns, O. (2013). Network attributes for segregation and integration in the human brain. *Current Opinion in Neurobiology*, 23, 162-171.

Sprigge, T. L. S. (1983). *The vindication of absolute idealism*. Edinburgh University Press.

Stace, W. T. (1960). *Mysticism and Philosophy*. London: Macmillan.

Stalker, D. (1994). *Grue! The new riddle of induction*. Open Court.

Stalnaker, R. (2012). *Mere possibilities*. Princeton University Press.

Stanford, P. K. (2006). *Exceeding our grasp: Science, history, and the problem of unconceived alternatives*. Oxford University Press.

Stanford, P. K. (2017). Underdetermination of scientific theory. *Stanford Encyclopedia of Philosophy*.

Stanner, W. E. H. (1979). *White man got no dreaming: Essays 1938-1973*. Australian National University Press.

Steel, J. R. (2014). Gödel's program. *Cambridge University Press*.

Stein, E. (1989). *On the problem of empathy* (W. Stein, Trans.). ICS Publications. (Original work published 1917).

Steinberger, F. (2019). Three ways in which logic might be normative. *Journal of Philosophy*, 116, 5-31.

Steiner, M. (1998). *The applicability of mathematics as a philosophical problem*. Harvard University Press.

Steinhardt, P. J., & Turok, N. (2007). *Endless universe: Beyond the big bang*. Doubleday.

Stenger, V. J. (2011). *The fallacy of fine-tuning: Why the universe is not designed for us*. Prometheus Books.

Stenmark, M. (2001). *Scientism: Science, ethics and religion*. Ashgate.

Stenmark, M. (2004). *How to relate science and religion: A multidimensional model*. Eerdmans.

Stern, R. (2000). *Transcendental arguments and scepticism: Answering the question of justification*. Oxford University Press.

Stillwell, J. (2010). *Roads to infinity: The mathematics of truth and proof*. A K Peters.

Stoljar, D. (2006). *Ignorance and imagination: The epistemic origin of the problem of consciousness*. Oxford University Press.

Stoljar, D. (2010). *Physicalism*. Routledge.

Strawson, G. (1994). The impossibility of moral responsibility. *Philosophical Studies*, 75, 5-24.

Strawson, G. (2006). Realistic monism: Why physicalism entails panpsychism. *Journal of Consciousness Studies*, 13(10-11), 3-31.

Strawson, G. (2018). The consciousness deniers. *The New York Review of Books*, 65(1-4), 46-50.

Strawson, P. F. (1952). *Introduction to logical theory*. Methuen.

Strawson, P. F. (1959). *Individuals: An essay in descriptive metaphysics*. Methuen.

Strawson, P. F. (1962). Freedom and resentment. *Proceedings of the British Academy*, 48, 1-25.

Strawson, P. F. (1966). *The bounds of sense: An essay on Kant's Critique of Pure Reason*. Methuen.

Street, S. (2006). A Darwinian dilemma for realist theories of value. *Philosophical Studies*, 127, 109-166.

Street, S. (2008). Constructivism about reasons. *Oxford Studies in Metaethics*, 3, 207-245.

Street, T. (2004). Arabic logic. *Elsevier*.

SStroud, B. (1968). Transcendental arguments. *The Journal of Philosophy*, 65(9), 241-256.

troud, B. (1989). *The significance of philosophical scepticism*. Oxford University Press.

Stroud, B. (2000). *Understanding human knowledge*. Oxford University Press.

Stroud, B. (2018). *Seeing, knowing, understanding: Philosophical essays*. Oxford University Press.

Sturgeon, N. L. (1985). Moral explanations. *Cornell University Press*.

Sugirtharajah, R. S. (2001). *The Bible and the Third World: Precolonial, colonial and postcolonial encounters*. Cambridge University Press.

Susskind, L. (1995). The world as a hologram. *Journal of Mathematical Physics*, 36, 6377-6396.

Susskind, L. (2005). *The Cosmic Landscape: String Theory and the Illusion of Intelligent Design*. New York: Little, Brown and Company.

Susskind, L., Thorlacius, L., & Uglum, J. (1993). The stretched horizon and black hole complementarity. *Physical Review D*, 48, 3743-3761.

Swinburne, R. (1997). *The evolution of the soul* (Rev. ed.). Oxford University Press.

Swinburne, R. *The Resurrection of God Incarnate*. Oxford: Oxford University Press, 2003.

Swinburne, R. (2004). *The existence of God* (2nd ed.). Oxford University Press.

Swinburne, R. (2007). *Revelation: From metaphor to analogy* (2nd ed.). Oxford University Press.

Swinburne, R. (2013). *Mind, brain, and free will*. Oxford University Press.

Swinburne, R. (2016). *The coherence of theism* (2nd ed.). Oxford University Press.

T

't Hooft, G. (1993). Dimensional reduction in quantum gravity. *Cambridge University Press*.

Taber, J. (2018). Dharmakīrti and the Mīmāṃsakas in conflict. *Oxford University Press*.

Tahko, T. E. (2009). The law of non-contradiction as a metaphysical principle. *Law and Method*, 7, 32-47.

Tahko, T. E. (2015). *An introduction to metametaphysics*. Cambridge University Press.

Takeuti, G. (1987). *Proof theory* (2nd ed.). North-Holland.

Talbott, William. "Bayesian Epistemology." *The Stanford Encyclopedia of Philosophy*, Winter 2016 Edition, Edward N. Zalta (ed.)

Taleb, N. N. (2007). *The black swan: The impact of the highly improbable*. Random House.

Tarski, A. (1944). The semantic conception of truth and the foundations of semantics. *Philosophy and Phenomenological Research*, 4, 341-376.

Taves, A. (2009). *Religious experience reconsidered: A building block approach to the study of religion and other special things*. Princeton University Press.

Taylor, C. (1989). *Sources of the self: The making of the modern identity*. Harvard University Press.

Taylor, C. (2004). *Modern social imaginaries*. Duke University Press.

Taylor, C. (2007). *A secular age*. Harvard University Press.

Taylor, C. (2011). Why we need a radical redefinition of secularism. *Columbia University Press*.

Taylor, E. F., & Wheeler, J. A. (1992). *Spacetime physics* (2nd ed.). W. H. Freeman.

Tayob, A. (2018). *Islamic ethics and the trusteeship paradigm: Taha Abderrahmane's philosophy in* comparative perspectives. Brill.

Tegmark, M. (2003). Parallel universes. *Scientific American*, 288, 40-51.

Tegmark, M. (2008). The mathematical universe. *Foundations of Physics*, 38, 101-150.

Tegmark, M. (2014). *Our mathematical universe: My quest for the ultimate nature of reality*. Knopf.

Tempels, P. (1959). *Bantu philosophy*. Présence Africaine.

Thagard, P. (1992). *Conceptual revolutions*. Princeton University Press.

The Univalent Foundations Program. (2013). *Homotopy type theory: Univalent foundations of mathematics*. Institute for Advanced Study.

Thiemann, T. (2007). *Modern canonical quantum general relativity*. Cambridge University Press.

Thomasson, A. L. (2015). *Ontology made easy*. Oxford University Press.

Thompson, E. (2007). *Mind in life: Biology, phenomenology, and the sciences of mind*. Harvard University Press.

Thompson, E. (2015). *Waking, dreaming, being: Self and consciousness in neuroscience, meditation, and philosophy*. Columbia University Press.

Thompson, E. (2020). *Why I am not a Buddhist*. Yale University Press.

Thornton, T. (2004). *John McDowell*. McGill-Queen's University Press.

Thurston, W. P. (1994). On proof and progress in mathematics. *Bulletin of the American Mathematical Society*, 30, 161-177.

Tillich, P. (1957). *Systematic theology* (Vols. 1-2). University of Chicago Press.

Timpson, C. G. (2013). *Quantum information theory and the foundations of quantum mechanics*. Oxford University Press.

Tinker, G. E. (2004). *Spirit and resistance: Political theology and American Indian liberation*. Fortress Press.

Tollefsen, C. (2008). *Biomedical research and beyond: Expanding the ethics of inquiry*. Routledge.

Tononi, G. (2008). Consciousness as integrated information. *Biological Bulletin*, 215, 216-242.

Tononi, G., & Koch, C. (2015). Consciousness: Here, there and everywhere? *Philosophical Transactions of the Royal Society B*, 370(1668), Article 20140167.

Torretti, R. (1978). *Philosophy of Geometry from Riemann to Poincaré*. D. Reidel Publishing Company.

Tracy, D. (1981). *The analogical imagination: Christian theology and the culture of pluralism*. Crossroad.

Traiger, S. (2010). Experience and testimony in Hume's philosophy. *Episteme*, 7, 42-57.

Trivers, R. L. "The Evolution of Reciprocal Altruism." *The Quarterly Review of Biology* 46, no. 1 (March 1971): 35-57.

Troelstra, A. S., & van Dalen, D. (1988). *Constructivism in mathematics* (2 vols.). North-Holland.

Tryon, E. P. (1973). Is the universe a vacuum fluctuation? *Nature*, 246(5433), 396-397.

Tucker, M. E., & Grim, J. (2014). *Ecology and religion*. Island Press.

Turing, A. M. (1936). On computable numbers, with an application to the Entscheidungsproblem. *Proceedings of the London Mathematical Society*, 42, 230-265.

Turner, D. (2004). *Faith, reason and the existence of God*. Cambridge University Press.

Turner, J. (2010). Ontological pluralism. *Journal of Philosophy*, 107, 5-34.

Turri, J., & Klein, P. (2014). *Ad infinitum: New essays on epistemological infinitism*. Oxford University Press.

Twenge, J. M., Cooper, A. B., Joiner, T. E., et al. (2018). Age, period, and cohort trends in mood disorder indicators and suicide-related outcomes in a nationally representative dataset, 2005-2017. *Journal of Abnormal Psychology*, 128, 185-199.

U

Uffink, J. (2001). Bluff your way in the second law of thermodynamics. *Studies in History and Philosophy of Science Part B*, 32, 305-394.

Unger, P. (2006). *All the power in the world*. Oxford University Press.

V

Vaidman, L. (2018). Many-worlds interpretation of quantum mechanics. *Stanford Encyclopedia of*

Philosophy.

Vaidya, A. J. (2017). Does critical thinking require meta-cognition? In J. Ganeri (Ed.), *The Oxford handbook of Indian philosophy*. Oxford University Press.

van Atten, M. (2018). The development of intuitionistic logic. *Stanford Encyclopedia of Philosophy*.

van Benthem, J. (2008). Logic and reasoning: Do the facts matter? *Studia Logica*, 88(1), 67-84.

Van Essen, D. C., Smith, S. M., Barch, D. M., et al. (2013). The WU-Minn Human Connectome Project: An overview. *NeuroImage*, 80, 62-79.

van Fraassen, B. C. (2002). *The empirical stance*. Yale University Press.

van Fraassen, B. C. (2008). *Scientific representation: Paradoxes of perspective*. Oxford University Press.

van Inwagen, P. (1983). *An essay on free will*. Clarendon Press.

van Inwagen, P. (2006). *The problem of evil*. Oxford University Press.

van Inwagen, P. (2009). Being, existence, and ontological commitment. *Oxford University Press*.

van Oosten, J. (2008). *Realizability: An introduction to its categorical side*. Elsevier.

Vance, A. (2015). *Elon Musk: Tesla, SpaceX, and the quest for a fantastic future*. Ecco.

Vansina, J. (1985). *Oral tradition as history*. University of Wisconsin Press.

Varela, F. J. (1996). Neurophenomenology: A methodological remedy for the hard problem. *Journal of Consciousness Studies*, 3, 330-349.

Varela, F. J., Thompson, E., & Rosch, E. (1991). *The embodied mind: Cognitive science and human experience*. MIT Press.

Vargas, M. (2013). *Building better beings: A theory of moral responsibility*. Oxford University Press.

Vasubandhu. (1991). Twenty verses on consciousness-only. *Buddhist philosophy*, 161-179.

Vavova, K. (2015). Evolutionary debunking of moral realism. *Philosophy Compass*, 10, 104-116.

Väyrynen, P. (2006). Moral generalism: Enjoy in moderation. *Ethics*, 116, 707-741.

Verlinde, E. (2011). On the origin of gravity and the laws of Newton. *Journal of High Energy Physics*, 2011.

Vilenkin, A. (1982). Creation of universes from nothing. *Physics Letters B*, 117(1-2), 25-28.

Vilenkin, A. (1983). Birth of inflationary universes. *Physical Review D*, 27, 2848-2855.

Vilenkin, A. (2006). *Many worlds in one: The search for other universes*. Hill and Wang.

Vilenkin, A. (2007). Measures of the multiverse. *AIP Conference Proceedings*, 878, 3-13.

Vohs, K. D., & Schooler, J. W. (2008). The value of believing in free will: Encouraging a belief in determinism increases cheating. *Psychological Science*, 19, 49-54.

von Neumann, J. (1932). *Mathematische Grundlagen der Quantenmechanik*. Springer.

von Neumann, J., & Morgenstern, O. (1944). *Theory of games and economic behavior*. Princeton University Press.

von Rad, G. (1972). *Genesis: A commentary*. Westminster Press.

W

Wagon, S. (1985). *The Banach-Tarski paradox*. Cambridge University Press.

Wainwright, W. J. (1995). *Reason and the heart: A prolegomenon to a critique of passional reason*. Cornell University Press.

Wald, R. M. (1984). *General relativity*. University of Chicago Press.

Waldron, W. S. (2003). *The Buddhist unconscious*. RoutledgeCurzon.

Wallace, B. A. (2007). *Contemplative science: Where Buddhism and neuroscience converge*. Columbia University Press.

Wallace, D. (2010). The arrow of time in physics. *Oxford University Press*.

Wallace, D. (2012). *The emergent multiverse: Quantum theory according to the Everett interpretation*. Oxford University Press.

Walton, J. H. (2009). *The lost world of Genesis one*. InterVarsity Press.

Wanderer, J. (2008). *Robert Brandom*. McGill-Queen's University Press.

Ware, K. (1993). *The Orthodox Church*. Penguin Books.

Watson, G. (2004). *Agency and answerability: Selected essays*. Oxford University Press.

Wattles, J. (1996). *The golden rule*. Oxford University Press.

Weber, M. (1946). Science as a vocation. *Oxford University Press.*

Weber, M. (1978). *Economy and society: An outline of interpretive sociology* (G. Roth & C. Wittich, Eds.). University of California Press.

Weber, M. (2006). *Whitehead's pancreativism: The basics*. Ontos Verlag.

Wielenberg, E. J. "On the Evolutionary Debunking of Morality." *Ethics* 120, no. 3 (2010): 441-464.

Weinberg, J. M., Nichols, S., & Stich, S. (2001). Normativity and epistemic intuitions. *Philosophical Topics*, 29(1-2), 429-460.

Weinberg, S. (1987). Anthropic bound on the cosmological constant. *Physical Review Letters*, 59, 2607-2610.

Weinberg, S. (1989). The cosmological constant problem. *Reviews of Modern Physics*, 61, 1-23.

Weinberg, S. (1992). *Dreams of a final theory*. Pantheon Books.

Weinberg, S. (1995). *The quantum theory of fields* (Vol. 1). Cambridge University Press.

Weinberg, S. (2008). *Cosmology*. Oxford University Press.

Weinberg, S. (2015). *Lectures on quantum mechanics* (2nd ed.). Cambridge University Press.

Weiskrantz, L. (1986). *Blindsight: A case study and implications*. Oxford University Press.

Westerhoff, J. (2009). *Nāgārjuna's Madhyamaka: A philosophical introduction*. Oxford University Press.

Westfall, R. S. (1980). *Never at rest: A biography of Isaac Newton*. Cambridge University Press.

Wheeler, J. A., & Ford, K. (1998). *Geons, black holes, and quantum foam: A life in physics*. Norton.

Wheeler, J. A. "Information, Physics, Quantum: The Search for Links." In *Proceedings of the Third International Symposium on Foundations of Quantum Mechanics in the Light of New Technology*, Tokyo, 1989, pp. 354-368. Published 1990.

Wheeler, J. A. (1990). Information, physics, quantum: The search for links. In W. H. Zurek (Ed.), *Complexity, entropy, and the physics of information*. Addison-Wesley

Wheeler, J. A. (1990). Information, physics, quantum: The search for links. In W. H. Zurek (Ed.), *Complexity, entropy, and the physics of information* . Addison-Wesley.

Whitehead, A. N. (1925). *Science and the modern world*. Macmillan.

Whitehead, A. N. (1978). *Process and reality: An essay in cosmology* (Corrected ed.). Free Press. (Original work published 1929).

Whitt, L., Roberts, M., Norman, W., et al. (2003). Indigenous perspectives. *Blackwell*.

Whyte, K. P. (2017). Indigenous climate change studies: Indigenizing futures, decolonizing the Anthropocene. *English Language Notes*, 55(1-2), 115-132.

Whyte, K. P. (2018). Indigenous science (fiction) for the Anthropocene: Ancestral dystopias and fantasies of climate change crises. *Environment and Planning E*, 1(1-2), 224-242.

Wielenberg, E. J. (2005). *Value and virtue in a godless universe*. Cambridge University Press.

Wielenberg, E. J. (2010). On the evolutionary debunking of morality. *Ethics*, 120, 441-464.

Wiggins, D. (1987). *Needs, values, truth*. Blackwell.

Wiggins, D. (2001). *Sameness and substance renewed*. Cambridge University Press.

Wigner, Eugene P. "The Unreasonable Effectiveness of Mathematics in the Natural Sciences." *Communications in Pure and Applied Mathematics*, vol. 13, no. 1 (February 1960), pp. 1-14.

Wilber, K. (2000). *Integral psychology*. Shambhala.

Wilber, K. (2000). *A theory of everything: An integral vision for business, politics, science and spirituality.* Shambhala.

Wilczek, F. (2015). *A beautiful question: Finding nature's deep design*. Penguin Press.

Will, C. M. (2014). The confrontation between general relativity and experiment. *Living Reviews in Relativity*, 17.

Williams, B. (1973). A critique of utilitarianism. *Cambridge University Press.*

Williams, B. (1978). *Descartes: The project of pure enquiry*. Penguin Books.

Williams, B. (2014). *Essays and reviews: 1959-2002*. Princeton University Press.

Williams, M. (2001). *Problems of knowledge: A critical introduction to epistemology*. Oxford University

Press.

Williams, P. (2009). *Mahāyāna Buddhism: The doctrinal foundations* (2nd ed.). Routledge.

Williamson, J. (2010). *In defence of objective Bayesianism*. Oxford University Press.

Williamson, T. (1994). *Vagueness*. Routledge.

Williamson, T. (2000). *Knowledge and its limits*. Oxford University Press.

Williamson, T. (2013). How deep is the distinction between a priori and a posteriori knowledge? In A. Casullo & J. C. Thurow (Eds.), *The a priori in philosophy*. Oxford University Press.

Williamson, T. (2013). Logic, metalogic and neutrality. *Erkenntnis*, 79, 211-231.

Williamson, T. (2013). *Modal logic as metaphysics*. Oxford University Press.

Williamson, T. (2016). Modal science. *Canadian Journal of Philosophy*, 46(4-5), 453-492.

Wilson, D. S., & Wilson, E. O. (2007). Rethinking the theoretical foundation of sociobiology. *Quarterly Review of Biology*, 82, 327-348.

Wilson, E. O. (1998). *Consilience: The unity of knowledge*. Knopf.

Wilson, M. D. (1978). *Descartes*. Routledge & Kegan Paul.

Wiredu, K. (1996). *Cultural universals and particulars: An African perspective*. Indiana University Press.

Wittgenstein, L. (2001). *Tractatus logico-philosophicus* (D. F. Pears & B. F. McGuinness, Trans.). Routledge. (Original work published 1921)

Wittgenstein, L. (1953). *Philosophical investigations* (G. E. M. Anscombe, Trans.). Blackwell.

Wittgenstein, L. (1969). *On certainty* (G. E. M. Anscombe & G. H. von Wright, Eds.; D. Paul & G. E. M. Anscombe, Trans.). Blackwell.

Woit, P. (2006). *Not even wrong: The failure of string theory*. Basic Books.

Wolf, S. (1990). *Freedom within reason*. Oxford University Press.

Wolf, S. (2010). *Meaning in life and why it matters*. Princeton University Press.

Wolfram, S. (2002). *A new kind of science*. Wolfram Media.

Wolpaw, J., & Wolpaw, E. W. (2012). *Brain-computer interfaces: Principles and practice*. Oxford University Press.

Wolterstorff, N. (1976). *Reason within the bounds of religion*. Eerdmans.

Woods, J. (2019). Logical nihilism and the logic of 'prem'. *Thought*, 8, 161-169.

Wootters, W. K., & Zurek, W. H. (1982). A single quantum cannot be cloned. *Nature*, 299, 802-803.

World Council of Churches. (1982). *Baptism, eucharist and ministry*. World Council of Churches.

Worrall, J. (1989). Structural realism: The best of both worlds? *Dialectica*, 43(1-2), 99-124.

Wright, C. (1983). *Frege's conception of numbers as objects*. Aberdeen University Press.

Wright, C. (1992). *Truth and objectivity*. Harvard University Press.

Wright, C. (2004). Warrant for nothing (and foundations for free)? *Proceedings of the Aristotelian Society Supplementary Volume*, 78(1), 167-212.

Wright, N. T. (2003). *The resurrection of the Son of God*. Fortress Press.

Wright, N. T. (2005). *The last word: Scripture and the authority of God—Getting beyond the Bible wars*. HarperSanFrancisco.

Wu, C. S., Ambler, E., Hayward, R. W., et al. (1957). Experimental test of parity conservation in beta decay. *Physical Review*, 105, 1413-1415.

Wykstra, S. J. (1984). The Humean obstacle to evidential arguments from suffering: On avoiding the evils of "appearance." *International Journal for Philosophy of Religion*, 16(2), 73-93.

Y

Yablo, S. (2010). *Things: Papers on objects, events, and properties*. Oxford University Press.

Yang, C. N., & Mills, R. L. (1954). Conservation of isotopic spin and isotopic gauge invariance. *Physical Review*, 96, 191-195.

Yazdi, M. H. (1992). *The principles of epistemology in Islamic philosophy: Knowledge by presence*. State University of New York Press.

Yoshino, A. (2012). The birth of the lithium-ion battery. *Angewandte Chemie International Edition*, 51, 5798-5800.

Z

Zadeh, L. A. (1965). Fuzzy sets. *Information and Control*, 8, 338-353.

Zagzebski, L. T. (1996). *Virtues of the mind: An inquiry into the nature of virtue and the ethical foundations of knowledge.* Cambridge University Press.

Zagzebski, L. T. (2009). *On epistemology.* Wadsworth.

Zagzebski, L. T. (2012). *Epistemic authority: A theory of trust, authority, and autonomy in belief.* Oxford University Press.

Zahar, E. (1973). Why did Einstein's programme supersede Lorentz's? *The British Journal for the Philosophy of Science*, 24(2), 95-123.

Zahavi, D. (2003). *Husserl's phenomenology.* Stanford University Press.

Zahavi, D. (2005). *Subjectivity and selfhood: Investigating the first-person perspective.* MIT Press.

Zahavi, D. (2014). *Self and other: Exploring subjectivity, empathy, and shame.* Oxford University Press.

Zee, A. (2016). *Group theory in a nutshell for physicists.* Princeton University Press.

Zeh, H. D. (2007). *The physical basis of the direction of time* (5th ed.). Springer.

Zermelo, E. (1908). Untersuchungen über die Grundlagen der Mengenlehre I. *Mathematische Annalen*, 65, 261-281.

Zhuangzi. (2009). *Zhuangzi: The essential writings* (B. Ziporyn, Trans.). Hackett Publishing.

Zhuangzi. (2013). *The complete works of Zhuangzi* (B. Watson, Trans.). Columbia University Press.

Zimmerman, D. (2010). From property dualism to substance dualism. *Proceedings of the Aristotelian Society Supplementary Volume*, 84, 119-150.

Zimmermann, M. (2002). *A Buddha within: The Tathāgatagarbhasūtra.* Biblotheca Philologica et Philosophica Buddhica VI.

Ziporyn, B. (2009). *Zhuangzi: The essential writings with selections from traditional commentaries.* Hackett Publishing.

Zizioulas, J. D. (1985). *Being as communion: Studies in personhood and the church.* St. Vladimir's Seminary Press.

Zurek, W. H. (2009). Quantum Darwinism. *Nature Physics*, 5, 181-188.

Zuse, K. (1969). *Rechnender Raum.* Friedrich Vieweg & Sohn.